Acclaim for **Miriam Horn**'s

REBELS IN WHITE GLOVES

"The book [provides] a context for understanding the mercurial first lady who has defied categorizing. . . . A candid snapshot of a generation in transition."
—*The Charlotte News & Observer*

"Horn reveals a group of women who arrived at the prestigious Massachusetts college at the end of an era and stepped out to pioneer another."
—*The Philadelphia Inquirer*

"Engrossing and beautifully written."   —*Biography*

"Offers a provocative look at the long way women have come and the longer way that is left to go."
—*The Hartford Courant*

"A story that speaks to more than one generation and more than one gender."
—*Patriot-News* (Harrisburg)

"Carefully written and intelligent. . . . The most appealing aspect of this book is the candor with which the women speak of their lives and the non-intrusive and nonjudgmental way in which Ms. Horn reports her findings."   —*The New York Observer*

MIRIAM HORN

REBELS IN WHITE GLOVES

Miriam Horn has been a journalist since 1986. She spent her twenties working for the U.S. Forest Service in Colorado and now lives in New York City with her husband and daughter.

REBELS IN WHITE GLOVES

REBELS
IN
WHITE GLOVES

*Coming of Age with
Hillary's Class—Wellesley '69*

MIRIAM HORN

Anchor Books   A Division of Random House, Inc.   New York

FIRST ANCHOR BOOKS EDITION, MAY 2000

A portion of this work was originally published in
U.S. News & World Report.

The Library of Congress had cataloged
the Times Books edition as follows:

Horn, Miriam.
Rebels in white gloves: coming of age with Hillary's class—
Wellesley '69 / Miriam Horn.
p.   cm.
Includes index.
ISBN 0-8129-2501-7
1. Wellesley College. Class of 1969—Biography.
2. Wellesley College—History—20th Century.   I. Title.
LD7212.6 1969.H69   1998
378.744'7—dc21   98-33331

Anchor ISBN: 0-385-72018-1

Book design by M. Kristen Bearse
Author photograph © Peter Serling

www.anchorbooks.com

Printed in the United States of America
10   9   8   7   6   5   4   3   2   1

For my mother,
and in memory of my father

Acknowledgments

For their support and help on this book, I wish to thank my present and former colleagues at *U.S. News & World Report*, especially Emily MacFarquhar, Wellesley '59, who had the inspired idea for the historical survey of Wellesley women (from which most of the statistics in this book are drawn), and her classmates, who conceived the questions, compiled the data, and were kind enough to share it with me. I also thank Chris Ma, whose idea it was that I should look closely at Wellesley '69, Mike Ruby and Merrill McLoughlin, Peter Bernstein, Kathy Bushkin and Sara Hammel. At Wellesley, I was given wonderful help by Laurel Stavis, Wilma Slaight, and Harriet Dawson. I also thank Peter Osnos, formerly of Times Books, for recognizing the potential for a book, and Betsy Rapoport, my wonderful editor. Of the many friends and family members who gave me encouragement and a room of my own to work in, I thank in particular Patricia Cohen, Elise O'Shaughnessy, Nachshon Peleg, Peter Serling, Randy Cohen, Maria Nation, Kinsey and Lilika and Sindri and Danae Anderson, Lucrezia Reichlin, Ruth Friedman, Laura Silverman, and David Horn. I thank my imaginative, exacting, beloved husband, Charles Sabel. Most of all, of course, I thank the women of Wellesley '69.

Contents

Introduction

On a cloudless spring morning in June 1994, eighteen hundred women in white wound their way through the serene and verdant campus of Wellesley College. A sweet breeze stirred the swamp maple, tupelo, and hickory trees, setting their leaves to trembling in the still mirror of Waban Lake. Pale ivory dogwood and scarlet rhododendron littered petals like confetti across the lush, sloping lawns. Led by 102-year-old Jane Cary Nearing, a graduate of Wellesley before women had the right to vote, the elder alumnae stepped regally through an arbor of their successors, skirts dancing about their ankles and class colors held high. The women of '29 shook blue-and-white pom-poms; '34 tipped purple gingham hats; '59 answered with a twirl of yellow parasols; and '69 fluttered green scarves. All cheered tribute to the silvery ladies who had led their way.

More than one returning alumna discerned in that river of white a symbolic pageant of female history. Yet missing that morning in Wellesley, Massachusetts, was the most prominent symbol of the dramatic transformation in the lives of American women in the late twentieth century. The Wellesley graduate who twenty-five years earlier had launched her classmates into the world with a now legendary commencement address was in Europe that June weekend with her husband and the other leaders of the Western world, commemorating the fiftieth anniversary of D day. In her place, her classmates bore—with obvious and antic pride—a cardboard cutout of the First Lady. Lifted from one of the photo hustlers who stalk the sidewalks around the White House, that effigy, too, was a fitting symbol. As America's most visible representative of the modern woman, Hillary Rodham Clinton is inevitably rendered, by those who love her and by those who don't, in two dimensions.

Her classmates, for the most part, have been spared a similar fate. Coming of age at a rare moment in history and with the equally rare privilege of an elite college education, the women who graduated from Wellesley in 1969 were destined to be the monkeys in the space capsule, the first to test in their own lives the consequences of the great transformations wrought by the second wave of feminism. Each has confronted the same questions as Hillary, but more privately, unburdened by the symbolic weight of the First Lady's role. How much would they embrace of their parents' values, and how much of their rebellious peers'? How reconcile their youthful aversion to the establishment and what Hillary called in her commencement speech "our prevailing acquisitive, competitive corporate life" with their determination to claim power for women, break into male professions, support themselves, provide well for their children, change the world? Could they create such a thing as a marriage of equals, combine the model of full-time motherhood they had been raised on with the demands of working lives? How would they confront the historically tragic realities in a woman's life: the loss of youthful beauty, the leave-taking of children, the end of fertility? And how manage all of that in a culture bent on defining on their behalf the nature of womanhood and the path to female happiness? "We are, all of us, exploring a world that none of us understand and attempting to create within that uncertainty," Hillary Rodham told her classmates on the day of their graduation three decades ago. "The only tool we have ultimately to use is our lives . . ."

This book is about how the women who graduated from Wellesley in 1969 created their lives at a moment when that river of female history surged to flood stage, tearing roots, collapsing once solid banks and familiar landmarks. Some would plunge headlong into the roiling waters, hoping to ride them into some newer Eden. Others would grasp at the riverbanks even as they crumbled. Yet even those who tried to resist the flood have ultimately used it to carry them free of the narrows in which women had long spent their lives. Nancy Wanderer, for example, wanted her mother's life and got too much of her wish, including a stifling marriage; the difference is that twenty years on, she attached herself to a radical social movement that not only broke her marriage but helped her realize, finally, the life girls dream of when they play house with other girls, a life where each gets a turn playing Mommy and Daddy. Virtually all in the class would repeat that pattern in some fashion: In the wider world, they escaped the intensely private and limited lives to which previous generations of women were consigned. For Hillary Clinton, claiming a public life has been a decidedly mixed blessing. She is, even by her classmates, pitied as much as admired. But what of the others? In breaching the domestic wall, have her closest peers mostly enjoyed, or mostly suffered, the new possibilities their generation created for women?

The years in which these women grew up and entered the world were a time of unprecedented change. In the decade that began in their high school junior year, a women's movement becalmed since the 1930s gained a sudden second wind with the publication of Betty Friedan's *The Feminine Mystique*. Challenging the postwar dogma that the only normal and joyful destiny for a woman was to be mother and wife—and voicing in public for the first time the unconfessed misery of countless white middle-class suburban housewives—Friedan's remarkable catalog of the propaganda aimed at women by advertising and the media and science was by 1964 the best-selling paperback in the country. That same year, the passage of the Civil Rights Act and creation of the Equal Employment Opportunity Commission provided the advocates of race and gender equality a powerful new legal instrument: When the head of EEOC publicly refused to act against sex discrimination, Friedan helped launch in 1966 the National Organization for Women. NOW lobbied and litigated against discrimination and in behalf of such needs as day care for the children of working women, but its goals extended well beyond workplace issues to a fundamental reconception of both men's and women's roles. "We believe that a true partnership between sexes demands a different concept of marriage, as well as an equitable sharing of the responsibilities of home and children and of the economic burdens of their support."

Following the lead of civil rights activists, who refused the deference and public invisibility historically demanded of blacks, NOW and its more radical sister organizations broke all feminine rules of modesty and took feminism to the streets. In 1967, when the women of '69 were sophomores at Wellesley, Mother's Day protesters descended on the White House. Brandishing signs reading END HUMAN SACRIFICE. DON'T GET MARRIED, they ritually discarded chains of flowers, aprons, and mock typewriters, emblems of the courted girl, the housebound wife, and the helpmeet in the steno pool. In their junior year, "women's liberation" made its first national splash when two hundred demonstrators arrived at the Miss America pageant in Atlantic City to protest its "propagation of the mindless sex object image" and set up a "freedom trash can" into which women were invited to toss "objects of female torture": hair curlers, girdles, bras, and high heels. Sex and underwear, the most private matters, were recognized as having political meaning. *Ms.* magazine was launched in 1971; by 1972 the Equal Rights Amendment had passed by overwhelming margins in both the House and Senate; in 1973, the Supreme Court found a constitutional right to abortion in *Roe v. Wade.*

NOW's demand for a wholesale remaking of marriage, child rearing, education, work, politics, law, medicine, religion, psychology, and sexuality has been in the brief lifetime of these women to a remarkable degree fulfilled. In the 1950s, when the women of '69 were girls, half of all women married as teenagers, and a third had their first child before age twenty; the average age of first marriage and motherhood dropped to the youngest in U.S. history and all but 7 percent of women eventually became mothers, typically raising three or four children. Only a fifth of students then in college were women; two out of three of those dropped out, and only 6 percent of all women completed their degrees. Fewer still went on to advanced degrees and professions. By 1966, women's share of college faculty positions was lower than in 1910 and women accounted for only 0.5 percent of engineers, 3 percent of lawyers, and 6 percent of physicians; throughout the workforce the gender wage gap was widening. A century's gains in women's education and employment were in fact reversed with the end of World War II as a million women were pushed out of jobs or into pink-collar ghettos to make room for 12 million returning GIs. Fewer than one in ten mothers with children under six worked full-time; in the suburbs, just 3 percent did so. Unless she was nonwhite or poor, marriage and child-rearing were a woman's lifetime career.

By the time the women of '69 were launching their own daughters into the world, all that had changed. In 1998, just 3 percent of families corresponded to the perfect portrait of the traditional nuclear family— dad bringing home the bacon to two kids and a stay-at-home mom. With women waiting longer to wed, and with half of all marriages ending in divorce, a woman today can expect to be married less than half her adult life. Child rearing, too, occupies a smaller portion of her adulthood: Though the number of children raised by single mothers has quadrupled since the 1950s to 24 percent, Hillary Clinton's generation has had fewer children than any previous generation of American women. With longer life expectancies, they will spend many more years in an empty nest. Twenty percent have never had children.

The shifts in family structure followed dramatic changes in women's education and employment. Women are now the majority among students pursuing higher education, and have made tremendous gains in high-earning professions. By 1990, a third of all attorneys, doctors, professors, and business managers were women. The median income of women in their forties has increased 31 percent over three decades, while men's remained nearly unchanged. Fifty-seven percent of women with children under six and 68 percent of women with school-age children are now in the workforce (though a third of those with children under eighteen work part-time); 48 percent of married women provide half or more of their family income; 18 percent are the sole providers, and 10 percent of husbands now describe themselves as homemakers. In 1992, those shifts were mirrored, somewhat belatedly, in the First Family: Barbara Bush, a grandmother of twelve who dropped out of college to marry and never again held a paying job, yielded America's most symbolic hearth and home to an attorney with a six-figure income and one child.

Having been girls in one world, the women of Wellesley '69 became women in another. They were "split at the root," in poet Adrienne Rich's phrase. Though they are more educated and less poor than average—as of 1994, 58 percent had an advanced degree—their lives mirror the new national norm to a remarkable extent: Just 5 percent are traditional homemakers; 42 percent of those who are married provide half or more of their household income; 12 percent have never married; 23 percent have no children.

Women's colleges have often provided a useful window into the present state of womanhood. Researching *The Second Sex* (1949), Simone de Beauvoir interviewed women "from Mary Guggenheim to Mary McCarthy to the many anonymous Marys who were students at Vassar, Sweet Briar and the women's campus of Tulane." *The Feminine Mystique* began with a fifteenth-reunion survey of Betty Friedan's own class of 1942 at Smith College—a group exactly the generation of the mothers of the class of '69. Mary McCarthy's cruel roman à clef *The Group* mocked her classmates of Vassar '33–and, by implication, their progressive descendants in 1963, the year of its publication; Sylvia Plath's autobiographical novel *The Bell Jar,* about a Smith student in the 1950s, held out a dark warning to the young women of the sixties.

All of these authors exploited the high degree of self-consciousness common among these well-schooled women. It is a quality particularly apparent in the hordes of baby boomers who came of age in the sixties: Theirs was a generation that imagined it would reinvent the world. Self-conscious iconoclasts and pioneers, the women of '69 would experiment boldly with sex and work and family and religion and politics. They would also develop the habit of seeing their own lives in historic terms. Having been analyzed endlessly by experts of every stripe, from psychologists and sociologists to marketers and gender theorists (some drawn from their own ranks), the way they are talked about is also the way they often talk about themselves. In their voices, one hears echoes of the diverse vocabularies of linguist Deborah Tannen and developmental psychologist Carol Gilligan, of New Age guru Clarissa Pinkola Estes and child-rearing expert Penelope Leach, of the New Left and the women's health movement and feminist jurisprudence. The women of '69 recognize themselves as characters in the present drama over the meaning of gender, over family structure and the rearing of children, over the relationship between the self and society, between the private and public realms.

The accounts of their lives offered here are more memoir than biography. Though I interviewed mothers and fathers, sons and daughters, husbands and lovers and friends, I was concerned most with what the women themselves make of their lives, what choices they celebrate or regret as they look back from the vantage of midlife. Where possible, I have tried to provide some context for their metamorphoses. These women, alert consumers of culture, are like slightly bent satellite dishes: They pick up most of the intellectual currents of the day, but the signal is frequently broken up or overlapped by contrary signals. Rather than impose coherence, I have tried to summarize the ideas they have absorbed while also preserving the idiosyncratic ways in which they have understood them. For the sake of narrative flow, I have sometimes knitted together several conversations, which can throw into relief the human habit of self-contradiction.

Memory, of course, has its own agenda: To the extent that these are self-portraits, they preserve both the kind and unkind cuts that enterprise invariably entails. In recounting their histories, each of these women has made a story of her life, finding with hindsight the fruit born of chaos and pain, mapping cause and effect, discerning motifs, imbuing events with symbolic and prophetic portent. They have rationalized misdeeds and also lacerated themselves with criticism; romanticized youthful adventures, swelling them to grand proportions, but also flattened their own past into anecdote.

They have not, however, kept many secrets. Reared in the tenets of consciousness-raising, most of the women of Wellesley '69 have been candid about their lives to an almost unsettling degree. To break the silence that prevailed in their childhood on such matters as sexuality and marital unhappiness and substance abuse, most believe, has a moral purpose. Though Hannah Arendt herself was hostile to feminism, her recognition that "if we do not know our history, we are doomed to live it as though it were our private fate" was developed by feminists into a central principle of the movement. The feminist insight that "the personal is political" meant that some seemingly solitary struggles were in fact shared, rooted in family, social, and corporate structures that had to be challenged by women in solidarity with one another. Personal testimony became a political act; speaking out was a way to join and sustain the sisterhood. "The personal is political" also meant that there was a politics, a power relationship, in the family and that therefore such public values as justice and equality had to be taken home. It meant that all sorts of seemingly intimate choices—what kind of underwear one wore, whether and how and with whom one had sex—were political as well as personal, a way of confronting social rules as to how a lady behaved and of interrogating the complicated relationship between power and sexual consent. "The personal is political" meant that disputes traditionally treated as domestic and therefore private—acts of forced sex or of violence against one's family members—would no longer be immune from public scrutiny. It meant that you had to "walk the talk," align how you lived in the world—earned your money, disposed of your trash—with the values you professed. It meant, as well, that the political is personal: that the public realm of work and law had to be tempered with such "womanly" values as nurturance and compassion.

The dissolution of the hard boundary that once separated the private from the public has had mixed consequences, and those consequences are the central subject of this book. Co-opted by commercial culture, the confessional impulse has grown grotesque on TV talk shows (though as David Halberstam points out in *The Fifties,* it was *The Adventures of Ozzie and Harriet,* the show that has come to stand for all the marvelous family values America subsequently lost, that first took "what was most private"—the lives of the couple's two sons—"and made it terribly public"). In politics, the idea that the personal behavior of a senator or president is a legitimate measure of his political character has often degraded civic discourse into scandalmongering. Hollywood has seized upon the openness toward sex and intimate violence as license to make them both staples of popular entertainment. Excessively shielded as girls from harsh realities, the women of '69 have raised children excessively exposed. They have also sometimes lost their way on the "twelve-step" path. "The personal is political" has sometimes degenerated into the notion that personal revelation and transformation are politics enough.

Yet it remains true that these women have taken great sustenance, like many women before them, from speaking truth to one another—it is a tradition still enacted at their class reunion meetings. The women of '69 have come out as debutantes. They have also come out as lesbians, as victims of domestic abuse, as alcoholics. At the same time, they have remained possessed of the manners and dutiful habits instilled at Wellesley—a wonderful combination for any biographer attempting to retrace their lives. So Dorothy Devine, '69, was not only able to promptly find and send me the 1970 report to the House Judiciary Committee on her subversive activities in the New Left and in Cuba—as well as snapshots of herself with bare-breasted celebrants at the Michigan Womyn's Music Festival and wreathed with laurel at a menopause rite. She also accompanied it all with a gracious note on flowered stationery in a lovely hand.

"Why do we have all these problems we didn't have in 1955?" Speaker of the House of Representatives Newt Gingrich asked in a speech in 1994. "Because a long pattern of counterculture belief . . . has undervalued the family." Nostalgia for the childhood world these women lost or abandoned, and disavowal of their generation's "revolution" as a destructive spasm, are central tenets of political discourse in the 1990s. In the present rendering of postwar history, the fifties marked the last golden moment of centuries of stable and happy families, a world of order and restraint tragically dismantled by the nihilistic assault in the sixties on traditional values. In this view, selfish ambition and wanton pleasure-seeking triumphed over a spartan sense of responsibility, precipitating the family's demise: Since the nurturance and moral education of family is traditionally the responsibility of women, it follows that they bear the greatest share of blame for this tragedy. It was for men to shoulder the burdens—and honor—of work and civic life. When women insisted on stepping into the public arena as well, they betrayed their calling as the keepers of a domestic haven in a heartless world.

When my brief portrait of five women of Wellesley '69 (U.S. attorney Kris Olson Rogers, Dr. Lonny Laszlo Higgins, and management consultant Janet McDonald Hill—all married working moms; Susan Alexander, a divorced working mom; and Kathy Smith Ruckman, a married full-time mom) appeared in *U.S. News & World Report* on the occasion of their twenty-fifth reunion, the letters received by the magazine reflected this sense of betrayal. A military man stationed in Europe wrote: "I submit that Kathy Ruckman, who got married, had children and stayed home, is the most successful career woman of the bunch. It's also a good bet her children aren't high school dropouts, drug addicts, unwed mothers, gang members, or in some other way a burden on society. . . . This is what the rest of these 'gifted women' . . . have given us." A woman in Hitchcock, Oklahoma, charged that "the group rebelled against more than the traditional family. Hillary and classmates rebelled against the Ten Commandments." To another woman, from Newton, New Jersey, Hillary's generation of women was the reason "we are in big trouble today—the most important word in their vocabulary is 'mine.' Look at how many are divorced. [Their parents made sacrifices in the armed services] so these ungratefuls could live, and now they are trying to destroy this great country."

They have destroyed the family and ruined America's children, defied the divine order and sabotaged morality, replaced self-sacrifice and duty with arrogant self-absorption and greed. That is the charge made against this generation of women. They have torn down American values, or sold out to them. In the process, they have ruined their own lives and created a nightmare for their daughters. A 1994 *Frontline* documentary on Hillary's class depicted these women as badly damaged by feminism: the career woman condemned to barren spinsterhood and remorse; the full-time mom to humiliation; the working mom to hyperorganized hyperactivity and her own daughter's disavowal of her hectic life.

These are the familiar condemnations and cautionary tales. "You know the rules," Hillary Rodham Clinton told the 1992 graduates of Wellesley. "If you don't get married, you're abnormal. . . . If you get married and have children but then go work outside the home, you're a bad mother. If you get married and have children but stay home, you've wasted your education." The "baby busters" may lament their generation's absence of a galvanizing identity, but their mothers suffer the opposite burden, as an endlessly caricatured generation.

Such caricatures well serve crusaders out to whittle history into a sharp ideological stick, but they are of little use for anyone wanting to understand another actual human being. Lives rendered as moral parable—whatever the agenda—are inevitably drained of the density and ambiguity and complexity and mystery of real life in favor of the broad strokes of social realism. "Generalities clank when wielded," Eudora Welty once wrote. "They make too much noise for us to hear what people might actually be trying to say. They are fatal to tenderness and are in themselves nonconductors of any real, however modest, discovery of the writer's own heart."

Those caricatured pay their own price. For Hillary's classmates, the recipe of the glass slipper and Betty Crocker domesticity on which they were raised remained enormously powerful, no matter how many countertales feminism told. More than a few have struggled to sort out their own dreams and experience from the dreams fed them by the common culture. Nonna Noto, '69, wrote every five years to her classmates of her enduring hopes for a husband and children and was wistful at her bad luck. But she now wonders whether she and some of her fellow childless classmates in fact chose the life they wanted but could not admit that choice even to themselves—whether they failed, as Hemingway put it, to "feel those things they actually feel and not the things they think they should feel." Those who deviated from the feminist recipe for happiness—at times just as fixed and tyrannical as the old pattern—have also frequently felt scorned or abnormal, equally mismatched with what Phyllis Rose calls the "limited and limiting plots" we impose on our own lives. "If I were to overcome the conventions, I should need the courage of a hero," Virginia Woolf once wrote, "and I am not a hero."

The women of Wellesley '69 are overwhelmingly feminists: 80 percent readily describe themselves that way. Are they, then, anti-men, anti-sex, anti-family, anti-motherhood, anti-religion? Have they been burned out and embittered by the changes wrought by feminism?

The aim of this book is not to supplant malicious caricatures with their opposites but rather to reflect the immense variety of these four hundred women, a variety that is itself the most dramatic legacy of feminism. Almost any adventure imaginable in the past fifty years can be found somewhere among their number: They have dropped acid, cheated on their husbands, had abortions, struggled to get pregnant, run away with the stableman, run away to be a Buddhist nun, made fortunes, lost fortunes, taken Prozac, started menopause, pushed a stroller through their twenty-fifth-reunion parade. In the sheer diversity and idiosyncrasy of their lives, the women of '69 resist the taxonomist. How does one type a Pentecostal Christian creationist physician with a house-husband? How make a cautionary tale of Catherine Parke, a college professor and poet whose late baby has not "stolen my time to write nor scattered my attention nor left me tired or overwhelmed nor damaged my career or sex life or self-esteem"?

To fairly reflect their diversity, I have gathered a larger cast than the usual three, four, or five characters typical of social histories. I have not, however, attempted to represent the class in any demographic sense: I did not divide the book among married and divorced, black and white, happy and unhappy, in proportional reflection of the class. Ultimately, I followed the stories that interested me most. If they are sometimes exceptionally dramatic, traversing what Oliver Sacks calls "the arctics and tropics of human existence," they are also the stories that the women of '69 tell each other and themselves. Having sailed into unmapped waters—and before the recent great surge in women's biography and fractured fairy tales and female picaresques—these women have frequently turned for inspiration to one another's often epic lives: to Lonny Laszlo Higgins's ten years at sea raising her family and training Micronesian public health workers; to Dr. Nancy Eyler's marriage to an uneducated cowboy and move to Montana; to Alison Campbell Swain's rejection of the ease she could have bought herself with her family fortune in favor of a life of ceaselessly taking care of other people.

Though each chapter charts a season or theme in their lives, their sagas are rarely linear. Motherhood, still, is the great track-switcher: For all their efforts to share with their husbands housekeeping and childrearing responsibilities, the demands of family have almost always upended their lives more radically than they have unsettled their husbands'. So three decades after they graduated from Wellesley, some are senior partners in major law firms and some are recent graduates from law school. Alongside women at the top of careers pursued unremittingly are women who have dedicated their principal energies to their children and are only now entering graduate school or the workforce, or reentering after a long time. Some have grown children, born as early as December 1969; one is caring for a toddler, born in 1997. The fluidity of their lives has not been without limits: The biological clock imposes its imperatives, as does the premium on youth in the workplace. But theirs are complicated intertwinings of work and marriage and motherhood and daughterhood, with interruptions and distractions and divided attention and necessary new beginnings. The boundaries between chapters therefore sometimes blur.

The confusion of realms presented a dilemma as to what to call these women throughout the book. In the 1950s, the use of first names generally indicated a subordinate status: A secretary was Betty or Carol; her boss was Mr. Thompson or Dr. Smith. That changed with the mixing by the sixties generation of personal and public life. The current president is referred to by his first name more than any of his predecessors because of the familiarity he has invited with public talk of such matters as his underwear, and because his presidency has seemed to be more novelistic than most. The phrase "Friends of Bill" is a perfect example of how intimacy and organized politics have become intertwined; another is the political controversy stirred by Hillary Rodham's youthful decision to carry her maiden name forward into her marriage. Like Bill, Hillary is often just "Hillary" in the conversations of ordinary people, including, of course, her classmates. For that reason, and because their stories weave in and out so often between private and public life, I have for the most part referred to Hillary and the rest of the women of Wellesley '69 by their first names. The one exception is in Chapter Four, where I deal at length with the work of two women in the class virtually in isolation from their private lives; in that case, it seemed appropriately formal to use their last names.

Chapter One looks at their years together at Wellesley, their first experience away from the domestic cocoon, and their first taste of loyalties divided between the world they grew up in and the new possibilities then emerging for women. Chapter Two goes backward, then, for a closer look at the circumstances of their girlhood and the nature of the imprint left upon them by their mothers' lives. Chapter Three focuses on those who dove deep into "the sixties," shaking radically loose from their past with all manner of political and personal transgressions of their parents' rule. Chapter Four—the first of three chapters on their lives at work— looks at how their encounters with a "man's world" reinforced or reshaped their ideas of what it means to be a woman and how, in turn, they have remade their professions. Chapter Five recognizes their struggles as pioneers—the lone woman in her medical school, the first vice-president at her bank—recalling the barriers present thirty years ago for women and the battles required to bring them down. Chapter Six takes on the subject that is both most discussed and most susceptible to ideological distortion—the dilemmas of balancing work and family. Chapter Seven looks at those in the class who have stayed home to raise their kids; and Chapter Eight, at those who have wound up single—by choice or luck. Chapter Nine is given over to two women whose journeys toward an authentic identity and life have been particularly arduous and wild. Chapter Ten focuses on the quest that increasingly defines these women's lives, for spiritual knowledge and serenity. And Chapter Eleven looks at how they are facing the mortal struggles of midlife—empty nests, erratic hormones, aging parents, aging selves.

Mary Catherine Bateson has argued that the constant improvisations and sustained peripheral vision required by the interrupted female life are not crippling to a woman's life and work but creative. She proposes "the knight errant as a better model for our times than the seeker of the grail." Dorothy Devine, '69, offers another model: She has taken up a classic woman's craft—needlework. "A patchwork quilt is like a kaleidoscope of your life; you're making something harmonious of all the disparate pieces."

Richard Holmes, biographer of Coleridge and Shelley, believes that a biographer should find a subject "that actually puts him on guard in the most extreme and delicate way—that, as it were, throws down a challenge." As a woman exactly ten years younger than my subjects, I have often felt that there was much at stake for me in their answers to my questions. There is no formula to derive here: The marrieds are not categorically happier than the unmarrieds—nor are the professionals or those with children or those without. Their happiness, where it exists, cannot be dissected or hunted with a map like buried treasure; it is not a destination arrived at ever after but one fleetingly won and lost. Though these lives defy the attempt to craft a certain recipe for a fruitful life, to listen to these women is nonetheless cheering. They are, for the most part, "in love with daylight," in Wilfrid Sheed's lovely phrase. "When I say a prayer," says the orphaned, unmarried, childless, too often celibate, more than once heartbroken Chris Osborne, '69, "it is a prayer of thanks."

REBELS IN WHITE GLOVES

CHAPTER ONE

The Wellesley Years

At Christmas break of her senior year, Dorothy Devine got married in a white tulle veil and a moiré silk wedding gown with a high Victorian collar and a micro-miniskirt, daisies in her hair.

A moon-faced, mild, middle-class girl from Winnetka, Illinois, Dorothy had never felt fully at home at Wellesley. The academic demands overwhelmed her, and she had made few friends among the sleek New York debs and midwestern heiresses in their cashmere sweater sets and gold circle pins. By sophomore year, she was spending much of her time across the river in Cambridge, where, at a meeting of the Students for a Democratic Society, she met Dan Gilbarg, an intense young radical with curly hair and a scraggly mustache. Though just a senior at Harvard, Dan was teaching "Socialist Critiques of American Society" with New Left political philosopher Herbert Marcuse and Black Panther Eldridge Cleaver. Dan upended Dorothy's fearful certainty of the "domino theory" of Communist hegemony. At his urging, she began writing for *The Liberation News*, covering "community work in the ghettos, third world revolutions, police brutality, and the truth of events in Havana and Hanoi." Together they painted placards and staged sit-ins in Harvard Square.

Dorothy had never had a date in high school, never even been kissed. So when she told her mother junior year that she had a boyfriend and was on the pill, her Catholic father "went bonkers." The first time she brought Dan home to meet the family, her father told her that he had hidden his navy sword to avoid killing the young man who'd compromised his only daughter. Mr. Devine wrote her twenty-page letters every day, telling her she was a ruined woman. He went to the dean of the college in a rage, excoriating her for failing to meet her responsibility to keep his daughter a virgin. "Wellesley was this castle in the woods full of princesses," says Dorothy. "My father was angry because the tower wasn't tall enough."

To punish Dorothy for her immoral behavior, her father took away all her money and demanded she get married if she hoped for any further support. "I had no idea what I wanted to do and how I would support myself. I believed I needed a man to get money. And marrying the future professor—that seemed like something to do with my life. So I married Dan. Then my father refused to come to graduation, because we were Communists. When Dan and I moved into a radical collective, he cut ties completely. That hurt a lot, because I felt harried into my marriage. It was not a particularly happy day. And my mother couldn't really intervene. She was always under my father's thumb. He ran the house, and you were either a patriot or traitor, right or wrong. Here I'd done what I was supposed to do: I had married the Ivy League man and set up housekeeping. But I got punished for it. The Vietnam War, the sexual revolution, it just completely pulled us apart. There was this huge, unbridgeable gap between generations."

Like reluctant seafarers, one foot aboard ship, the other still reaching for familiar ground, the women of the Wellesley class of '69 spent their years at college poised precariously across a chasm between two worlds. Lagging a breath behind the rest of America's campuses, physically isolated and archaic in its traditions, Wellesley inhabited at the end of the decade an odd crease in time, where everything meant by *the fifties* and all that would come to be called *the sixties* existed for a moment side by side.

Parents with traditional notions of femininity had sent their shining girls into pastoral quietude to be cultivated into graceful mothers and wives. In this "hothouse for purebred flowers," as Kris Olson, '69, remembers it, the girls would chastely await the arrival of their Ivy prince. Their campus guidebook neatly summarized centuries of feminine destiny. "We are the sought, rather than the seekers. How do we begin being sought?"

At the same time, even high in their Gothic towers, the young women of Wellesley could not help but hear the countervailing messages in the culture. Already in the decade of their girlhood, the civil rights movement had insisted on a broadened definition of equality and demonstrated a grassroots mechanism for social change; by the late sixties, its principles and practices had been embraced by the movement for women's equality. The joys of sex were being publicly celebrated as never before in advertising, Hollywood, and rock 'n' roll. And though few would feel the sting of tear gas, most of these girls admired the rebellion under way against their parents' values by antiwar activists, student protesters, New Left intellectuals, consciousness expanders, Whole Earthers, humanist psychologists, spiritual pilgrims, sexual adventurers—all promising a doorway out of what Hillary Rodham would call in her graduation speech "inauthentic reality" and into "a more penetrating . . . existence." The Wellesley college newspaper regularly covered Timothy Leary's lectures at Harvard, in which he urged all his "well-adjusted" young students to jettison their "parochial psychic stability," drop acid, and complicate their ways of seeing and experiencing the world.

In the odd crease in time Wellesley inhabited, such radical injunctions inevitably took on a pastel hue. Reporting on her interview with Frank Zappa junior year, Wellesley *News* correspondent Chris Franz, '69, duly reported the rock star's standard advice: "Freak out, Suzy Creamcheese. Drop out of school before your brain rots." What Zappa meant, Chris reassured her readers, was merely that the "supersocialized product of the education system should cast off outmoded and restrictive thinking and etiquette." His call to drop out, she wrote in a profile tucked into the paper between an ad for Brooks Brothers clothiers and a notice for the collegiate queen competition, "was aimed at students in public school." And the Mothers of Invention, she added, were all exceedingly "well mannered and clean."

Living on the cusp between the age of the feminine mystique and the age of feminism, it is characteristic of this class that its most radical member, Dorothy Devine, borrowed her politics from her boyfriend, like a letter sweater or a fraternity pin. It is characteristic of the times that her rebellion was taken seriously only when it impinged on sex, marriage, and home. There would be many deep estrangements between the women of '69 and their mostly Republican moms and dads. Nearly all would erupt over domestic concerns. At their root was a fundamental question: What is a woman's essential nature, her proper place and role?

In the late forties, when the women of Wellesley '69 were born, the answer to that question was being radically re-formed. In the two decades after the war, sex roles temporarily loosened by the first wave of feminism, the Depression, and the demands of the war economy were circumscribed again within bounds as narrow as any in the century. Freud's Victorian conceit—that anatomy is destiny—recovered, in the fifties, its status as Truth. At the same time, Freud's descendants in the social sciences ruled femininity a fragile possession. True womanhood—fecund, nurturing, compliant—did not exist simply by virtue of being female: It required protection and cultivating and could easily be jeopardized by excess independence or a too-willful mind. Masculinity, too, could be readily deformed, if Father was a Milquetoast and Mother too strong; man's God-given superior strength existed only by the grace of female weakness.

If, as the experts attested, passivity and domesticity were fundamental to female identity, then education—the right to which the first-wave feminists had fought their earliest battles—could only be damaging. The women who entered Wellesley in 1965 were America's best little girls: 90 percent had been their high school newspaper editor, student body president, or valedictorian. Yet in the odd moment they inhabited, the pursuit of higher education for a woman could itself be regarded defiant. In a short story entitled "Revelation," published in 1965, Flannery O'Connor captured how grotesque a studious girl then seemed to much of the world. In the waiting room of a doctor's office, a fat, ugly girl "blue with acne" wearing Girl Scout shoes and heavy socks "scowls into a book called Human Development . . . annoyed that anyone should speak while she tried to read." The girl smirks and glares with dislike, "her eyes fixed like two drills" on the country wives who surround her, making a loud ugly noise through her teeth. "Mary Grace goes to Wellesley," her ladylike mother apologizes to the increasingly discomfited women around them. "Just reads all the time, a real bookworm. . . . I think it's too much. I think she ought to get out and have fun."

When Kathy Smith, '69, of Wilmington, Delaware, came home from high school with a perfect report card, as she never failed to do, she knew she would have to face her mother's fury. "Mom thought I should be like my sister, who was a majorette and not much of a student and wildly popular and married her high school sweetheart. All the women in her bridge club ever wanted to know was, Doesn't Kathy have a boyfriend yet? I was supposed to look attractive to men at all times, but my mother always told me that I was not attractive, that I was a failure on that score, and it was a matter of great concern. When I applied to Wellesley, she told me that I didn't belong with those kinds of people, that I'd get my head filled with fancy ideas and come back thinking I was better than the rest of the family. She was very clear: My job was to find a husband, and a smart girl would scare boys off."

In her concern that education would jeopardize her daughter's future, Mrs. Smith echoed the most estimable psychologists and doctors of the day. A passionate intelligence, the experts advised, was distinctly unfeminine; if encouraged, it would certainly condemn a girl to a life "unsexed." *Redbook* and *Ladies' Home Journal* were full of cautionary parables about the too-clever young lady who loses her young man to a helpless, charmingly addle-brained creature in need of his protection. Even if she avoided the tragedy of spinsterhood, the educated woman would become "masculinized," in the words of a standard 1950s text, with "enormously dangerous consequences to the home, the children dependent on it and to the ability of the woman, as well as her husband, to obtain sexual gratification." *Brain* was an epithet, applied to a girl: Hillary Rodham's high school newspaper predicted she would become a nun, called Sister Frigidaire.

Spinsterhood and frigidity were not the only lurking dangers. The near-certain consequence of education was dissatisfaction for a girl with her place—ordained by God and science—as mother and wife. Medical experts cautioned against thwarting what a group of male doctors told *Life* magazine was a healthy woman's "primitive biological urge toward reproduction, homemaking and nurturing. She deeply wants to be able to submit to her husband." In 1960, *The New York Times* scolded the presidents of women's colleges who "maintain, in the face of complaints, that sixteen years of academic training is realistic preparation for wifehood and motherhood. . . . The road from Freud to Frigidaire, from Sophocles to Spock, has turned out to be a bumpy one." Like those who argued against educating the Negro lest it confuse him as to his proper place—fomenting restlessness and menacing the social order—the critics of women's education couched their warnings in benevolent terms. "To urge upon her a profession in the man's world can adversely affect a girl," wrote a Yale psychologist, advising against the admission of women to the college. "She wants to be free of guilt and conflict about being a fulfilled woman." A Harvard psychiatrist, also opposed to coeducation, saw social dangers: "Only when women enter upon motherhood with a sense of fulfillment shall we attain the goal of a good life and a secure world." Still others warned against wasting resources: The education that girls would not use as housewives was urgently needed by boys to do the work of the atomic age. In 1971, Radcliffe president Matina Horner described the consequence of this relentless message: A "double bind" entraps a bright young woman, she wrote. "If she fails, she is not living up to her own standard; if she succeeds, she is not living up to societal expectations about the female role."

Concerned for their survival, some women's colleges attempted to appease the experts and allay parental fears, instituting curricula in family life and urging girls into home economics degrees. By the time Friedan published *The Feminine Mystique,* Mills College had adopted a slogan: "We are not educating women to be scholars, but to be wives and mothers." Rather than promote such masculine and "vastly overrated" qualities as creativity and individualism, the college's president promised, Mills would nurture the feminine talent for "relationship."

In the midst of this debate, Wellesley was singled out for praise among the Seven Sisters for managing not to disturb the serenity of the young women in its charge. Wellesley girls, said Princeton's 1965 guide to coeds, remain "strikingly traditional." The class of '69 looked like a group of "nice young future den mothers" to a Harvard critic's eyes. While the rest of the campus world was going "madly mod," the *Boston Globe* reported, "Les Wellesley Femmes go blithely on with the basics." They are not given "to the long hair, bulging book bags and breathless brilliance found at Radcliffe . . . or the compulsive egalitarianism of Barnard students," *Time* magazine wrote of Hillary's entering class, adding what, at a time when "adjustment" to one's given life role was counted the highest form of mental health, could only be read as glowing praise. "Their distinguishing characteristic is that they don't stand out. They are simply wholesome creatures, unencumbered by the world's woes, who make normal, well-adjusted housewives."

Wellesley had in fact taken pains to be certain that Hillary and her classmates would grow up to be normal housewives, preserving traditions long jettisoned elsewhere. Like their mothers and grandmothers, the women of '69 would be "finished" as ladies. Among their required courses were figure training (instruction in how to stay shapely and pert) and fundamentals of movement, which included learning how to get out of the backseat of a car while wearing high heels. Wednesday afternoons, they practiced the proper pouring of tea. A good portion of the campus guidebook was devoted to appropriate attire: Suits were ideal for dates; "one cocktail dress is usually all you'll need until Christmas." Skirts were mandatory at dinner—"a good incentive to neaten up and make the table more attractive." For after-dinner demitasse and trips into town, the girls were to add white gloves to the ensemble. Their girlish purity was often on display as they paraded in green beanies, sang hymns on the chapel steps, or donned the gossamer white gowns of "tree maidens" to form a W, sing the alma mater, and skip and dance across Severance Green. A helpful "Wellesley lexicon" focused on what its author assumed was the girls' principal preoccupation: "A 'caller' is an eligible male at the Bell Desk. A 'visitor' is a father-image caller or a lady. 'Harvard' is not strictly part of Wellesley. We share it with the 'Cliffies. The pavilions around Waban Lake are 'spoonholders,' because they hold spooners. 'Gracious living' is what we all aspire to."

Girls of good breeding, many of them descended from several generations of Wellesley women, were being cultivated to marry and rear the men who would run America. That they were in fact being groomed for breeding was not always subtly expressed. When Rusty Steele's mom graduated from Wellesley in 1943, she and her classmates had been told: "You are the cream of the crop. If we want to improve the species, it is your job to go out and reproduce." By the time Rusty was a freshman in 1965, that message had been muted, but it had hardly disappeared. The annual "marriage lecture"—which offered guidance on such matters as how to converse with your husband's boss and how long to let the baby cry—was still mandatory. The psychology department offered a curriculum heavy on abnormal child psychology and its roots in maternal failure. Seniors still rolled giant hoops down a hill on May Day in a race to see who would be the first to marry. And, in a strange exercise with links to the eugenics movement, the girls were required to have a posture picture taken soon after they entered school. Wearing only her underwear, with reflective stickers marking her spine, each freshman was put in a small pitch-black closet and told to stand very still. When the doors flew open, a flash of light captured on film her shivering form, then the doors slammed abruptly shut—presumably to protect her from prying eyes. The pictures were then scrutinized to see how well each young lady's figure and posture conformed to the ideal, which, according to guidelines put out by the college's department of hygiene, was characterized by "the buttocks being neither unduly prominent nor having that 'about to be spanked' look." Like similar pictures taken at elite colleges around the country, the pictures were later sought by a man of questionable science intent on determining what physiognomy signified the superior genetic material possessed by these girls. Wellesley, to its credit, was one of the few colleges that refused his request.

Few of the young ladies protested Wellesley's efforts to polish them into choice mothers and wives. Accustomed to doing what they were told, reared on *Cinderella, Marjorie Morningstar,* and *Donna Reed,* most of them dutifully embraced as their primary purpose at Wellesley the pursuit of a "ring by spring." Eldie Acheson, '69, granddaughter of Truman's secretary of state Dean Acheson, recalls "a big social premium on getting the right guy. When Kate Pillsbury [of the Doughboy fortune], who lived in a suite full of seniors as rich and socially prominent as she, got engaged to Godfrey Wood, all the talk on campus was about her ring, which was the size of a pool ball. He'd frozen it in ice and dropped it in her drink." In several of the yearbook pictures, diamonds grace folded hands. Most girls, says Kris Olson, "expected to marry and raise families and use their educations to be serious adjuncts to their husbands' careers."

In their first weeks as freshmen, those keen to be quickly settled in a suburban split-level, a bridge foursome, a car pool, and Junior League pored over the Wellesley College newspaper's guide to the nearby "shrines of masculine learning." Boston College was to be avoided; those boys "were not going to take you home to meet their mom, would never marry a Methodist or Episcopalian and only want one thing." Not all MIT men had stooped shoulders, slide rules, and pocket protectors, but Princeton boys, in their Weejuns and tweed, "would worry all evening that you look better than they do." Girls headed to isolated Dartmouth "should expect to be greeted with open arms, and take a hat pin." Without question, the best spot for seeking a mate was a Harvard mixer, the

News advised. Harvard felt the same way about Wellesley: At elite clubs like the Porcellian, the young men scanned Wellesley's freshman face book as if looking over a paddock full of thoroughbred fillies. The *Harvard Crimson* offered a more acidic tribute: It dubbed Wellesley "a school for tunicata—small fish who spend the first part of their lives frantically swimming around the ocean floor exploring their environment, and the second part of their lives just lying there breeding."

To Wellesley to Wed

As she packed her daughter, Nancy, off to Wellesley, Marge Wanderer, a round woman with pink cheeks and hair silvered like frosting, quietly nursed her fears as to the future of her beautiful, ebullient girl. "What we hoped we would get from Wellesley is that we thought it would develop her into a fine wife and a wonderful mother," she told *Frontline* in the documentary that aired in 1994. But Marge also worried that Nancy wouldn't make the extra effort necessary at a women's college to meet eligible men. In high school, she'd had to press her daughter to put on a bit of makeup and go out on dates. Even after Nancy began dating a man I'll call Thomas in the spring of freshman year, Marge worried that she would "send him to the shower before he had a chance to pitch a full inning."

For all her mother's worries, Nancy's storybook wedding at the end of junior year seemed, to her classmates, inevitable. Button-nosed, with her mother's bright blue eyes and a gap-toothed, sunshine smile, Nancy was her schoolmates' vision of the all-American girl. They elected her class president freshman year, and chose her over Hillary Rodham for junior representative to the National Student Association (this just shortly after *Ramparts* magazine disclosed that the NSA had received $3 million from the CIA, a fact that apparently dampened neither girl's enthusiasm for the post). She planned to run against Hillary senior year for student government president, and believes she might have won. Though it is the rare class member who does not remember being courted by Hillary— invited to join her at a Young Republicans mixer at Harvard Law School or asked to dine in her dorm—"she was somewhat intimidating," says Nancy. "I think people were more comfortable with me."

It was Thomas's unpretentious ways that captured Nancy's heart. "He seemed more mature than the others. He was handsome and ambitious, taller and maybe smarter than me—all those things a man was supposed to be. He had this unfashionable haircut, a kind of buzz cut, and a frayed collar. He talked about things besides how many beers he could drink, and invited me up to Bowdoin—not to party, but to show me the Maine coast, where he worked on fishing boats in the summer.

"Thomas picked the timing—for our engagement and wedding and then for our baby. It was a beautiful wedding, just the way my mother wanted it. We had five hundred people in the Wellesley chapel, four hundred of them Wellesley friends."

Nancy had just one moment's doubt about her choice to take refuge in marriage. "When I began to get politically aware at Wellesley, Thomas belittled me. I went to hear McGeorge Bundy debate the Vietnam War with [Eugene McCarthy speechwriter] Richard Goodwin and was so excited I immediately called Thomas. He was completely patronizing, 'Oh, Dick Goodwin,' he said. 'I knew about him years ago.' He thought he knew it all. Maybe he did, but I wanted to know it, too. It dawned on me that he intended to do the thinking for both of us." Gnawed by foreboding, she finally shrugged off her doubts and at age twenty became a bride. "When I told Jan Krigbaum I was getting married, she said, 'Why are you doing this? You haven't done anything in your life.' I said, 'Oh no, I really love him. I want to iron his shirts.' I had heard Betty Friedan speak freshman year, and thought, This has nothing to do with me. I just didn't get that being married so young would limit me. I wanted to be in the Junior Show; it would have been great fun to collaborate with those women, but Thomas didn't want me to be in it. He said it would distract from the announcement of our engagement. I dropped out of choir to spend my weekends at Bowdoin, then got engaged and dropped out of the race for student government president. But I really didn't know myself. Marriage provided an answer. I escaped into it with a great sense of relief."

Gazing upon her daughter's seven bridesmaids in their pale blue dresses and the promising young groom, Marge Wanderer knew her every wish had come true. "What she came home with was beyond a mother's wildest dreams. And I just thought, Wow. Whatever it cost us, it was well worth it, because look what she found at Wellesley. She was a traditional bride, with veil and train, and her mother was pleased as punch because here was the end of a dream. This young lady dressed in white was my daughter, and she was beautiful."

In 1968, however, no Cinderella story could be so simple, even at Wellesley. The fantasies about marriage offered in literature and movies and music were growing ever less sentimental and more parodic or dark—in the poetry of Anne Sexton and the erotic diaries of Anaïs Nin (both cult figures to 1960s college girls), in the bad-girl songs of the Ronettes and Martha Reeves. The skeptical female voice then emergent in rock 'n' roll is catalogued in Susan Douglas's *Where the Girls Are:* Lesley Gore's warning to a boyfriend that "You Don't Own Me"; the satire of suburban small-mindedness in "Harper Valley PTA"; a preference for bad boys over husband material in "Leader of the Pack"; the flaunting of female sexual appetite in "I'm Ready" and "Heat Wave." In film, the pathetic spinster—bun-headed and frigid—metamorphosed in 1961 into the beautiful, winningly nonconformist, and nonvirginal Holly Golightly, smoking and drinking all night and vowing not "to let anyone put me in a cage." Helen Gurley Brown took up the cause a year later with *Sex and the Single Girl,* and then the *"Cosmo* girl"—spinning glamorous fantasies of the liberated bachelorette, with her own studio apartment and edible panties. Even Barbie, introduced in 1958 when most '69ers were ten, eschewed marriage and motherhood for an independent life. In 1963, six years ahead of Hillary, Barbie became a college grad, with a cap and gown. By 1969, she had a job, black girlfriends, velvet bell-bottoms, and long, straight hippie hair. Throughout, Ken remained a mere accessory. The doll's cruel measurements aside, M. G. Lord, in her biography of the world's most successful toy, makes a persuasive case for Barbie as a "decidedly subversive heroine."

Though their mothers' generation found a sense of common cause in the best-selling *Feminine Mystique,* and though most of the class of '69 would eventually read it, no book spoke more directly to these young college girls facing compulsory suburban happiness than Sylvia Plath's *The Bell Jar.* Heroine Esther Greenwood, a gifted student at a northeastern women's college, imagines marriage to be a dreary affair "for a girl with fifteen years of straight A's . . . dawdling in curlers, washing the dirty plates while her husband went off for a lively, fascinating day." Devoting herself to "baby after fat puling baby" seems an equally bleak prospect: Drained of her desire to write poems, she would become "numb as a slave in some private, totalitarian state." As for suburban life, Plath drew on her hometown of Wellesley to describe a journey in her mother's Chevrolet: ". . . white, shining, identical clapboard houses with the interstices of well-groomed green proceeded past, one bar after another in a large but escape-proof cage."

The Wellesley girls voiced their own resistance to their compulsory marital aspirations with riffs on the college motto. *Non Ministrare, Sed Ministrari*—"Not to be ministered unto, but to minister to"—is an unquestionably admirable call to good works. But to women reared in the fifties, it also evoked the endless handmaidenry of the traditional homemaker's life. "Not to be ministers but to be ministers' wives" seemed to the '69ers a more truthful rendering of their Latin credo. That skeptical view of their inevitable destiny was the inspiration for the showpiece of their college career, the Junior Show.

For director Chris Osborne, '69, the show was her first chance to make use of a new, painfully won freedom. Raised in a "foul corner" of Rochester, New York—paved with strip malls and gas stations and shabby little tract houses—Chris had been rigidly disciplined and confined as a child. Though books were her first love, her father forbade her to read Alan Watts on Zen or J. D. Salinger's *Catcher in the Rye*. His iron rule followed Chris to Wellesley, until Sophomore Father's Day, when, to the girl's great horror and shame, Mr. Osborne dropped dead of a heart attack on campus. A droll creature, Chris tells how her dad "quit in front of the whole class" as abruptly as Nabokov dispenses with Lolita's father ("picnic; lightning"), though she adds almost in passing that every misery since has descended from her failure to face her pain then. Chris transmuted her grief to wildness—"If my father had been alive, I would never have smoked pot; I would have been certain he would catch me and punish me brutally"—and a detached, black wit that has remained with her ever since.

For the Junior Show, Chris and her classmates crafted a goofy account of a bunch of natives on an island as remote as Wellesley hoping to be discovered by Columbus so they can "sell their wares" with some "Madison Avenue Injun Guile." After a brief show of independence, its two heroines arrive at their inevitable fate. Sizzynine, the tribal prophetess, runs off with an incongruously WASP ship astronomer: "No injun brave/could make me rave/It's a man from a classier league that gets me.

. . . No toothless chief compares with Leif/Blond, with no odor of horse/Really Norse/but of course I'd love him." She joins the expedition, promising to contribute somehow: "I can cook up a storm." Meanwhile Jade West, who had been the lone voice of caution—"They'll either make slaves of us or commercialize us"—swoons for Captain Miguel d'Ivy Leagua, who makes her his bride. Inverting yet again the Wellesley motto, Columbus instructs Miguel he is "not to minister unto, but to be ministered to."

A more flamboyant dissent against their suburban future erupted among the precocious feminists in the class. In December 1968, the Women's International Terrorist Conspiracy from Hell (WITCH), including some "parolees from Wellesley," infiltrated the Wellesley Alumnae Club luncheon and bridge party at Grace Episcopal Church in Brooklyn. WITCH founder Robin Morgan had led the Miss America Pageant protest earlier that year and, with her "coven," had recently pronounced an incantation on Wall Street, erupting in a jubilant clamor when the stock market dropped five points. Now "disguised" in Villager dresses, the WITCH girls settled sweetly into their bridge foursomes with the Wellesley alumnae, then interrupted their own bidding with cries of "Oh my God, all those years pounding my brains out and here I am playing bridge!" They were there, they explained, "to contact Wellesley sisters, whose witch powers were eliminated when they were shackled in velvet chains and placed in protective compounds," and, paraphrasing Thorstein Veblen's theory of the leisure class, to protest "the phallic culture which imposes on women the empty life of a consumer class." As they were ushered from the church garden by horrified alumnae, they chanted the latest television ad for diet Jell-O. "What's the difference between a career girl and an old maid? . . . Nothing!"

The Politics of Manners

For girls raised to be ever well behaved and demure, to make such a scene was an insurrection akin to suffragists shingling their hair and baring their bloomers to the world. Flouting feminine behavior and fashion has, in fact, always been a rebellious woman's first move. Long before they explicitly declared the personal to be political, feminists had recognized that the seemingly private and trivial matters of decorum and dress were in fact weighted with political meaning. Rules about what a lady wore or said or did served to define what a woman could be— capable only of mincing steps, for instance, or shameful in her sexuality and having to be covered or concealed.

The '69ers' fashion rebellion began the first moment they were out of their mothers' sight. Tossing away their Peter Pan collars and box-pleated skirts, emblems of girlish innocence, they tried on the androgyny and mobility offered by boys' jeans, the unfettered sexuality of miniskirts, or such antifashion statements as Hillary's Coke-bottle glasses and unkempt hair. Nancy Gist recalls her classmates Eldie Acheson, who spent winters at her grandfather's retreat in Antigua and summers sailing and playing tennis with the Kennedys on Cape Cod, and Nancy Rowe, daughter of a prominent midwestern steel family, "rebelling against where they came from" by a willful dishevelment. At the wedding of Huali Chai, '69, to a young Mormon graduate of the Harvard Business School, says Nancy, the roommates all "wore skirts halfway up our asses," and Kris Olson, now U.S. attorney in Oregon, "had her hair piled up on her head like a streetwalker." The whole picture proved too much for the groom's mother, who wept for three days.

Several of their battles with Wellesley authorities centered on fashion. In 1968, the girls won permission to wear slacks to cafeteria meals, as long as they were wool, and overturned the requirement that long hair be wound in a bun for graduation. An official history of the college written that year recognized a genuine protest. "A generation brought up by TV . . . became distrustful of words and images. Students appeared in the dean's office with bare feet, cutoff jeans and an old shirt tied around the midriff. . . . This seeming lack of respect was in reality an inchoate attempt to express the very sincere belief that appearance did not matter and that what was important was the inner man."

For the five black women in the class, hair was loaded with yet another layer of political meaning. Fran Rusan and Nancy Gist both adopted Afros. "A lot of black women decided there was no longer a need to have the long, flowing locks that were the cultural ideal until 1968," says Nancy. "I had a long flip, but I cut my hair and stopped straightening it. Only, I forgot to tell my mother. When I got home to Chicago for the summer, she almost died. I had not been at all politicized when I left for school, at sixteen. My parents had bought me a

first-class airplane ticket. They were so proud I was going off to Wellesley. It seemed to validate all their expectations of my success, so it mortified them to see me return with a headful of kinky Angela Davis hair.
Symbolically, my mother was losing control of me. She is fair-skinned
and has pretty straight hair. The whole straightening biz was to suggest
that I'd inherited that. I said, 'Ma, I got kinky hair and I like it.' I understood that I could put aside all that was involved in the pretense of
straight hair, that I could reject that other standard. But even twenty-six
years later, when I told my mother that [Attorney General] Janet Reno
had asked to meet with me [regarding a job as director of the Bureau of
Justice Assistance, for which Nancy was later confirmed], the first thing
she said is, 'I hope you'll do something nice with your hair.' "

Men, of course, also rebelled in the sixties against what Eldridge
Cleaver called "their old crew-cut elders who don't dig their caveman
mops." If in the fifties hair had to stay in its place, in the sixties its uncut
unruliness would symbolize freedom. But for women such a rebellion
was both more precedented and more charged: A woman's appearance
has always been her most vital currency in the world and fraught with
social meaning.

Women's rebellions against the constraints of fashion are also more
likely to boomerang and do them harm. To invest questions of manners
and dress with too much attention, even rebellious attention, can drain a
woman's energy and keep her trapped in self-consciousness; in Simone
de Beauvoir's words, such a preoccupation "rivets her to the ground and
to herself." It is the danger ever present in a politics focused too concert-
edly on the personal—of self-trivialization, the neglect of larger questions, the squandering of whole books on whether lipstick is feminist.

A preoccupation with fashion also makes women easy targets for
mockery, providing more evidence, as historian Anne Hollander has
written, of a "distinctively female superficiality and moral weakness."
The 1963 New York Review of Books parody of The Group made just that
point: "squinty, pink-cheeked Maisie," having just been deflowered on a
tacky flowered couch ("Mother would have minded the couch somehow
more than the event"), puts on her "Lord and Taylor bias-cut cocktail
dress (all the rage this year, just as Hitler was threatening to reoccupy the
Rhineland) and slips out."

Whatever social rebellion women might have thought they were engaged in, politics would wind up a mere footnote to fashion, attention to their clothes and looks eclipsing all else. Coverage of the early women's movement inevitably lingered over Gloria Steinem's "long blond-streaked hair falling just so above each breast" or wrote off Kate Millett as an ugly woman who hated men because they never asked her out. "Poor Betty," *The New York Times Magazine* said of Friedan in 1970. She would "happily have traded 30 points on the IQ scale for a modicum of good looks."

The Wellesley rebels fared little better. In a *Boston Herald* story on a rally led by Hillary Rodham protesting course distribution require-ments, the reporter linked female disobedience with that other great threat to the American way, ignoring the substance of their complaint and noting only that "they looked like the Bolshevik women's auxiliary, in their fur caps and high boots, conspiring." When the young women joined a national student hunger strike in 1967 to protest the war in Viet-nam, young men calling themselves "frequenters of the campus" wrote a letter to the college newspaper lauding their initiative. "We like you nu-bile; we like you fresh. A bit of fasting tones the flesh."

"Protest boxy suits," urged ads in the *Wellesley News* for Nehru jackets and paper dresses adorned with peace signs, appropriating the groovy new language of dissent in a tactic that would soon be standard on Madison Avenue. "Protest big ugly shoes!"

In 1968, the *Wellesley News* vented the students' frustration at such frivolous treatment, lambasting *The New York Times* for its regular items on the "clinging Ivy" League, which perpetuated "the revoltingly cute and socially serene image society editors have long assigned to us, all blondes and bustlines, dates and debs."

These women were, in fact, behind the times. The fight for "student power" had begun much earlier on most campuses, inspired by the 1963 Free Speech Movement at Berkeley; while many of their peers had moved on to planting bombs and barricading buildings, Hillary and her classmates were requesting, nicely, that the college eliminate parietals. The young ladies overturned a rule restricting male guests in dorms to Sunday afternoons only, with the door kept open, as well as an 11 P.M. curfew, a prohibition against cars, and an official admonition to married seniors not to reveal to the younger students any "secrets of married life."

Again, such victories were easily mocked. In March 1968, four Princeton boys wrote the *Wellesley News* regarding the "recent history of growing student disobedience and immorality at Wellesley as evidenced by radical changes in parietals and dress . . . oh Wellesley, no longer may America look upon you as an impregnable bastion against drugs, booze, atheism, crime in the streets and pinko Communist libs. Go, we say, abolish your Bible requirements, lock yourselves in your bedrooms with strangers, dress like slovenly hoodlums instead of young ladies of breeding. We will never suffer our daughters to enter your sin-filled portals."

Easy targets though they were, the battles fought by the class of '69 were perhaps not so trivial: The demand for cars on campus seems somewhat less so when one considers how many of these girls' mothers were literally imprisoned in their suburban homes each day when their husbands took the family's only car to work, and how enamored the culture then was of the freedom promised by the open road—and the backseat. Nor was it frivolous for these women to seek the same personal freedoms that had always been allowed college men: Even in the 1990s, campus rules serve symbolically for the fundamental question of whether a woman can take responsibility for herself, alone with a man, without a chaperone. "We were determined to be treated not as girls but as adults," says Nancy Gist. The radical freedom for which they ultimately fought was to control their own sexual behavior at a time of immense upheaval in social mores.

Good Girls and Bad

As with marriage, the messages about sex were, in those years, profoundly mixed. These women had grown up well aware that an American tragedy awaited the girl who went all the way. Women who had sex before marriage, like Dorothy Devine, were damaged, used up, even criminally delinquent. "There were good girls and bad girls, and bad girls did things good girls wouldn't," Ann Sherwood Sentilles, '69, recalls. "You didn't smoke or drink or go beyond petting. My father, who was a surgeon in Geneva, Ohio, would come home every so often and say, 'Another one of your friends is in trouble. I don't want to be embarrassed by that. Don't do anything that would bring shame on the family.' We all knew what happened if you got pregnant. You were disappeared—sent away to a home for wayward girls to have the baby under cover of night and give it up for adoption. That sort of thing didn't happen to a Wellesley girl. We were good girls. That's how we got there in the first place."

And yet. Something changed between freshman year, when Ann Landsberg, '69, was "shocked" to find birth control pills in a senior's room, and junior year, when she lamented that she was one of the last virgins on campus. The senior yearbook, designed by Alison "Snowy" Campbell, '69, flaunted the girls' new sexually knowing ways. Making a lewd pun on '69 in what she looks back on as "the naughtiest thing I ever did in my life," the angel-faced, willowy girl with soft brown eyes and white-blond hair put an acid–pink and green Mae West—in the psychedelic Art Nouveau style common to rock posters—right side up on the front cover, upside down on the back. (One of the many cheers for this class includes the line: "upside down, right side up, one-nine-six-nine Wellesley," though that was before oral-sex jokes became a source of public torment for Hillary.) A picture meant for the yearbook frontispiece was pulled at the last moment by the college administration: It featured the bare-assed figures of Snowy and Eldie and two other girls standing atop their dorm roof surveying the lush landscape. With a self-importance typical of their generation, they left the frontispiece blank but for a small, somber note about censorship by official powers. Yet for all their bravado, an innocence lingered at the marriage lecture in their senior year, which, against the wishes of the dean, addressed the subject of sex both inside and outside of marriage. The invited speaker, Carola Eisenberg of MIT's department of psychiatry, advised the girls that "if intercourse does occur, it is usually at first disappointing, often horrifying." The many young women in the audience who wanted to know what an orgasm was were chastised. "This is a medical question and will not be answered here. Go to the infirmary."

Like everything else, the sexual revolution reached Wellesley on a kind of time delay; elsewhere it had been gaining momentum since the end of World War II. A culture in the thrall of Freud anointed sexual fulfillment the best yardstick for measuring psychic well-being. Talking about sex became an acceptable, even necessary, proof of modern thinking: The Kinsey studies, first published in 1948, became runaway bestsellers with their accounts (however reliable) of rampant sexual experimentation in mainstream America. In 1953, the year the new *Playboy* magazine offered advice to men on how to outsmart "Miss Gold Digger" and get sex without getting trapped, half of American women said they were having premarital sex; from 1940 to 1961, the number of illegitimate births to mothers under twenty-five increased by 300 percent. "It seems that all America is one big orgone box," proclaimed a *Time* magazine cover story in January 1964, referring to the libido-enhancing machine conceived by Freud disciple Wilhelm Reich. "Day and night from screens and stages, advertising posters and newspaper pages it flashes larger-than-life-sized images of sex . . . with the message that sex will save you and libido make you free." Everything from "incest to inversion" could be found in novels like *Tropic of Cancer, Peyton Place,* and *Valley of the Dolls,* complained *Newsweek.* In Hollywood, taboos were crumbling, which in 1967 the head of the film production code deemed "the most healthy thing." Anaïs Nin offered her recipe for happiness: "Mix well the sperm of four men in one day." Even the leader of the National Council of Churches joined in, urging couples to "conjure up various positions" for their mutual pleasure. And no longer was carnal knowledge the exclusive province of girls of the lower classes. A psychologist at Radcliffe estimated that in the fifteen years after 1950, the proportion of girls having intercourse in college had risen from 25 to 40 percent. Where a generation earlier college boys had of necessity strayed off campus, "today they're looked down on if they can't succeed with a coed."

Though the sexual revolution is now remembered as a legacy of the sixties, it was not the younger generation that had launched this "orgy of open-mindedness," in *Time*'s view, but their elders, "who embrace the Freudian belief that repression, not license, is the great evil . . . and Ernest Hemingway's manifesto that 'what is moral is what you feel good after, and what is immoral is what you feel bad after.' " Cynthia Gilbert, '69, recalls an unsettling trip to the psychiatrist to deal with crippling bouts of depression during her sophomore year at Wellesley. "I'd just gotten engaged; our family had never been quite the *Father Knows Best* scenario, and I wanted the 'real family' that I hadn't had. The psychiatrist felt my childhood had been totally repressed and that I should be sleeping with my fiancé. I told her that in my family you simply didn't have sex, and she said, 'Why not?' I told her a story my mother had told me of going to a back alley with her best friends for an abortion in the thirties. She told me I could always go to Mexico if I had to. That psychiatrist's 'Why not?' scenario turned my already upside-down world totally inside out. Maybe a more gradual change would have been more helpful. My father was authoritarian; when I took that psychiatrist's advice and threw it all over, it was like adding fat to the fire."

Even at home, youngsters were pushed toward adult behavior too soon, *Time* warned in that same 1964 story, "by ambitious mothers who want them to be popular; with padded brassieres for twelve-year-olds and pressure to go steady at an ever younger age." Nancy Wanderer had balked in junior high at her mother's insistence that she wear heels and a girdle and makeup; she fought in vain against her mother's demand that she perm her hair. "She thought I should be more interested in dating, and though I didn't want to date, I did want to please her. So in eighth grade I had a torrid romance with a guy at my brother's school, who was three years older than me. He initiated me sexually, though I was so inexperienced, I didn't even realize it. My mother had never told me what not to do."

With her parents' blessing, Nancy and her beau talked about marriage and opened a joint bank account, a serious form of playing house in a decade when one out of every two girls was a teenage bride. But the sex had unnerved Nancy. "I quickly wised up that getting pregnant at thirteen was not the way to a great life. I broke it off, and after that I stayed in control. I just wouldn't have intercourse. At Wellesley I went out with this guy from MIT, a jazz pianist who was completely full of himself and was always telling me I should trade in my skirts and turtlenecks for something slinkier. Another guy, from Harvard, broke up with me 'cause I wouldn't have sex with him, then called me later to boast that he was sleeping with a girl at a local trade school. I lost so much valuable time at Wellesley with all my involvement with men. On weekends, the men's schools would send scouts to campus to pick up as many girls as they could fit in their cars to bring us to parties. It was like going for provisions. I was sick of all the smoothness, sick of the pressure not to be myself, worn-out by the struggle of: Will I have sex? Will I get birth control? I decided the important thing was to settle who would be the best husband. I wanted to get marriage over with, and put to rest all those questions about sex."

Useful Women

If the culture of the late sixties sent these women contradictory messages about marriage and sex, their alternatives—for financial self-sufficiency, professional achievement, worldly adventure—were no clearer. Again, Wellesley offered muddled guidance. The only one of the Seven Sisters to have always had a woman president and a charter mandating female faculty, Wellesley offered in its deans and scholars the first model that many of these girls had encountered of women committed to an intellectual and public life. For all its lingering scent of a finishing school, the college maintained rigorous academic standards and afforded an opportunity for its students to exert leadership without competition from men. Wellesley also had a remarkable history of educating "useful" women. In 1892, the college had graduated twelve doctors and twenty missionaries; by the turn of the century, it was sending substantial numbers of women into social work. Many became heads of settlement houses and trade unions or suffragists. Carolyn Wilson, '10, covered the First World War for the *Chicago Tribune*. Marguerite Stitt Church, '14, went to Congress from Illinois. Madame Chiang Kai-shek, '17, served as liaison between Nationalist China and the U.S.: In 1943, she went before Congress to plead for help in her nation's war against Japan, and, ever the Wellesley girl, described the lawmakers as "clodhopping, boorish and uncivilized." Patricia Lockridge Bull, '37, landed with the marines at Iwo Jima and was the first woman correspondent to enter the Buchenwald concentration camp. Jocelyn Gill, '38, was chief of in-flight science at NASA; Selma Gottlieb, '41, designed helicopters. Madeleine Albright, '59, would become U.S. ambassador to the United Nations and the first woman secretary of state. Cokie Roberts, '64, and Diane Sawyer, '67, would have spectacular journalistic careers. A 1962 survey of all alumnae found that more than four fifths had been employed, the vast majority in teaching. Though 62 percent had stopped work at marriage, 18 percent had worked for twenty years or more.

Still, "old maid" professors offered a warning as much as a model to the class of '69. And in a cultural climate so inhospitable to the education of young women for anything but future domestic roles, Wellesley joined other women's colleges in actively discouraging professional ambition in its charges. Though the deans consistently assured the girls that they were the cream of the cream, America's smartest young ladies, in the marriage lecture during their freshman year, the dean of the college advocated that the girls pursue work only as volunteers, to avoid competition—professional or financial—between husband and wife. During a debate over going coed, the director of admissions, Miss Clough, defended their single-sex education on the grounds that it prepared them for a "post-college life in community affairs with mostly women." An editorial in the college newspaper found "it probable that most Wellesley girls see professional careers, not marriage responsibilities, as the diversion" from their true and ultimate path in life. Jacqueline Kennedy was held out as the ideal: A "certifiable egghead," multilingual, a painter and art lover, educated at Vassar and the Sorbonne, she had been above all else exquisitely gracious and ornamental at her husband's side. "Those of us who graduated from Wellesley in the sixties weren't ever meant to have futures . . . or opinions," recalled writer and director Nora Ephron, '62, "we were meant to marry them. If you wanted to be an architect, you married an architect." Even the campus architecture underscored the message, as classics professor Mary Lefkowitz has noted. The Wellesley library doors are ornamented with two figures: Wisdom is a man; his female companion is Charity, comforting a child.

In the late sixties, the college newspaper was full of advertisements for engagement rings, padded bras, and pantie girdles, for a new computer dating service at MIT and Princeton tryouts for go-go girls for the Yale game. "Taking your M.R.S.?" asked a regular ad. "Do your cramming with *Modern Bride*." Recruitment notices were limited to those for Katherine Gibbs secretarial school ("the best way to get started in any field"); Braniff flight hostesses ("wear world-famous Pucci fashions as you fly in the most fascinating career of women today. You must be under 27, single and weigh less than 135 pounds"); and the CIA.

Outside of Wellesley, there was little more encouragement. Nearly half the women in America were working in 1965, but three quarters of them held clerical, sales, or household jobs. A report that year by the President's Commission on the Status of Women detailed widespread wage discrimination and a rapidly declining ratio of women in professional and executive jobs. Though in 1966 NOW condemned the custom that men carry the sole burden of supporting a family—"for a girl as for a boy, education can only be serious when there is an expectation that it will be used in society"—and launched lawsuits against employment discrimination, not until 1973 would the Supreme Court bar help-wanted ads listed by sex. In sum, the working world offered little but frustration to the college girl. As Radcliffe graduate Julie Hayden wrote in a 1965 *Atlantic Monthly* essay that was excerpted in the *Wellesley News:* "We wind up the Kafka readers in the typists' pool, the seekers after truth making coffee."

The "experts" were just as discouraging about work as they had been about education, diagnosing a woman with career aspirations as neurotic and unfeminine and a danger to society. The panel of male doctors gathered by *Life* magazine warned that "the disease of working women leads to children who become juvenile delinquents, atheists, Communists, and homosexuals. Daddy understands business. Mommy understands children." Even anthropologist Margaret Mead, who inspired numerous feminists with her argument that "personality traits we call masculine or feminine are as lightly linked to gender as are the clothing, manners and form of headdress that a society at a given period assigns to either sex," also argued that a girl's flickering ambition toward "compensatory achievement" dies down with the certainty of maternity. "It is of doubtful value to enlist the gifts of women if bringing them into fields defined as male frightens the men, and unsexes the women."

The popular culture offered few depictions of women at work, except for those unfortunates who had so far failed to snare a man. The secretary setting a trap for the promising young executive was a stock character of the time, in films like *The Apartment* and stories like John Cheever's "The Five Forty-Eight." The "organization bimbo," *Newsweek* called her. "Miss B.A., who has failed to catch a husband, is in New York seeking men," reported *Look* magazine in 1966. "She will be asked just one thing. 'How's your steno, dear?' Nimble fingers are of more interest than her nimble mind." Burdened with aspirations stirred up by college, she'll likely find herself "beaten out for jobs by docile high school grads, who win secretarial desks because college women grow restless too soon." The lucky ones will "end up typing letters, watering the boss's rubber plant and earning $65 a week." But never mind, the editors consoled, defying the conventional wisdom that a girl educated herself out of the marriage market. "The college girl holds one advantage. While the

Katie Gibbs grad lands the higher pay, it's the B.A. who succeeds with the college man."

Even women who had committed to serious work voiced ambivalence at the price. In her essay "Silences," published in *Harper's Magazine* in 1965, Tillie Olsen demonstrated how nearly impossible it was for a woman to do creative work and also be a mother and wife: Jane Austen, George Eliot, Emily Dickinson, Eudora Welty, Virginia Woolf— all had remained childless throughout their lives. Sylvia Plath wrote of her fears that a woman dedicated to creative work would "sacrifice all claims to femininity and family." Anaïs Nin worried that she would shrivel a man were she to "steal his thunder [and] outshine him."

At home, for many of these women, the message was much the same. Mary Day Kent's mother had dropped out of Wellesley at the end of her junior year, in 1945, to get married, and she made it clear to her daughter that the aim of college was not to prepare herself for work but "to be a more interesting person to meet a more interesting husband." Marilyn Hagstrum's mom urged her daughter to focus less on her grades and more on her bridge: She, too, was at Wellesley "to fit in socially, to meet somebody nice with good prospects and get married."

The Wellesley girls took such admonitions to heart. The majority of seniors in the class of '69, like most women in college that year, expected to work only until they married or had their first child. Few graduated with professional goals and plans. Most still believed it best for men to be breadwinners and women to be wives.

The Ruling Class

Inevitably entangled with the question of work were matters of money and social class, issues as complicated in the sixties as all the questions regarding women's proper role. Only a fraction of this Wellesley class anticipated that they might actually *need* to make money: the quarter who were on financial aid knew that they would need to support themselves if they failed to marry well, and even a middle-class girl like Rhea Kemble, '69, was advised by her father that since a woman who was smart might not be a social success, she should prepare herself at Wellesley for "self-supporting spinsterhood."

For most, however, money had never been a concern in their lives.

Though by the late sixties Wellesley had shed some of what Nora Ephron, '62, called its "hangovers" from an earlier era, "when it was totally a school for the rich as opposed to now when it is only partially so," of the 470 freshmen who entered the class of 1969, a fifth were legacies— daughters or granddaughters of alumnae, beneficiaries of the most enduring form of affirmative action in higher education—and 40 percent were from private schools. Most of those were eager to take their certain place as matrons of society, passed from rich daddy to rich husband.

But the late sixties were also a time of strong antimaterialist sentiments, with personal wealth viewed by many as politically suspect: Fortunes were too often made through exploitation, leftist critics argued, and were in any event obscene in a world where so many were poor. Many in the class would renounce their inherited or anticipated privilege and join in their peers' denunciation of the hollow pursuit of the dollar. "Money was what the military-industrial complex was about," recalls Susan Alexander, '69. "We were interested in higher things." For some, that repudiation would be temporary: Susan would become a Presbyterian minister in her twenties, and then, a decade later, a Wall Street trader. For others, their moral doubt about being members of the ruling class would have lifelong consequences.

Alison "Snowy" Campbell had grown up in Oyster Bay, Long Island, with Rockefellers and Bouviers, but had little desire to return there and would eventually turn her back on that world for good. "I had ideas besides marrying some promising trust lawyer and going to cocktail parties. That's probably a stupidly egocentric thing to say. I just knew that I was definitely not attracted to people living off their ancestors' earnings, playing golf, clipping their stock coupons, and drinking like fish." Having gone to Wellesley against the wishes of her grandmother, who would have preferred to see her among the older, more traditional money at Vassar or Smith, Snowy was thrilled to find what seemed to her "a melting pot" after her years at the excruciatingly elite Miss Porter's School: One of her Wellesley dormmates grew pot in their dorm; another married a black man and was disowned by her parents. An incandescently beautiful girl (classmate Catherine Shen remembers her as "a vision, a Caucasian vision"), with no trace of the brittle sophistication and hard sexiness that often hung about the boarding-school girls, Snowy was relieved to "quit the competition on looks and makeup and clothes." After a brief romance with a Green Beret, she began spending her time with a band of hippie poets and computer pioneers at Wesleyan University in Connecticut, gingerly breaking propriety's rules. "They were taking acid trips by the dozens. I experimented a little to be polite, but I was too sensitive. Drugs made me feel yucky. And though I was glad that 'free love' took the fallen-woman onus off a girl enjoying her body, I was uncomfortable that my boyfriend wanted to have an open relationship. I was loyal and old-fashioned and monogamous. He was a poet, and kept trying to persuade me that I was hung up. He would say I was laying my trips on him."

Less timid was Lorna Rinear, '69, who, a decade after the publication of *Lady Chatterley's Lover,* chose the surest means to escape the constraints of her class. Raised by a nurse and nanny on Manhattan's exclusive Sutton Place, dressed at her mother's insistence like a doll with long, golden Shirley Temple ringlets, Lorna was forbidden in high school to venture into the streets except with the family chauffeur, who took her each morning to the Spence School. "While my brother had complete freedom, I made exactly one decision in my life—and that was whether I was going to have braces. My parents knew where I was every minute of the day. It was a typical WASP family. No one talked about anything: I didn't know that my mother was my father's fourth wife until I got involved in genealogy at Wellesley and discovered half-sisters I'd never known existed. And no one ever touched. When my mother died years later, my uncle gave me a tap on the shoulder to express his sympathy."

Though a few of her Spence classmates had working moms—modeling tycoon Eileen Ford, actress Kitty Hart—Lorna could not imagine a life "except the kind my mother had, supported by an incredibly rich man. Though it always struck me as bizarre that you would put that kind of money into private school for your daughter so she could be accomplished, but at nothing in particular. I was a reflection of them, part of the furniture. Here is my perfect house, my perfect wife, my perfect child."

The surest escape for such a princess was into the rough arms of the wrong man. Most in the class fled from their safe, respectable destinies only in their fantasies—falling for Elvis or James Dean, dangerous boys from the wrong side of the tracks. Lorna arrived at Wellesley, "and the second I was sprung, I went wild. I hitchhiked to Rolling Stones and James Brown concerts. And I discovered that the sexual revolution was just my cup of tea. There were many overnights not recorded by Mrs. Jones of Cazenove Hall. I was into roulette, making up for my previous seventeen years of abstinence."

After so sheltered an upbringing, however, Lorna was poorly equipped to handle such freedom. "I was not very wise about people, and about men in particular. Going to girls' schools my whole life had left me somewhat naive. I ended up getting pregnant sophomore year. He was twenty-seven, in the middle of a divorce, and broke—his wife had split with their kid and all the furniture. He was at Wellesley working as the stableman."

Six years before *Roe* v. *Wade,* Massachusetts state laws on sexual behavior, birth control, and abortion were the most conservative in the nation. An unmarried woman could not spend the night in a man's room "even if he was her uncle." Though the pill had come on the market in 1960 and 6 million American women were by then using it, the pope's encyclical *Humanae Vitae* in 1968 explicitly prohibited the use of contraceptives. In predominantly Catholic Massachusetts, contraceptives could be distributed only by physicians and only to married women; anyone prescribing birth control to an unmarried woman under twenty-one could be prosecuted for contributing to the delinquency of a minor. Abortion, except to save the life of a woman, was a felony punishable by life imprisonment. Even a doctor who gave a gynecological exam to a girl under eighteen could be prosecuted for statutory rape. So while pamphlets circulated on campus quoting Masters and Johnson on "the myth of the vaginal orgasm" and urging coeds to learn to masturbate, others warned girls not to try to abort themselves by inserting objects in the vagina, falling down stairs, swallowing quinine or lead, or douching with gasoline, vinegar, potassium permanganate, or kerosene.

Still, a third of the women in the class have had abortions, many of them before *Roe* v. *Wade.* They would pass secret knowledge from dorm to dorm, of gas stations in New Jersey where five hundred dollars— cash—would buy them an operation. In a motel room. Without anesthesia.

A girl from Sutton Place had better alternatives. "I felt trapped and not strong enough to make any decision on my own, so I told my parents. They wanted to know who it was. I lied." Lorna's father made all the arrangements. "In New York, if you're rich, you can find people. My father was a very pragmatic man. He also had his own checkered sexual history, though I didn't know that at the time. Being of the generation where they never admitted mistakes, my parents didn't say, 'We know how it can be.' They did what they had to do to spare themselves embarrassment, then punished me with their scorn. Looking back, I'm struck by the incredible hypocrisy of their disdain."

At spring break, Lorna's father took her to Puerto Rico. They drove to a small pink adobe building, where she was led upstairs to a spare, clean room. "I didn't see anyone else; we were all kept separate and concealed. A male doctor and two nurses put me on a table and, with a shot, induced labor. I was awake for hours through incredibly painful contractions. I remember throwing up from the pain. Afterwards, I didn't think about it much. I couldn't afford to. It was just something that had to be done. All my parents said to me was, 'We were going to send you to Europe for graduation. Too bad we spent that money on your abortion.' "

Lorna didn't tell anyone at Wellesley where she'd been or what she'd done. And though she continued to visit Neil at the stables, she wouldn't have sex with him again. The next January, however, she succumbed. Four weeks later, when she went to get birth control pills, she learned she was pregnant. "This time I didn't tell my parents, not till it was too late, in June. I did call somebody in a Boston back alley, but it sounded so iffy and weird that I chickened out.

"I began to think I should just have the baby. This was spring of my junior year, but I had no goals and couldn't imagine what my degree would do for me. I'd wanted to be a vet, but then decided that was out of reach after a discouraging conversation with the dean. My father would say every summer, 'Why don't you take typing so you can always be a secretary?' I didn't want to be a secretary, or a teacher. Both seemed like being a wife and mother, with none of the perks. I was undirected. Neil wanted to marry me. I thought it'd be neat to have a baby. I had no other plans."

Jamey was born September 20 of what would have been Lorna's senior year. "I don't know why my parents didn't say, 'You will finish college.' I needed less than a year." Instead, Lorna dropped out of school and got married. She wore a white and yellow dress she'd bought at

Filene's Basement and carried yellow roses. About ten people from the Wellesley stables came; they chipped in to buy her an A-line wool coat as a wedding present. A forty-year-old nurse from the Wellesley infirmary was her matron of honor. Jamey was with the baby-sitter, so they all went out to dinner afterwards.

"When Neil and I presented my parents with a fait accompli, they were horrified. My mom just told me not to come home, and hung up the phone."

For a while the couple lived in upstate New York, where Lorna stayed home with Jamey. But after a falling-out between her husband and his genteel bosses, they had to move, as they would have to move many more times. They landed finally in Kentucky, where Lorna went to work at a racehorse farm, leaving Jamey with a girl who had no schooling beyond the fourth grade. Lorna worked mucking out stalls and taking care of mares and foals, earning ten dollars extra a week because she could read and write.

The Outsiders

If many of the rich girls found Wellesley unpleasantly familiar, those students who were not wealthy, Protestant, and white—or those with working moms or families that otherwise departed from the norm—often felt like utter misfits at the school. The cultivation of "traditional" feminine graces and aspirations, they discovered, was not the only way in which Wellesley worked to preserve the postwar social order; the college also persisted far longer than most in a 1950s conception of class, religion, and race.

For most of the poor girls, the years at Wellesley were an exercise in humiliation. The college had only recently discontinued the practice of having scholarship girls wait on their social betters. "In the first week of school, they gave us a trash can and red rain boots," recalls Kathy Smith Ruckman, '69, "a gesture of charity that I found insulting. And we were continually reminded that the administration looked on us as lower-class and thought we should be endlessly grateful for all they'd done."

Nancy Young, '69, the daughter of an auto mechanic from the shabbiest corner of Boston's north shore, "really, really, hated" Wellesley. "There is almost no way to describe how bad it was for me. It was the worst four years of my life. I was unprepared for how isolated and inadequate I would feel. And angry. It's all very well to bring in people like me and give us scholarships and say, Aren't we doing wonderful things—but not if you don't give us the tools to catch up. My classmates were refined and cosmopolitan; they'd been to Florence and had season tickets to the symphony. I'd never been anywhere in my life. I was just a local girl with none of the clothes and polish. My freshman roommate, who'd lived all over the world, was mortified to be rooming with the likes of me. She would constantly correct my pronunciation. I dumped her midyear, she was so scornful of me. But I couldn't escape it. I remember a discussion with my best friend—who was all hung up on her coat of arms and her family's descent from Charlemagne—and a bunch of other girls at dinner about whether you should ask your maid to wash out your underwear or was that too intimate and should you wash it yourself. I said, 'Don't you understand that there are people at this table who do not have personal maids?' I thought there should have been understanding that for the great bulk of humanity this is not an issue. Wellesley was a bastion of privilege without people understanding that they were privileged, that there was another world out there. I felt immense anger at being thrust into their value system; I always felt I had to represent the oppressed classes."

Nancy's father had not wanted her to go to Wellesley. "It was my idea, and anything that was my idea he wanted to squelch just for the sake of it." He had ignored her achievements in high school, paying attention just long enough to criticize her "unfeminine" aggressive style. When she won debate competitions and made valedictorian, he told her she was "mouthy." Asked to contribute a paragraph to her college application, he wrote one sentence: "Nancy is impatient, impulsive, and inconsiderate." "It stayed with me forever," says Nancy, "that he would say such a damning thing." At Sophomore Father's Day, Nancy got a glimpse of the reasons for her father's scorn. Mr. Young turned to Nancy and said, "You know, these [other] men all went to college." It was clear, says Nancy, "that he was terribly embarrassed, mortified." Still, when Nancy grew desperate to leave Wellesley, her father would not let her go. "He said, 'I will never see you again. I will give you no support.' He had no expectations of me, but wanted to make sure I would not be a financial burden. I think he thought that at Wellesley I had the best chance of marrying someone successful and being well fixed. He finally told me he'd give me a thousand dollars if I'd stay and finish senior year. I took the deal."

Eager to get away from Wellesley, Nancy "split" from campus as often as she could. She began acting in Boston with professional theater groups, rehearsing every night—a kind of revenge on her father, who had hated his actress mother for her neglect of him and what he imagined to be her "promiscuity." Nancy was also the first unmarried girl permitted to live off campus on her own, though she had to produce a psychiatrist's report to win that freedom. "I wanted to be in the city, not in this stupid suburb with all these stiffs in the Villager look, these Johnny Appleseed prim, flowered blouses. Everywhere else everyone was getting groovy. At Wellesley, they were playing bridge all afternoon. Except for the fact that they had more money, these women were like my mother, without curiosity about the world. What am I saying? Hillary was in that class. But even then I thought she was way too mainstream, talking the language of the administration, co-opted, all about politics and visibility. I thought, Why are you talking to these people? We should do everyone a favor, burn this college down.

"I tried to find other women who I could be friends with, but the only thing I ever had in common with any of them was that we were on the fringes. I was a working-class Catholic; they were overweight or unattractive or Jewish. That set us outside the in crowd. The tone of my life was set by that time. I felt alienated, and that feeling has stayed with me ever since."

As archaic on matters of religion as it was on class, in the late sixties Wellesley housed Jews in dorm rooms with Jews and Catholics with Catholics, offering the rationale that such an arrangement would make it easier for the girls to go together to synagogue or mass. In 1967, the *Amherst Guide* reported that Wellesley maintained a Jewish quota of 12 percent. Such a policy was by then sufficiently unacceptable that Hillary's mentor, Professor Alan Schechter, was called upon to make a public denial. Yet the following year Wellesley was still struggling with its "Jewish problem." Worried about persistent public perceptions that Wellesley was a "Jewish school," chairman of the board John Quarles publicly affirmed that "Wellesley was founded for the glory of God and service of the Lord Jesus Christ" and that "with a view to maintaining the Christian purpose of this college . . . the faculty, administration and trustees should be predominantly Christian." The statement outraged students and alumnae; under pressure from both, the college finally altered its stance. By Nancy Young's senior year, Bible class was eliminated as a requirement. Religion professors no longer had to be Protestant. Quarles announced that a Catholic was joining the faculty, and promised to add a Hindu and a Jew.

The question of race proved less susceptible to appeasement. During the four years these women were at Wellesley, the civil rights movement radicalized: Roxbury erupted in riots, one of fifty-eight urban ghettos to do so: Eldridge Cleaver issued his violent manifesto *Soul on Ice;* assassins murdered Malcolm X and Martin Luther King, Jr. The fight on campus for racial equality served as the first political education for many of the women of Wellesley '69, with the five black class members exerting an influence on their white classmates out of all proportion to their numbers. Though all of the black women came from middle-class families, their personal histories were otherwise different enough from the white students' to have developed in them a much bolder female voice. All had educated, working mothers, reflecting the norm: Black women have been better educated than black men since the Civil War, and in 1965, 70 percent of black mothers of school-age children worked for wages. All were already initiated into political activism—and in alliance with, rather than in opposition to, their parents. And all had inherited a different historical legacy, one that included female heroes, from Sojourner Truth to Rosa Parks, but excluded women from the gilded cage. While white women's ostensible fragility had been invoked to justify keeping them home, black women had been granted no such weakness. The consequence, novelist Toni Morrison has written, was that "aggression was not as new to black women as it was to white women. Black women seem able to combine the nest and the adventure. They are both safe harbor and ship."

Though they would prove to be powerful leaders among their classmates, feminism was, for these women, secondary. "I identified much more as a black person than as a woman, and I didn't get the double bind at all," says Nancy Gist. "I thought of feminism as a white woman's issue. I remember hearing Shirley Chisholm say she felt more discriminated against as a woman than as a black, and I thought, 'What, is she crazy?' In later years I came to think maybe she had a point."

The fiercest voice in the class of '69 was that of Francille Rusan, now director of the African-American Studies program at the University of Maryland. Though she came from an integrated school in Chicago, Fran was amazed at her Wellesley classmates' crude naïveté. "People would say, 'I know one black person,' or, 'Do you know my maid?'—the kinds of questions we couldn't imagine they would say to other people." Fran replied in the pages of *Keynote,* the college literary magazine, introducing to the campus the militant themes then sounding in the larger movement. "*Today* I'm not evil. *Today* I'm not dangerous. Usually I'm alienated by their simple ignorance and gross lack of everything else important except money. Pale fey mommas bore rather than threaten. WHERE is the fire of Columbus; of all those other great honkies who line the history books? . . . But today I will keep my heroes apart and my tastes distinctly watermelonsweetpotatoeseatchittlinsyesmam!"

With Nancy Gist and Karen Williamson, Fran led the protest on campus against grouping students in housing on the basis of religion and race. "I don't think anything is strange at all," Fran recalled for *Frontline* about meeting her roommate, Susan Liebowitz, freshman year. "And over the next few days as I'm meeting the other students I realize that all the other black students have black roommates, and when I talk to my own roommate, I discover that the college has called her and asked her if she would like to be part of an experiment. And I'm pretty upset, because they never called me and asked me if I would like to be a part of an experiment." The girls founded a student organization, Ethos, to protest "the rooming of Jews with Jews, Negroes with Negroes, Chinese with Chinese." Ethos complained to the National Scholarship Fund for Negroes that the college had offered the class of 1970 the chance to request a roommate with a "certain background" and "when no white student requested a Negro," had put each black freshman in a single. The Fund responded with a letter advising Wellesley president Ruth Adams that other colleges, including Harvard and Dartmouth, had remedied their segregationist housing policies fifteen years earlier and that "Wellesley is as anachronistic as could be."

In 1968, after the King assassination and the report of the Kerner Commission documenting the damaging persistence of white racism, Ethos threatened a hunger strike if Wellesley failed to join the new national movements toward affirmative action and multiculturalism. The college finally agreed to all of the group's demands: It increased its recruitment of black students and staff, allocated funds for black speakers, created an Afro-American Studies department, and desegregated its dorms. With the girls' assistance in recruitment, Wellesley admitted fifty-seven black women into the class of '73.

In the course of the debate, however, a remark by a faculty member sparked the most intense protest of all their four years. Echoing the public debate over whether racism or degenerate values best explained the failure of some blacks to succeed (a debate rekindled in 1965 by Daniel Patrick Moynihan's doleful assessment of the deteriorating black family), a Wellesley professor complained that it was difficult to recruit "colored" students when so many came from homes "where the only literature was comic books." Attempting to calm the resulting furor, the dean of students, who called herself Mrs. Harold Melvin, instead compounded the insult, asking: "What will happen to students from a community not on the cultural level with other Wellesley students?" and promising to bring students with "deficient backgrounds" up to Wellesley standards.

Ethos responded with a scorching letter denouncing "an atmosphere of bigotry and ignorance, an effort to destroy our pride and unity. We are deeply insulted by the deans classing us a lower race. We will not accept the idea that the existence of two different cultures calls for the superiority and more Wellesley-like qualities of the lighter one. . . . We realize the majority of the faculty and students has associated itself with African-Americans in a master/servant relationship, and may find it difficult to adjust to more equitable arrangements, but we insist on being called blacks or Afro-Americans, never colored girls, which alludes to latter day Prissies. . . . Wellesley is an institution whose function is to perpetuate the nature of white society under the guise of higher education. . . . This cheaply disguised bigotry is indicative of the morally bankrupt nature of this college. . . . We are tired of having our culture described as 'comic book reading.' Must the administration be changed or is there a good honkie in the house?"

Over time, Fran Rusan's message grew increasingly separatist, focused more on the need for public solidarity among blacks than on private strivings. In the aftermath of the Detroit riots, she explained Black Power to the *Wellesley News:* "Hitherto worried about meshing carefully in the establishment, the African-American is now concerned with preserving his negroness, his fraternal ties to the ghetto. The college-educated negro has an obligation to go back to the ghetto, not to a white environment. We have a foot in the door, and are the only ones who can push it open to other black people. We want to start black theaters, read black poets, teach American history that includes the history of the negro." Her voice then grew less ladylike and more hostile to her liberal Wellesley classmates. "When slaves were freed we were promised 40 acres and a mule. That's all we want, with interest. Violence is one means to what we want. We don't like to use it, but we are not afraid to. It's important to remember that the American tradition is a violent one and not see black nationalist activity as deviant from the norm. The objective is not to ease racial tension. The time when whites could play a significant role in negro affairs has passed. We don't want white support anymore."

Nancy Gist, also from the urban North, shared Fran's misgivings at slipping too thoroughly into the world of the white ruling class. Nancy's father was a Housing and Urban Development administrator, and in high school she'd gone to the University of Chicago's prestigious Lab School, becoming adept at crossing back and forth across the divide between her white schoolmates and her black after-school friends. But by the time she reached Wellesley, such assimilation was suspect. "With the Black Power movement came a premium on being more 'street,' being from the proletariat," she said. "Those of us who didn't come from that background had to feel—and sometimes be—apologetic. At the same time, of course, we were expected to pay for everything."

As the one black class member from the segregated South, Janet McDonald, then a somewhat awkward parochial school graduate from New Orleans, brought a substantially different perspective, one still rooted in the integrationist, pacific, aspirational vision of Martin Luther King, Jr. "My mother decided I'd go to Wellesley after she read of it in *Time* magazine. She wanted me to understand things like fine art and medieval history, wanted me to be forced to integrate and others to be given the opportunity to learn something other than their narrow understanding of black people." Having never before known a white person who wasn't also a nun, Janet found Wellesley utterly intimidating. "I'd never been in the North except to visit relatives in Harlem. The girls made fun of me when I'd ask for the bread and 'buttah.'" Within days of arriving on campus, she called home, hoping her father would answer the phone. "I was going to say, 'Daddy, I hate it here. Everyone's white.' And he would say, 'Yes, baby, hang on. I'll come and get you and bring you home.' But my mother answered instead. She said, 'You can do it, and you are going to stay.' I didn't crumble again." By senior year, Janet was chief justice of the college court. "Wellesley taught me that all white people were not like those I'd encountered in Louisiana. But I was also not as upset as the other black women that we were all roomed together. It didn't bother me, because I'd come from an all-black environment. They all came from integrated schools, and were more militant and radical. They felt we needed to demonstrate and signify that we were black. I knew I was black. And I didn't think an Afro or a dashiki was going to look good on me. It wasn't that I was so anxious to assimilate. I had been perfectly happy being all black, and now that I'd had a glimpse of the other side, I wasn't intrigued. But when we helped recruit the class of '73, I opposed creating a relative standard for blacks. I think Wellesley made a mistake that way."

Perhaps because the struggle for equality felt familiar—as Nancy Scheibner, '69, would write in an editorial in the *Wellesley News,* "Wellesley was founded to serve an underprivileged population—women"—even for many of the white students, racial injustice became the defining issue of their college years. Fran Rusan's polemic aside, "the black women could have separated out, but instead they remained good friends with us," recalls Eldie Acheson. "Fran and I were in Roxbury together when King was killed. She drove me out to safety, then went back in. A lot of us would never have encountered anything outside of our suburban, white, intensely private experience if we hadn't been there in our long Bermuda shorts and shell sweaters watching Fran take on the admissions office, battling for inclusiveness, questioning authority." The white students' allegiance to their black classmates did not always sit well at home. After Hillary Rodham took Karen Williamson with her to church, she called her parents, who listened to Hillary's excited account with chilly disapproval. "I was so disappointed in their reaction," she wrote to her hometown minister, Don Jones, who in 1962 had taken Hillary to hear King preach in Chicago. "My attitudes toward so many things have changed in just three weeks, and I think I expected Park Ridge to have undergone a similar metamorphosis."

"All of us talked about the difficulties of going back home again," recalls Kris Olson. "We were asking ourselves, How can we be the children of these parents?" In high school, Kris had been the sole girl in her affluent New York suburban community to opt out of the home economics club and join the boys' service group working in Harlem settlement houses. At Wellesley she organized a political theory group to read Thoreau on civil disobedience, and wrote her thesis on John Rawls's theories of compensatory social justice. A co-founder of Wellesley Against Racism (WAR), she organized students to tutor and baby-sit in Roxbury, worked for the black candidate running against segregationist Louise Hicks, and helped organize a boycott against Kodak to force the company to hire and train black workers. At an Ethos rally, she picked up a megaphone to condemn Wellesley's "tokenism and gradualism" and the college's expectation that the black students would simply "be patient and grateful for all we've done in the past."

As she became more of an activist, Kris learned a lesson that she and many of her classmates would later apply in larger political and professional arenas: that the feminine demeanor which trapped them could also serve as protective coloration, and even be turned to their own ends. Kris gathered some like-minded classmates to pay calls on Boston-area corporate executives. "We'd go in our little Villager dresses and heels, meet sweetly with the board of trustees, and then confront them on institutional racism." Pounding their little white-gloved fists on the table, these budding radicals camouflaged as ladies would demand of the stunned corporate leaders that they divest.

Vietnam

If the young women of Wellesley were stirred by the era's first great defining issue—equality—the second registered more faintly on campus. Lonny Laszlo Higgins's husband, David, who graduated with Al Gore from Harvard in 1969, believes the greatest difference of mind between his classmates and his wife's is that for the men, vulnerable to the draft, the war in Vietnam eclipsed all else. Only a few Wellesley girls marched for peace, riding in buses from Harvard to the Pentagon. Chris Osborne, who had switched to the religion department the day after her father's death to pursue her previously forbidden interest in Zen Buddhism and wrote her thesis on Yale's pacifist chaplain William Sloan Coffin, helped support the "sanctuary" movement at Harvard, bringing meals and blankets to draft resisters and AWOL servicemen taking refuge in churches. Nancy Gist got calls from home about neighborhood boys who had died in the war. Blacks accounted for a quarter of all casualties in Vietnam. "So many boys I knew were coming back in boxes. I was overwhelmed and confused."

For Nancy Wanderer, the war came intimately home. In the summer of '68, just months after her big wedding in the Wellesley chapel, the graduate school deferment was eliminated, and a year later her husband, Thomas, was drafted. She and Thomas were opposed to the war—"We felt like you were going for no reason and would come back dead"—but going to Canada seemed out of the question; Nancy was too close to her family to bear leaving them. "For me it was so complex. It involved my relationship with my family, and also Thomas's dream of running for office. He was afraid that if he dodged, it would come back to haunt him someday." Thomas rejected the more drastic alternatives proposed by a friend, who had recently severed all the tendons in his hand. Drafted into the mortar division of the army infantry, he shipped out and Nancy returned to her parents' home.

Thomas did stay out of combat, landing a spot as a clerk-typist in Bien-Hoa, processing arrivals and orders home. "I wrote to him every day, and he wrote to me, describing how he had to notify families when someone died. He couldn't bear to tell people the truth if their kid had been blown up on the latrine or in a whorehouse, so he'd invent a gallant death. He'd torch these little paper planes they got from the Red Cross so he could describe what they looked like crashing in flames. He also wrote to me all the time about what he was going to buy. Vietnam was a shopper's war, a war of great deals on cameras and stereos. When he wrote that he'd tried marijuana, I went into a tailspin. I was convinced beyond all persuading that he would come home addicted to heroin."

Nancy's first big fight with her parents was about the war. "All of their friends' kids had managed to get out of serving. They were proud that their son-in-law had gone, and insisted he was there out of patriotism, fighting for his country. I was ashamed he was there, and felt like our friends scorned us for not standing on our principles, that we lacked the courage of our convictions."

Nancy's rift with her family was a common one in the class. Most of these girls had arrived at Wellesley in 1965 with conservative politics, a reflection of their overwhelmingly Republican elders. A survey that year found that the majority supported U.S. policy in Vietnam and, having grown up with civil defense drills and the McCarthy hearings on television, fervently believed that Communism had to be stopped. Only a quarter felt the war to be morally wrong, less than 10 percent thought a U.S. withdrawal feasible, and only 5 percent said they would go to jail in protest. Two years later, confirming many of their parents' fears that their daughters would fall under the sway of "pinkos" in the radical Northeast, just 20 percent of the Wellesley juniors supported the Johnson administration and feared Communism. Half now called the war morally wrong, and 22 percent said they would go to jail in protest. By 1968, with 538,000 American troops in Vietnam and 30,000 Americans dead, a majority of the class were "clean for Gene" (McCarthy) and 91 percent favored immediate and unconditional withdrawal from Vietnam.

Flower Children

Counterculture would, nonetheless, be too strong a word to describe life at Wellesley in the late sixties. The girls did try to get hip in the Wellesley newspaper: The Beatles movie *Help!* was reviewed as "crispy fab." And in an interview with Country Joe McDonald, Chris Franz, '69, reported that the guitarist "felt hassled by the commercial music circuit" and sought "inner happiness joined to self-actualized living in a Maharishi cum Maslow ideal." In April 1966, Hillary Rodham wrote home to her minister, Don Jones, to say how exciting college was because it enabled her to try out different identities. In what she described as "an orgy of decadent indulgence—as decadent as any upright Methodist can become," she had gone "hippie," painting a flower on her arm.

The young ladies' venture into recreational drugs was likewise tame, though how tame is somewhat hard to judge, since substance abuse—both their own and their parents'—is the subject about which these women are most circumspect. A junior-year poll found that 37 percent of the class had smoked pot and 58 percent would do so if given the opportunity. The Junior Show was full of knowing references to "grasses and acids and a whole pot of Ashbury juice" dispensed by Poppadoc (played by Fran Rusan), the tribal witch doctor. (At the 1995 White

House reunion Hillary hosted for her classmates, all joined in on a reprise of one of the show's numbers: "You'll soon be communicating, commence hallucinating, on the grassroots level.")

A certain avant-garde academic credibility had recently been bestowed on drugs by the LSD experiments of Harvard's Timothy Leary and Richard Alpert (later Baba Ram Dass), both of whom regularly spoke on Boston-area campuses, and by Aldous Huxley and R. D. Laing, whose books many of the Wellesley women read. Conventional normalcy, Laing argued, was "the condition of being asleep"; chemicals could "break the ego," opening it to the transcendental that sometimes breaks through in psychosis. The idea that a deeper truth might be found in drugs or madness was popularized in such best-sellers as the highly romantic account of schizophrenia *I Never Promised You a Rose Garden* (1964) and Carlos Castaneda's accounts of his trips on hallucinogenic mushrooms with the visionary Indian Don Juan.

One Wellesley student did a hundred acid trips for a course in Christian Ethics, and said she saw God. Another, now a health professional in the Bible Belt, remembers swallowing whole bottles of Robitussin DM, a cough medicine, to achieve "a zombielike state." She went to Woodstock the summer after graduation but remembers little beyond dropping cellophane acid and learning to meditate with hippies from a commune in the Carolinas called the Farm. Acid was a revelation for the art history major: "In the fifties, what you were supposed to feel and say was so stilted. What you became aware of on acid is that 80 percent of communication is nonverbal. I would get intense creative urges. LSD lifted my inhibitions and liberated a whole new style." At the same time, she believes that smoking lots of pot helped defeat her aspirations to get a medical degree. "I thought that to be a doctor would be class collaborationist. And I was afraid. I think drugs had something to do with that. Drugs tend to magnify whatever feelings you have. If you don't know if you can get into med school and no one's encouraging you and it's all scary, marijuana magnifies your fear."

For some students, their classmates' rebellious adventures were tedious or grating. Charlynn Maniatis, who describes herself as a Goldwater girl to this day, "lived in my own little hermit world. We were the nerds. We knew Vietnam was going on, but we were more concerned with, What do we do tonight? I never even went into Boston for the first year. It was just like being at home, the same four walls; I'd come home and do my homework, eat dinner, and go to bed. I was afraid to go to mixers, and I certainly wasn't interested in the wider world. I was living in a dreamworld, with four or five other dreamers, at the Wellesley of the proper gloves and hats and teas. Civil rights and feminism were beyond our horizon." Virginia Blankenhorn found her classmates' orthodoxy oppressive. "Wellesley was a place for me to study Renaissance music, Chaucer, medieval history. I loved it. Hillary Rodham and I might have been on different planets. I didn't have time for politics, and I loathed the political correctness of some of my classmates, the rigidity of thought and language that went into some of their positions. I recall being castigated by one classmate, who insisted that music was simply not a 'relevant' thing to be doing." Kathy Smith was embarrassed to announce her engagement senior year to medical student Roger Ruckman, a serious young man from a wealthy Delaware family, and still more reluctant to admit to her classmates that motherhood was her dream. "By the end of Wellesley I felt burned-out and was looking for comfort, the comfort of having a baby. But feminism devalued anything related to caring for children."

More often, however, the women of '69 found Wellesley insufferably tame, their classmates too much the good girls, patronizing or timid in their commitments to social change. Senior year, the class published a twenty-page critique of the college. "Our good students are well-disciplined automatons who play by the rules," wrote Marilyn Hagstrum. "The good deedism of the motto is condescending and inadequate," added Jan Krigbaum. Students wrote to the newspaper with scorn for "housewives putting in time, superficial and risk averse" or suffering from a "rich girl complex, at this prissy finishing school. . . . To assuage the guilt there are threats of hunger strikes. Is Wellesley an intellectual community or an extension of Junior League?" When a student strike to protest the war in April 1968 was only feebly honored, Hillary Rodham lamented the "large gray mass" of the uninvolved. To Professor Marshall Goldman's belittling suggestion that the girls make a real sacrifice and give up a weekend mixer instead, she responded: "I'll give up my date Saturday night, Mr. Goldman, but I don't think that's the point. Why do these attitudes have to be limited to two days?" In fact, many of her classmates lay at Hillary Rodham's feet credit, or perhaps blame, for the genteel nature of their protests. Typical was her response as college government president to California governor Ronald Reagan's March 1969 demand for a federal investigation of student protesters and order for the arrest of nearly two hundred San Francisco State demonstrators. Hillary stayed up all night to talk students out of staging a protest "that would embarrass our college." She would "co-opt the real protest," in one classmate's words, "by creating an academic one."

Returning from her tenth reunion in 1972, Nora Ephron wrote a derisive account in *Esquire* of her alma mater. What Wellesley wants for its graduates, Ephron wrote, is "for us to avoid the extremes, to be instead that thing in the middle: an example to the community, a Samaritan. . . . How marvelous it would have been to go to a women's college that encouraged impoliteness, rewarded aggression, encouraged argument. Women by the time they are eighteen are so . . . tyrannized out of behaving in all the wonderful outspoken ways unfortunately characterized as masculine. . . . A college must do remediation, force young women to define themselves before they abdicate the task and become defined by their husbands. . . . We all tend toward tiny little rebellions, harmless nips at the system. We will never make any real trouble. Wellesley helped see to that."

In "Silences," Tillie Olsen had lamented the near impossibility for a woman, trained always to please, to believe in the right to speak her mind or the importance of what she might have to say. Mary Day Kent recalls a lecture attended by five hundred Wellesley women and five male guests: Three of the visiting men asked questions; not one of the young women said a word.

Hillary Rodham Versus the Washington Establishment

For girls so deeply ingrained with the feminine habits of silence and docility, the audacity of Hillary Rodham's speech on graduation day was unimaginably liberating.

Few anticipated her bold performance. Hillary had always been a great practitioner of procedures and rules, undaunted by long meetings and complex policy wrangling; she had won the admiration of faculty and administrators, even more than students, for her skills at conciliation, damping unruly passions by finding common ground among divided campus factions. But if Hillary had already proven her political skill, on that sunny spring afternoon she revealed a capacity more electrifying to the gathered young ladies. Massachusetts Republican senator Edward Brooke had spent his long-winded speech praising Richard Nixon and America's "strength abroad," and scolding the assembled girls for their generation's resort to "coercive protest," calling it a perversion of democratic privilege. It would be tragic, he said, if they adopted dissatisfaction as a way of life.

The gathered parents were still nodding their assent when Hillary Rodham, the first student speaker in the history of Wellesley graduation ceremonies, stepped to the podium. Enraged by Brooke's speech, she set aside her prepared remarks and proceeded extemporaneously to upbraid the senator. Her 420 classmates, who had chosen Hillary to be class speaker, felt their pulses race and their parents turn to stone. "I find myself in a familiar position, that of reacting, something that our generation has been doing for quite a while," she began, her voice ringing. "For too long our leaders have used politics as the art of the possible. The challenge now is to practice politics as the art of making what appears to be impossible, possible."

That she had plowed through her course reading lists was evident in the echoes of Kierkegaard and Heidegger throughout her speech: In Kierkegaard's warning that the "despair at not willing to be oneself" was the first form of "sickness unto death"; and in Heidegger's description of the "inauthenticity" that comes from fleeing the terrifying necessity for self-creation by "allowing others to direct my life . . . when I surrender to 'them,' " Hillary found her vocabulary and philosophy. "Our love for this place, Wellesley College, coupled with our freedom from the burden of an inauthentic reality allowed us to question basic assumptions," she told a stunned crowd of two thousand, among them Nina Nitze's father, Paul, and Eldie Acheson's grandfather, Dean. "I would like to talk about reality sometime, authentic reality, inauthentic reality, and what we have to accept of what we see. . . . To be educated, the goal must be human liberation, enabling each of us to fulfill our capacity to create. . . . We're searching for more immediate, ecstatic, and penetrating modes of living. So our questions about our institutions, our college, our churches, our government, continue. Every protest, every dissent, is unabashedly an attempt to forge an identity in this particular age." She read a poem by her classmate Nancy Scheibner: "And the purpose of history is to provide a receptacle/For all those myths and oddments/Which oddly we have acquired/And from which we would become unburdened/To create a newer world/To transform the future into the present./We have no need of false revolutions/In a world where categories tend to tyrannize our minds/And hang our wills up on narrow pegs./It is well at every given moment to seek the limits in our lives./And once those limits are understood/To understand that limitations no longer exist./Earth could be fair. And you and I must be free." She called on her fellow students to emulate the protesting French students whose slogans covered the walls of the Sorbonne. "Be realistic, they say. Demand the impossible. We will settle for nothing less." And she acknowledged the generational breach opening up before her. "Yesterday I was talking to an older woman who said that she wouldn't want to be me for anything in the world. She wouldn't want to look ahead, because she's afraid."

When Hillary finished, her classmates rose to their feet and for seven minutes stood and cheered her defiant words. Or most did: Ann Sherwood sat still, "terrified that my father would be furious with me that one of my classmates had the temerity to rebut an adult, much less a U.S. senator." Mary Day Kent also cast a cautious sidelong glance at her father, who had before that day never seen an Afro or a miniskirt, and was in shock well before Hillary opened her mouth. Charlynn Maniatis recalls her father whispering furiously, "What a disrespectful young lady," and feeling the same way, "I was cringing." "I would have liked to have stopped her," Marge Wanderer told *Frontline*. "I'm sure her mother would have liked to have stopped her, but her class absolutely encouraged her."

That a speech which was often incoherent and meandering could be so galvanizing and polarizing said much about the way these girls had been raised. "When we were growing up, it was unseemly to have confidence if you were a girl; it was considered insolence. I remember times I felt great about something I'd done, and my parents would cut me down," Jan Dustman Mercer recalls. Hillary's speech "was brash, it was brilliant, it was unplanned, and it was disrespectful to Senator Brooke. And I can remember squirming in my seat at the same time the inner me was saying, 'All right!' "

That a young woman would contradict a man of authority was also,

in 1969, front-page news. SENATOR BROOKE UPSTAGED AT WELLES-
LEY COMMENCEMENT read the *Boston Globe* the next day, adding that
Dean Acheson was sufficiently impressed that he had sent Hillary a note
requesting a copy of her speech, an excerpt of which was published in
Life magazine. A handful of parents were equally cheered: Jesse Branson,
whose daughter, Johanna, was Hillary's roommate at Wellesley and an
attendant at her wedding and remains one of her closest friends,
"thought what Hillary was saying was great. I didn't want to stop her; I
was unhappy with Brooke myself. We were just startled that she had the
courage." Vern Branson remembers that Hugh Rodham—who had
come alone to graduation in the family Cadillac while his wife, Dorothy,
stayed home with Hillary's brothers—was altogether unfazed, talking
that evening with great enthusiasm about "blue onions," his best-selling
textile design.

"I will never forget it," Marge Wanderer told *Frontline*, "because
Nancy said to me at the end of graduation, 'Take a good look at her. She
will probably be the president of the United States someday.' And that
shook me up. . . . It kind of frightened me, the whole group frightened
me, because this was the beginning of a whole new era, and these women
were going to go out and take over the world. Not my daughter, because
my daughter was very safely married. I thought she was going to be
home sweeping the floor and taking care of the babies, so I wasn't going
to worry about her. But I worried about the other ones, because they
were so sure, they were so sure of themselves, and that is something that
Wellesley instills in these women. I just hope that they are all successful
and happy. No, I'm going to restate that. I just hope that they're happy."

In the pursuit of happiness, few of these women would in fact ever reject
so entirely Marge's dreams; many more have swept floors and taken care
of babies than have taken over the world. But from the vantage of a
smart, ambitious girl in 1969, the fifties did not look anything like the
wholesome paradise of 1990s political memory. To the degree these
women allied themselves with their generation and against their parents,
it was not out of a desire to destroy traditional American values but because those values seemed to them to have been betrayed—by "faceless
bureaucrats" drained of a sense of personal responsibility for their political actions, by a suburban existence that the *Christian Century* de-

scribed as a "handkerchief soaked in chloroform on the mind and spirit," by a willful blindness to immense social injustices. "My country right or wrong" seemed less noble to most than what Senator Fulbright called "a higher form of patriotism," the insistence that their country, and each one of them as a citizen, live up to its ideals. There was hubris in this generation, certainly, in the notion that they would utterly remake home and family and politics, that their morality was unlike the shabby stuff of most men and women. But there was no nihilism. "Men with dreams" had shaped their consciousness, Hillary said in her speech, "men in the space program, the civil rights movement, the Peace Corps." Earlier that year, she had given her boyfriend, Jeff Shields, a copy of Thoreau's *Walden,* one of the earliest American testaments to the idea that a person's political integrity is measured by how he lives each day in his own home and by whether he dissents when his government fails to honor its stated principles. "There's a strange conservative strain that goes through a lot of New Left collegiate protests that I find intriguing, because it harkens back to a lot of the old virtues," Hillary said in her speech. "We feel that our prevailing acquisitive and competitive corporate life is not the way of life for us." These women's political convictions and personal aspirations began, before all else, in an immensely ambivalent rejection of their girlhood world.

CHAPTER TWO

Mothers and Daughters

A woman is her mother. That's the main thing.
—ANNE SEXTON, "Housewife"

What Nancy Wanderer loved best were the car trips each summer from Pittsburgh to her father's childhood home in Illinois farm country. Stretched out in the Chrysler's big backseat with her small blond head nestled in her mother's lap, Nancy would close her eyes and listen contentedly for hours as Marge recounted stories Nancy had heard a thousand times. Marge told of her own visits as a girl to her grandmother's house in the "Germantown" of St. Louis, with "Aunt Elsie and the whole family, those first-generation immigrant women who weighed three hundred pounds, babies running around, everyone out on their porches on hot summer nights with big, foaming pitchers of root beer." Hearing her mother's strong, exuberant voice, feeling her link to all the women in her past, Nancy says, "I felt very well loved."

New Kensington, just outside of Pittsburgh, was a slightly down-at-the-heels, gritty mill town. But dads were securely employed at Alcoa Aluminum, moms were always home, front doors were open, and grandmas and big brothers were nearby. No one ever had a baby-sitter. The kids clambered over fences and front porches, went in and out of one another's houses, raided refrigerators, played in the woods over the hill with never a thought of danger. "All my best friends lived on my street. My mother knew that any place I was, somebody's mom would be around. Even our dads seemed close by. When we walked home from school for lunch every day, in our kneesocks and letter sweaters, we'd stop to salute as the Alcoa trucks went by." Nancy and her big brother and her mom and dad always sat down together for breakfast and dinner; Mrs. Wanderer would set out a spaghetti casserole with Velveeta cheese, or pot roast and potatoes, then take off her apron and smooth her skirt before joining her husband and children at the table. She did her cooking and cleaning in a dress and heels, her hair just done at the beauty parlor. On weekends, Nancy's dad would putter about the house or cut the grass, and then they'd all go to a potluck dinner with friends.

Nancy and Marge were rarely separated. A pillar of the church and president of the PTA, Marge became a Girl Scout leader when Nancy was in the third grade, and every one of the twenty-two girls in Nancy's class joined the troop. They met Thursday evenings for knitting competitions and learned to bake chicken potpies and put on spirited performances: A picture of a twelve-year-old Nancy playing Curly in *Oklahoma!*, in a red plaid shirt and cowboy hat, with her freckled snub nose and mop of blond curls and jubilant grin, is pure sweet-corn Americana.

Marge's family had been hit badly by the Depression; her memories of poverty left her determined that her tomboy daughter would learn the proper feminine graces and marry well. She sent Nancy to get "polished up" at a private high school, scrimping money out of the household budget and going back to work in the classroom she'd left when she got married. "Sometimes I was a bit embarrassed by her," says Nancy. "She had a big, loud laugh, and always a funny story to tell. But she has a kind of inner class; there is nothing money could buy that she didn't already have. In my eyes she was the ideal woman—really out there, getting people excited. I wanted to be just like her, a leader. She is like the sun; she has such warmth and energy. That's why when she turned her back on me later it was so cold."

An honors student and class president at every school she ever went to, Nancy remembers being in trouble just once. Climbing to hang like a bat in the rafters of a half-built house, she left behind a jacket, which gave her crime away: It had, of course, a name tag sewn in. More unsettling to her conscience was an attempt, hiding behind a garage door with her friend Michelle, to light a match. She'd been told not to play with matches and was thoroughly tormented by her misdeed. As she walked home in the snow, she decided she deserved no Christmas presents that year. Most of the time, she kept busy with her civic activities, among them founding and serving as president of a neighborhood dog club. "I'm still a club starter. It all feels like the dog club to me, so I'm amazed when someone sees the way I live now as antisocial. I don't think I've done an antisocial thing in my life."

Nancy's rigorous sense of honesty came from her father, a company man with unwavering standards of rectitude and sobriety. When Nancy golfed with her dad, he insisted that if she missed a swing or the ball moved a quarter inch, she had to count that stroke. When for her older brother's twenty-first birthday Nancy's mother impulsively bought a celebratory bottle of champagne, her father refused to permit it in his car. Marge ended up walking home from the store with it while he drove alongside hollering, "We don't need this, Marge." "He would have had a dumb life but for her," says Nancy. "He was always at a slight remove from the family, going to get the car or standing behind the camera taking home movies. But he thought she was too loud and ate too much. She was squelched by him, but she did it all anyway. That's really been my guide, that back- and-forth—my father, ramrod-straight, serious, and diligent, my mother, warm and enthusiastic. I learned so much from my parents: Be yourself, be honest, don't lord it over anyone—things I live by that now drive them crazy."

Innocent of danger, snug in a deep-rooted family and safe community with a big, stern dad employed for life and a soft, warm mom wholly dedicated to her children's well-being: How precious it must have seemed for the parents of the class of '69 to be able to provide their children a safe and predictable world, a small, separate peace, after knowing in their own youth the fear and deprivation of the Depression and a world war.

For a fortunate few in the class, childhood was so sweet: scented with new-mown grass and cinnamon toast, as shiny as a red bicycle and freshly whitewashed picket fences. In such a cheerful palette has Hillary Clinton's youth been painted: Like pages of a Norman Rockwell calendar, here is Hillary home from school to have lunch with her mom, here playing Parcheesi with her family, here baking chocolate chip cookies on Christmas Eve, here at Ted and Pearl's Happy House for Cokes, here sewing yet another merit badge on her Girl Scout uniform as she dreams of marrying a senator and decorating her Georgetown home.

For many in the class, however, such Arcadian childhood portraits concealed deeper discontent. "Hers was not the life I wanted." There is for these women no more common refrain. Most saw mothers who were not happy homemakers but were frustrated and suffocating: Barely girls themselves when they had their babies, isolated from the world by the geography of suburbia and from each other by the need to "keep up appearances," they spent their days playing bridge and shopping and vacuuming, sipping pale coffee and opening boxes of macaroni and cheese as they waited for the sound of crunching gravel in the drive. The Wellesley graduates remember their fathers as often distant from their families: organization men overburdened with the demands of breadwinning or salesmen forever on the road—and sometimes seeking a comfort there they no longer found at home. Flipping through their childhood memories, these women tell of drawn curtains, bottles of Valium, and cold silences. "The smell of home," one says, "was the smell of gin and tonic." A few tell a third story, one neither rosy nor unremittingly bleak but also largely erased from present renderings of the postwar years—of parents who set themselves against the conformist pressures of the time, instilling in their daughters radical aspirations, or daring dissent at a time when it could be deemed criminal disloyalty.

The Unhappy Homemaker

"My mother was dressed in a dress, baking cookies and unhappy," says Kathy Smith Ruckman, a suburban mother who stayed home to raise her four kids. "I don't think my mother could have named her unhappiness—that generation wasn't terribly introspective. But she was miserably bored and unable to see other choices. She never had the self-confidence to go into the community, even as a volunteer. She felt she had nothing to offer." Though Mrs. Smith had earned straight A's in high school, she had not attended college; her father would pay only for his son's education. Married young to Kathy's father, she raised three daughters in Wilmington, Delaware, on the modest income Mr. Smith earned as a DuPont engineer. "My father was wonderful, but not bright or ambitious. He worked so we could eat; his goal every day was to get home and be with us. If they could have made their choices, my mother would have worked and my father would have stayed home. He was the more maternal figure, much more willing to change diapers or take care of the house. It bothered us as kids—we thought it was weird. And in those days, for a woman to work made the man look as if he couldn't provide; it was an insult to her husband." Unable to afford a second car,

Kathy's mom was quite literally trapped in her suburban home. "It was an awful life to be stranded at home with kids and no car for someone like her, someone by nature not at all close or nurturing. She was home all the time, watching the soaps all day long. To this day, when I hear that theme music, it makes me feel sick."

The suburban house became for many a postwar homemaker a sort of alter ego, a reflection of her essential self. "My mother's life was very much focused on appearances—how her house looked, how she looked," says Ann Landsberg, '69. "She took on dinner preparation as a demonstration of what she was as a mother and wife. She never let go of that, her entire life. Even when I was grown and had a house of my own, she'd walk through our big, old shambling Victorian with its threadbare rugs and need of a paint job and say to me, 'If you loved your family, you would do something with this house.' "

But if the suburban house was a woman's sacred creation, it was also, as Sylvia Plath wrote, "a mausoleum," a place to bury a woman alive, granting her existence only vicariously through the lives of her husband and children and her new best friend, the TV. Woman "the house-jailed and child-chained," Christina Stead called the mid-century mother in *The Man Who Loved Children*, a 1940 novel that became a best-seller in 1965; kept by "the keycarrier, the childnamer" in a house full of "leprosies of disillusion, abscesses of grudge, gangrene of never-more."

The suburban house reflected and reinforced the post-war family's growing appetite for privacy. Over the course of these women's child-hood, sociable front porches and town sidewalks were replaced by fenced backyards and highways, and families increasingly retreated be-hind rolled-up car windows and locked front doors. *House Beautiful* magazine offered typical praise of that inward turn: In the "privacy of home life are produced men and women strong in themselves, rather than taught to lean on each other as in the more socialistic communi-ties." What was exposed to the neighbors was in fact carefully con-trolled, with the consequence that an unhappy woman like Kathy Smith's mother believed herself to be alone. "The problem that has no name," Betty Friedan called the affliction. "So ashamed to admit her dis-satisfaction that she never knew how many other women shared it," the suburban mom "matched slipcover material, ate peanut butter sandwiches with her children, chauffeured Cub Scouts, and was afraid to ask even of herself—Is that all there is?"

Sometimes the secrets were kept even within the home. One class member, still protective enough to ask to be unnamed, describes growing up in an upper-middle-class community "like Ozzie and Harriet's" neighborhood. "We were, to all appearances, the perfect family. My parents were childhood sweethearts. My father was a successful business-man who had provided his family with a lovely home. My mother was on the school board and active in Junior League.

"When I was growing up, I assumed that everybody, like my mother, had friends over every afternoon for a few drinks. I never realized how deeply unhappy she was. When she left my father after I got married, the very first moment she felt she could, it took me totally by surprise. They had never fought. It was unsettling to realize that so much of what we thought was true, wasn't. Imagine the shock when we realized the rot beneath the perfect facade.

"There was no reality. If there were any negatives—death, divorce, financial failure—parents felt it best to hide it from their children, to insulate them from harshness. We were supposed to believe that every-thing was wonderful all the time. I think a lot of our generation has been less able to deal with failure as a consequence, and we all sooner or later meet it in our lives. We never saw our parents cope with the difficulties of real life."

For children so sheltered in their youth there were, no doubt, advan-tages: Their generation's abundant optimism could only have been nourished in such protected ground. But many of these girls of the fifties felt, like Pam Colony, '69, that they "learned nothing about relation-ships" from the model of their parents' marriages. Even in private, dis-content went unexpressed; conversation was often formal, superficial, austere. "My mom and dad didn't interact that I ever saw," says Pam. "They never fought, they just coexisted. I picked up that pattern of not confronting a problem." Matilda Williams, '69, recalls her mother's overprotectiveness as, "in an odd way, a kind of neglect. On the one hand, you're so precious that you can't do anything they don't approve of. On the other hand, there's a denial of anything that doesn't fit the ac-ceptable story. It's all hush-hush and taboo and not to be talked about, which is not very helpful to actually prevent stuff like sex from happening. You were expected to be a certain way. If you deviated from that path, you became invisible; no one could see you or hear what you were trying to say." In a poem published freshman year in Wellesley's literary magazine, Cheryl Ann Lawson, '69, wrote of "the gray chill of my father's house. . . . The cats and I were soldiers/Who did not hear my mother's silences. . . . She set her mouth and washed the blinds."

Graceful and well behaved, the girls of '69 were often pressed into service as emissaries of family normalcy; their parents trotted them out like a flattering mirror or their own marvelous invention. Their goodness and achievements were meant to compensate for the disappointments in their parents' lives. Matilda Williams's mother had studied painting in Europe after college but gave it up at her husband's insistence shortly after the wedding. "He put her on a pedestal, which proved to be a stifling kind of love. She resented all along that she had given up her work as an artist to have children, so she programmed us to complete her life."

Where the miseries were acute, these gifted girls were sometimes looked to as the most able-bodied person in the room—to contain the damage, or to somehow justify a painful family arrangement by publicly demonstrating its success. Growing up in New Haven, Connecticut, Elizabeth Michel, '69, was in love with books by age three. Her father was a committed pediatrician, who made house calls at all hours for his working-class patients. Her mother, who had met her husband at age fifteen, was a stay-at-home mom. All in all, says Elizabeth, "the family looked great from the outside." But Mrs. Michel suffered from severe depression, which jeopardized the wholesome picture. "She was given amphetamines to raise her spirits, then needed barbiturates to sleep, and wound up addicted to both," says Elizabeth, a small woman with a birdlike face and shaggy bangs veiling her eyes, who is now a physician herself. "Lily May, the cleaning woman, told me years later that she would go the house sometimes when we were at school, and wouldn't be able to get in, because my mother would be knocked out. That lady had an eighth-grade education, but she knew there was something wrong, with so many pills around."

Elizabeth understood what she was expected to do. "I became one of those kids who did extremely well in school. I hid behind books, got quiet, and stayed out of trouble. My diligence was rewarded by my mother, though it also always had the potential for being used. I became her trophy to display."

Mother's Little Helpers

Though her experience is not uncommon in the class, Elizabeth Michel is unusual in her willingness to talk openly of her mother's drug dependency. Most others in the class, after speaking of such matters, would ask that I not use their name. One, the daughter of a salesman, recalls her father going off on road trips for weeks at a time. "He also used to go away on cruises—by himself, he said. My mom would stay home, pacing circles. He would never let her get a job. 'No wife of mine is going to work,' he would say. She would have terrible bouts of depression. When he'd go away, she would quit eating and pass out. I knew my father had a drinking problem, though that was one of our many 'undiscussables.' I began to wonder whether she might also be hiding a bottle.

"My mom had three nervous breakdowns, as they called them then, dazed spells when she was not all there. When I was six she was hospitalized for three months, and they wouldn't let me in to see her. I was always afraid for her. I fell off the jungle gym once, and rather than bawl as most kids would, I rushed to my mother to tell her it was all right.

"My mother was taken terrible advantage of by the medical community. Her doctors were incredibly remote; they expected to be treated like gods. And in those days women with 'nervous ailments' were medicated out of their misery. My husband's mother was prescribed Valium by her doctor for twenty years and was then urged by him to have a brandy if she was having trouble sleeping. As for my mother, well you name it, she was given it. She died at age fifty, of what may have been a drug overdose. When she died, I was away at boarding school, and they didn't even tell me till the next day. It was another of those silences that had been maintained all along. I felt she was robbed of her life. I think she'd been a hopeful girl, but by the time I came along, I knew a very different person, one worn down by life. If my father would say, 'Jump,' she'd say, 'How high, dear?' She was always controlled, all her life—by her father and then by her husband. What a tragic waste of life."

Though it is Hillary's generation that is famous for its drug culture, her classmates turn out to have been no more prone to substance abuse than were their parents. The fifties were a boom time for cocktail shakers and pharmaceuticals. The introduction of Miltown, Librium and Valium launched the golden age of tranquilizers: The consumption of "mother's little helpers" reached 462,000 pounds in 1958 and 1.5 million pounds a year later. "The housebound," wrote Jane Davison, a 1954 Smith College graduate, who wrote a wonderful memoir of her family home, "committed mini-suicide by Fudgsicle or popped Valium or hit the vodka."

Doctors were quick to pathologize unhappiness and to prescribe a chemical cure: A woman, after all, was first and foremost her biology. Because "woman's life is entirely dependent upon her reproductive functions," wrote Dr. Noel Lamare in a widely read book of 1957, "she is in a state of constant physiological unbalance [and] psychical inconstancy. The consciousness of this frailty may give rise to an inferiority complex. So woman appears temperamental, devoid of sense and of the barest faculties of judgment . . . a vain being, stupid and designed to be dominated. Doubtless man, whose physiological life ensures him an unquestionable stability, must show forbearance, a little charity, towards his companions of the weaker sex." Dr. Lamare advised "psychotherapy under narcosis, that is after injection of Pentothal, sedative treatment (valerian, phenobarbitone), or electroconvulsive therapy for the extremely hyperemotional or hypermoral and prudish woman." A guinea pig for such wisdom, Sylvia Plath wrote repeatedly of its effects: In her poem "Lesbos," amidst the stink of cat and baby crap, mother is "doped and thick" from her last sleeping pill; father hugs his ball and chain but is able to slump out.

A startling number of women of Wellesley '69 remember mothers (and fathers) courting oblivion with drugs and alcohol. It is perhaps not unrelated that one in ten also reports having been physically or sexually abused as a child. "When I was four," says Elizabeth Michel, "my mother beat me really badly and I became totally submissive. My sister and brother were always fighting with each other, but I learned to be a very good girl. It didn't protect me. She abused us in all ways—physically, emotionally, and sexually. My father wasn't home much—he worked most days, and evenings as well—and says now that he wasn't really aware of what was going on. None of her friends knew of her addiction and abuse. People just didn't talk about it then. I remember sophomore year at Wellesley a friend telling me that her mother had once hit her. I became very, very ashamed, and didn't say a word."

Elizabeth would later speak of the sorrows in her family. Her mother never would, sealed away to the end by concern for appearances. Such isolation had tragic consequences. Shortly after Elizabeth's younger sister joined her at Wellesley in 1967, their mother made her first suicide attempt. She soon made several more, and was briefly hospitalized, which left Elizabeth's father feeling "terribly ashamed." During Elizabeth's junior year at Wellesley, her mother went into a brief drug-induced coma. In 1973 she walked out of the house and disappeared for good.

Looking back, Elizabeth wonders whether all the stellar grades and awards she brought home were entirely welcomed by her mother. While they offered a kind of Potemkin facade, helping Mrs. Michel win and keep the admiration of her neighbors, Elizabeth's achievements were perhaps a complicated blessing. In medical school, Elizabeth discovered that she struggled to speak up in front of other people, to look smart in public. "I feared people would abandon me. And I realized then that my success had been threatening to my mother. It meant separating from her, ceasing to identify, being disloyal. It was a crazy-making bind."

Even now, Dr. Elizabeth Michel doesn't fully understand her family's still-unfinished story. It had been difficult, she says, for her mother to grow up Jewish in New Haven in the thirties. She had both suffered and absorbed the prevalent anti-Semitism: Jews were vulgar, she told her daughters, then insisted that they date only Jewish boys. Denied her own chance to go to college—though her grandfather was wealthy, he saw no reason for a girl to go to school—she grew jealous when her daughters went off to Wellesley. When they came home from college, she taunted them relentlessly, accusing them of thinking themselves too good for the likes of her. Such maternal jealousy can cripple a young girl, Elizabeth learned. In the daughter's joy is implied her mother's deprivation.

In the end, most of the mothers and fathers of the women of '69 hoped that their daughters would be, not exceptional, but average, unambitious—*normal*. For a girl to be smart or to remain single was to be "thrown out of all the better-worn social grooves," wrote Anne Parsons, the unmarried daughter of Harvard sociologist Talcott Parsons, the most famous 1950s advocate of the nuclear family. "Being in that category is like being a Negro or Jew."

"My mother simply did not want me to be the person I was," says Kathy Smith Ruckman. "She kept telling me not to stick out, because people wouldn't like me. 'Be as average as you can be.' She never wanted to seem as if we were trying to be better than anyone else. When I asked for music lessons, she told me they were a wealthy person's luxury. So I bought five-cent plastic flutes and built piano keyboards out of paper to try to teach myself. When I signed up for a second language at school, she was furious. My dad didn't understand my desires, and thought my mom was always right and never intervened on my behalf. My mom was determined not to ripple the water. She needed to be liked, and hung with people she knew she could fit with, who posed no competition— uneducated people who she never had to worry would be smarter or richer than she. She was anti-intellectual, and so was her milieu. Intellectuals were people with pretensions and no common sense. 'You're supposed to be so smart, and look at the stupid thing you did.' I heard that all the time. She didn't like the fact that my friends were mostly Jewish. She told me I should find friends of my own kind. By the time I was in college, my mother and I had given up talking about anything of real meaning to me. I felt as if she didn't remotely understand who I was. I still feel that way about the rest of my family. I got away from Wilmington and lived a very different life, and that seemed to make my family uncomfortable. Maybe they feel threatened by what I did. What was good enough for them should have been good enough for me."

A mother "saddles her child with her own destiny," wrote Simone de Beauvoir, "a way of proudly laying claim to her own femininity and also a way of revenging herself for it." The mothers of the class of '69 bequeathed to their daughters their dreams of domesticity to affirm the worth of their own busy lives, and sometimes to squelch the girls' threatening aspirations. But they did so, also, as a gesture of love: A brilliant marriage seemed the only route to success for their beloved girls. And if the older women were themselves unhappy in the sort of lives they were championing, it was not because they found family life unrewarding, but only because they were excluded from everything else. In a country that celebrates nothing so much as money and independence, they were unpaid or barely paid and wholly dependent. Gallup polls in the early sixties found a majority of women rating motherhood the chief joy of womanhood but also wanting their daughters to have more education and to marry later.

There were numerous external barriers that kept these mothers from stepping into the world on their own: The lapse of the 1943 Lanham Act brought an end to federally funded child care; colleges were filled up with men on the GI Bill; most jobs and credit, even FHA mortgages, were available only to men. But it was the internal barriers that were most powerful. Even if their own experience contradicted the "feminine mystique's" message—that a reliable breadwinner and babies and a sparkling linoleum floor were all a woman needed for perfect bliss—postwar women could not easily resist the newly powerful opinion-making machine.

Between 1945 and 1960, advertising in America increased 400 percent. Perfect homemaking was vital, Madison Avenue's new advertising wizards told the young postwar mom; like a scientist in a laboratory, she must bring her expertise to the fight against unhealthy germs and unsightly "ring around the collar." Her children would be tragically deprived if she was not home every minute. The dinner she gave the boss was crucial to her husband's career. Above all, shopping was the answer: Buying things would win her neighbors' envy, recapture her husband's attention, fill the unnameable emptiness.

The entertainment media joined forces with advertisers in purveying the feminine mystique. Harriet flipped Ozzie's pancakes on the Hotpoint stove the show was devised to sell. For a decade, the most popular daytime show was *Queen for a Day,* which social historian Susan Douglas calls "a monument to the glories of female martyrdom: Its message is that there is nothing more admirable in a woman than suffering, no tragedy that couldn't be fixed by a Naugahyde recliner and a year's supply of Rice-a-Roni." In prime time, the top show was *Father Knows Best,* which regularly found Dad sharing his higher wisdom with little Kathy: "The worst thing you can do is try to beat a man at his own game. You just beat the women at theirs." Women's magazines ran articles asking: "Are You Training Your Daughter to Be a Wife?" and "Do Women Have to Talk So Much?" Pop music produced hits like "I Will Follow Him." And the master of fantasy, Disney, set beautiful young paragons of selflessness against old and powerful stepmothers or queens. "Cinderella was abused, humiliated, and forced to become a servant in her own house," that movie begins, "and yet she was ever gentle and kind."

When the women of Hillary's class describe their mothers, they return again and again to images of confinement and suffocation. They speak of women squelched, trapped, controlled, stunted, childlike; collectively, they conjure an image of bubbling springs stopped up, silenced. Such language might suggest daughters still wallowing in adolescent grievance, except that most of these women have in midlife developed a mutual regard and intimate understanding with their mothers, and tell their childhood stories more in sorrow than in anger. Rather, such images of a swaddled existence reflect the radical shrinking in the fifties of a woman's responsibilities and domain. As the extended family disappeared and as such domestic arts as clothes making and baking were increasingly outsourced to commercial enterprises, housework was reduced to its least creative parts: vacuuming, scrubbing toilets, doing the laundry. The moral work of the 1950s household was also badly attenuated. Though the postwar family resembled its Victorian predecessor in delegating to Father the Hobbesian world and to Mother the tender dependencies of home, in the Victorian notion of "True Womanhood" mothers were not just moral guardians of their nests but also of society, expected to soften the ruthlessness of capitalism by sustaining churches, orphan asylums, and settlement houses. In the fifties, those broader social and religious functions of the home eroded. Volunteerism and national women's organizations dwindled: The League of Women Voters was by 1960 half the size it had been in the 1920s. A woman squirreled away in suburbia increasingly labored only for the personal comfort of her husband and children. Without the more expansive understanding of "family" that had once defined her responsibilities, a suburban matron found herself living in a very small world.

While the world of the Wellesley girls' mothers shrank, critical scrutiny of them grew. Shadowed by the Freudian specter of the bad mother, the most idealized figure of the period also became a scapegoat. Full-time mothering was essential, they were told, but one false step could mean disaster: Behind every psychopathic, delinquent, sissy, or impotent man—and behind every frigid or promiscuous female—was a repressed or shrewish or rejecting or overprotecting mother. In *The Bell Jar,* Esther's mother is certain that she is to blame when her daughter lands in a mental hospital, because the doctors ask her a lot of questions about Esther's toilet training. Lectured on the latest "scientific principles" of child rearing, mothers discovered another competition to divide them; they compared their children as if discussing the new furniture in the den.

Daddy's Little Girl

As a very small child, Nancy Young lived with her family in her maternal grandparents' triple-decker home. She was, she says, fortunate to get out of there at a tender age. Her grandfather, a Polish immigrant factory worker and truck farmer, was a "tyrannical presence," a volatile and paranoid man. He ringed his house with chain-link fences and a pack of vicious German shepherds to guard his extended clan. Outsiders were barred from the property. Inside, all lived in constant fear of enraging him. Nancy's mother didn't work, but fled the house nearly every day, leaving her children in the care of aunts and cousins. She hated being there, hated being tied down by kids.

As a young girl, Nancy scorned her mother. "I thought she had no interest outside of what was on sale in the stores," she says. "Her life was my model of what not to have." It was her auto-mechanic father that the girl emulated and admired. A fervent Democrat who read serious books, he avidly discussed politics with his bright little girl. When Nancy became a teenager, that relationship changed. Now her father would talk to her only of her mother's failings; he repeatedly complained to Nancy that her mother wasn't interested in sex. He also worried out loud about money. In an effort to move up in the world, Nancy's father had quit fixing cars and taken over a photo business from one of his mother's ex-husbands. But he hated managing people and glad-handing customers, and chronically struggled in his new enterprise. "He had five people to house and clothe and feed. It was a terrible burden for one person to bear all the responsibility for earning the family's keep."

Like her grandfather, Nancy's father believed in rough demonstrations of his authority. "I got away with being a tomboy as a kid. But by the time I was in high school, my father made it a point, regularly, to put me in my place. He told me all the time that my strides were too long, that I was too noisy when I ate, that I was unladylike. He saw me as too big for my britches. I was supposed to be obedient and well behaved. We couldn't wear red or dance, because that was for whores. He would tolerate no challenge to his rule."

Paternal authority often fell harshly on the women of '69; the much vaunted respect for their elders of these postwar kids often seemed a sentiment more akin to fear. Still, many of Hillary's classmates would look to their fathers as a model for their lives, rather than to their hypervigilant or underdeveloped mothers. Betty Demy fell in love with classical archaeology, a field to which she has recently returned, at the family dinner table. Her father, "a real intellectual, who reveled in teaching us and in the sheer joy of knowledge," thrilled her with tales of Troy. When Nancy Wanderer played house with her best friend, both insisted on dressing up in jackets and ties. One would play Uncle, and the other, Father. "Neither of us wanted to be the mom. I knew I was smart, and I guess that seemed like my dad."

Charlynn Maniatis was named after her grandfather Charles. Her father, disappointed that he had no sons, had determined to raise his daughters as boys. Charlynn never had dolls. Her father taught her to shoot skeet and took her to World War II movies and Yale football games and pushed her hard at school. Every day, she was required to come right home and do her homework; if she dawdled, he smacked her. "I was afraid of him, but I accepted it as the way life was supposed to be. I knew how to stay out of trouble. I knew I could please him with my straight A's. Once I came home with a C in physical education, which was so unheard of that the principal called my father. I was never rebellious. I was very staid."

Charlynn's father had fought the Communists in Korea with the marines. Stern and still military in demeanor, "he was very patriotic," says Charlynn, "with great respect for authority and politics to the right of Genghis Khan." He forbade his daughter to go to Radcliffe with "that bunch of hippies," wanting her under the watchful eyes of Wellesley housemothers. In the fearful atmosphere of the Cold War, Dr. Maniatis wanted his wife and daughter safe, within domestic or at least wholly female bounds, well away from dangerous influences. He flatly refused his wife permission to learn to drive. Though he gave Mrs. Maniatis a weekly household allowance of twenty dollars, he went along with her to the grocery store in their Connecticut hometown to ensure that she spent his money on cube steak instead of sirloin. "He had a parental relationship with her," says Charlynn. "All her social life came through him. She didn't dare not be there when he came home. In my life, she was kind of a zero. Whatever my father said, she agreed. My mother is a very timid woman. Until the day he died, she didn't ever want to leave the house."

A surgeon, Dr. Maniatis encouraged his daughter to pursue her schooling, though at Wellesley he forbade her to study such "liberal nonsense" as political science or economics or art. Just sixteen when she went to college—she had finished high school in three years—Charlynn then skipped a year of college and graduated at nineteen. The Harvard Law degree she had by the age of twenty-one didn't satisfy her father. So she enrolled in Johns Hopkins Medical School, graduating with a master's in public health and an M.D. at age twenty-five, while also serving as a commander in the naval reserve and running her own real estate company in New York.

Dr. Lonny Laszlo Higgins's father filled his daughter's imagination with tales of practicing medicine in far-off places. For months at a time when Lonny was small, her father would vanish into Africa to provide medical care and practice a kind of anthropology—exchanging medicines with indigenous healers and documenting puberty rites, clitoral excisions, and birthing practices. Home in Connecticut, he took his daughter along on house calls, letting her carry his mysteriously powerful black bag.

Lonny's mother had been a gifted artist as a girl, but was pressed to abandon her study of sculpture at eighteen to marry the dashing Hungarian Dr. Laszlo, fourteen years her senior. From then on, her life was that of a doctor's wife. "I saw resentment in her thwarted ambitions; she preached adventure but stayed home," says Lonny. "My father was a fist slammed on the table. My mother was passive and remote. I never felt she'd earned the right to discipline me. She seemed like another child. After the death of my father, when I was fourteen, I left home. My hero had been snatched. The wrong one died."

If most of the Wellesley girls had either to turn away from their mothers or embrace the feminine mystique, not all did. Their mothers were not all quiescent. Nor were they all white middle-class suburban housewives.

The very rich were sheltered by their coterie of servants from the postwar compulsion for homemaking, though money did not buy them perfect freedom from conventional women's roles: The world of private clubs and girls' boarding schools had its own narrow horizons and rigid rules. Alison Campbell's mother was beautiful and stylish and classically educated; as a girl, she was tutored in Latin and Greek, and she finished a year at Vassar before dropping out at nineteen to marry. "My mother was a person who should have done something," says Alison (who has shed the nickname Snowy, along with the other vestiges of her high-WASP youth). "But there wasn't a lot that women like her felt free to do, except organize charity balls. My father provided well for his family; that was the mark of a good husband. He always believed that money equals success, and worked long hours. Mother was bored out of her mind and terribly lonely. But women simply didn't have the choice of combining career and family. My aunt Scilla chose a career, but married late and never had children. She was a Bryn Mawr graduate, nearly blind—the brilliant, awkward one, while my mother was the gorgeous, graceful one, though that does justice to neither." Author of a 1977 biography of the Oswalds, *Marina and Lee,* Soviet historian Priscilla Johnson McMillan [Aunt Scilla] has made a brilliant career: She has taught at Harvard, and was one of the few women to make it onto Nixon's enemies list. When Svetlana Alliluyeva, Stalin's daughter, defected to the U.S., Aunt Scilla hid her at Alison's grandfather's "posh Long Island estate," as *The New York Times* described it, where she received such "gentleman callers" as George Kennan, Harrison Salisbury, and George Ball. "I was sent to Bergdorf's to buy Svetlana a size 16 navy-blue suit, to set off her red hair and blue eyes. I loaned her hair curlers and took her shoe shopping one day, to Lord and Taylor. Scilla wanted us to avoid anywhere too expensive, too . . . capitalist, I guess."

At the insistence of her maternal grandmother, Alison was sent into "the thick air of social prominence" at Miss Porter's School. Alison hated Miss Porter's, with its endless policing of her grooming and manners and diction. Permitted to leave the campus just once a year, she felt like a prisoner and couldn't wait to escape the mean-spirited competition among the vain girls. "When you're locked up like that together, it doesn't bring out the best in people. There was lots of cruelty." She chose Wellesley after her interview with Radcliffe seemed to promise more of the same. "This bulldog lady, up above me on a platform, made me sit on a rickety lawn chair to see how I would handle it. I didn't think I should just lie back on it, so I perched there precariously on the edge. I found it all too tense."

Like velvet curtains drawn at the carriage window, the extraordinary privilege of Alison's youth rendered her deaf and blind to much of the world. "It was painful for me later, when I came to understand how much suffering there is in the world. I should have realized it sooner, but I'd been in a bubble, this rarefied atmosphere. I was both protected and confined." Lovely, with pale, powdery skin and white-blond hair, sheathed in Lilly Pulitzer shifts of pink or sky blue, Alison was an ethereal presence at the skeet shoots and polo games at Piping Rock—Long Island's most exclusive club. She had private lessons in piano, ballet, horseback riding, sailing, and golf; studied painting with Jacob Lawrence and drawing at the Sorbonne. On holidays, in a new ball gown, she made the rounds, in the family limousine, of the best parties in New York. But she always felt like an interloper. "That was not my home; these were not my people. I saw so many in the older generation who were terrible drunks, and that did not appeal to me. My own peers were also getting drunk, totaling their new Jaguars, getting pregnant. Boys were expected to be cads, you know: 'Upper-class boys will be upper-class boys.' Girls spent their time getting their hair done and buying expensive clothes, so they would fit in. My mother would drop me off at the club and want me to mingle, and I would hide in the locker room with a book."

Alison's breeding was nearly impeccable. Her maternal grandmother, Eunice Clapp Johnson, was old-line aristocracy. A Daughter of the American Revolution, with no fewer than three ancestors from the *Mayflower*, Eunice had danced with Rudolph Valentino and John Barrymore at her debutante ball. Her family's ball-bearings fortune had secured for the family an immense estate with a farm and several houses staffed by live-in maids, butlers, chauffeurs, nannies, and governesses, though it was still not as fancy, Alison says, as the neighbors' spreads. Alison's mother, a fine-boned woman with a refined, sonorous voice, recalls "thinking we were poor, because when our chauffeur took us to school, we didn't have detectives. This was shortly after the Lindbergh baby kidnapping, you see, and I was in the Green Vale School with terribly likely targets—Dina Merrill, then Nedenia Hutton, the daughter of Marjorie Merriweather Post and E. F. Hutton; a young Vanderbilt; the daughter of Princess Xenia of Russia. Most of them had two or three bodyguards. The school had to set aside a special room for the men to play poker while we were in class."

Alison's mother considered her own household more modest still. She had married a working man, a doctor, who was not from Newport or Boston and whose money, while ample, was new. The only spanking Alison recalls was when she visited her paternal grandfather's coal mine and disobeyed her parents' prohibition against playing with the miners' children. She was caught on a sagging front porch peering through a torn screen door, watching TV. "At home, we had maids come in," says Alison, "but since my mother grew up with live-ins, that seemed to her a simpler life. And my coming out party had only two hundred guests, not six hundred like most of the other girls'."

Still, until the day she died, Alison's maternal grandmother ensured that proper appearances were preserved. For Alison's sixteenth birthday, Grandmother Johnson sent her to Europe on the *Queen Elizabeth,* first class, with eight long gowns to dress for dinner each night, silk day dresses for visiting museums and cathedrals, and two elderly lady escorts. When *Glamour* magazine wanted to feature Alison as one of its debutantes of the year, Grandmother said no. "A lady is in the paper only when she is born, when she marries, and when she dies." Alison was stunned the day she learned of Eunice Clapp Johnson's death; the family had kept from her news of her beloved grandmother's declining health. She had always dressed up to see Alison, even the very last time.

Though she sometimes bristled under her grandmother's tutelage, Alison also deeply admired Mrs. Johnson. She had "the guts" to leave her scoundrel husband in the early 1900s and initiate a then-scandalous divorce. She'd then had the resourcefulness to go to work with society designer Elsie De Wolfe, pay off the rogue's gambling debts, remarry, have four children in her thirties, and help found the local library and fire department in Oyster Bay.

Grandmothers were often an important influence on the women of '69. Born in the first years of the century, they had themselves come of age with the first feminist wave. International lawyer Kaitlin Thomas, '69, the granddaughter of a suffragist, modeled her life on "those women who lived early in the century who managed to have some influence culturally or politically while also embarking on great adventures." Kris

Olson spent many afternoons over tea listening to her British grand-mother tell of her travels around the empire and her life in Bombay and Africa and the logging camps of Canada. Alison's paternal grandmother, Ruth Commack Campbell, was a concert pianist, athlete, and activist, who set out to clean up the local mental institutions and jails in West Virginia, where her family lived. "My grandmothers were ahead of their time, or at least more independent and self-determined than most of their peers. Both could have led self-absorbed lives of prominence and ease, playing bridge and ordering about lots of servants," says Alison. "North-shore Long Island's environment and that of Miss Porter's School tacitly prepared me for a narrow range of life choices, as society wife, CEO's wife, diplomat's wife. I am fortunate to have had great women predecessors, who found their own way to make a difference, to make their lives more meaningful than society and the time allowed. They gave me the freedom to reject my class."

If Alison's life was set apart from the fifties norm by her extraordinary wealth, Johanna Branson's was distinguished by her parents' aversion to social ambition and their powerful civic conscience. Though she let her daughter choose her own college, Johanna's mother, Jesse, hoped it would be the University of Kansas. Where other mothers saw Wellesley as a place for their daughters to climb the social ladder, Mrs. Branson worried that a school full of wealthy girls would change Johanna, today an art historian in Boston, mother of three daughters, and frequent baby-sitter over the years of Chelsea Clinton. "I wanted [Johanna] to keep that breadth of tolerance for people who aren't just from the upper echelon," said Jesse Branson. "I grew up on a farm in the Depression and drought. Johanna spent a lot of time there as a child, and I think she ad-mired the character of Kansas farmers. I probably pressed on her some of my principles of tolerance. She had opportunities I never had, but I hoped she would understand those who were disadvantaged."

Like so many of her contemporaries, as a girl Jesse had seen her aspi-rations dashed by parents who "clearly valued their son more highly" and reserved for him the widest scope of educational opportunities. Though she had shown promise as a pianist, they insisted Jesse be a nurse. "She was forced to be a doctor's wife in the 1950s and had the goods to do anything she wanted and was miserably frustrated," says Johanna. "I remember a mom-sits-on-the-side-of-the-bed conversation, and she said, 'I think I'm going to go crazy if I have to be a housewife anymore.' I think my mother really wanted to be a mother but had way too much drive to do that and nothing else."

Johanna's only brother was brain-damaged at birth. "You can't imagine the pain that puts in a family, especially in an era when everyone keeps it shrouded in secrecy. My mother became head of the Kansas Association for Retarded People, though she always felt she wasn't taken seriously as a volunteer, and she was right. This was not the model repressed mom but the chomping-at-the-bit repressed mom, forced to be at home with a damaged son when nobody really understood what was the matter. She was considered the town eccentric. She didn't toe the line, but flamed out about facilities for the retarded. She has a ferocious sense of right and wrong, and was determined to bring things out in the open. I'm just sorry she got treated the way she did, and grateful she lived long enough to see things change. At fifty-nine she was elected to the state legislature by 230 votes, going door to door in sneakers. It was a remarkable win, especially in Bob Dole country. We used to joke that we were related to all eleven Democrats in the state."

Johanna was taught by her mother to take chances for what she believed. "She was goddamned if anyone was going to treat her daughters as if they were second-rate. She had this burning, fierce determination to protect me and my sisters, had large ambitions for us. There are downsides to that, but by and large I'm grateful." Johanna's father, Vern, a pediatrician who cares for low-income families, also encouraged his daughter, urging her to go to graduate school so she would never be dependent on a man. He gave Johanna every book she ever asked for, though he recalls that a few were "what you might call racy." " 'We've raised you to be a responsible adult,' " Johanna recalls him saying as she packed to leave for school. " 'From now on, I'll never give you advice unless you ask. But I'll support you no matter what. You're a good person.' It made me take myself very seriously," she says. "I couldn't blame anything on them. I was responsible for myself."

A small minority of the Wellesley class of '69 had moms who worked for pay. Jan Krigbaum Piercy, a classmate who has remained a Friend of Hillary and is now the U.S. executive director of the World Bank, was raised by a single mom who worked for the Cook County Welfare Department. Jan found in her mother a model of both female economic self-sufficiency and commitment to service. Dr. Nancy Eyler's physician father told her she'd go to medical school over his dead body, that a woman should stay home and care for her family. But Nancy's mother was herself a doctor, sought out by the women of Lancaster, Pennsylvania, to treat their children. She called herself Mrs. rather than Dr. Eyler, to preserve the appearance that her husband was boss. But she also explained the function of kidneys to her daughter at the kitchen table and gave Nancy lots of freedom. "Without somebody always breathing down my neck, I was left to entertain myself with a book, or to go pick berries in the woods to bake a pie."

Among the nonwhite girls, working mothers were the norm. Catherine Shen's mother, a hematologist trained at Tulane University and already forty-one years old when her only child was born, taught her daughter that she'd better learn to take care of herself, because nobody else would. "It never occurred to me," says Catherine, "that anybody else would ensure my economic well-being." Bent on her daughter's assimilation—a desire that for the black and immigrant mothers frequently overwhelmed any impulse to dampen their daughters' aspirations—Mrs. Shen pushed her only child to go to an Ivy League school. She refused to teach her Chinese or to talk about her own past. Only when Catherine stumbled upon her mother's uniform in an attic trunk did she learn of her service in the Chinese Nationalist Army. Catherine's high school in Belmont, Massachusetts, was almost entirely white. "I ended up pretty deracinated, as my mother had hoped I would. When I got called *chink* on the street, it was discombobulating. I had an Asian body but a WASP cultural lens."

Though political dissent was anathema to most of the parents of Wellesley '69, a few girls learned the art of resistance at their parents' knee. Growing up on a farm in Wisconsin, Cherry Watts learned from her parents that faith in God compelled a strong sense of public responsibility. Cherry's father was a Christian Scientist and an outspoken man. The day after he was quoted in the *Milwaukee Journal* criticizing Wisconsin's popular senator Joseph McCarthy, a third of the accounts at his family's business were canceled. When he joined the NAACP and hired blacks into front-office positions, he lost most of the rest.

Until she graduated from high school, Janet McDonald lived in a New

Orleans segregated in its own fashion, with white people on the city's wide and shady boulevards and black people out of sight but close by, on the narrow side streets and in the alleys. Close as she was to her white neighbors, Janet didn't know a single one. She walked past them without speaking to take her place in the back of the bus, drank from a different water fountain in the park, and went for a soda through a separate entrance at the snowball shop. Her friends made a sport of "passing" as white and sneaking into segregated facilities. Most were Creoles, including Janet, whose paternal grandfather was white. "Many of my friends were very fair, with white features and French surnames. They would come to school and say, 'I passed last night and went to Sanger Theater.' They would speak a French patois at the ticket window and see a movie that would not come to black theaters for several weeks. They considered it a notch on their belts to be able to pass as white." Janet did not join in. "It was too dangerous," she says, "and it would have been like stealing, because it was against the law." Now the co-owner of a D.C.-based management consulting firm, Janet makes a point of going to the famous New Orleans restaurants that she could have entered as a girl only through the back door, and then only to wash the linen tablecloths and scrub the linoleum floors.

Janet's father, like many of his generation, had left the South to seek work in Chicago after finishing high school in the 1920s. He came home again two decades later, after picking up a black newspaper, seeing a picture of the Arkansas Agricultural, Mechanical and Normal School's homecoming queen, and falling in love. He immediately went to Arkansas to introduce himself to the young woman, sixteen years his junior, who had just completed her master's in music. They soon married and moved back to New Orleans, into the house Mr. McDonald's family had owned since before he was born. Together they launched a business making dentures and crowns, and three years later, Janet was born. Every day after school, Janet would come to the lab, which was attached to the house, to do her homework while her parents worked. After supper, when she was in bed, her mother would go back to work, often putting in eighteen-hour days. Fifty-one years later, Janet's mother still runs her denture business; her own mother had shown her the way, practicing nursing in Arkansas for fifty years.

An only child, Janet was her father's pride and joy. When she was three, he taught her how to count money. For twelve years, he sat with her every day for two hours while she practiced piano. Former UN ambassador Andrew Young, who grew up with Janet and calls her his "country cousin," teases her that she is a BAP—a black American princess. Janet's parents were intensely protective. To insulate her from the racial strife in the public schools, they sent her to Catholic school with the Sisters of the Blessed Sacrament, who devoted their lives to teaching blacks and Indians. By the time efforts at school desegregation turned intensely violent, Janet was safely at Wellesley. Janet interviewed for Wellesley with a former Mardi Gras queen, who did little to veil her surprise at the girl's scholarly aspirations but failed to humiliate her nevertheless. "My parents taught me that we were separate but superior, that whites had more to learn from me than I did from them. I knew about white people from TV, but they didn't know about me."

The McDonalds had high hopes for their daughter. "But my parents were outraged and bitter about the circumstances of their own and their friends' lives. They believed that discrimination diminished everyone's quality of life, deprived the whole society of the rich contributions black people can make. A lot has changed, but ask my son, Grant [Hill]. He'll tell you that a lot hasn't changed."

In 1961, the year the Freedom Riders first set out from Washington, D.C., heading for New Orleans, Janet's father became active in grassroots civil disobedience and encouraged his daughter to get involved. On the steps of city hall, father and daughter together joined picket lines protesting the continued denial of voting rights to portions of the black populace. During one such demonstration in 1962, the same year the New Orleans Citizens Council offered free one-way transportation to blacks wishing to move north, Janet was arrested with a group of other teenagers. Only the intervention of a sympathetic judge kept her from landing in jail.

When the women of '69 say, "I always expected to have my mother's life," they are often describing an ambiguous frame of mind, both happy anticipation and dread. Women could blame on their mothers the feminine self-effacement they despised in themselves, see in them colluders with a society that restricted women. "What had our mothers been doing then," wondered Virginia Woolf, chafing at her exclusion as a woman from the lawns and libraries and "High Tables" of Oxbridge, "that they had no wealth to leave us?"

The contempt for her mother's capitulation might propel a girl to outdo her. At the same time, to reject her mother's example was to be a traitor to her love; to step out into the larger world might arouse a daughter's guilt and her mother's rage. Literary historian Carolyn Heilbrun has argued that the heroines of most novels by women have no mothers, or ineffectual ones, because they reflect the female dream of taking control of one's life without injuring the much loved and pitied mother. Outside of fiction, the dilemma was not so easily resolved. For most of the women of '69, their relationships with their mothers are a work in progress. As they reach middle age and each hears her mother's voice in her own, she can still feel compelled to resist the vortex of her feminine history. More often, both women have evolved toward each other and a grateful peace.

Before that rapprochement was possible, however, their break with the past required a good number of these women to give the pendulum a hard swing. In the years that followed Wellesley, in that loose-bordered epoch typically called the sixties (though it spilled well into the seventies), a number of the women of '69 chose exile or estrangement, taking off like runaways with no forwarding address, moving into communes or marriages so unacceptable as to guarantee broken ties. Like George Eliot's fall from austere bluestocking into mistress of a married man, which made it possible for her to write, a woman wanting to escape the conventional role into which she was cast had to transgress.

CHAPTER THREE

Rebellions and New Solidarities

In the summer of 1970, Alcohol, Tobacco and Firearms special investigators Clyde Curry and Robert d'Orsa and Sgt. Ronald Andrade of the Fall River, Massachusetts, police department testified before Senator Strom Thurmond and the Senate Subcommittee on the Internal Security Act. Their topic was the "Extent of Subversion in the New Left." Though the testimony ranged widely, the questioners were most keenly interested in the members of the Regional Action Group (RAG), who had settled into several communes in Fall River in order to conduct political education and organize among the mostly white working-class residents. "The landlords complained that these individuals were using narcotics and wanted to overthrow the country," Mr. d'Orsa reported.

The "red squad" listened with grave concern as the witnesses testified about a twenty-two-year-old female, Dorothy Devine Gilbarg, who had recently returned to the collective after traveling to Cuba with the Venceremos ("We shall overcome") Brigade for reasons she subsequently described to the *Providence Journal:* "We helped break the U.S. information blockade, supported the Vietnamese struggle and advanced the cause of Internationalism." RAG was devoted, she said, to "the destruction of U.S. imperialism and to the eventual communization of the world."

Mrs. Gilbarg's Cuban sojourn was what "brought the heat on the collective," she believed. "The ATF told our neighbors we were dangerous, and enjoined them to rent their front bedroom so they could set up cameras to monitor our activities." The investigators' pictures—shot with a long lens, they are grainy and gray and clumsily composed—were posted in the Fall River Police Department with a warning that the young woman might be dangerous. Dorothy's lank hair is tied back in a bandanna. Otherwise, she is much the same soft, shy girl who smiled out of her Wellesley yearbook in a picture taken just twelve months earlier.

A year and a half had passed since her father had forced her down the aisle; Dorothy was cut off from her parents, but she was still struggling to make her new home. Swept into Dan's leftist circle, the young bride was repeatedly frustrated in her wish to have time alone with her husband to solidify their new marriage. Though for a time the couple had their own apartment, they never made dinner together at home. Every night they were at someone's house, "organizing." Their thorough entanglement of the personal and political greatly enlarged Dorothy's world, but it also menaced her sense of safety and would eventually sabotage her efforts to create a lasting intimate bond with her husband.

Dorothy tried to play homemaker for her radical husband, valiantly hanging new Marimekko curtains and laying their breakfast table with Danish-modern flatware. She also dutifully supported her husband's career, following him to Fall River though she had no work of her own there, and reliably parroting his political ideas. Her husband taught at a community college; he teaches there still. "His idea, 'our idea,' was that working-class people would change America, that if the working class wanted blacks to have equal opportunities and they wanted the war to end, then the world would change. We'd find real alienated Vietnam vets and talk to them about how they got used," says Dorothy, "or try to get street toughs hanging on corners to not just be punks but to want to change their country and their town." Several of the street kids, she believes, later informed on them to the ATF and FBI.

There are at least three versions of the life Dorothy lived as Dan's wife and a member of RAG. The first is that described by the Senate Subcommittee on Internal Subversion. Dorothy and her comrades, in the committee's rendering, were seditious and highly dangerous. The group was out to indoctrinate children: Dorothy and occasional RAG associate Susan Hagedorn (a former member of the Weather Underground) frequented the YMCA to show Boston Newsreal Co. documentaries about the Black Panther party and labor unions and Vietnam. Hagedorn, a youth counselor and teacher at the Fall River junior high, also consulted with Dan on "revolutionary propaganda" with unalarming titles that she might sneak into her class. "She said 'I cream my jeans when I think of the stuff I can show the kids,' " reported Sergeant Andrade, adding that he didn't much cotton to her "trooper's language." Andrade reported further that Dan had distributed leaflets to workers in the garment industry. When a worker he'd recruited at the King Phillip Mill complained that his co-workers called him a Communist, the sergeant said, Dan had snapped back: "Well, what the hell do you think you are?"

The witnesses described a progressive turn toward violence in the group. "The members of RAG were advised by their Cuban companions as to the best tactics for revolution and informal indoctrination," the investigators told the Senate. Venceremos Brigadiers "have a propensity toward the use of bombs and incendiaries." In a New Bedford demonstration in November 1969, the ATF agents said, RAG member Michael Kevin Riley (whom they inaccurately identified as chairman of the Weatherman faction of SDS) burned a live pig. They produced as evidence leaflets they said were being produced by Mike Ansara, "one of the twenty most dangerous white revolutionaries in the U.S." and distributed by Dorothy. The leaflets advocated violence, condemning the "Amerikan government's attempts to suppress dissent" and calling for the emulation of Third World revolutions, "where poor people are taking what's theirs." "The Man is out to pull a fast one," reads one of the leaflets reproduced in the report, "accusing us of being duped by outside agitators. We are going to take power back to the people. We are going to drive the cops, politicians and bloodsucking businessmen out. Free Bobby Seale. The black struggle against the rich rulers is white working people's fight too."

The investigators' account grew increasingly alarming. By the spring of 1970, they testified, just a month after two members of the Weather Underground blew themselves up building bombs in a Greenwich Village town house, the collective began planning a violent May Day demonstration in Fall River. Sergeant Andrade reported that Dorothy and another woman had been caught in the police station and could offer no explanation for their presence. "They are suspected of reconnoitering to take it over or to bomb it on the night of May 1st, 1970." The police said they had also detected an unusual number of sales of gasoline in small containers and road flares called fusees, exactly like those that had been used to ignite buildings in Harvard Square. An informant who claimed to have infiltrated the collective reported that the group was anticipating "heavy action" on May Day. This was the same group, he claimed, that had organized the "April window-smashing riot" in Cambridge; now they "wanted the Hell's Angels and the Panthers in their May Day parade, and were not afraid of a shoot-out. David Miller [another RAG member] thought he might die, and Dan Gilbarg said he would take some pigs with him." Claiming that the group had threatened to kill him if they found him, the informant absconded. The group did not renounce violence, according to the police; the next month, they claimed, Mike Riley bought a semiautomatic gun.

The second version of those years comes from Dorothy's ex-husband, Dan Gilbarg, a straightforward, reflective man who still teaches at the community college in Fall River. Dan disputes much of the Senate report. Though there were some in the group who wanted to be "militant," what that meant was "chanting loudly while we marched, instead of singing folk songs or 'Give Peace a Chance.' If there had been anything like bombs, guns, or Molotovs, I would have been gone." The burned pig, Dan says, was made of papier-mâché and decorated with the names of all the corporations making money in Vietnam. The two women arrested in the police station were strangers to the group. And the informant, Dan says, must have been someone at the fringe of the group, given how wrong most of his information was; alternatively, he may have exaggerated RAG's violent intentions to curry favor with authorities eager for a rationale for a harsh police response. The Fall River city council president did in fact promise to "take the wraps off of the police," insisting he would not be bound by the rulings of "a senile kangaroo court [a reference to the U.S. Supreme Court] supporting the radicals." That promise came despite the fact that RAG had no contact with the Black Panthers at all prior to the May Day march in 1970, according to Dan; it was the police who spread rumors that armed Panthers would be "landing on the beach at Westport," causing frightened residents to begin buying guns. It was that influx of guns, in turn, that caused RAG to call off the demonstration, fearing someone would get hurt. "The pig power structure tails us and stakes out our home," RAG announced. "They sent us bomb and death threats, told us they'll use their clubs and guns." The event effectively marked the end of RAG, Dan says. Most members decided their efforts to mobilize the workers were hopeless, and turned away from politics to their private lives. Dan sought to recast his appeal: "Rather than expect the locals to get interested by talk of the Panthers, I started to speak to people about their everyday concerns."

The third version is Dorothy's. Early on, she says, she felt a mounting sense of aimlessness in her new life with Dan. She did not have a job or a burning sense of mission of her own, and her attempts at traditional wifeliness fit only awkwardly into the collective's structure. For the second time, therefore, she left home to experiment with a new kind of family. Without Dan, and with about two hundred fellow travelers, she joined the Venceremos Brigade, violating U.S. law by traveling to Cuba. Though she now calls the Brigade "a propaganda thing" by Castro, she also recalls her months working in the cane fields alongside Cuban comrades as a time of "more energy and sense of direction than I'd ever had." She was impressed by the free clinics and schools and loved the physical labor and wholesome life. The revolution was like a generous and protective father: "They clothed me and fed me, and insisted we not use drugs." Castro himself, who visited the Brigade on Christmas Day, seemed "charismatic and kind," with none of her own father's tyrannical will. "Fidel doesn't sit in Batista's palace and issue decrees," she told the *Providence Journal.* "The people have to want a certain thing to happen, then Fidel asks that it happen, and it happens." Describing the absence of violent crime, she added: "Why should you steal anything? All the essentials are free. Police are not needed. The populace will pursue a thief, because anything he steals belongs to everyone."

Dorothy's parents had not spoken to their daughter in almost a year when the FBI showed up at their door to tell them that she was "Fidel Castro's guest" and being taught to make explosives. She returned home from Cuba soon thereafter, and though just eleven weeks had passed, she found nearly everything changed. Dan had been evicted from their old apartment for political activities, and though he had found them another place to live, he had let their houseplants die and had not unpacked a single box. He was waiting for Dorothy to do it when she got home. "I walked in the door, and here was this big radical leader acting utterly dependent on me. I guess you could say we were starting to have problems with our roles."

Women throughout the New Left were by this time growing impatient with their men; many, like the thwarted abolitionists who became suffragists a century earlier, would become key figures in feminism. Why is it, wondered Mary King of the Student Nonviolent Coordinating Committee (SNCC), "that men in communes still gather around five to ask, 'When's supper going to be ready?' " At meetings of the Students for a Democratic Society, women who demanded to speak were often greeted with ridicule. A June 1967 plea "for our brothers in SDS to root out the male chauvinism within themselves" ended with, "We love you!" It was reprinted in the official SDS newsletter accompanied by a derisive drawing of a young woman wearing a polka-dot baby-doll dress and matching panties. Dan Gilbarg looks back with regret on the movement's failure to confront its sexism. "There was a lot of macho stuff, and nobody ever bothered to ask why women weren't in leadership positions. It was also sexist that I set the agenda in our marriage, that I didn't encourage Dorothy to find a project or job of her own."

There was more change awaiting Dorothy when she got home. In her absence, Dan had become involved with another woman—though she was a lesbian, he said, and he had waited to ask his wife's permission before having sex with her. (He felt licensed to ask, Dan says, when Dorothy told him she'd had an affair of her own in Cuba.) Dorothy wasn't much surprised. "The collective did not value fidelity or have any regard for marriage," she says.

In fact, the experiments in collective living in the late sixties were to a great degree a reaction against traditional marriage and an attempt to craft alternatives that might be less unequal and inhibited and isolating. Many of Hillary's classmates would spend months or years after Wellesley participating in such experiments, pursuing an ideal first described by Plato in *The Republic*. Families, Plato wrote, should "live in common houses and meet at common meals. None of them will have anything specially his or her own, [thus ending] the tearing of the city in pieces by differing about mine and not mine. . . . All will be affected . . . by the same pleasures and pains . . . and all tend towards a common end." Plato's vision included free love: "They will all be together . . . and so they will be drawn by a necessity of their natures to have intercourse with each other." He also championed a radical kind of collective parenting, in which "no parent is to know his own child, nor any child his parent." In 1948, B. F. Skinner had resurrected those ideas in *Walden II*; in 1961, *Stranger in a Strange Land* gave the theme a sci-fi spin, and in 1966 the best-selling *Harrad Experiment* transplanted the idea into

Wellesley's backyard at a fictional New England college (Harvard-Radcliffe). All explored the central question: where the boundary should be between public and private life.

In Dorothy's version, her collective viewed marriage as a capitalist effort by one human to own another; fidelity was repressive, and those who insisted on it were uptight. "The Weather Collective actively busted up couples, made them break up and go out with somebody else. Some collectives got rid of individual bedrooms entirely and everyone slept together on a mat on a floor. We all smoked lots of marijuana, which was definitely a sex aid. But I felt completely alienated from Dan, and when he told me he wanted to sleep with the lesbian, I said, 'I don't care what you do.' By that time we'd moved into the collective house on New Boston Road. We lived in separate rooms, and he had a series of affairs. I understood that at that moment I'd lost all my protection. Another big honcho in the movement came to me and said, 'I'm delighted you're not into monogamy,' and I just burst into tears."

The Sexual Revolution

Do It!, Jerry Rubin titled his 1969 Yippie polemic. "Puritanism leads us to Vietnam. Sexual insecurity results in a supermasculinity trip called imperialism. America has a frustrated penis trying to drive itself in Vietnam's tiny slit to prove it is the man." For all the heedlessness with which many of the Wellesley women were then leaping into numerous beds, sex was a heavily laden thing in the early 1970s. It was no longer private, a sacred covenant between man and wife, or solely procreative. But it was far more than a recreation to pass the time in hot tubs: With drugs and rock 'n' roll, it was the path to liberation. Men were sick, said Wilhelm Reich and Norman Mailer and Woody Allen, because they did not have enough or good enough orgasms. Sex was personally liberating: primitive, consciousness-expanding, transcendent. Sex was also politically liberating: transgressive, the last wild freedom in the prison of repressed industrialized society, a tool for world peace ("Make love, not war"). That sexual liberation was politically subversive was a view shared by the establishment: In 1967, J. Edgar Hoover ordered his agents to publicize the "depraved nature and moral looseness of the New Left," and the deviant sexual behavior at RAG's collectives described by investigators seemed to Strom Thurmond solid evidence of sedition.

As an act of social rebellion, the sexual revolution was far more important for women than for men: The public policing of sexual behavior had never been very much focused on men. If loosening their corsets had been for women an act of political defiance, unbuttoning their Levi's was much more so. Women would claim control of their own bodies—especially their sexual, reproductive bodies. They would demand their freedom to feel pleasure like men. Germaine Greer preached that the denial of female sexuality was "the chief instrument in the deflection of female energy" and urged women to put away their makeup and engagement rings and underpants and "celebrate Cunt." Nancy Friday cataloged female sexual fantasies in *A Secret Garden*. For a century, female lust had been dirty, perverse; now young Wellesley alumnae studied *The Joy of Sex and The Sensuous Woman* by "J" (who called herself "a lady in the living room and a bitch in bed"), committing to memory such techniques as "the butterfly flick" and "the hoover" and the "whipped cream wiggle." Sweeten and apply, the best-seller instructed, "then lap it all up with your tongue. He'll wriggle with delight and you'll have all the fun of an extra dessert. If you have a weight problem, use one of the new artificial whipped creams in an aerosol can. And avoid gnawing."

In the consciousness-raising group Cherry Watts, '69, joined right after Wellesley, she recalls, they talked about little except sex, "about what gave us pleasure, about orgasms and the best way to have one and how it was your right to have one and if he couldn't pleasure you that you should take matters into your own hands, literally." Feminist presses churned out papers, rigorously arguing that women should insist on being on top, or championing clitoral orgasms as a means to liberate women from their dependence on the penis.

The sexual revolution was unquestionably liberating for a woman like Dorothy, who had been made a "ruined woman" and an unwilling bride by the repressive morality it sought to overthrow. Many of her classmates recall fondly those days of what Chris Osborne, '69, describes as "fucking like bunnies"; they are not anything like the sex-hating banshees of antifeminist lore. But the revolution was also a mixed blessing: Girls raised like hothouse orchids *had* grown up, often, to be fragile flowers, woefully unprepared for the flood of sex let loose upon the land. "It was the first time we felt we had the right to feel good," says Dorothy Devine. "We didn't have to ask, 'What's his portfolio?' or, 'Does he want the same number of kids?' At the same time, the idea that a man would invite you out simply for the pleasure of your company was made, overnight, obsolete."

While women were struggling to escape the ideology that their biology rendered them bundles of natural feeling unfit for the hardheaded world, the focus on sex reduced them once again, before all else, to their anatomy. Moreover, the revolution was incomplete: Women were still more object than subject, "the sought, rather than the seekers," as the Wellesley guidebook had said. Outside of the truly radical voices like Greer's, most of the new sex gurus were still teaching young women how to arouse male desire, not how to awaken their own. The 1969 best-seller *Advice to a Young Wife from an Old Mistress* (reissued in 1995) suggested that female sexual liberation meant the freedom to shed passivity for the tricks of the courtesan's trade. "We were designed to delight, excite and satisfy the male species," wrote "J."

There were other complexities for women in the sexual revolution, many of which are still being sorted out. The social surveillance of women's sex lives had afforded a kind of protection, which was now suddenly gone. "I was really buxom as a college student, and got lots of attention," says Dorothy. "It felt icky, invasive. Men felt this new kind of permission. They would reach out of a crowd and grab my breast." As Gloria Steinem had predicted in *Esquire* in 1962, "Betty Coed" was now "morally disarmed." The old social code had given way to a new one: Dorothy felt unable either to demand fidelity or to refuse the demands of other men for sex without being deemed "uptight."

The recognition of that new intrusion on their sexual autonomy led some feminists to shift focus away from the politics of pleasure and toward sexual coercion and the nature of consent. "The sexual revolution is a reinstitution of oppression." So Robin Morgan, editor of *Sisterhood Is Powerful* and, later, *Ms.* magazine, concluded in her "Farewell to the New Left," published in *Rat*, a radical underground newspaper, just weeks before Dorothy's return from Cuba. "Goodbye to the Weather Vain with the Stanley Kowalski image and theory of free sexuality but practice of sex on demand for males. . . . Abbie Hoffman dumping his first wife and kids when he's Making it; Paul Krassner reeling off in alphabetical order the names of people in the women's movement he's fucked, as proof he's no sexist oppressor." In 1970, Kate Millett introduced in *Sexual Politics* what remains the single most controversial polemic in feminism: that sexual intercourse itself is political, an expression of male power. Her analyses of the novels of Henry Miller and Norman Mailer found their heroes pursuing sex not for love or even desire but as a means to master and humiliate women.

That sex could be brutal and frightening had for Dorothy become clear at an early age. As a six-year-old, Dorothy was raped by a teenage baby-sitter, a story she volunteers. "My parents got me away from him and said, 'We're going to put him in jail.' They did the best they could with it, had me checked medically, then tried not to make a big deal out of it, thinking it would only be worse for me. But it left me panicked and angry and terribly shy. Sexuality is a precious thing. And women take the brunt of promiscuity: They're so much more vulnerable to disease and pregnancy and violence if they're out there looking for Mr. Goodbar. When I split from my husband in the collective, I was afraid. I didn't want to be preyed on sexually."

Dorothy's new sense of vulnerability away from the protection of her husband's bed was only heightened by what she saw as her collective's recent turn toward violence. She describes the events of November 1969 much as the police had: Members of her collective, she says, had gone into New Bedford with Molotov cocktails to inflame a smoldering racial conflict; their intention, she says, was to demonstrate to America that even in seemingly conservative neighborhoods dissent was brewing. The group was busted, and then defended by William Kunstler. (They got off, says Dan, suggesting that the charges were unfounded.)

Dorothy had also developed a distaste for what she calls "the swagger" of the Weather Underground, whom she'd encountered in New Brunswick; delayed by U.S. authorities en route home from Cuba, she'd spent several nights in a barn with fellow Brigadiers. "Mark Rudd [who as a junior at Columbia had led the 1968 occupation of university buildings and was by then a leader of the Weathermen] came and instructed us to go underground." Fearing the spreading net of FBI surveillance and arrest, "a lot of people obeyed his orders and disappeared. But the Weather People had offended me. 'We're going to make a revolution in America,' they'd brag to the Cubans. 'We'll go back and tell the truth.' These kids from Columbia University were trying to out-revolutionary Castro."

Of the many adventures and commitments in the larger world that have been recognized to forge male character, few have been more honored than the taking up of arms in service of a passionate cause. Becoming a soldier has been for men the classic coming of age: By risking himself for the common good, a man could transcend himself, join the brotherhood, arrive at the fullness of manhood. In the sixties, violence seemed to some a particularly fertile necessity—to overthrow colonial oppression and resist the vast, bureaucratized military-industrial complex killing hundred of thousands in Vietnam.

With rare exceptions (the Manson girls, the debutante terrorist Patty Hearst), no such feminine, or feminist, romance with violence ever got very far. Feminism, rather, has often been strongly linked to pacifism: The earliest second-wave marches were protests against nuclear weapons and the Vietnam War. Some saw violence as a betrayal of female "nature": Robin Morgan accused those few women in the left who did adopt "the machismo style and violence" with making "a last desperate grab at male approval." Contemporary eco-feminists have resurrected the idea that women have a more protective, maternal instinct toward living things.

Though the Wellesley women of '69 would join men in almost every other public activity, doing violence was where all drew the line. Nancy Gist did some work with the Black Panther party after finishing Yale Law School with Hillary. With Bobby Rush, later chairman of the party and a member of Congress, Nancy worked with the People's Law Office in Chicago on the wrongful-death suit brought against the FBI and Cook County for the December 1969 killing of Chicago Panther party chairman Fred Hampton, murdered by the police in his sleep. It took her a while, Nancy says, "to understand the implications for women of the Panthers' symbolic statements about black manhood," a statement best captured in the famous picture of Huey Newton with his spear and gun. "From my particular vantage, I didn't see the disparity in treatment. There seemed an equal regard for women. Women were central; we always are. We're the ones with the mimeograph machine in the basement cranking out leaflets, though nobody ever hears of our work. Then we got Stokely Carmichael telling us that 'the best place for women in the movement is on their backs.' "

As her collective prepared for the May Day march in solidarity with the Panthers, Dorothy grew increasingly scared. "These military, radical men just seemed to be picking a fight and would probably get us hurt. A few of the women, very few, were just as macho. [Weather Underground member] Kathy Boudin came and met with my husband, and said, 'If you're a real man, you'll go and make bombs.' I didn't like her at all. Dan never did get a gun; he was afraid to, though that wasn't something he could admit." (Dan responds that it was not just fear that kept him from getting a gun but principle, and that he never hesitated to express how scared he often was.) "I resented him for putting us in danger," Dorothy says.

In middle age, Dorothy is a big, doughy woman with a hesitant, gentle voice, watery, blinking blue eyes, and a nervous habit of running her hand through her fragile cap of wispy brown hair; it is easy to imagine how, as a very young and bewildered woman, her efforts to please her husband, Dan, might have taken her places she never meant to go. "I was in the left because of my boyfriend. I hadn't thought much beyond 'War is bad. I'll work for peace.' I was neither anti-imperialist nor pro-Communist. I was opposed to violence, and afraid. We all were being followed. The cops would harass us and arrest us for spray-painting on buildings to announce demonstrations, or for smoking pot. And once we staged a demonstration in Lynn, and one guy said to me, 'Dorothy, you get on the car and speak.' A panic washed over me. I tumbled out a few words. Then bikers and vets started throwing rocks and bottles at me. I was terrified."

By June 1970, just weeks after the killings at Kent State made credible all the paranoid fears that armed authorities would gun down dissenters, Dorothy was out the door. "I was leaving, but I didn't want my parents to know that. I sort of divorced my parents and my husband at the same time. My relationship with my father was completely severed, and it would be a while before I could see my mother as being my family. For two years they had no idea whether I was alive or dead, though then I settled down a bit and let them know where I was. After that, once a year my mother would visit me wherever I was, in a commune or the tepee I sewed to live in, in the woods or, later, in households with uncertain relationships that she didn't understand. Visiting me cost her dearly in her own marriage.

"I ended my marriage by buying a car with my husband's money and going cross-country with three other women who'd gone to Cuba after me on the Brigade; one was a dropout from Wellesley. I had no family, no marriage, no job, no skills, and no money."

Arriving in Haight-Ashbury, Dorothy "crashed with a bunch of hippies" and her husband's roommate from Harvard. "We went to the Fillmore and to lectures by Steve Gaskin, who was this spiritual leader and vegetarian farmer, and did a lot of psychedelics. That all felt good and spiritual. But none of it helped me to think I was the kind of person who could get a job."

She did have one offer to earn money. San Francisco was then home to a counterculture porn industry presided over by the Mitchell brothers, who ran a hands-on sex theater and made counterculture "beaver" movies like *Behind the Green Door* (1971). "A bunch of the people I was hanging out with, including some Wellesley girls, were making softporn movies with a guy named Russ Meyer. They tried to persuade me to make them too. 'You do it stoned. Making love is fun.' They talked about it like free money. Fortunately, I had just enough self-preservation instincts left to say 'Naaaah.' "

After a few months, Dorothy moved back to Cambridge with a "hippie boyfriend." Her husband asked her to come back; when she refused, he divorced her for desertion. "I think my husband loved me. I didn't love him. And I wish young women were taught about what you give away and what you keep. He'd offered me a ready-made identity. He was the professor in Harris Tweeds and a respected leader who knew what he wanted to do. And I didn't. I was in this intense milieu, but I was drifting. I wasn't assertive or confident. I believed my dad that I was ruined. I avoided my Wellesley classmates. I was ashamed to be divorced, ashamed I was not successful in anything. It'd been four years since graduation, and I'd never held a job."

Moving from one commune to another, Dorothy tried to become "more liberated about sex, to have no expectations. In the best places, we were essentially a whole bunch of friends that slept together. I'd come home from a camping trip and jump in the shower and somebody else would jump in with me. It didn't mean you belonged to them.

"I did have a few boyfriends—long-haired, soft, pretty young things who'd never gone to college. Then I started having girlfriends. It seemed much simpler and less confusing. It took me a few years to learn that women can be cruel as well. At the time, our community of women with our long skirts and hair and bare feet seemed safer than the movement where people got teargassed and beat up. Instead of picking up rocks and guns, we held hands around the dinner table and drank herbal tea and raised chickens. I took refuge in a softer place."

Dorothy was not alone among her classmates in seeking a more authentic existence by going "back to the land." The Wellesley fifth-year reunion book is full of flights from future shock into cooperative vegetarian restaurants and organic farms. Armed with *Small Is Beautiful* and *The Whole Earth Catalog*, class members taught themselves about electricity and plumbing, put up preserves, raised goats, made pottery and quilts.

With two gay men and her lesbian lover, Dorothy moved to Randolph Center, Vermont. "We didn't last. We had chickens and sold eggs and always had the cigar box of pot on the kitchen table. But none of us could deal with the isolation; in Cambridge we'd had food co-ops and women's writing groups. Our whole house was on food stamps. My friend was on welfare. She had a baby while we were together, and I was her labor coach. Our neighbors were all hippies but were uncomfortable with us because we were gay. We finally gave it up. Then I ended up homeless for a while, just because I was spacey. I'd been squatting in an apartment in Cambridge and got thrown out, so I slept in the boiler room under Indian bedspreads.

"Here my classmates were networking and going to graduate school. My friend Audrey Melnick, whose values were nearly identical to mine, was working for Dukakis. And I was pretty much unemployed. I didn't want to pretend I was someone else to get a job, but when people figured out who I'd been married to, it made them uneasy. And none of us had career preparation from Wellesley—I had classmates who were working as typists all over Boston. I was a social worker in a hospital for a while for $2.50 an hour. I'd still wear real hippie clothes on the weekends, but I'd put on costumes for work to look just like everybody else. But I didn't want to get a real job and become part of the system. I became very bohemian, willfully staying outside the mainstream. We thought that by being bad at managing life we were refusing to be part of the establishment."

Dorothy's experiments in the sixties and seventies were among the wildest in the class. Her foundation was also one of the shakiest, given her estrangement from her parents and her sheltered and undeveloped nature. Her ex-husband believes she was attracted to political activism precisely because "she was unformed, uncertain of who she was, and took up politics as a way of trying on identities, some of which were more militant than I ever was." Dorothy's disillusionment, therefore, probably says more about her personal fragility than it does about the sincerity of the movement's aims or the wisdom of its tactics. Nor was she ever so thoroughly disheartened as she sometimes sounds. Thirty years later, settled in Rhode Island with a full-time job and long-term partner, she boasts in a note that she is "an activist" again, though no longer antagonistic to the system: "Just received a State Senatorial Citation for my work as a river advocate." Like many of the women of '69, she is still engaged in the search she began in those years, and even now remains uncertain as to which experiments will prove fruitful, which destructive or barren.

Dorothy's story illuminates some of the difficulties in trying to recover the real experience of the sixties. Given how polarized the debate remains over the meaning and consequence of that era, it is hard not to fall into one of two camps—either defending the activists and counterculture, or assuming the present chic attitude of ironic detachment and derision, which regards the political and social experiments of those times as frivolous theatrics. The difficulties are compounded by the way these women, like most eyewitnesses, often turn their own histories into yarns, larks, adventures—romantic or foolish but, either way, emptied of the real terror and exhilaration of the times.

Many in the class, of course, kept their distance from "the sixties." Others, as Nancy Gist says, "dallied with radicalism" but ultimately circled back to their well-adjusted destinies. But many took up tough work, against lots of odds. Cherry Watts worked for the Teachers Corps in Philadelphia, tutoring kids for whom gunfire was a part of daily life, then helped found a rape crisis center in Nashville. Nancy Eyler helped poor people avoid being evicted in New York City, then became a doctor providing care to Native Americans in Montana. Many sustained a deep commitment for years, or a lifetime. When an heiress gives away her fortune, or a girl from Oklahoma takes Buddhist vows and spends years sleeping on the Thai forest floor and begging for alms, those are not tourist trips but acts of great courage or desperation. These women were alive, they believed, at a moment of great moral danger for the United States, but also at a time when the greatest possibility existed to reinvent the world and transcend themselves. The personal was truly political: How they lived their lives each day was of historic, even cosmic, consequence. And then, from that same small group, there were women like Hillary Rodham—as integrated into the status quo as a girl could be.

The Fifth Column

Kris Olson, '69, was the kind of liberal that Dorothy's Devine's radical associates would have scorned. In the heart of the heart of the establishment, at Yale Law School with Hillary Rodham, Kris did not shun the system as a corrupt and corrupting fraternity but determined to infiltrate it and undertake its repair. Rather than take to the streets on May Day in solidarity with the Panthers and Bobby Seale, who was then in jail awaiting trial with seven codefendants on kidnapping and murder charges, Kris settled into the courtroom to monitor the proceedings for the American Civil Liberties Union. That experience became the basis for her law school thesis on politically motivated trials: Socrates, Christ, Joe Hill, the Wobblies, the Chicago Seven, Angela Davis—all were prosecuted, the future Clinton-appointed U.S. attorney argued, with faint justification but for the wish of the government of each "to rid itself of a thorn in its side."

Kris worked for Legal Aid in New Haven jails and mental hospitals and juvenile institutions, monitoring inmate conditions and developing alternative sentencing and rehabilitation programs. With Hillary Rodham, she edited the *Yale Review of Law and Social Action.* She did not, however, put to rest the question of whether she was "selling out" by getting her law degree; in late-night conversations with Hillary, she wrestled with the tension between conscience and pragmatism, between moral purity and political effectiveness. When Oregon U.S. attorney Sid Lezak came to talk to the students, Kris was among those who heckled him for being Nixon's henchman and prosecuting draft dodgers. He responded by describing the possibilities open to a prosecutor: to divert first offenders out of the system so they would not have a record and to influence policies at the Justice Department. His insistence that "you can do more on the inside" fell on fertile, if still ambivalent, ground.

Kris had grown up believing in a "responsive government" but had direct experience as well of the ill uses to which the forces of law and order could be put. She had seen Bobby Seale bound and gagged in the New Haven courtroom and had herself been put under surveillance by the FBI after going in and out of Panther headquarters several times for documents on the case. (The agents were easy to spot, she says, because they "always kept their shoes shined.") She'd heard a firsthand account of the brutal police beatings at the '68 Democratic Convention from Hillary, who'd ridden a bus downtown that summer from her suburban Chicago home. Kris herself was working in a prison in 1971 when the police stormed Attica under orders of Governor Nelson Rockefeller, killing thirty-nine people and wounding eighty more. The same year, she helped wade through the Pentagon Papers for the *Boston Globe*, learning with the rest of the nation of covert bombing missions in Laos and Cambodia and the widespread discrediting within the State Department and the military of their own geopolitical rationales for the war.

Through her boyfriend, Jeff Rogers, the son of Nixon secretary of state William Rogers, Kris also came under the sway of Jeff's mentor, Charles Reich, author of *The Greening of America*. Dedicated "to the students at Yale and their generation" and first excerpted in *The New Yorker, The Greening* was an influential synthesis of the ideas that would enduringly shape many of the bookish women of the Wellesley class of '69.

Following on Marx and Marcuse, Reich argued for the central significance of "consciousness" in social change, and mapped three kinds of consciousness in America. He rejected the essentially libertarian "Consciousness I," with its faith in self-reliance, as naive, suitable for the craftsman and small landholder in the eighteenth century but a hoax in the context of advanced industrial capitalism. He praised the liberal "Consciousness II" for recognizing that large corporations robbed ordinary people of their full humanity and autonomy, turning employees into factory parts and the public into dupes to be manipulated into consumerist excess and political docility. But Reich questioned the liberal faith in government's ability to subordinate corporations to the public interest by making laws to protect labor and the environment, redistribute wealth, ensure fair competition, and weave a safety net for the weak. The efforts by Progressives and New Dealers and Great Society–makers to use law and politics to restore equality and individual liberty, he argued, had only enlarged the reach of the Kafkaesque organizations and hastened their creation of a streamlined "new man," cured of all vitality and resistance like the lobotomized McMurphy in Ken Kesey's *One Flew Over the Cuckoo's Nest.*

The IIs had failed to touch the fundamental problem of the "loss of meaning" in America. But a new consciousness was dawning, Reich said. Flower Power marked the dawn of a new age. Hippies were the prophets of Consciousness III and would save the world: "Woodstock in time will include not only youth, but all people in America." In a society that was dead, he argued, the only ones alive were those who were "antisocial" in the conventional sense: Hippies refused to be made into "instrumental beings" in organizations, rejected rankings by wealth or merit, threw over a "legalistic view of marriage" in favor of a higher natural law that recognized that to observe "duty toward others, after the feelings are gone, is not virtue and may be a crime." Through their clothes and illegal activities, hippies became models of independent consciousness, of a self broken loose from the constraints of society. At the same time, Reich's hippie was a natural communitarian, living "as if the corporate state did not exist and some new form of community were already here," opening free schools and free clinics and the door of his pad to anyone wanting to "crash." In short, the personal was the only useful politics: "When liberal reform and radical tactics prove powerless, the hippies' new lifestyle will dismantle the corporate state." That was not, remarkably, a fringe view. Even *Time* magazine, two years earlier, had decided that in their "independence of material possession, their peacefulness and honesty, their calls for an end to profits and empire and violence," hippies are "considerably more virtuous than the great majority."

When it came to Kris and Jeff and their classmates at Yale, Reich was divided. While he singled out the college graduates of 1969 as "the harbingers" of the new age, he also insisted that his favorite fictional icon of the new consciousness, Holden Caulfield, would surely "reject the legal profession." To secure a Yale Law degree, he warned, was to buy a place in the meritocracy and probably be doomed for the big chill: "Reformers risk nothing and opt out in their stylish private lives."

Kris had made at least one gesture worthy of Consciousness III when she moved into the Cozy Beach commune her first year at law school with an architect who designed Buckminster Fuller–inspired inflatable domes, and actor Henry Winkler, then a student at Yale Drama School. (The FBI would later interview "the Fonz" while clearing Kris for confirmation as a U.S. attorney.) Cozy Beach had ties with Ken Kesey's Hog Farm in Oregon, whose members came for a visit soon after their Magic Bus had been given immortal life by Tom Wolfe in *The Electric Kool-Aid Acid Test.* The Beach also had its own little road show: Hauling their geodesic dome around to the neighborhoods of New Haven, they put on psychedelic light shows and political plays. They all wore jumpsuits with their names stenciled on the back; Kris was called Package Deal. "I was the radical with the la-di-da Wellesley manners and middle-class hang-ups and white gloves," she explains. "I could pour tea in the afternoon and put on a psychedelic light show at night. They were teasing me, but I've always believed that mixture of qualities enabled me to do more."

The move into Cozy Beach cost Kris the financial support of her Goldwater-Republican parents, who refused to fund a lifestyle they abhorred; she put herself through law school, working forty-hour weeks and taking evening and Saturday seminars. By the time she announced her engagement to Jeff, however, a tall, rangy, somewhat taciturn young man of the finest Republican stock, Kris had been welcomed back to the parental fold. The couple had fallen in love at first sight. Jeff's friend Bill Clinton was living with Kris's friend Hillary, and the four spent a lot of time together, hanging out at home listening to Janis Joplin, the Jefferson Airplane, and the Rolling Stones. Engaged a week after meeting Jeff, Kris had a wedding shower in September 1971 attended by Mrs. Spiro T. Agnew, Mrs. George Bush, Mrs. John Connally, Mrs. John Ehrlichman, Mrs. H. R. Haldeman, Mrs. John Mitchell, Mrs. Elliot Richardson, Mrs. George Romney, and Mrs. George Shultz. Jeff and Kris were married two weeks later on Shelter Island. Secretary of State Rogers, acting as best man, read passages from *The Prophet* by Kahlil Gibran; Secret Service men listened solemnly in their boats lined up along the shore. Among the four hundred wedding guests were most of the Nixon administration, Chief Justice Warren Burger, Charles Reich, and all of Kris's commune friends.

Going to the Chapel

A wedding is, of course, the happy ending of every fairy tale, the ultimate feminine fantasy come true. By the early 1970s, with feminism blooming into the American mainstream, it was a ritual begging to be remade. Those Wellesley graduates who did not simply disdain the "bourgeois convention" entirely often subverted or symbolically transformed the ceremony or at least remained half indifferent to the whole affair. By re-making the public ritual—discarding vows of obedience; rejecting the name change, with its historic echoes of a wife's legal status as her husband's property; refusing the white dress, with its symbolic representation of virginity—perhaps they would get a head start on remaking the institution of marriage itself. Hillary Rodham lived with Bill Clinton before she married, and then forgot to collect her Empire-waist cotton wedding dress, picked out by her parents in a Fayetteville department store, until the night before. Nancy Gist refused to register for silver and china, "much to my everlasting regret." Nan Decker sent out photocopied invitations (a picture of a couple on lawn chairs about to be crushed by a flaming blimp); her husband wore shower thongs, and a lesbian minister presided, and for a year after the wedding the bride continued to live in her Cambridge cooperative while the groom went off to medical school in Cincinnati: "My mother had been afraid I was going to move in with a man without getting married; instead, I was married and not living with him." Jenny Cook, who had won the hoop-rolling contest that presaged the first Wellesley bride, skied into her December 1971 wedding in a log cabin in Alaska. She received no toasters, but ended up with three fondue pots: "That was a countercultural gift," her husband says. Fran Rusan's June 1972 wedding was a ceremony traditional to the Yoruba people of Nigeria. The groom, Ernest Wilson, was an aide to Representative Charles Diggs of Michigan, chairman of the subcommittee on Africa, and the couple had spent long periods of time on that continent, including a full month in Ghana at a religious shrine. Their two hundred wedding guests, most in African dress, participated in the ritual. With their shoes in hand, women lined up behind the bride and men behind the groom, and the whole congregation moved in two columns into the ballroom, singing ceremonial songs led by priests of the Temple Bosum Dzemawodzi. All two hundred knelt before the

priest while vows were spoken. Then, led by a chorus from the temple
and a band of drummers, everyone stood and began clapping their
hands while doing an improvised tribal dance around the floor. "The
whole idea is to celebrate a feeling of community," Fran told a reporter
sent by *The New York Times,* while having her hair braided into an intri-
cate arrangement. "The significance is not just that two people are getting married but that two families are being joined, with the approval
and blessing of the community." The daughter of a St. Louis doctor,
"the bride did have a china pattern registered in a department store," the
Times noted, "and a white tiered wedding cake."

Feminism II

In the five years after the graduation of the class of '69, the second wave
of feminism reached its crest. Between 1968 and 1973, more than five
hundred new feminist publications appeared, with names like *Broom-
stick, Options for Women Over Forty,* and *off our backs.* Many were
printed at the SoHo women's press where Nancy Eyler, '69, worked, and
were sold at a cooperative feminist bookstore in Cambridge founded by
Jean MacRae, '69. In 1970, the fiftieth anniversary of the passage of the
suffrage amendment was marked with the first major demonstration in
half a century: In the "Strike for Equality," thousands of women un-
plugged telephone switchboards, put down mops, or dumped their kids
at their husbands' desks while they marched in New York, Boston,
Washington, and San Francisco demanding day care, the opening of all
jobs to both sexes, and greater involvement by fathers in parenting.
Women staged sit-ins at women's magazines and urged the boycott of
products with sexist ads. They also made inroads into politics: In 1971,
the National Women's Political Caucus and National Women's Education Fund were founded, in part due to the efforts of Jan Krigbaum and
Betsy Griffith, both Wellesley '69.

The Wellesley women fit the classic profile of the moderate feminist
activist—young, white, middle class, well educated—and in great numbers they were active in such organizations as NOW and the movement
to ratify the ERA, as well as in women's health and reproductive rights
and the education and welfare of children; only a very few involved
themselves in either "radical" feminism or its opposite. Alison Campbell

remembers experiencing "the click," as feminists called the moment that politicized a woman, when she learned from *Ms.* magazine of the aggressive marketing to Latin America by U.S. makers of infant formula: Mothers would let their milk dry up, then watch their infants waste away with dysentery from unclean water. That click propelled her into a conscientious study of natural maternity. Kathy Smith Ruckman, home with the first of her four kids, also found in feminism a guide to changing her domestic life. "Betty Friedan's discussion of how women are slaves to housekeeping freed me right up. It let me reject many of the demeaning 'housewife' chores that I didn't enjoy or think important— ironing, throwing the perfect dinner party, waiting on my husband and kids."

Class members had varying views of feminism's public style. Kathy thought their "stridency" a "disservice" to women—both self-defeating and fake. Jan Krigbaum, who with Betsy Griffith worked to increase the number of women delegates to the 1972 presidential nominating conventions (they succeeded in tripling the proportion to 40 percent), was also not entirely comfortable with the confrontational style of leaders like New York congresswoman Bella Abzug: "But I recognized then and feel even more strongly now that without their aggressiveness, none of the rest of us would have been free as quickly and as fully to adopt different styles. The barriers are real and enormous, and the front guard has to go through with enormous velocity to break them down and then the others of us coming behind have far more flexibility than the vanguard. I wince sometimes when younger women caricature Bella. I believe that the times forced her to those extremes, and then she made it possible for all of us to succeed—not just by wearing the three-piece suit that was the model for making it in the corporate sector, but by holding on to our individuality."

Seekers

For Matilda Williams, '69, graduating from Wellesley "was like being launched on a ship without a rudder." After several "self-criticism sessions" with her SDS group, she too had gone to Cuba with the Venceremos Brigade and for years afterward refused to tell her parents where she was as she careened through numerous jobs and towns and loves. "I turned my back on Wellesley and all the privilege it pretended," she wrote to her classmates, "and 'cast my lot with the poor people of the earth,' as in José Martí's song."

She came to rest finally in Thailand, where she had gone to do public health work in a refugee camp. There she met a Buddhist monk who was trying to save the rain forest by ordaining trees as monks; confronted with a sacred being, the loggers would have to bow and show respect and let the tree stand. "Within half an hour of our meeting, we felt we'd known each other for three thousand years. He was convinced that in some previous incarnation we had known each other. He said to me, 'You have to live here for seven years.' So that's what I decided to do." When she finished her work with the refugees, Matilda went to his temple, the Wat Nam Phud in the Dong Yai forest, and took the vows of a Buddhist nun. She shaved her head and donned white robes, forgoing all adornments and perfumes so as "not to call attention to myself or be imprisoned in my ego." Having vowed not to sleep on a high bed and to eat only what she was given, she went out with a begging bowl, and slept on a grass mat in the woods, on a platform raised just enough to be out of reach of the snakes and rats. "I meditated seven hours a day, wishing compassion to all living things, trying to be one with all creatures. As nuns we had few possessions—a couple of robes, underwear, soap, toothpaste, a toothbrush, and a *gloat*, which is like an umbrella with a mosquito net attached, which we slept under when traveling. I snuck a camera into mine, and had my picture taken with a fully opened lotus— an arrogant move, because it implies enlightenment. A few Thais were hostile to me as an interloper, but some were perversely proud." They could not, in any case, miss her: With her large pink nose and apple cheeks and bright blue eyes in a big, bald, moon-white head, she stood out like a bare lightbulb among the small, nut-colored nuns.

She would spend just two of her seven promised years. Matilda received word at the temple that her father was in a coma and dying, that his insurance had run out and her mother needed help. "I recognized the hypocrisy of praying for the rain forest and the benefit of all living things while ignoring my own mother's needs, so I came home to Oklahoma. I saw how much I had hurt my mother, and felt I couldn't do that anymore." Still, a sense of alienation deep enough to inspire so extraordinary a pilgrimage was not easily overcome. Giving her life over to

Buddhist practice had been an attempt by Matilda to escape from the personal—both the stifling, oblivious love of her mother and the "ego" itself. The two years in Thailand freed her enough to go home but not to be happy there. She describes her maternal caretaking as a thankless task. "Everything is still a cause for a fight, from why do I want to be an idol worshiper to why don't I like Lawrence Welk."

The "third great religious awakening," Tom Wolfe would call the early seventies. Badly soured on politics, young Americans increasingly vested their faith in those years in the promise made by Charles Reich and many others: that the transformation, or transcendence, of self was the true avenue to transforming the world. Watergate had been the single greatest wound to the civic spirit; the humiliating fall of Saigon, a rash of skyjackings and terrorist attacks, the first Arab oil embargo, and the abrupt end of the twenty-five-year postwar economic boom all added to the sense that the American age was at an end.

Many in the class of '69 now turned away from their efforts to redeem the world and toward a more intimate encounter with the sacred, or to what Wolfe would call "a new alchemy: changing one's very self." As the human potential movement launched in the early '60s by Abraham Maslow and Gregory Bateson and Alan Watts and Carl Rogers came to full flower, Hillary's classmates could be found lying on the floor of one of the sea cliff rooms at Esalen listening to dolphin sounds; studying astrology or transcendental meditation; enduring est seminars, encounter groups, and Rolfings; or living in Zen monasteries or Hindu ashrams. "Up against the wall" was replaced on the lips of many with Fritz Perls's Gestalt prayer: "I do my thing and you do your thing . . . and if by chance we should meet, that's beautiful." The '69ers were far from alone: *Jonathan Livingston Seagull* sold more copies in the early seventies than any work of fiction since *Gone with the Wind*. Hippies became Jesus freaks or Hare Krishnas or Scientologists, read Hermann Hesse or had their auras read.

Though she was invited to go, Alison Campbell had skipped Woodstock. That summer, after graduating from Wellesley, she was working in the brooch department of Tiffany's, next to Princess Hohenlohe (a member of the German nobility) at the diamond counter, and was "just too straight an arrow" to call in sick. Alison did make it to the infamous Rolling Stones concert at Altamont that December, dressed like a nymph in a gauzy Empire-waist dress and sandals and flowers in her hair, but she remembers little except the fear. "I was glad to get home. It was not nice. When the Hell's Angels killed that guy, it was like watching barracudas descend on bait."

Alison had moved to San Francisco just a few months earlier with her poet boyfriend, Michael, and had found a job at a gallery making kinetic sculpture. For a brief time, she experimented with the freedom she felt, cut loose from her family's fortune and the expectations and shelter that came with it. She earned only enough to live in a basement apartment for fifty dollars a month. Her father sent her generous checks. She sent them back.

But things were falling apart with Michael. He continued to be unhappy with Alison's "hang-ups" over fidelity and keeping the house clean. When she received a job offer at home from one of her father's patients, she abandoned her self-exile and for a time returned to the fold. For the next six years, Alison would be a kind of court artist for the Paul Mellon family, flying about in their Gulfstream jet—its walls hung with Braques and Van Goghs—to do watercolors of the family's Virginia and Washington and New York and Antigua homes. "I felt strange painting for wealthy people when I had wanted to make a difference in the world. I had marched after King's assassination and protested against the war and wanted to go into the Peace Corps; I always identified more with people who were hurting than with those who were not. But when Nixon was reelected, I was so disillusioned. I stopped paying attention to politics, stopped believing we could change the world."

A near-member of the family in those years, Alison did Mrs. Mellon's Christmas shopping every year: buying gifts for John Jr. and Caroline Kennedy or a toothbrush in gray and yellow—his racing colors—for Mr. Mellon. When she married an aspiring medical student, in a wedding as grand as her debutante ball, with eight bridesmaids, six hundred guests, and her father in tails, she wore a dress given her by Mrs. Mellon—a Givenchy gown.

It was a short-lived marriage. Supporting her husband both financially and emotionally left Alison drained and in search of rejuvenation. She earned a black belt in Tae Kwon Do. Then, one afternoon in Washington in 1976, she went to a New Age fair and met some visitors from Findhorn, a spiritual community on the Scottish North Sea coast with vaguely Celtic beliefs and remarkable gardens. A few days later, Alison was sitting reading a Findhorn garden book when an odd thing occurred. "A butterfly landed on me, several times. I'd been reading about the secret life of plants and why you should talk to them, about how angels direct all things. Oh dear, I'm worried how this will sound—you can't describe a spiritual experience. But I felt I'd had proof many times of the benign forces in the world, in the flowers and hummingbirds. As a child I had felt it was magic to be alive, that there must be a soul that made your body move. What other people tried to accomplish with drugs, I already felt I had—a heightened sense of color and shapes. I always felt there was consciousness in everything. I thought if there's a place they believe in angels and try to grow plants the way the plants want to grow, I've got to check it out."

Alison had found the religion of her upbringing uninspiring. "My parents sent us to an Episcopal church, but they never went. And life didn't match what I learned in Sunday school. I saw pious ministers who wouldn't rile their wealthy congregations, weren't agitating to change corporate behavior. I felt guilty about being confirmed when I didn't believe.

"Though I hadn't managed it yet, I still wanted to live closer to my ideals, and after four and half years, I needed a separation in my marriage. So I gave away almost everything, including the French handpainted china Mrs. Mellon had given me, and went to Findhorn. They had one place open, in the kitchen—it was slogging work, four of you feeding three hundred people—but I decided I'd do it and asked to stay. I met unbelievable people there: Swami Satchidananda, Pier Vilat Khan, who was the head of the Sufis, Dr. Frederick Leboyer [a French obstetrician who advocated gentle birth, in a darkened room and under water, so as not to traumatize the baby]. After some months, I realized I couldn't go back to my marriage. Fortunately, we had no children yet, though we had tried. I agonized over not going back. But I knew I had to pull myself back together and make my own happiness instead of propping up somebody else." A year later, Alison returned to America, having met Bruce Swain, a journalist who shared her interest in the spirit world and with whom she would soon establish a middle-class Middle American home.

The turn in the early seventies from the political to the personal has been seen by some as a kind of defeat for women. Since the beginning of time, women have sought consolation for their sorrows in the company of other women or the comforts promised in the afterlife; some radical feminists saw consciousness-raising and New Age pieties as merely sustaining those traditions, providing group-therapy sessions or a new opiate of the masses that dissipated anger rather than mobilized it to political ends. In 1969, Anaïs Nin was booed at Smith for being apolitical and self-involved.

Of course, in Wolfe's "Me Decade," everyone was "polishing one's very self . . . observing, studying and doting on it." The human potential movement had barely begun before it was swallowed up by a marketplace increasingly adept at capitalizing on what was hip. Entrepreneurs turned the counterculture into a kind of epicureanism: fern bars, free-range chickens, *The Whole Earth Catalog* selling gorgeous hand-wrought "tools for intimate personal power" and promising a cybernetic utopia. Self-anointed therapists and gurus saw the moneymaking opportunities in spiritual seekers as well and were soon trafficking in an expensive kind of navel-gazing.

The co-optation of the sixties would have particular consequences for women. Sexual liberation had been the first movement to be seized upon by the entrepreneurs. Quickly drained of its millennial politics, it became the capitalists' favorite tool, exploited to arouse appetites for all sorts of curved and aromatic and glistening things. The sex industry came aboveground and flourished; rape and other forms of sexual violence, rarely spoken of until confronted openly by feminists, became the stuff of made-for-TV movies and MTV. The emergent multimillion-dollar recovery movement would also affect mostly women; its market is 85 percent female. The self-help business perfectly reverses feminism's central insight: Rather than challenging the structural impediments (workplace inflexibility, inadequate public support for parents and children, economic dislocation) to individual success, it turns every problem into a psychological or spiritual illness, a private failure.

Even feminism, which had assimilated Veblen's insights and rejected consumerism as a means for confining women, was co-opted by Madison Avenue. Equality became a "lifestyle." "The ad industry encourages the pseudoemancipation of women," Christopher Lasch wrote in *The*

Culture of Narcissism, "flattering them with its insinuating reminder 'you've come a long way, baby' and disguising the freedom to consume as genuine autonomy."

Feminism was to a degree complicit in the shift away from social action to self-improvement and advancement. From the beginning, the women's movement had been split between those like Ti-Grace Atkinson and Kate Millett, who sought a fundamental social and economic revolution, and those like the "bourgeois" Betty Friedan, who were more interested in simply securing for women a piece of the status quo. By 1972, Joan Didion would conclude that the Friedan faction had won and that the original, radically egalitarian and collectivist idea that had animated feminism was lost. "The have-nots, it turned out, aspired mainly to having. . . . It was a long way from Simone de Beauvoir's grave and awesome recognition of woman's role as 'the Other' to the notion that the first step in changing that role was Alix Kates Shulman's marriage contract ('wife strips beds, husband remakes them'), but it was toward just such trivialization that the women's movement seemed to be heading. Of course this litany of trivia was crucial in the beginning, a key technique in politicizing women who had perhaps been conditioned to obscure their resentments even from themselves . . . but such discoveries could be of no use at all if one . . . failed to make the leap from the personal to the political."

The world of paid work would permit and require most of the women in the class to make that leap. Some would find in work a tremendous liberation from the personal: It would offer a way out of the feminine expectations that were so deeply ingrained at home and the financial dependency that had trapped many of their mothers, and a way in to useful work and citizenship. Others would find the "man's world" too alien for comfort: These would have to reconsider what it means to be a woman, and have to alter either the workplace or themselves.

All would face critics on both sides. From the feminist left would come charges of elitism and careerism and selling out. From the traditionalist right would come charges of selfishness. If a man raises a family, performs productive work for society, and engages as a citizen, that is honorable. For a woman to attempt the same would be denounced as a greedy effort to "have it all."

CHAPTER FOUR

Reinventing Womanhood

Of all the revolutions made by the members of the class of '69, none has been more radical than their wholesale entry into the professional world. Though many of the women had experimented with political activity in the sixties movements, work would set them, unlike any previous generation of women, firmly within the public sphere.

Work promised many freedoms and possibilities: independence, adventure, the chance to pursue passionate curiosities, even perhaps some influence on the world. Most of all, work afforded an escape from their mothers' small domestic chambers into the larger spaces where they might become "self-made." But entering the workplace also required of these women their first serious negotiations between the personal and political. Individually and collectively, they had to consider anew what it meant to be a woman, in harmony with or opposition to the expectations of what had long been men's worlds.

For some, work would fulfill all their hopes. Entering into worlds where women had not been before, they discovered a liberating absence of the clear expectations laid out for them at home and in relations with men. On this tabula rasa, women could experiment with new ways of being: more competent and controlled, less racked by the complexities of domestic and emotional life. For others, the world of work would prove unexpectedly hostile, alien in its values, and isolating, with neither the community of women they had known at Wellesley nor the solidarities of the sixties movements. Nearly all, having breached the border between men's and women's separate spheres, would struggle for a deeper integration of those two worlds: importing into the workplace the gentler habits associated with home, bringing home such "public" values as justice and equality.

It was 1984, fittingly, when Kris Olson Rogers began to doubt the moral possibility of remaining obedient to the government she served. Working as a federal prosecutor in Portland, Kris was ordered by Oregon U.S. attorney Charles Turner to get an indictment on a former Black Panther then living in town. The evidence against the man was flimsy but adequate for the task: Informants, disguised as housepainters, had ransacked his home and found in an upstairs closet a box containing a disassembled gun, which they had stolen and turned over to the Department of Alcohol, Tobacco and Firearms. Kris knew, as did her boss, that in five minutes she could run an ATF agent before the grand jury and indict the defendant on hearsay, no matter the merits of the charges.

It was no accident that Charles Turner, a conservative Christian and Reagan appointee, had chosen Kris for this task. From the moment of his arrival, Kris had felt Turner's disdain for her, the "liberal lady prosecutor," as she puts it, now in his charge. There was no doubt who would win their contest of wills: In an administration recently censured by its own Civil Rights Commission for having reduced by half the numbers of women in the judiciary and the White House, Kris could count few allies. Nor could she easily afford to jeopardize her job, with two small children to support and both parents seriously ill.

The story of her confrontation with Turner is one Kris has told many times. In the course of those many tellings, she has shaped it into an allegory, a parable on the question that has also plagued Hillary Rodham Clinton: how much to compromise personal principles in order to get and keep power to do things in the world.

Kris and her husband, Jeff, had gone to Oregon soon after law school, drawn by their love for the great northwestern forests and mountains and sea. They settled first in a country house all overgrown with blackberries, then moved into a big, silent house ringed by hemlock and Douglas fir at the edge of Portland. It was, in the early seventies, a common pilgrimage. Celebrated in the best-selling novel *Where the Wasteland Ends* as a secessionist "ecotopia," the shadowy woods of western Oregon offered perfect refuge for dreamy back-to-the-landers and radical environmentalists and marijuana growers in exile from California. More than a few imagined themselves founding the kind of alternative society proposed by Charles Reich and elaborated in the *Yale Review of Law and Social Action* when Kris and Hillary were contributors: One article called for "the migration of large numbers of people to a single state for the purpose of effecting the peaceful political takeover of that state through the elective process." These "alienated or 'deviant' members of society" would then test the elasticity of such traditional institutions as marriage and democracy, "providing a living laboratory for social experiment through radical federalism." The radical federalists already in residence—loggers and fishermen, most of them—did not see in the newcomers kindred spirits, and their mutual hostility made for a volatile mix. Even today, the Northwest remains a place of extremes reminiscent of those times. With Earthfirsters and the Oregon Christian Association both committed to principled violations of the law, it is a perfect place for a woman with complex notions about the proper balance between accommodation and dissent.

When she accepted a job as a federal prosecutor in Oregon, Kris told herself that it would be a brief, strategic sojourn: She would go inside as "a fifth columnist" only to become a better defense attorney by "learning the enemy's ways." As it turned out, she remained through three administrations, persuaded over time by the justification offered by her first boss and mentor, U.S. attorney Sid Lezak—that, as a prosecutor, she "could do more." While a defense attorney could react only to other people's legal initiatives, Kris could initiate her own: against white-collar and environmental crimes, for civil and tribal rights. The last would become a principal focus of her work. Having first fallen in love with Oregon on a visit with Lezak to the Warm Springs Reservation to watch ritual dances and feast on buffalo stroganoff—the same year that the American Indian Movement seized Wounded Knee and brought native rights to the foreground of left consciousness—Kris became one of the nation's experts in tribal courts and the protection of cultural traditions and religious freedom. She was also the first woman in Oregon to prosecute high-profile criminal cases: kidnappings, bank robberies, and drugs.

Kris did not get an indictment on the former Panther. Sabotaging Turner's goal, she brought the phony housepainters in as witnesses, encouraged the grand jury to fulfill its role as a "shield" for the individual from the state, and ultimately persuaded the jurors not to indict. Turner was furious. "He spluttered that I had embarrassed him with the local police chief, to whom he had made a promise that the Panther 'thorn' would be removed." He complained to Washington that Kris was insubordinate, a complaint he repeated a few months later, when she chaired a committee for an organization of local business and civic leaders on how to deal with growing street prostitution in Portland. She recommended decriminalization to limit pimping and public health dangers, and the provision of alternative programs for those who wanted to leave the life. When she then spoke out against Attorney General Ed Meese's antipornography campaign, she incurred the wrath of some feminists and, again, of Turner, who attacked her on the front page of the *Portland Oregonian* as "unfit to represent the United States" and demanded that she resign. Kris felt she had no choice but to do so, and was sure her government career was at an end.

Nine years later, in 1993, when Bill Clinton asked Kris to leave her job as professor and dean at Lewis and Clark Law School and become the first woman U.S. attorney in Oregon, her appointment roused her local enemies anew. Turner led a campaign to defeat her nomination, persuading the state's leading newspaper to reprint his letter of a decade earlier denouncing her to Washington and to editorialize against her appointment, branding her "soft on crime." At her swearing-in, Kris retaliated with a bit of political theater reminiscent of her commune days. While Turner's conservative Christian fellows were gaining legislative victories against gay rights around the state, Kris invited members of the Warm Springs tribe to say the invocation prayer and the Gay Men's Chorus to sing a song by the Grateful Dead.

As the chief federal law enforcement officer in Oregon, Kris has watched her life take several ironic turns. Having once been known in her commune for baking delicious hashish brownies to serve with English tea, she has become, in America's prime marijuana-growing region, a frontline soldier in the war on drugs. She is an outspoken critic of efforts to expand government surveillance of citizens, including the antiterrorism bill supported by Clinton, but it is frequently her signature that authorizes wiretaps and search warrants. And though a lifelong champion of civil disobedience, she has come down hard on what is at present the nation's most active antiestablishment movement, prosecuting a string of antigovernment militants. Among her targets have been the "Posse Comitatus," radical advocates of property rights who refuse to pay taxes and menace federal employees; operators of a Corvallis, Oregon, methamphetamine lab, who stockpiled diesel fuel and ammonium nitrate in quantities sufficient for a bomb like the one used to blow up the federal building in Oklahoma City; and a survivalist in the Columbia Gorge, who nearly burned down a small town when his booby-trapped arsenal of 1,400 pounds of plastic explosives blew up.

Even as she has busted marijuana growers and civil disobedients, however, Kris has also used her office to aggressively pursue what local critics deride as her "liberal agenda." In 1995, her office negotiated the plea with Shelly Shannon, the mother of two who shot an abortion clinic doctor while awaiting sentencing for firebombings at Lovejoy Surgicenter in Portland; the information they got from Shannon helped flush out the leaders of the "justifiable homicide" movement and forestall other planned attacks in the region. In disputes over grazing rights and dam construction pitting the Environmental Protection Agency and Native Americans against property rights groups and the Forest Service, Kris has frequently chosen to intervene on behalf of the EPA and the tribes, winning her the admiration of local environmental activists.

She has several times scorched local bridges. She contributed to the Packwood 26, the women bringing sexual harassment charges against former Oregon senator Bob Packwood, and denounced the "weak-kneed" Republican chairman of the National Endowment for the Arts, Oregonian John Frohnmayer. And she has raised the ire of Republican senators Orrin Hatch and Charles Grassley over her handling of pornography cases. Disturbed at what she considered a "reverse sting" by the U.S. Postal Service, which would buy mailing lists from gay magazines, peddle child pornography to their readers, produce and mail the materials, and then secure search warrants and arrest recipients when it arrived, Kris issued guidelines to her office that they would not prosecute for receipt of government-produced porn.

Kris has also offended law enforcement officers and the FBI (though she depends on both and pleaded the Fifth when I asked if she had ever called a cop a pig). In a speech to the Yale Club of Oregon, she recounted her experience in 1994 filing a Freedom of Information request to look at her own FBI file. She waited two years without a response;

when she finally asked again, the agency said it had been eager to help but couldn't find her, because she'd moved to a new address. Kris was a U.S. attorney at the time. At last she received the file, which was more than five hundred pages long and stretched back to her days at Yale, though chunks had been withheld and redacted "for national security." In her speech, she detailed the shabbiness of the investigation—the agency's reliance on rumor and ludicrous sources and its clear pursuit of the political agenda of the J. Edgar Hoover era.

After more than twenty years in Oregon, Kris looks like a westerner: Her straw-colored hair hangs long, with schoolgirl bangs; her eyes are a wide, clear blue; her square face is tawny and scrubbed. She wears flowing skirts the colors of jewels, dangling turquoise earrings, silver Indian bracelets, and thick ropes of beads. Though she spends much of her time amid good old boys with slicked-back hair and bolo ties, her manner is neither coquettish nor tough but rather patient and soothing—almost motherly. She has a soft voice and a calm, direct gaze and, like Bill Clinton, a highly developed capacity to calibrate the effect she has on people. Having not forgotten the usefulness of her little white gloves as cover in her years as a rebellious coed, Kris remains calculated in her demeanor and style. "I'm not going to be flirtatious and manipulative, but I also don't want to out-men the men, in my hobnail boots. It jolts them when the federal prosecutor shows up in ethnic clothes." A tribute to her political skills, presented by her law school colleagues, hangs on the wall of the private bathroom that adjoins her large, formal office: a "bulletproof" bra made of kitchen strainers, suggesting the protection from political enemies her earth-motherliness affords.

Though Kris was never radical, her thorough integration into "the system" has caused her, in various public settings, to recite the guilty refrain of her generation: that in her life perhaps expediency has too often won over principle, that the price she has paid for power has sometimes been too great. "When I was young, I played at radical chic, but all along I preserved my conventional options. I went to demonstrations but also to an Ivy League law school. I did drugs and experimented sexually but quit both when I married Jeff." As a prosecutor, Kris says, she has been to some degree "co-opted" by power. "I censor myself a lot, bide my time, package things in more palatable terms. My environmental work is in large part a way to appease my guilt over having to defend the Forest

Service in its destructive logging practices. And there are prosecutions that make me cringe: When we've got real down-and-out defendants, up for robbery or drugs, I know we're putting them away so that as a society we don't have to face our racial and economic problems." At such times, law enforcement ceases to seem to her "a moral calling."

Against those self-inflicted charges, Kris has in turn defended herself in public forums with the claim that she has used her power as a prosecutor to temper the rigid values of the law with a kind of womanly empathy. She has challenged, for instance, mandatory sentences as contravening a higher justice, which "requires the consideration of particular human beings and their circumstances. We shouldn't be operating from abstract theory but from local knowledge and experience."

The notion of a law less impersonal in its enforcement is one of the central tenets of feminist jurisprudence, which Kris taught at Lewis and Clark. So is her belief that the law should reach beyond defining rights to impose a duty of mutual care, like that understood to be a part of family life. In her speeches, Kris has called "cold" the provision in tort law that absolves a stranger of the duty to rescue a drowning child, lest the good samaritan incur liability. Rather than forgiving the self-protective refusal to help another, she believes the law ought to "forgive the consequences of trying to do the right thing."

Kris is uneasy calling her approach to law enforcement feminine: "I reject the dichotomy that associates the jurisprudence of rights with men and the jurisprudence of care with women." But she does, in fact, credit women—with their deeper access to the heart, their stronger ties to the hearth—with a moral advantage in the struggle to reconcile power and conscience. Like Hillary Clinton, she often turns to Native Americans for models of societies in which women are the moral guardians. "Woman elders in Indian tribes can say things others cannot say," she told the Oregon Women Lawyers in a speech in early 1994. "Among the Iroquois, the matron chose and could impeach the chief. Among the Cherokee, it was up to 'the beloved woman' to decide questions of war and peace, of punishment and pardon. Nine of the fourteen western U.S. attorneys in the Clinton administration are women; the top layer of the department is all female. Our role is to hold the feet of male law enforcement officers to the fire and bear witness to our leaders' shortcomings."

Kris has borne such witness against her White House patrons: When Janet Reno helped derail the appointment of Portland's former chief of police, Tom Potter, to head a community-based policing project because of his advocacy of gay rights, Kris gave an interview to the local paper saying the department had lost sight of its principles. She has also been openly critical of her friend Bill Clinton for dumping their old Yale Law classmate Lani Guinier and "for bowing to conventional wisdom and trying to out-tough his political opponents. It is time for the profession to stand up and condemn timid leaders pandering to a public whipped into a hysteria about crime.

"Woman in ancient society was the truth sayer, the one who strips away hypocrisy, the keeper of the collective conscience. Her presence inhibited the puffing of others' vanities. If that means saying the emperor has no clothes, so be it."

The Question of Difference

In the early seventies, when the women of '69 first began to work, most shared the aspirations then central to feminism: the end of discrimination and the securing of opportunities for women in every way equal to men's. Many pursue those aims still: Janet McDonald Hill's consulting firm helps corporations bring blacks and women into upper management, above the glass ceiling; Cynthia Gilbert-Marlow has played a key role in organizing stewardesses; Catherine Ravinski works as a judge to "defend the underdog."

But if equity remains a prime motive for most of the working women in the class, many have also moved in step with feminism toward more complex ambitions. Simply securing a place in the public arena, it turned out, was not enough: Too often in their role as pioneers, these women felt misfitted to the "man's world" they had joined, insufficiently swaggering or detached or bold. Some assimilated, becoming one of the boys. Others left. The great majority, however, became, like Kris Olson Rogers, persuaded of the possibility of bringing a "woman's way" to medicine and business and law, a way they advance as more cooperative, empathetic, flexible. From the simple pursuit of equal representation in the professions, they set out to redefine the problems addressed in Congress and research laboratories and then, further still, to question the "man-made" methods and values and languages of those cultures. Far from fulfilling the experts' predictions that the world of work would "masculinize" them, many would have their consciousness of themselves as female heightened by work. Their sex would cease to be a constraint to be transcended and become the basis on which to claim moral advantage. Here was the key to resolving their generation's central dilemma—how to take hold of the world's levers while also holding fast to their personal ideals.

At its extreme, the debate over sexual difference sets culture against nature: Those who believe that there are no essential female traits but only socially constructed differences—the product of historical circumstances and acculturation—stand opposite those who believe that real and profound differences were forged by nature or God and are the source of the sexual divisions of labor and behaviors found across cultures and throughout history. A few in the Wellesley class of '69 take the second position, that women are eternally and essentially different from men: Fundamentalist Christian Dr. Katherine Shepeluk Loutrel financially supports her children and husband but considers her stay-at-home husband the unquestioned head of the family—as the Bible commands. A few take the first stance: Janet Hill says, "I simply don't know what a female attribute is." Most, however, believe in some measure of difference, seeing aspects of their femininity as learned but speaking also of woman's distinct nature.

The women of '69 have been influenced by the work of such feminist psychologists as Dorothy Dinnerstein, Nancy Chodorow, and Carol Gilligan, who see the construction of sexual identity as a process that begins in infancy, and as crucially shaped by the primacy of maternal care. Because boys must split from their mother to establish their masculine identity, they succeed well at individuation and autonomy but fare less well at intimacy. Girls, experiencing no such abrupt separation from their mother, develop less distinct ego boundaries. While better at empathy and close relations, they remain weaker in their sense of self, more inclined to shoulder blame, to doubt their convictions, to accommodate and appease. Involving men fully in parenting infants, these developmental psychologists propose, would alter both men's and women's capacities for power and love. Gilligan has extended those arguments to claim for women a different moral calculus, less abstract and adversarial, more personal and particularist and concerned with reconciling conflicting interests to preserve relationships over time. Deborah Tannen, a favorite of Hillary Clinton's, describes a similar gender gap in communication: Men talk to affirm status and hierarchy; women, to offer support, share information, and fortify connection.

Because it deals directly with questions of equality, the law has been a particular focus of analyses based on the difference between women and men. Critical legal theorists began the process, challenging the faith that the law as written embodies timeless principles of justice and contending rather that "all law is politics," serving the powerful and disserving the powerless—including women. The courtroom, too, has been deemed biased for want of a woman's point of view. Stanford political scientist Susan Okin complains that because judges are often recruited from among partners in prestigious law firms or from academic law—both of which make their greatest demands during child-rearing years and so "discriminate against those who participate in parenting"—there is a built-in "absence of mothers" among those making judicial decisions regarding abortion, rape, divorce, and sexual harassment. Legal education is similarly challenged: Not long after Kris Olson Rogers's speech there, Yale Law School formed a committee on the status of women in response to a law review article by Lani Guinier indicting the Socratic method for sabotaging women with their "more deliberative" habits of learning and public speech.

Law school was a misery for many of the lawyers in the Wellesley class of '69. Rhea Kemble, who would become the first woman chief prosecutor of narcotics and organized crime in New York City, felt completely shut down at Harvard Law, where at the time less than 10 percent of the students were women. "Unless I had something extraordinarily meaningful to say, there was no point in saying anything. I would be rolled over by the professor or would hear snide comments from classmates. I felt alienated and eventually just disengaged. I now regret I wasn't more of a feminist. I could have resisted better had I spent more time with other women."

Worse was the sense of displacement many felt once they entered a firm. In a law journal article in 1978, Priscilla Fox, '69, wrote of the struggles she faced in her first years after graduating from Stanford University Law School. She began with a critical assessment of her own learned timidity as a woman. That she had been "socialized to avoid conflict . . . to be weak, dependent, more passive than my male peers" was a handicap in court, she wrote, noting with dismay the long exclusion of women from the bar on the grounds, as an 1875 ruling by the Wisconsin Supreme Court put it, that the "tender susceptibility, purity and delicacy" of a woman disqualified her for "forensic strife."

Having denounced such stereotypes, however, Priscilla went on to describe herself growing overwhelmed and depressed in her work on child abuse cases seemingly because of just such a "tender susceptibility." "I tended to become too emotionally involved in the cases . . . felt a looming sense of responsibility, strong sympathy for many of the so-called 'child neglecting' families, who were inevitably plagued by a constellation of problems. . . . Emotion (except in a highly stylized, controlled form), compassion and altruism are out of place in the world of courtroom lawyers. . . . The skills one needs to win are typically male ways of behaving: bluffing, strutting, subtle verbal put-downs." Priscilla concluded that she had none of that ruthlessness and too much of the "female qualities of understanding and nurturing." Those qualities might not get her very far in litigation, she wrote. "But deep down I simply do not want to lose that part of my humanity that feels terrible when someone I care about loses one of life's battles." She wondered: "What would happen if women stopped adopting male models of behavior . . . stopped playing the game by the men's rules?" Priscilla left her job and went to work for the Massachusetts Public Health Department investigating the use of pesticides, lead paint, food safety, and housing standards. She has since moved with her family to Vermont and joined a goddess group, joining with other women to celebrate pre-Christian female deities.

Priscilla's complicated relationship to her "female qualities" is not uncommon among the women in her graduating class. Having rebelled as girls against their schooling in tender selflessness, many of these women have grown increasingly ambivalent about what to discard and what to keep. They have come to see their "feelingness," whether innate or learned, as an admirable quality, better shared with men than shed. Many have groped toward some version of androgyny, though often conceived in terms that reversed the assimilationist effort to "turn women into men," as Kathy Smith Ruckman puts it. "I would like my sons to gain some qualities of women: nurturing, enjoying family, spiritual things."

One of twenty women in her class at Yale Medical School, Elizabeth Michel was criticized by her professors for not being aggressive enough. "I could see the other students developing a coldness, which was what we were taught. [Professor] Bernie Siegel talked about patients as real people with lives affected by their illness, but that was different from the way most of our teachers talked about patients, as essentially anonymous hosts to what was really interesting—their disease. Doctors would talk about patients right in front of them, a lot of the time just to show off to their colleagues. I didn't have the temperament for it at all. I was involved in the women's movement—it was my consciousness-raising group that gave me the courage to go to medical school—and as a woman living from a feeling level, I would not go along with their socialization."

Elizabeth did not, at any rate, believe assimilation a winning strategy. Articulating a classic double bind, she recalls that the aggressive qualities her professors valued in a doctor were not the same qualities they admired in a woman. "If a woman is forceful, she's called a bitch. If you're outspoken, you're unfeminine. What I did was just try my best to be invisible. I dressed in tailored, neutral clothes, did nothing to bring attention to the fact that I was a woman. For me, being seen was a setup for being humiliated."

The tender, holistic impulse was not, in Elizabeth's eyes, a "strictly male-female thing." Her husband, a fellow medical student, was as distressed by the reigning culture of medicine as she. The couple had their first child halfway through their residencies, "because we both felt emotionally barren," and did volunteer work at every possible turn. Treating survivors of a coal-mining accident in Appalachia from which many bodies were never recovered, Elizabeth, whose vanished mother had never been found, recognized the anguish of women unable to cease grieving until they knew their story's end.

In 1980, Elizabeth was hit by a car that shattered both her legs. Though one healed askew and required surgery, she delayed the procedure for months rather than neglect her medical students and patients. In this case, it was her "female socialization" that she believed ill served her. "As women, we're taught an empathy that requires we not think

about ourselves. I was harming myself to do the right thing for others."
When she finally had the operation, Elizabeth quit medicine. In chronic
physical pain, she found herself consumed with childhood memories
and the enduring mystery of her mother's disappearance—and persuaded of the therapeutic necessity to confront those memories. "The
gift of my accident," she wrote to her classmates in 1989, "was that it
forced me to face my child abuse honestly; this work has been painful
but has freed me from a prison of shame." Writing poetry and doing
yoga and studying "bioenergetics," which she describes as "psychotherapy that includes body work," Elizabeth nonetheless could not escape
the depression brought on by her belated attending to her past. Over-
coming the wariness of drugs she'd developed as witness to her mother's
unhappy fate, she joined the 10 percent of her class that has taken anti-
depressants. "Prozac helped me make good decisions for myself. I finally
faced the fact that I didn't like working in the hospital, being responsible
for people who might die. After my accident I was working with victims
of child abuse, and realized I couldn't endure that either. For the first
time in my life I felt able to say, 'I don't have to expose myself to everything horrible that's happening to people.' "

Yet again displaying the ambivalence common among her classmates,
from a critical scrutiny of her own socialization into feminine self-
sacrifice, Elizabeth slips into an almost mystical understanding of her
woman-ness. Though she describes her husband as a wonderful and devoted father, she believes that carrying and birthing and nursing a baby
give a woman an organic connection to others not possessed by a man.
"There are things my husband doesn't think about that are always in my
consciousness. When the kids were little, he wouldn't think whether
they were hungry. I would—which, I think, is a natural outgrowth of
nursing. It's a way of feeling into another person's life. In medicine that
translates to listening more. Rather than simply seeing them as an array
of symptoms, women doctors are more sensitive to how patients carry
emotions in their bodies and how illness affects the whole structure of
their lives."

The view of women doctors as more holistic, patient, humble, collaborative, and gentle seems to be widely held in the Wellesley class of '69.
Forty-three percent of these women have switched to female doctors in
the years since graduating; in their life stories, unhappy encounters with

male doctors are a recurrent theme. And the same qualities claimed by these women in law and medicine—an ecological sensitivity to relationships and systems, a willingness to share information and find common ground—are held up by many as their distinctive gifts in business and politics and diplomacy as well. Christian Scientist Cherry Watts, '69, who calls God "she" because Cherry believes divine love is unconditional and therefore "maternal," is the first woman to run her three-generation-old family business and has introduced an "egalitarian, cooperative, feminine" organization. Hillary Clinton's relationship with her aides, nearly all of whom are women, is invariably described in similar terms: anti-hierarchical, mutually supportive, informal, intimate, inclusive of all views—habits described by her former chief of staff Maggie Williams as "sex-linked traits." Adrienne Germain, '69, president of the International Women's Health Coalition, recently took part in a seminar at the Council on Foreign Relations on the "women's lens in foreign policy," proposing that from "different values and different views" would come new policy. (In the staff portrait in her organization's brochure, secretaries and top officers stand side by side, recalling the picture of the Watergate impeachment committee in which Hillary Rodham refused to stand in front with the other lawyers, calling it elitist, and instead stood in back with her friends on the support staff.) Jan Piercy, U.S. executive director at the World Bank, believes that "women on the whole have a more highly developed capacity for finding win-win solutions, reconciling diverging interests rather than trouncing the opposition. You see it in the different language men and women use when talking about comparative positions in international negotiations." Betty Demy, who raised $400,000 from Democratic women in New Jersey for Bill Clinton's first presidential campaign, also believes women seek consensus over "win-lose" situations. "Otherwise, you just erode relationships. It's what we learn by being so focused on our families, where you love one another and have to live with one another over time."

A whole literature has emerged defending this "woman's way" as better suited to the requirements of a global economy and the information age. Books with titles like *America's Competitive Secret: Utilizing Women As a Management Strategy* argue that women's team-building and ability to assimilate information coming from many directions at once give them an advantage over territorial and single-minded men in the new decentralized, high-tech economy. Women-owned businesses, which now employ far more people than all of the Fortune 500 combined, are held up as models of flexibility and "nurturing" management styles. Though he does not make the gender link explicit, Daniel Goleman argues in *Emotional Intelligence* that success is no longer best predicted by a person's IQ or credentials but by his or her capacity for empathy, cooperation, and consensus building—those same "feminine" skills. At Harvard Medical School, the "New Pathway" curriculum puts a premium on "communication, collaboration, and collegiality," giving "women applicants the edge," according to a dean for admissions.

The commercial opportunities to tap this blooming fascination with the difference between the sexes have not been missed. The longest-running best-seller in the 1990s has been John Gray's *Men Are from Mars, Women Are from Venus*. In packaging the 1996 Olympics, NBC sought to win female audiences by appealing to women's "natural empathy" with intimate probings into athletes' lives. Uncompetitive by nature, women don't care who wins or loses, sports research director Nicholas Schiavone told *New Yorker* writer David Remnick, but want their heartstrings tugged.

For all the cashing in, however, the often self-contradictory understandings of sexual difference expressed by the women of '69 mark them as creatures of equally confused times. Though Ruth Bader Ginsburg once argued landmark cases against unequal treatment based on sex, in writing the Supreme Court's majority opinion forcing the Virginia Military Institute to admit women, she felt it necessary to acknowledge the " 'inherent differences' between men and women," which "we have come to appreciate remain cause for celebration." Wellesley tied itself in knots deciding whether to join twenty-six other women's colleges in filing an amicus brief: VMI's defense of its "uniquely male" and "adversative" teaching style and its creation of a separate women's institute using "cooperative methods which reinforce self-esteem" seemed close correlates to the belief in a "woman's way of knowing" propounded by a number of Wellesley faculty. Even Justice Antonin Scalia's dissenting argument that VMI's exclusionary traditions reflected Virginians' "shared understandings" seemed almost feminist, echoing Kris Olson Rogers's defense of context and "local knowledge."

It is not surprising that the women of '69 would simultaneously embrace and reject the idea of a distinctly female nature. Even as they lament that "though they are feminists they never intended for women to act like men," they seem to hear themselves echoing all those postwar experts who warned that a woman who was too logical or ambitious would become "unsexed." The veneration of women's different voice, many suspect, is double-edged, restoring honor to such devalued "feminine" qualities as compassion, but also opening the door to the renewed confinement of women in the gentler virtues.

Most treacherous in women's claim to greater tenderness and rectitude is its essential nostalgia: for an ideology Victorian in origin and carrying deep implications for social and family life. The idea of woman as antidote to the selfishness of man has its roots in the era of political and industrial revolution: The end of feudal dependencies and the splitting of work from home combined to dissolve much of the connective tissue of community life. To preserve social cohesion against the centrifugal forces of liberal capitalism—forces compounded in America by frontier individualism and a particularly fevered commercialism—the Victorians arrived at the ideology of separate spheres, which gave to men the public, material world and to women the private and spiritual. Men could be perfect economic actors, pursuing pure self-interest, only if women preserved interdependence by sustaining their last refuge—the family. Feminist historians have argued that from this sexual division of labor came our modern conception of what is masculine and what is feminine. Men were assigned the traits deemed suitable for their public sphere: reason, will, appetite, a capacity for coldheartedness; women were given feeling, pliancy, self-denial.

First-wave liberal feminism, rooted in eighteenth-century rationalism, protested the persistence of an arrangement still essentially feudal, with responsibilities and privileges distributed in accordance with "innate" differences and "natural" hierarchies. But their efforts to rout the ideology failed. A century later, conservative scholar Alan Bloom would still pine for the days "before feminism freed women from their duty to protect men from their own natures." Pope John Paul II would invoke women's "special capacity to care" as justification for "their special role in the family, where the feminine genius can have a humanizing influence against the demands of efficiency and productivity." Robert Bly would long for the days when gentle women yielded the iron qualities to men. When the women of '69 cast themselves as curative to the dog-eat-dog habits of a man's world—when Hillary Clinton calls women society's "glue"—these are the forces they join.

The determination of this generation to breach the wall between women's domestic domain and the world of men was born of the recognition that the persistence of the separate-spheres ideology has important social consequences. It explains why children and families are defined as "women's issues" and relegated to the political margins; why a "traditional family" is defined as one where fathers go off to work and mothers (at least non-poor mothers) stay home, even though such a family has rarely existed in American history; and why studies of the (detrimental) effects of child care define it not only as day care or baby-sitters but also as care by the children's fathers.

The lingering ideology has consequences in the workplace as well. Because the domestic sphere remains the primary responsibility even of working women, children trail their mothers into the workplace in ways they rarely trail their fathers, creating child-care traumas and mommy tracks and guilt. Even in choosing their occupation, these women seem attentive to their domestic role: That so many in Hillary Clinton's class work in health care, child welfare, and education may reflect their inherent inclination to nurture, or it may be a way for them to legitimate their entry into the wider world. Becoming "social housekeepers" is another Wellesley tradition: The college's progressive founders were in the vanguard of women's movements to soften or clean up the evils of industrialization and urbanization by founding maternal associations, temperance groups, and campaigns against child labor.

Finally, the persistence of the ideology affects the telling of these women's lives. Jill Ker Conway has written of biography's evolution from eighteenth-century accounts of the political and military triumphs of great men to, after Rousseau and the ascendance of the Romantic idea of the inner genius, more personal records of self-creation. For women, the evolution has been reversed. Because she was expected to merge her identity into a man's and find all meaning in relationships, a woman's memoirs were invariably about her private (though rarely her intellectual) life; if she had a public life, it was interesting principally for how it disturbed her role as mother and wife. That convention endures. The

Frontline documentary on the class of '69 all but ignored the substance of its subjects' work and focused only on how it conflicted with their personal lives. Once again, the question was whether they could "have it all," a question almost never asked of a man.

Remapping Female Destinies

In addressing the question of what measure of sexual difference derives from nature and what from culture, two women in the class of '69 have rare expertise; both have participated, as few women of previous generations could have, in remaking the scientific and anthropological doctrines that help map female destinies. Ellen Reeder is a classical archaeologist who has taught at Johns Hopkins University and is at present curator of ancient art at Baltimore's Walters Art Gallery. In 1995, she curated the most comprehensive exhibit ever to explore the depiction of women in fifth-century Greece, the source culture of Western civilization. Martha McClintock is chair of the committee on biopsychology at the University of Chicago and teaches courses on the biological foundations of gender and gender differences. A former student of Harvard entomologist and sociobiologist E. O. Wilson, McClintock has more than once completely upended long-held certainties regarding female biology and behavior with her studies of sex and reproduction in rats and humans.

The currently dominant biological account of woman's nature was well summarized in Robert Wright's 1994 best-seller on evolutionary psychology, *The Moral Animal.* The underlying principle of evolutionary psychology is this: that the same Darwinian mechanisms of natural and sexual selection that shaped our physiology over the course of 2 million years of evolution also shaped our minds. Adaptive yearnings and behaviors—those that maximize the survival of genes by enhancing the survival and reproductive success of their host individual and its offspring—endure, while maladaptive urges are gradually diluted out of the species. Biologist Richard Dawkins has put it most bluntly, calling human beings "robot vehicles that are blindly programmed to preserve the selfish molecules known as genes."

Wright reiterates several standard descriptions of female nature. The theory of the "coy female," first proposed by Darwin, holds that in most species the female is less sexually eager than the male because she can reproduce only a limited number of times and at high cost. She must therefore be far more selective about her mates, securing not only good genes, but also a long-term commitment of his resources to the survival of her young. A male, conversely, improves his chances of passing on his genes by having sex with as many partners as possible, even if he invests heavily in the survival of only some of his progeny. Wright chides feminists who have supported divorce for failing to see that it licenses men to act on their promiscuous carnal desires and robs women of the long-term claim on paternal resources that is allegedly their chief desire. He cites anthropological research as proof of the asymmetry of desire. "Can anyone find a single culture," he asks, "in which women with unrestrained sexual appetites aren't viewed as more aberrant than comparably libidinous men?"

The second argument Wright recycles is that competition and dominance are far less important for a female, because status does not determine her capacity to get sex as it does for a male, who if powerful gets lots of mates but if weak risks being shut out of the reproductive game. Females may be underrepresented in high-paying jobs not as a result of discrimination, he concludes, but because they lack the genetic predisposition to seek power.

Two kinds of evidence are summoned to support such hypotheses. Studies of animal behavior, especially primates, are used to illuminate human evolutionary antecedents; studies of human culture seek universal attributes across cultural and historic lines, focusing particularly on hunter-gatherer societies, the dominant form of social organization throughout most of the period in which human beings evolved. The evidence, that is, comes from both the archaeological record (and modern anthropology in relic hunter-gatherer societies) and from biology.

The myth of Pandora's box gave Ellen Reeder the central insight for her exhibition on women in antiquity. Though the Greek Pandora was the mother of the human race, she was not, like the Judeo-Christian Eve, a gift to cure man's loneliness but rather a punishment for Prometheus's theft of fire. Before Pandora, men dined with the gods and suffered neither sickness nor sorrow; without women, they were not born and did not die. Only when the defiant and devious Pandora opened her "box"—the jar that is also her body, her womb, her genitals—were all the miseries released into the world.

With her collaborators on the exhibition (including her former professor, Wellesley classicist Mary Lefkowitz), Reeder reconsidered the central Greek stories of divine and mortal women as told visually in classical vase paintings and sculpture. What Reeder found was an ancient conception of female nature as far from the "coy female" as one could imagine. Woman was, in the judgment of the Greeks, insatiable and indiscriminate in her carnal appetites. More animal than human, ruled by instinct and not reason, she was a danger to civilization, a "hungry mouth" devouring man's strength and menacing the social order. Like Pandora, she was adept at concealing secrets, a weaver of disguises and entrapping webs. She was the Medusa, with her snaky locks like pubic hair and her paralyzing gaze; Circe on her all-female island making a consort of Odysseus and impotent pigs of his men; Omphale, buying Heracles for her sex slave; Phaedra lusting for her stepson; Helen and Clytemnestra, whose adultery brought the heroic age to an end. Man is not sexual predator, in this conception, but prey. Tiresias the seer, who spent part of his youth as a girl, testified that a woman derives nine times as much pleasure from sex as a man. She may mask her lust with love, but only men grow truly lovesick and need to be cured.

The artifacts Reeder assembled were designed to alert the men of Athens to the dangers of an ungoverned woman, but also to demonstrate that her sexuality could be brought under male control. In the end, in these illustrated morality plays, the Greek heroes slay the she-monsters, break the spells, exact revenge for women's sins. The defeat by a male hero (Heracles, Theseus, Achilles) of the Amazons—those fierce female archers who refuse to marry, have sex when it suits them, slay their enemies, and rear their children without men—is a favorite tale, ending as it does with the proper restoration of male domain.

The marriage rite was, for the Greeks, the most important symbolic enactment of the taming by man of the female will. Performed at the onset of puberty, when a girl awakened sexually, the ceremony culminated in the groom's grasping the bride's wrist in a gesture of abduction while she, trained by older women to show submission, disarmed her most potent weapon by dropping her gaze. Through the transformative power of art, the female predator is thus made prey. Her reproductive powers were also ritually usurped: After each birth, the child's father decided whether the infant would be reared or abandoned in the woods to die, overriding the power of her womb with his legal authority.

Over the course of the century traced by Reeder's show, the advance of Greek culture brings a refinement of this triumph by civilization over the natural sexual order. Archaic period vase paintings of Odysseus's encounter with Circe focus on her power to seduce him, while later classical vases capture the moment he makes her submit to his will. The myth of Pygmalion marks man's ultimate triumph through culture over female nature: The sculptor who despises real women carves of ivory a perfect female, entirely subject to his control.

Whether or not Reeder's work provides a convincing rebuke to Darwinian theories of coy females, it does suggest that claims to document universal qualities of female nature by resort to history and anthropology require more subtlety of interpretation than the evolutionists sometimes bring. A vase painting of a husband abducting a wife is not, as Reeder shows, a historical account of "natural" fifth-century B.C. sexual behavior—proof of the coy female who must be forcibly taken—but an example of the central function of art and ritual: to assert man's will *against* the state of nature, to school the minds of the public to accept civilization and its discontents. Wright misses that distinction when he claims that the view across cultures of libidinous women as aberrant is proof that a powerful female libido *is* abnormal. Surely it is equally possible, as Freud suggested, that a culture's definition of female lasciviousness as aberrant, its need to impose a taboo, suggests not the absence of a natural impulse but the reverse, an impulse so powerful and dangerous as to demand social control.

Reeder's work illuminates other careless uses of the archaeological record. The dependence of females on male resources in hunter-gatherer society is assumed in most "nature" arguments about her sexual selectivity, but such dependence was not always the case. Massive climactic and technological changes during the last 2 million years more than once radically altered the human economy and women's place in it. Bronze Age women, Reeder points out, produced most textiles and therefore controlled an important segment of economic life. And though during ice ages women and children did depend heavily on what men could hunt, much recent archaeology suggests that for most of prehistory, female gatherers were the primary "breadwinners." The evidence that women had a crucial provider's role was long overlooked, says Reeder, because of academics' bias: She recalls digs on which senior archaeologists simply tossed aside Neolithic female figurines as uninteresting. Women's place in Greek society was similarly obscured, she says, because of a scholarly preoccupation with politics and war, both activities reserved for men. The record of sexual behavior has been particularly distorted by archaeological bias; until recently, "obscene" artifacts were frequently destroyed.

Of course, selective interpretations of cultural history are not the exclusive province of biased males. Mary Lefkowitz has written an entire book aimed at undoing reductionist accounts by feminists of antiquity, including efforts by acolytes of the goddess movement to make cartoon heroines of the complex women of Greek myth and tragedy. Her scoldings earned her the distinction of being cast in one of Wellesley alumna Carolyn Heilbrun's Amanda Cross mysteries as that "damn classics prig" who disparages the Amazons and Antigone.

Martha McClintock was just twenty years old when, perched at the edge of a room full of the world's top biologists, she broke into their conversation with an observation that would become the basis for a study of major scientific importance. It was the summer after her junior year at Wellesley, and Martha was invited, with a handful of other students, to attend a conference at Jackson Laboratory in Maine. The scientists were discussing pheromones—chemical messages that pass between organisms without their conscious knowledge—and how they cause female mice to ovulate all at the same time. McClintock recalled the event for *Chicago* magazine: "Driven by curiosity despite my self-consciousness, I mention that the same thing happens in humans. Didn't they know that? All of them being male, they didn't. In fact, I got the impression that they thought it was ridiculous. But they had the courtesy to frame their skepticism as a scientific question: 'What is your proof?' I said it was what happened in my dormitory. And they said unless you address it scientifically, that evidence is worthless."

Her Wellesley faculty adviser, Patricia Sampson, encouraged Martha to take up the challenge, and the 135 women in her dorm agreed to participate. Each woman recorded the dates of her menstruation and also how often she spent time with men. The data confirmed that the cycles of roommates and friends became synchronous, and that women who had little contact with men ("You could only do this study at Wellesley,"

Martha jokes) had longer cycles, suggesting that ovulation was not taking place and was perhaps influenced, as in mice, by casual contact with males. She wrote up her results as her senior thesis and the next year, in graduate school at Harvard, was urged by E. O. Wilson, the sociobiologist famous for his studies of chemical signaling among ants, to submit her findings to *Nature* magazine. Published in 1971, when Martha was twenty-three, the paper was the first scientific evidence ever presented of the functioning of human pheromones.

Though she now works in a $12 million laboratory built by the University of Chicago to house her research, Martha McClintock has for three decades continued to pursue the question first posed in the Wellesley study: How do social interactions and environment affect female reproductive physiology? And, more broadly, how does the mind work on the body? Her top-down, outside-in approach inverts the usual link explored by scientists between biology and behavior, and complicates the notion of biology as destiny. "A common bias among biologists is to approach reproduction from the bottom up. Someone interested in the timing of ovulation begins with the hypothalamus, then individual neurons in the hypothalamus, then proteins that regulate one calcium channel in each neuron," McClintock explains. But as demonstrated in the Wellesley study, a woman's social behavior also affects the neuroendocrine mechanisms that regulate the timing of ovulation. Though "the molecular level of analysis is important, so are higher levels."

The notion of mind over body is a favorite of the New Age but one rarely studied with the scientific rigor that McClintock brings. In 1995 she was invited to join the MacArthur Foundation's Mind-Body Network, which sponsors collaborative studies among specialists in psychophysiology, endocrinology, and immunology of how states of mind affect health. With psychiatrist David Spiegel of Stanford University, McClintock has built on her lifelong interest in the protective function of strong social relationships by studying the effects of group therapy on women with metastatic breast cancer. The studies have shown that terminal patients who clearly voiced their needs and discussed their fears of death lived twice as long after the study began as those who did not, results comparable to those patients who take tamoxifen, a drug made to slow tumor growth. "It wasn't Norman Cousins, 'Will away your cancer, envision yourself cured,' " says Martha. "If it suggested anything, it was that denial is toxic."

From the outset, McClintock's interest in the effects of environment on biology has required her to invent unconventional experimental strategies. At the University of Pennsylvania, where she did her Ph.D. (and was also a resident in psychiatry), she decided not to study the specially bred rats used by every lab in the world, hypothesizing that their behaviors did not mimic that of rats in the wild. She asked a "kindly Mr. Herbert," who supervised the Philadelphia public health patrol, if he could live-trap twelve rats for her from the sewer. He delivered them dead, not believing that anyone could want his vermin alive.

Mr. Herbert was finally persuaded to deliver live rats to McClintock, which presented a second problem: how to house the creatures, which can bite through quarter-inch steel, in something resembling their natural habitat. The daughter of an engineer, McClintock contrived for her rats a home built of sticks, rocks, and wire mesh, with trails and places to nest and hide, all monitored by cameras so that even while the rats scurried through heaps of litter and nooks and tubes, they could be constantly surveilled. Tagging the rats posed another problem, since the marker used on the typically albino domestic strains of rats was invisible in the wild ones' gloomy fur. McClintock tried bleaching fur patches with Clairol Nice 'n Easy, but nothing happened. "In such a case, scientists consult an expert," she told *Chicago.* "So I called Bonwit Teller's hair salon. I said, 'I'm working with animals, how do you bleach their'— I didn't want to say it was rats, so I used the word *pelts."* They transferred her to their colorist, Mr. Andre, who advised shampoo, followed by peroxide and then dye. "He said, 'Why don't you bring the animals in, so I could help?' I had fun thinking of taking sewer rats to the salon, but said, 'Thank you. I couldn't possibly.' "

Keen to observe rat sex as practiced in nature, McClintock again created a little piece of home for her subjects at the University of Chicago, where she joined the behavioral sciences faculty in 1976. Until then, scientists had studied rat sex by putting a single male and female together in a small cage, unconsciously reflecting human norms. The male rat's behavior—pursuing and copulating repeatedly with the female—became the basis for numerous conclusions about sexual initiative and relative appetite in females and males.

But this behavior, McClintock found, was almost entirely a construct of the artificial environment. By examining hundreds of hours of videotape, often a frame at a time, she found that a female rat was not at all passive or coy. In fact, it was she who initiated sex by entering a male's personal space. Scientists observing rats in small cages had never witnessed this behavior, because the female was already within that space. The male's response was misunderstood as initiative.

Still more intriguing was her discovery that sex was not a private matter between two consenting rat adults but a kind of orgy, with females working as a group to maximize each of their chances at conception, enticing the males and then passing them around. McClintock discovered yet another instance of female reproductive choice in the rats' postcoital behavior. If she has succeeded in being inseminated by a dominant male, a rat rests so the sperm can get to the uterus. If she has ended up with "a loser," she immediately seeks a new mate and interrupts the sperm transfer. The male attempts to influence her decision by urinating pheromones communicating his status and by crying at a pitch that turns out to be just at the threshold of hearing for a woman in her twenties. (When McClintock first reported the cry to her senior colleagues, all of them men for whom the pitch was inaudible, they thought she was nuts.)

Her discovery that females were initiating and controlling sex brought great notoriety to McClintock's study. Because it made much previous work obsolete, it took years to get published and then, to her dismay, was dubbed the "rat feminist" paper. To McClintock, female initiative was only the second most interesting finding; the first was the role the group played in female reproductive success. Observing that her rats, like her Wellesley classmates, synchronized their estrus with pheromone cues, she set out to find out why. The first advantage she observed was that females who ovulated together could not only cooperate sexually but could also give birth together and nurse their litters communally, freeing each mother to spend more time foraging. The more critical advantage was the prolongation of the female's reproductive life span. Rats in isolation, she discovered, entered menopause 30 percent sooner. They also got sick and died sooner, of breast cancer and even of infectious diseases, despite their isolation from contagions.

Interested in the implications for humans of her rat studies, McClintock devised a study to see whether women also behaved in ways to enhance the success of reproduction. She radio-collared couples, beeping them randomly over the course of the woman's menstrual cycle to find out what they were doing and feeling. Sure enough, in the days prior to ovulation, when sex was most likely to lead to pregnancy, female initiation of sex increased sharply.

McClintock also set about isolating what she calls "eaudor," or "eau d'ovulating rat"—the pheromone that synchronizes estrus by delaying or accelerating ovulation. If she could distill the chemical signals, she would have compounds that affect ovulation directly and could be used to treat infertility or for contraception. In 1998, she published the results of a similar experiment with human females in *Nature*. She found that by exposing a group of women to a whiff of the pre-ovulatory or ovulation-phase sweat of other women, she was able to shorten or prolong their menstrual cycles by as much as fourteen days. She has also looked at humans to see if they enjoy the same protective effects of the group on reproductive success. Though human menstrual synchrony might, as in rats, have emerged through evolution to facilitate communal child rearing in lean times, McClintock has come to believe that synchrony is in fact a side effect of a mechanism that extends the length of reproductive life as much as 50 percent.

Well aware that her work on female sexual behavior and the biology of "difference" enmeshes her in several contentious debates of the day, McClintock has written many times on the ideologically motivated misuses of "science," particularly on the new biodeterminism. Her own consistent attention to the "openness" of biological systems makes clear the fallacy in claims to genetic predestination of intelligence and other complex traits. Genes are not "master molecules"—untouchable totalitarian rulers sending out orders that shape an organism's immutable fate. Rather, genes are themselves malleable participants in a complex, interactive system of hormones, environment, and mind.

In fact, women and men are almost identical in their genes: Just 2 percent of their total genetic material differs. What generates most difference are the hormones that regulate those genes, but even with those endocrine effects, innate sex differences remain small. "As a rule of thumb," says McClintock, "only about 15 percent of variance comes from gender and 85 percent comes from individual differences within gender." The nature argument is complicated further by the particular difficulties in assessing which sex traits are inherited and which learned, "because males and females immediately enter different environments the moment someone answers the question 'Is it a boy or a girl?'"

McClintock began her efforts to clarify what it means to speak of gender traits as "genetic" or "innate" two decades ago in a piece on sex differences in parenting published in *Signs: Journal of Women and Culture*, a University of Chicago publication that has been a principal forum for feminists writing about science. McClintock challenged the evolutionists' argument that females are "naturally" more invested in their young. She disputed, first, the claim that there are universal maternal behaviors: "Of the various interdependent mating and parenting strategies . . . which is taken by the male and which by the female varies widely among species and across cultures." She also challenged the premise of a dramatic sexual division of labor among humans in prehistoric societies, citing evidence that maternal and paternal roles were far more alike in agricultural and hunter-gatherer cultures than in modern industrial society, adding that "it may be that a return to less sexual difference in parenting would be more successful in the context of new selection pressures created by the changing social structure." Far from violating the natural order, she wrote, a move toward more equally shared parenting would continue "the evolutionary process which selects behaviors in the context of many social and physiological systems."

Married since 1982 to Dr. Joel Charrow, head of clinical genetics at Chicago's Children's Memorial Hospital, Martha has two children—a son, Ben, born in 1986, and a daughter, Julie, adopted seven years later. She chose to stay home with each for the first six months, and says she would have "fought her husband" if he'd pressed for that role. In explaining her more powerful desire to care for her infants, she dismisses the classic account of "maternal attachment" rooted in pregnancy and nursing. "I know from my own experience that lots of what people attribute to pregnancy really comes just from being wildly in love with your child." Her explanation is that it is both nature and nurture. "I think there is a strong inborn component. And it's the way I was raised."

McClintock does believe "that females are hardwired to pay attention to relationships." She describes watching her daughter playing with her older brother's action figures. "She puts them in the bucket of his front loader and rocks them like a cradle. They're his figures and his front loader and he never did that. She does it because she has two X chromosomes and ovaries and hormones, and also because from the moment she was born, culture came crashing in. Her genes are interacting with a high level of hormones in a very particular environment of caretaking; it's extremely interactive."

But what begins to seem like an argument for "natural" motherhood quickly takes one of McClintock's characteristic turns. To say that a female is hardwired to attend to relationships does not mean that she is better fitted to parenthood. "You might argue that being exquisitely sensitive has negative effects, causing you to be overprotective. Maybe the less attentive parent promotes adventurousness by letting the kid do something he or she is scared to do, because the parent simply doesn't perceive the kid's fear."

In other words, one should mistrust reductionist stories, particularly those that turn out to justify the status quo. McClintock scoffs at stories like Robert Wright's about the greater innate drive in males for dominance and how it might explain their persistence at the corporate top. "These stories are so glib, and so biased; they're always told from the point of view of the alpha male. Look, imagine you're studying baboons and you drive out in your Land Rover. This is what you see: a dominant male, hugely bigger than the females in his harem. There might be a few subpuberty males hanging around, but the other adult males are pushed to the edge and don't approach. When any female is in heat, the dominant male does all the mating. You think, Okay, there's no cultural bias in this description: it's a clear male hierarchy."

But that is not the story told, McClintock says, by the work of her colleague Jeanne Altmann, chair of the committee on evolutionary biology at Chicago. For several years running, Altmann has returned to the same group of baboons. "And what do you know? She found the same group of females, but each year she found a different dominant male. She also saw that some females get access to water first, that some get their babies snatched and others don't. It turns out that whether a female has power is of vital biological importance, affecting the mortality rate of her offspring and therefore the survival of her genes. So, do you take your yearly snapshot and describe a male hierarchy, or do you say, Here's a matrilineal coalition where the key hierarchy is among the females. Do you use the word *harem*, which conjures up *Arabian Nights* and sex solely for male pleasure and all kinds of cultural meshegos, or call it a *female coalition* with a clear, linear dominance hierarchy and transient studs? Then the question becomes, Why would females form coalitions? and suddenly you're spinning a very different story." Wright's description of a male who comes and goes as he pleases is inverted: Now the females have agency, using the male as long as they need him and then sending him on his way. Armed with such primate evidence, an evolutionary psychologist might argue that for females with adequate resources, single motherhood has proven a successful strategy—that it is a behavior "in our genes."

McClintock herself would be cautious in proposing such extrapolations, having seen her own science too often turned to foolish ends. Thirty years after proving the function of pheromones in humans, she is blackly amused by an ad for Jovan perfume, which claims to combine the pheromone androstenol with beautiful floral notes to send "attractant signals so powerful that there can be only one response." Androstenol, she points out, is a compound produced by the male pig that causes the female to stand motionless so he can mate with her. Cans of it are sold through veterinary catalogues, with instructions to spray it directly into the nostrils of the sow. "To extrapolate wildly from insects to pigs to humans this way runs counter to everything good and powerful in science."

McClintock was equally dismayed when her rat sex study was branded a feminist paper, because, she says, "to say I did feminist science suggests that I had a political agenda ahead of time to demonstrate that female rats could be independent and assertive, just like males, and then designed studies to prove that hypothesis. That would be bad science. The fact is, my studies could be repeated by the most misogynist, chauvinist scientist, and he would be forced to come to the same conclusion." She does believe, however, that her work can and should serve political ends, that she is actively rewriting the biological doctrine that has been so powerful a force in defining women's nature and lives. "I am a feminist and I do science and I think my good science can certainly be used for feminist purposes. I think it's fun to subvert the dominant paradigm."

McClintock's history is proof of one of the central tenets of the feminist analysis of science: that a woman scientist's experiences will often lead her to ask different questions or to see phenomena previously overlooked or to interpret data differently. She would not have discovered the role of pheromones in humans if not for her own experience menstruating in synchrony with the other women in her Wellesley dorm. Her lab is often disproportionately populated by women students, and she has supervised their studies of such "female subjects" as girls' inhibition in competition; the perception of domestic violence by perpetrators and victims; self-esteem in mothers; and the psychology of daughters caring for elderly parents.

Martha attended Wellesley at her mother's urging. "She said, 'Whether you marry or not, you'll depend on women and should go somewhere you'll learn how to do that.' She said that with a good education I'd have something interesting to think about while folding diapers, which has also proven true. I had no plans when I arrived there, beyond maybe being a first-grade teacher. I was fourth-generation Wellesley, and thought the women who'd gone before me were what I'd grow up to be—a well-educated mother and community volunteer. My grandmother got engaged at Wellesley and knew she would move to western Massachusetts, where my grandfather farmed. She took astronomy because she figured in the country she'd see the stars and could teach her children their names."

After Wellesley, Martha found the "no-woman's-land" of Harvard's graduate program in sociobiology disconcerting. "Title Nine hadn't happened yet. I wasn't allowed to eat in the faculty club with my chairman or to use the stacks in some libraries or the squash courts. I was explicitly told by faculty that they admitted me only because the field needed people to do parametric studies, which are essentially the housework of the discipline, and that women kept nice neat lab notebooks. There were no women faculty, which was demoralizing."

At Penn, there were no women either, "but by that time, I didn't expect them. It's hard to describe how schizophrenic you had to be. Some conflicts you didn't even try to resolve, like preparing to be a faculty member even though there were no women faculty." The University of Chicago, where she got tenure, was happier. "Chicago had a long tradition of equal regard for women. It was one of the first research universities to go coed, a hundred years ago. When I got there, Hannah Gray was president and a third of the faculty were women. Though even now in many departments there are no women. And if you look at tenure decisions across the university, you see that in cases that are at all ambiguous, they turn down the women and accept the men—which means that to get the same treatment, women have to be better than men."

In the profile of McClintock that ran in *Chicago*, biopsychologist Esther Thelen described the best strategy for women in science: "Do as

Martha does. Just shut up and do the work." In fact, says Martha, "my strategy is to do the work and keep talking. You can't spend the energy necessary to be a creative scientist and fight those political battles all the time. And I would rather do the science that makes the point than spend my time working on sexual-harassment policy. But I'm delighted there are women faculty doing the latter, and I completely support them. It's absolutely appropriate to pick fights on behalf of women. But it takes a lot of energy, and you can only do it if you have a lot of emotional and intellectual support."

That support, Martha has always had. Refusing the formula that sets a woman's public, professional life against her private life, Martha not only studies the protective effects of strong social relationships, she has also always depended on such relations. "Everything important I've ever done was with the support of a man in my life. There is a myth that someone like me has gotten where I have by being ruthlessly single-minded and cut off from social contact. But I was never off by myself, some brave woman in glorious solitude. I've always had a close, committed relationship and lots of affirmation from men that what I was doing was interesting and was a big part of what they liked about me. Of course, I got the reverse. Are you kidding? Most of the time. But every one of my major professional decisions has been made in the context of a relationship; that's always been right up there as a determining factor in what I did. I don't think I'd have had the courage to do it otherwise. It would be asking a lot to have the personal strength to pursue a professional or intellectual passion without that emotional support. I couldn't have done it, nor should anyone expect themselves to."

Breaking discriminatory barriers, finding a way to integrate professional and family life: Even as the graduates of Wellesley '69 set about reframing ideas about women and work, they had to negotiate a world built on the old ideas about where women belong.

CHAPTER FIVE

Breaking the Barriers

W hen the women of Wellesley began their working lives, most had fairly uncomplicated aims: equality, self-determination, and, of course, money—necessary for all the rest. Virginia Woolf counted an income "infinitely more important" for a woman than the vote, because "intellectual freedom depends on material things." While there has always been a strong antimaterialist strain in feminism, protesting women's role as a symbol of wealth for men and advertisers' exploitation of their boredom and self-loathing, it was something else again for these women to go to work to win the autonomy their mothers never had. Rosalie Kiki Clough, '69, an "accidental feminist," whose only dream at Wellesley had been "to have enough chest to wear low-cut velvet dresses and then get married and have kids and be active in my church and drive a Country Squire station wagon and advance my husband's career," instead worked her way into a vice-presidency at Dean Witter after "Prince Charming failed to show. . . . Now I couldn't tolerate a husband who was weak and needed chains on me or constant adulation. I have independence and freedom. Money buys me that."

Many of the women of '69 have become breadwinners because they had to: Their husbands were downsized or low earners or left them, or they never married. These women had to support themselves, their children, and, increasingly, older relatives—a quarter now give regular financial help to parents or in-laws. Barbara Furne Simmons, one of the few women in the class whose mother became the family's breadwinner after Barbara's father left, had, in turn, to largely provide much of the support for her two sons after her own husband left. Though Barbara thought him a "great gene-pool type" with an MBA from Harvard and an engineering degree from CalTech, his intense commitment to work left her lonely; at night, when she wanted his companionship, "he wanted a wall around him" so he could unwind. "We just stopped talking to each other, and one day he came home and said he was moving out. I kept hoping we would reconcile, thinking, There are babies. But Jim was working in Silicon Valley, where the reigning belief was that if you're not getting satisfaction, then there are other places to get it. It was a time when marriages were disposable, like houses: This is my starter home; this is my starter marriage."

More than half these women have been the principal breadwinners, and a fifth have been the sole breadwinners in their family. Fifty-eight percent have held a job with higher pay than their husbands'. Forty percent keep some of their money separate from that of their partner; of those, half keep it all separate. The majority share equally in their family's spending and investment decisions. The Wellesley microcosm reflects a global trend. Collectively, women's incomes have won them power in the world: All told, women earned more than $1 trillion in 1994, a fivefold increase over 1975. They have also earned other currencies of power: Television correspondent Martha Teichner, '69, has repeatedly been slammed by conservative organizations for proffering the kinds of favors that once only men were in a position to grant. When she interviewed Hillary Clinton on *CBS Sunday Morning* in January 1997, for instance, she was criticized for commiserating with Hillary on the "nonstop bashing" her former classmate had endured.

Avenging Angels

Catherine Kostick Ravinski, '69, is a judge for the Social Security Administration in Miami. Until 1994, she was an appeals judge at the agency's headquarters in Virginia. "I'm a driven, competitive, aggressive person. I'm a star at what I do. At headquarters, my support group was mostly men. At lunch we'd head for the health club, get on adjacent Stairmasters, and bat around legal issues or vent frustrations. In a sense, I am my work. I chose to do one thing extremely well, abandoning my mother's belief that a woman should be well rounded and dabble. I'm a very physical person, which my mother was not. I love sports, white-water rafting (the more dangerous the better), driving; I don't enjoy reading, sewing, knitting, or anything that requires sitting still. My nicknames at head-quarters were the Cattle Prodder, the Bionic Woman, the Beastmaster. I am self-absorbed, focused, impatient, driven, rude, irreverent, mean, a loyal friend, a vicious infighter, a defender of the underdog."

Catherine has been married since June 1973. "My husband, Richard, is much more easygoing than I am, interested in antiques, gourmet cooking, gardening. He is accommodating and flexible and has little drive; since 1989, he's been a self-declared househusband, and has taken over all the shopping, cooking, cleaning, and yard work. He also makes jewelry, wreaths, stuffed animals, flower arrangements, and is known for his fine luncheons and dinners. He has made three major moves to follow my career. We're almost inseparable and share most activities, though he does tolerate my going 'out with the boys' and is generous about inviting my colleagues to the house for meals and special treats."

It would be hard to fit Catherine into any model of essential female character traits. If she seems, at first, to have perfectly reversed roles and temperaments with her husband, she then inverts the formula again, talking of how her "heart sings" to be with her present colleagues— "three other female judges and one male, who considers himself 'one of the girls.' " Though she fails to conform to most notions of a "woman's way" of working toward gentle compromise and conciliation, her role as a kind of avenging angel—ferociously representing the weak against the strong—has its own history as a woman's way of being in the world. Nineteenth-century feminists frequently fought on behalf of the poor and exploited and enslaved, channeling anger born of their own private experience of constrained liberty into public battles on behalf of other trapped human beings. Most of the people who come before Catherine for hearings, she says, are poor, disabled, poorly educated, and terrified. "So, while patience is not one of my virtues, I take pains to ensure that I have it while at the bench, and strive to be kind, compassionate, and respectful. While a very intense person, I try to turn that intensity toward good and useful objectives. While somewhat hard and opinionated, I have gone to the mat many times for people who lack the power to fight for themselves."

Like her predecessors', Catherine's pursuit of public justice is in part a way to redress injustices first experienced in private. It is a motivation she shares with many of her classmates: Abby van Alstyne, for instance, dropped out of Wellesley to work on the Poor People's Campaign and has spent twenty years as a civil rights lawyer in Alabama, impelled, she says, to rebel against the arbitrary exercise of power she had witnessed as a girl at home, but been helpless to fight.

Catherine Ravinski explains her ferocity with a grandly bitter tale of her mother's life. Raised in "colonial splendor" in the Philippines, Catherine's mother married in America and was "abused physically and emotionally. Her in-laws hated her for not being Russian, poor, and like them. She suffered abject poverty, starvation, and lack of medical care—without complaint. Though charming and fair-minded, with deep religious convictions, she was unable to control her six children, or 'savages,' as we were called. We lived on a small farm, often on the brink of starvation, with nearly nonexistent medical and dental care, somewhat like wild animals. Five of us were girls ('another girl,' my Russian Baba would say with disgust). Since we were 'only girls,' we had to do chores and work like dogs while we went to school. There was tremendous pressure for perfection, an A-plus in everything, yet with an underlying message from my father that we were, by nature, incompetent and inferior and would never make the grade.

"My mother spent her days doing household chores, which she was ill equipped to handle and did poorly. She died at fifty-one of metastatic cancer, which had gone too far because of her trait of not insisting on her needs—she did not fight back.

"All of this instilled in me a fierce desire for financial and personal independence, accompanied by a less than gracious attitude toward would-be oppressors, abusers, and users. I advise young women to immediately challenge anyone who tries to step on them. Anyone who tries to hurt me or those I care about I will swiftly 'decapitate' (preferably by verbal means, but if necessary, by any means); if a would-be abuser raises his or her ugly head in my presence, I'll be only too happy to cut 'em a new asshole."

In 1969, Cynthia Gilbert became a stewardess for Pan American Airways. The skies had always drawn her with their promise of freedom. She would have been an astronomer, she thinks, had she not absorbed as a girl the certainty of feminine failure in physics and math. A glamorous blonde, with a bright, sweet manner, the kind of woman who likes flowered dresses and full-length mink, Cynthia loved her vagabond life; she relished testing her wits in strange and sometimes treacherous places. It did not seem too onerous, as the price of her ticket to ride, to cut her hair, wear a girdle, and stay single and childless and underweight.

Cynthia was at first horrified at the idea of joining a union—"you know, wid dese guys and dose guys." But she slowly came to realize that while her professional classmates might cut individual deals with their employers, women in jobs like hers bargained collectively or not at all. She soon found herself "backing into" a leadership role in a women's labor movement freshly invigorated by the new organization of clerical workers, Nine to Five, and by the forging of a coalition among pink-collar unions. The movement was then focused on two goals. The first was to break down single-sex labor ghettos: Women sued AT&T to open lineman positions to women and operator positions to men, and sued the airlines to replace their girlie (young, unwed, slender) stewardesses with flight attendants of both sexes. The second was to secure decent treatment and fair pay for women who would never get anywhere close to the glass ceiling. At times, the aims of Cynthia and her colleagues were at direct odds with those of her professional classmates. While NOW opposed protective labor laws as discriminatory, or sought to extend protections equally to men (replacing maternal leave with parental leave, for instance), many union women opposed the ERA out of fear that it would jeopardize those same protections.

It is ironic, then, that the galvanizing event for Cynthia at Pan Am revolved around the denial to the women pushing coffee carts the protections reserved for the men in the cockpit. When the airline added the 747–SP to its fleet for long flights, the pilots were provided bunks, while the stewardesses were given nothing. "We were also starting to learn about ozone poisoning on these higher-altitude-flying airplanes; there was no air quality control in the cabin. And flight attendants were not covered by OSHA. The FAA cared only about the cockpit." The industry's "Fly Me" sexism was so blatant that it served as a crucible for numerous feminists: Just a few years before Cynthia took to the skies, Pan Am flight attendant Patricia Ireland—who would serve as president of NOW in the 1990s—had also been "jolted into feminism" when the airline told her that her medical insurance did not cover her husband, though male employees' wives were covered.

The Transport Workers Union was not much more sympathetic to its female members' needs. "They called us 'the girls,' and ignored us," Cynthia recalls. "When I suggested that we survey all the flight attendants about their concerns, they decided not to understand English. We almost outnumbered the other councils put together, and they didn't want to see the girls have too much power. They finally expelled 'the San Francisco Seven'—a group of women who were trying to form a new union just for flight attendants. I still wasn't into radical change, and kept trying to work with the TWU, going to all their meetings. But it was short-lived. We finally had to take matters in our own hands.

"A lot of women at Pan Am wanted to strike just to hurt the company, they were so mad. It takes a lot to get women angry, but it also takes more to appease them. Men can get angry and blow it off, but women take it more personally. In the end we had a 'blue flu,' and I ended up being served the court papers, which we thought we'd dodged by not making me an official. I'd started taking labor-relations classes like mad, and found wonderful mentors at the School of Industrial Relations. I wrote our sixty-five-page contract opener. Fortunately, there was at Pan Am a more gentlemanly code than at United, where women were getting their tires slashed—though some of my colleagues were careful about checking their suitcases, in case illegal drugs were put in. But eighteen months of negotiation did teach me that those in power get to write the rules."

Though they did not recognize it at the time, these women were preparing the future of a labor movement that was in mortal decline elsewhere. In 1970, 30 percent of all American workers in private industry were unionized; today just 11 percent are, and those troops are increasingly female and minority. Cynthia is proud of that legacy but has never quite shaken the feeling that she failed as a Wellesley grad. "While most of you sport your MBAs, L.L.D.'s, M.D.'s or Ph.D.'s," she wrote to her classmates in 1994, "I have my union card, which may account for my metamorphosis from Goldwater Republican to liberal Democrat." Later, she explains: "I thought maybe if I'd been president of a bank, the rest of the world would recognize me. At times I still imagine it would have been nice to have been born with a silver spoon, or married one. But then I think maybe you don't get in tune with the rest of humanity by being removed from it.

"I do know that my life is better than my mother's because I have more, not power exactly, but choice." Even after the birth of her daughter in 1986, Cynthia continued to fly and maintain an income separate from her husband's. She also kept control of the condo she'd bought in her early thirties. "My father didn't want me to buy it, but I'd begun to think I might never get married and decided I needed roots. I also got a loan much larger than I should have on my paltry salary, from a bank officer who winked and said, 'I imagine you don't have to buy most of your dinners, dear.' I've refused to refinance it because then it would become joint property, and I made my husband sign a quitclaim deed on it when we got married in 1981. I also insisted on keeping a flight fund, ten thousand dollars in my own separate bank account. My mother had always been trapped. To have no exit is hell. I wanted to always be sure I had an out."

The Barriers

In 1969, the Equal Employment Opportunity Commission was using *his* to describe job functions for its directors and investigators and *her* for all clerks and secretaries. In many states, women could not establish a business, buy stocks, or get a loan without a male cosigner. At many professional schools, quotas were still in place—quotas of the old sort, which capped the numbers of admitted women (or Asians or Jews). Thirty years later, though white males comprise just 43 percent of the workforce, they hold 95 percent of senior management positions. Less than 6 percent of all law partners and less than .5 percent of top corporate managers are women. Male executives' median earnings remain 57 percent higher than females'; male professors', 41 percent higher; male economists', 25 percent higher.

No surprise, then, that one in four women in the Wellesley class of '69 says she was discriminated against in hiring and promotion and half say they would have earned more if they weren't women. Mary Day Kent recalls personnel departments and help-wanted ads designating jobs open to women and those only for men: The former were typically clerical and specified that applicants should be young, single, and good-looking. Holmes Bridgers Ramsay, married two weeks after graduation, was asked what her family plans were, and when she admitted to wanting children, was turned down for bank-management-trainee jobs. Nancy Brenner was turned away from Grey Advertising, despite her Harvard MBA, because Grey executives believed clients like General Foods would not work with a woman—a not unreasonable assumption, given that the Harvard Business School's own survey of a thousand male executives that year found only a third in favor of women in management positions. When newlywed Pat Sinclair interviewed for her first job at Shawmut Bank, they asked what kind of birth control she was using. She told them. Lonny Laszlo Higgins was turned down by seven medical schools because "we don't want to give you the place of a man who will support his family and waste a spot on someone who'll just go out and get pregnant."

A third of the class reports having been sexually harassed. After her work with the Poor People's Campaign, Abby van Alstyne went to New York in the early 1970s to became a Medicare investigator for HEW. Several months after her arrival, one of her superiors in the Office of Civil Rights, a married man, told her that she had to join him on an overnight trip inspecting hospitals in Washington, D.C. After a dinner with colleagues, he asked her to step into his hotel room for a minute. Once behind closed doors, he pulled her toward him and tried to kiss her. She extricated herself "as tactfully" as she could. The next day, she was removed from cases she'd worked on for months; in the weeks thereafter, what had been consistently "excellent" performance evaluations of her work now consistently came up "poor." She filed a complaint, a two-year investigation found probable cause, and the superior was reprimanded. But he made life so unpleasant for her—excluding her from meetings, interfering with her cases—that she finally left the organization.

For her classmates, the consequences have not often been so dire. Their education and relative affluence have buffered them from much of the worst. Few have worked in the environments where sexual harassment is most pervasive and aggressive—manufacturing, police work, the military. And unlike the majority of working women, most had the resources to walk away from a job. Nearly all of those who were harassed simply put up with it and—whether because they'd been taught as girls that they simply had to endure boys being boys or because they'd been tempered by the sexual revolution—remained relatively untraumatized by the event. Elizabeth Michel simply laughed at an embryology professor at Yale who was clearly perturbed to have a woman in his class and taunted her with cartoons of breasts captioned as melons, peaches, and pears. At Dean Witter, Rosalie Kiki Clough ignored regular pats on the ass and requests from men to "Bring me some coffee, would you, doll?" When Constance Hoenk Shapiro was named chair of the Department of Human Service Studies at Cornell—where even now just 9 percent of full professors are women—she was asked by a dean during salary negotiations if she needed some time to get her husband's approval. Several years earlier, an administrator had suggested that "we discuss your tenure review materials over a late dinner at my house." In both cases, Connie declined.

Pam Colony had completed a Ph.D. in anatomy at Boston University and a postdoctorate at Harvard Medical School when she got her first faculty job offer at Hershey Medical Center in Pennsylvania. Despite warnings from colleagues that several senior faculty in the department were "antiwoman" and would be dead set against her getting tenure, she accepted. She knew job and tenure opportunities for women were scant in all institutions. Though in 1970 women composed 40 percent of the students at top universities, they made up just 10 percent of the faculty. At Columbia, just 2 percent of tenured faculty were women, and of six hundred tenured professors at Harvard, just three were women. The sciences were the worst, but so far Pam's work experiences had been good. She had spent years running a lab for her mentor, whom she considered unwaveringly respectful and fair. Once in ten years, he had made an advance, but "when I said no, that was it, and we both let it go."

As her advisers had warned, Pam's difficulties at Hershey would prove neither so minor nor so easy to overcome. Her colleagues, she says, impeded her progress at every turn. Her orders for chemicals wouldn't go out, her lab animals would disappear. After she waited four years for a computer critical to her work, when it finally arrived, it was given to a man who had just joined the faculty. Other department chairs—all of them men—did support her, giving her equipment and small grants, but there was only so much they could do. "There was little recourse. Each department was a fiefdom; if your chair was not supportive, you were up the creek. People told me I should document things, and I said, 'Oh no, it will work out.' I loved my work and had consistently good reviews from students and funding from the National Institutes of Health and the respect of my colleagues: A number of professors had expressed admiration when I failed the chairman's Ph.D. student, who was later thrown out of the program. At that point, I still believed that tenure wasn't personal but professional.

"I was denied tenure on grievously erroneous grounds. I was supposed to review and sign my dossier, and never saw it: There were omissions on my bibliography, teaching assignments left out, miscalculations of my teaching evaluations. When I appealed it to the committee on the main campus, the problems were so transparent that I immediately won a new tenure review. But I knew it wasn't going to change at Hershey, so I started looking for a job." Pam accepted a position as premed adviser and researcher at Franklin and Marshall College. "I went with the highest expectations and did a good job. But I got burned there as well, this time by a woman dean, who felt I didn't play by her rules. The day the grant that paid my salary ended, she gave me one day's notice that I was fired."

With hindsight, Pam recognizes the naïveté of her expectation that the workplace would reward, with perfect blind justice, dedicated teaching and innovative research. The dashing of such expectations was a common experience in the class. "In our world of women at Wellesley," recalls Ann Sherwood Sentilles, "we were endowed with a sense that we could do anything. I spent a lot of time believing in a meritocracy—that if you're good and a nice kid and work hard, you'll be rewarded. I was woefully unprepared for the way the world still regarded women." It was not just their belated encounter with the harsher realities of a coed world, however, that slapped these women out of their romantic notions of work. Though one admires Pam's refusal to compromise her principles, it's hard to say how much of her mistreatment was sexist and how much was the price exacted of lots of people, male or female, who refuse to play the political game.

Pam's personal life no doubt fueled her enemies' disapproval. Her first marriage, to a cab-driving Harvard Ph.D. unraveled painfully and somewhat publicly. "When I found myself sitting at work crying all day, I knew I needed to move on." Throughout, she remained remote from her colleagues, spending her free hours riding horses in endurance competitions, a perfect solitary pursuit.

Pam married her second husband soon after joining the faculty at Franklin and Marshall. He was in law school after thirteen years as a social worker, and Pam supported him. "I didn't mind. I decided how the money was spent, and he never crossed me." After two miscarriages, Pam was forty-two and pregnant again when she was fired. "We were screwed. I was bleeding a lot and terrified I'd lose the baby and now we'd lost our health insurance. I got a job offer back at Hershey in surgery. They agreed to let me work half-time with flexible hours and run my own research lab, so I accepted, though because I'd quit once, I'd relinquished my rights to a new tenure review. The first six months were rough. The dean of the medical school didn't allow me to be paid until the chief of surgery, a completely fair and honest man, went to him in support of me.

"To this day, I'm not sure if all that I went through was about me individually or would have been turned on any woman, but I would push a woman to do the opposite of what I did, which was to let it go by. I'm much too trusting. I either have to believe in people or give it all up. Our mothers had learned to acquiesce, to not expect to be on a par and to not demand anything. I had assimilated a lot of that. Way too much."

That they are insufficiently bold in the world, still too much the deferential girls groomed at Wellesley, is a worry for many of the women of '69. When Jan Krigbaum was hired by Family Planning International to be associate regional director in Bangladesh, she became paralyzed with fear that she would fail. She relived that feeling in 1992, when the Clintons asked her to go to Little Rock to assist in their transition into the White House. As a deputy assistant to the president, assigned to bring in diverse personnel, "I spent the whole first year waking up at two in the morning feeling terrified—literally physically terrified. I had this kind of lockjaw, where I couldn't open my jaw all the way. I don't think that would have happened to a man. Men are so audacious. They don't seem to think twice about whether they can do something or whether they're the best person for the job."

If these women have contended with barriers both external and internal, however, they have also recognized their immense advantages. The first was Wellesley. Women's colleges consistently turn out graduates successful in arenas traditionally underpopulated by women: One third of the female board members of Fortune 1000 companies and half of all female math and engineering Ph.D.'s are graduates of women's colleges, even though they constitute less than 4 percent of total graduates in the country. And Wellesley has been particularly strong. In 1995, *The New York Times* reported that "more than any other college, Wellesley has groomed women who shatter the glass ceiling . . . and hold more seats in executive suites and corporate boardrooms. Of 390 women directors of the Fortune 5000, including the presidents of Colgate North America and the Seagram Beverage Group, seventeen went to Wellesley, more than any other college."

The second advantage these women had was the timing of their entry into the professional world. The Vietnam War was their first perverse stroke of luck. When in 1967 military deferments were eliminated for male graduate students, it became vastly easier for women to get into top graduate schools. It became easier still in the early seventies when women began winning the first big sex-discrimination suits against universities and such companies as *Newsweek* and AT&T, with the consequence that both schools and firms felt significant pressure to let women in. At medical schools, quotas that capped female admissions were ruled illegal. Elsewhere, female quotas were imposed. Nonna Noto, '69, was admitted to Stanford's graduate school of economics, she says, only because the Ford Foundation had given the school money on the condition that it admit five women. She credits affirmative action with getting her a first job as well. No group, in fact, has benefited more from affirmative action than women like these—mostly white and headed for the professions. A very few in the class resent that fact. Charlynn Maniatis, M.D., L.L.D., entered the Navy Reserves as a lieutenant thanks to affirmative action but regrets that she "was not held to the same standard as men. I believe men are discriminated against when employers are forced to meet a female quota. I take offense at unqualified women who use the fact that they are women to advance. I have a colleague at New York Hospital, who sued when they advanced a man far more qualified [in their field]. People like that insult people who really are discriminated against."

As a vanguard, these women have had yet one more advantage. During her months in the White House contending with "people's ambition at its most raw, power play in its most aggressive form," Jan Piercy quickly learned some of the necessary arts of politics. Her most useful discovery in the game was that she could exploit that vestige of the ideology of separate spheres which grants women superior virtue. "Women's voices can have exceptional weight. Because of our rarity, when women do take a position with conviction, we carry a special moral authority, an authority that can have a disarming effect. That's been especially true at the [World] Bank. Much more than it would for a man, the office makes me appear larger, like a magic wand has been waved."

Breaking the Glass Ceiling

Janet McDonald Hill and Eldie Acheson have both helped women make it into the upper ranks of corporate and political power, and both have made it there themselves, though with differing degrees of ambivalence toward their bounty. Both are also, unlike most of the women in the class of '69, fairly reluctant to discuss their private lives. Some of that reticence is no doubt a consequence of their both having lived in families that are in the public eye. It may also come from their having been reared with the habit of public activism: For these women, the political is the political, and so they are less needful of the self-revelation that for many classmates is their form of public activism.

Janet is unapologetic about her personal success. The aspirations instilled in her as a girl in New Orleans—her father's lessons in piano and money counting; her mother's insistence on her attending a fancy northern school—remain intact. Advanced education, professional skills, and economic achievement, she believes, are the only reliable sources of safety and improvement—for blacks and for women: Social change happens not principally in the public sector but in the corporate world. Since 1980, Janet has owned a consulting firm with former EEOC chairman Clifford Alexander, advising such clients as IBM and Major League Baseball on bringing women and minorities into management's top ranks.

The language Janet speaks to her clients is devoid of moral appeals. She counsels companies to boost women over the glass ceiling—not because it's right, but because it's smart to seek out talent beyond the 35 percent of the population that is male and white. A high earner herself, and a woman whose husband, Calvin, and son, Grant, have both made millions as professional athletes, Janet calls herself "a capitalist who appreciates and understands money." Those at the bottom, she says, are "not my thing." A thoroughly assimilated believer in assimilation, Janet understands personal identity as something to be defined not by standing against society but rather by full integration and "excellence." Though she regards racism and sexism as America's gravest problems, she suspects social rationales for personal failure. Taught by her parents that no amount of contempt from others can diminish a person's dignity, Janet does not support such multiculturalist innovations as diversity training, believing that "the treatment and expectations of blacks and women should be indistinguishable from those for white men."

Eldie Acheson, who has spent her whole life in the land of privileged and powerful progressives, is both more self-conscious (where Janet was schooled not to count herself less, Eldie was taught not to count herself better) and more unconscious about her status. Her father, David Acheson, was Washington, D.C., U.S. attorney in the sixties and helped elect John Kennedy president. Her mother publicly tangled with Washington's posh private schools over their exclusionary admissions. Though the family summered at Eldie's maternal grandparents' hunting camp in Canada and spent weekends at grandfather Dean Acheson's Harewood Farm in Maryland and winter retreat in Antigua, Eldie describes her upbringing as essentially Calvinist. "There were cocktails and cigarettes, of course—it wasn't grim Calvinism—but my parents conveyed the message that life is not frivolous, that you can't coast on who you're related to and on your money. Mother insisted we live 'downtown' in Woodley Park, rather than in some elite white suburb. I did have a coming-out party at sixteen and we all went to private school, but I remember in sixth grade at Potomac School fighting with my classmate Sandra Auchincloss over her stepfather Carleton Putnam's neosegregationist tracts; she was spouting his theories about black inferiority while I spouted my parents' views on equality. Mother was adamant that we not belong to a country club—Chevy Chase, Kenwood, they all discriminated—and she took a dim view of us even going with a friend; she would send us off with a lecture about the injustice of social barriers."

Urged on by her prominent grandfather, Eldie graduated from George Washington Law School in 1973 and, after a year clerking for a federal judge in Maine, became one of the first women partners at the white-shoe Boston law firm Ropes and Gray. In her nineteen years there, Eldie coordinated the firm's pro bono activities and served as a trustee of Roxbury Community College, a fund-raiser for the Clinton campaign, and a board member of Women, Inc., a nonprofit treatment center for women drug addicts and their children. She also drafted the firm's parental-leave policy, a task in which her aristocratic origins proved useful: While many women of her generation were so grateful just for admission into the "old boys' club" that they wouldn't dare ask anything more, Eldie had been born to a sense of entitlement that overwhelmed any hesitancy to make demands. That she did not have children herself also made it easier for her to fight on behalf of the women in the firm who did; her efforts on that front contradict the conventional scenario of wars at work between childless women and moms.

Eldie's most persistent crusade at Ropes and Gray was to recruit and advance women and minorities. She set out to demonstrate to the clubbiest of the old boys that diversity was not bitter medicine. "It's just bullshit that you don't see qualified women or Hispanics or African-Americans, especially in law, which doesn't exactly take a rocket scientist. It takes people skills, the ability to form a relationship that makes a client feel secure; as our clients become increasingly diverse, it only makes more sense for a firm to have a diverse group of attorneys. And if the federal government is truly discredited as a values leader, as it seems to be in many people's eyes, then the private sector has to step up to it."

In 1993, Eldie joined four of her Wellesley classmates in the Clinton administration, becoming associate attorney general in charge of the Office of Policy Development, which screens candidates for positions as federal judges and U.S. attorneys. Again, she has used her power to advance equality: Half of the several hundred appointments she has shepherded have been women or minorities or both, almost twice the proportion among those chosen by President George Bush.

Eldie's appointment to the Justice Department was nearly derailed because of an episode that illustrates the slippery slope of assimilation into the old boys' club. In a perplexing moment of forgetting the link between the personal and the political, Eldie had joined the Country Club of Brookline. The club had no black members and a history of discriminating against women, a fact which Eldie had to have known, since just a year earlier a group from Ropes and Gray that included a black woman had been denied access to the men's grill. "All my male tennis and golf buddies were urging me to join the club, and I thought, Okay, this fits into the image of a partner at Ropes and Gray." Again, being a woman muddled the issue: Was it progress for her to make it into a place traditionally walled against women, or co-optation? Such clubs, after all, like the fabled "men's room," stood for all the places from which women were barred. "Somehow, I didn't hear my mother's voice echoing. It ended up being a Wellesley friend of mine, Cindy Stebbins, ['67] who got pissed off and pressed the club to abolish its segregated facilities. But if not for Carol Moseley-Braun, I don't think I would have ever understood the 'sin' of my joining. What then Senator Braun objected to, rightly, is that social lines are drawn. Business gets done in a place and way that keeps outsiders out."

Not to Be Served, but to Serve

If a few in the class of '69 have focused on securing women's access to the highest positions and perks, less than a fifth are in the classic yuppie professions: business, finance, advertising. The greatest number work in teaching, followed by law and government, not-for-profit work, and medicine. (In the class of '94, by contrast, a third of all graduates headed into business and only 13 percent went into education.) More than half earn less than $50,000, and just 7 percent earn more than $150,000—compared to 36 percent earning over $150,000 in Harvard '69 (though of course many of the Wellesley class married high-earning men—more than half have household incomes over $100,000). Asked why they work, only a handful deem status and power "vitally important"; most name personal fulfillment, earning a basic livelihood, and service as their principal motivations.

A remarkable number are, thirty years later, engaged in just the kinds of good works sanctioned in their idealistic youth. Mary Murtagh, '69, is the first woman executive director of the nonprofit Ecumenical Association for Housing in California, building homes for low-income elderly and disabled persons; previously, she directed the renovation of a hotel in San Francisco to house recovering alcoholics. Adrienne Germain, '69, was director of all Ford Foundation programs in Bangladesh before becoming president of the International Women's Health Coalition, a nongovernmental organization working for reproductive and sexual health and rights for women in Asia, Africa, and South America. Jan Krigbaum Piercy also worked in Bangladesh, for Family Planning International and the Grameen Bank, the latter a pioneering lending organization founded in 1976 to make small seed loans to microenterprises, most of them founded by women. In the 1980s she brought that model of community investment back to the U.S. to create Southshore Development Bank in Chicago, then helped the Clintons take the same model to Arkansas, raising capital for the Southern Development Bank. Now one of three women out of twenty-four executive directors at the World Bank, she has helped push through $3.5 billion for assistance programs to women, including $200 million in a new microcredit program. A friend of Hillary Clinton's ever since working on her campaign for student government office at Wellesley, Jan has had a significant influence on Hillary: In her husband's second term, the First Lady has often focused on providing microloans for women and importing to inner cities the development lessons learned abroad.

If many of these women have worked on behalf of women poorer and less powerful than they, few have actually worked at the kinds of jobs most women hold: Just 20 percent of Wellesley '69 work in pink-collar ghettos and earn less than $20,000, as 75 percent of all working women do. Some in the class have wondered, as they've rapped at glass ceilings, whether it was enough that their success trickled down (winning, for instance, job protection for all women who became pregnant) or whether their main achievement has been merely, as radical black feminist bell hooks charges, "achieving for white women of privileged classes social and economic equality with men of their class," ultimately strengthening a system that ill serves poor women.

Dressing for Success

Rhea Kemble Neugarten Brecher Dignam (she married in 1989 for the third time—in her first church wedding and first white gown) has the lank hair and big wire-rim glasses of a New England college girl circa 1969. As the first woman ever to be chief federal narcotics prosecutor in Manhattan and chief of the public corruption unit (she was a protégée of U.S. attorney Robert Fiske, who would later investigate her classmate

Hillary's involvement in the Whitewater real estate development deal), Rhea frequently depended on testimony from unsavory witnesses. She tried the first case in which Nicky Barnes, dubbed "Mr. Untouchable" in the narcotics trade, agreed to testify as a government witness after being handed life imprisonment without parole. "It was always a question whether the jury would accept such a witness. So I wore my standard trial outfit, which I called my parochial school uniform—a plaid skirt below the knee, a black blazer, and a white blouse with a little black bow. A common defense technique is to argue that the government framed the defendant. But it's hard for the defense to make that argument if the government representative comes across as though she couldn't possibly tell a lie. So I played a young girl who would never engage in tricks and shenanigans. It's a wonderful way to present a scuzzy witness. You can't vouch for him, but it's an undercurrent. Women lawyers on the defense side, of course, had a different strategy. They needed just one juror to hang the jury. I knew one who intentionally wore flashy clothes, with one too many buttons unbuttoned—anything to win that one guy. I was always Miss Prim and Proper, never wore pants in court, always had high necklines. I didn't want to make any waves with the jury. And it just never bothered me to dress a part."

How to fashion themselves for the world has of necessity preoccupied each of the working women in the class of '69. Leaving the private world for the public sphere meant having to choose a persona, a new set of manners, a style. They might draw on feminine models—like Rhea Dignam's schoolgirl, or Kris Olson Rogers's earth mother—or try to signal professionalism by mimicking masculine demeanor and attire.

Some have found those demands oppressive. Ivy Walker Parish wrote to her classmates in 1979 that she had "quit wearing underwear and shaving." Nancy Wanderer, who earned a law degree in her forties, left one of Maine's most prestigious firms in part because she did not want to fit herself to the requisite mold: "I've tried right through my life to be myself. Anytime I've had to wear a costume or appear something I'm not, I struggle. I resisted the heels and girdle and makeup and curls my mother pressed on me in high school. Even as a kid, my goal was to be natural. I hated Barbie because she was unnatural. I absolutely never wanted to have a hairdo. Now, panty hose represents to me all the repressive aspects of what women get into when they enter the professional world. They're expensive and confining and give you a stomachache. If I couldn't be myself, I didn't want money or power or prestige. It struck me again watching Hillary: It all comes down to hair. Hillary has to spend time worrying about it. I can do whatever I want with it. To me, that's freedom." Nancy now goes to work in trousers and close-cropped hair.

Many in the class share Nancy's resistance to the dictates of acceptable female fashion, seeing it as physically debilitating (the eating disorders, the migrating silicone), self-hating in its abhorrence of the "natural" female body, and a perpetuation of women's dependence on winning the admiration of men. These women have viewed Hillary Clinton's much-attended-to experiments in reinvention with dismay. In the old Hillary of the frizzy hair and Coke-bottle glasses they saw a principled refusal to trade on her appearance or mask her confidence and power. (Hillary herself has said, "It wasn't just that I didn't wear makeup; it was a statement.") These classmates lament what has seemed to them her capitulation: "I worry about the kind of message your highly publicized makeover may send to young women," Louise Carter wrote in the alumnae magazine in a collective offering of advice to Hillary from the class. "Don't be afraid to reveal your complexity."

This has been one feminist stance: Erica Jong liked "Hillary's fuck-you attitude, not giving a damn about clothes, proudly displaying her hillbilly taste in decorating, refusing to play her role as national saleslady. HRC may be chilly, but must all women be restricted to womanly warmth as defined by Pillsbury . . . simper to make Al D'Amato and William Safire feel potent?"

Others, who like Kris Olson Rogers and Rhea Kemble Dignam have discovered the usefulness of feminine manners, commend Hillary for wising up. "If Hillary has to change her hairstyle to get her ideas across, to get Mr. and Mrs. America to listen to her, then I admire her for having the guts to do it," says classmate Michelle Lamson, a former top fashion model. "In politics you have to choose," says Susan Alexander. "Do you play to perceptions to get in a position where you can really make a difference? I think yeah, since we're paying prices whatever we do." On similar grounds, Jan Piercy supports Hillary's decision, seven years after her 1975 wedding, to assume her husband's name. "Her name just wasn't more important to her than returning Bill to office and making a difference on education and health care. It wasn't a sellout or a giving up; it was a trade-off." It is not only politics, after all, that has demanded of women that they wrap themselves publicly in soft raiments. In a 1996 survey, female vice-presidents at the one thousand largest U.S. companies—women earning an average of $248,000 a year—said that after exceeding performance expectations, the second key to their success was developing a personal style with which their male colleagues were comfortable—a style they described as "nonthreatening . . . not too smart or assertive."

Hillary Clinton is also not the first White House wife to strike a useful pose. Nancy Reagan's besotted subservience was skillfully performed, and because she was "small and decorative and pippy poo," as Germaine Greer put it, "she got away with running her husband." Even the unvarnished Eleanor Roosevelt employed a kind of rhetorical camouflage, according to biographer Blanche Wiesen Cook, never missing an opportunity to discount her immense influence or to cast it as wifely caretaking of her invalid husband.

Just as the old unapologetically strong Hillary was damned by some as abrasive and praised by others as genuine and bold, so the flossier, more ingratiating Hillary has been both admired and despised for her skills as a real "pol." Camille Paglia, at least for a while, liked both "the bitch with a quick sharp tongue" and the girlish "Southern blonde," seeing both as "personae" useful to Hillary at different times. Connie Bruck admired Hillary for her agility at "invoking her familial roles—as mother, daughter, sister, woman, a wife there to help her husband—to soften her . . . using the myth to her advantage," but also damned her as a chameleon, opportunistically mirroring her surroundings, and saw in her performance a kind of deceit: "What are we meant not to see?" *New York Times* columnist Maureen Dowd repeatedly tore at the "apple-pie and motherhood" scrim behind which the "real Hillary hid." The cover of David Brock's *The Seduction of Hillary Rodham* features her in sixteen different hairdos, presumably a map of her gradual corruption, like the picture of Dorian Gray. The attacks are often self-contradictory: In his book on the Clintons, Roger Morris depicts Hillary as both politically inept and slick as Willy. On one page she is a "cold-blooded heifer," unfailingly condescending, on the next she is a charmer who schmoozes rural bosses with the best of them.

Whether there is something craven in a public figure's image-making has been a vexing question at least since Shakespeare's Coriolanus agonized over whether to parade his heroic war wounds before the Roman masses. The scars were real, but Coriolanus refused to pander, insisting that such a circus would express only contempt for the people, treating them as easily bedazzled children. His refusal proved disastrous. The dilemma is greater still in a culture so built on the machinery of publicity that it is merely foolish to imagine that simple, unadorned goodness will shine through without active manipulation of that machinery. "An eternity of false smiles . . . is the price you pay to lead," Joe Klein wrote in a backhanded defense of the Bill Clinton character in *Primary Colors:* "You don't think Abe Lincoln was a whore before he was a president?" He smiled his "backcountry grin . . . so he'd get the opportunity to appeal to the better angels of our nature."

In the end, it seems that Hillary Rodham Clinton's repeated refashionings of herself for public consumption have earned so much scorn not because she plays the image game but because for so long she played it badly. When she stitched together her image, the seams frequently showed—unlike the more adept Elizabeth Dole, who during the 1996 campaign was endlessly admired for "how well she hides her toughness and ambition" behind self-deprecation (her success is a mystery, as she tells it, something that merely happened to her), buttering up everyone she met with her honeyed drawl and the gracious manner of a southern belle. Lyndon Johnson called the former Duke University beauty queen a "sugarcoated steel magnolia." In her autobiography, Dole recalled that during her years in the Reagan administration, she "seduced" her husband over a candlelight dinner into voting to sell planes to the Saudis. Though she has run an organization with a $1.8 billion budget and 32,000 employees, during the 1996 Republican convention Mrs. Dole stepped away from this "very imposing podium" to speak about "the man I love." A decade older than Hillary Clinton, Elizabeth Dole comes from a generation of women who had little choice but to slip through quietly, to feign "traditionalism" even if they were shaping the world. Phyllis Schlafly successfully led the Stop ERA campaign in 1972, all the while carrying gifts of homemade jam to state legislators. Hillary herself has increasingly adopted the manners of an old-fashioned wife, standing by her man even as he publicly confessed to yet another infidelity, this one with a woman half Hillary's age. That demonstration of forbearance has had its own political benefits, winning Hillary—for the first time— the admiration of older, conservative women, who finally recognized a kindred spirit.

It is true that some styles are disastrous for women: The same caustic humor and brusque stiffness read as integrity in Bob Dole was despised when it surfaced in Hillary. But the constraints on women are probably no greater than they are for men: Bill Clinton is ridiculed for a moist style that when worn by Elizabeth Dole wins rapturous praise. What, then, is craven and what simply politically savvy? One is left, perhaps, to distinguish degrees of bad faith, to question whether the fabricated images are somehow faithful to the underlying truth and are in the service of some authentic purpose, or whether the initial conviction has evaporated and the quest to seduce and win (or simply survive) is all that remains.

Of course, the very idea of a "real self" revealed or concealed is dated. Postmodernists see a liberation of the self, not its betrayal, in the "masquerade." Fashion, writes Anne Hollander, is "a costume trunk to express a woman's complicated private character, a means of escape from fixed roles. A woman may keep wholly transforming through clothing with no loss of personal identity or consistency." To be many things to many different people may be an expression of fluidity and wide-ranging empathy. Or it may be Machiavellian. Or it may be both.

"My hair has always been influenced by my life," Chris Osborne wrote to her classmates in 1984, offering a chronology of hairstyles as the sum total of her entry in that year's reunion book. "Short and lavender in '65, it was by '69 an inoffensive light brown . . . left scraggly in protest. By '72, it was long enough for people to sit on. Cut and permed it in '74, a huge mistake. I was fat then too. . . . By '76, I was making big money in advertising so I used to take it down to New York and have Mr. Bobby at the Carlyle streak it. Much gray during my stint as a writer, then Associate Creative Director at J. Walter Thompson in San Francisco. I tried fighting back with wider streaks, but glare began causing mishaps on the Bay Bridge. At Doyle Dane Bernbach in New York . . . instantly more gray. I joined the Clairol group in 1982. While selling Nice 'n' Easy Medium Golden Brown, I became one. This is the true me. Back in San Francisco as a senior writer at Foote Cone and Belding. . . . I breathe clean air, support causes and date many men who don't suspect about my hair."

Chris's shape-shifting paralleled her "careening" path out of Wellesley in 1969. Fatherless and "plumb out of money" she had to get a job, though, like most of her classmates at graduation, anticipating a domestic destiny, Chris had spent little energy contemplating what she wanted to do. "Most of us were pretty lost about our choices; it's a mistake to assume, for all the achievers, that we were a bunch of directed student council types like Hillary." Chris took a secretarial job at Harvard but was soon bored, so she became a live-in housekeeper and cook for five male students at the business school. "I was supposed to be like a little sister. Oh, all right, I did sleep with one of them; I kind of shared him with one of my Wellesley classmates. It's perfectly okay to tell the truth. My father was dead and I could do anything I wanted."

Another year, and Chris was "running off" to California. "I worked temp jobs in Berkeley and lived with twenty-two people in a house at the edge of the campus. Everyone was fucking like bunnies, which wasn't the number-one appeal of living that way but was a great way to get to know your friends. It was not uncomplicated; somebody was always pissed at somebody else for sleeping with her boyfriend. I got really tired of it, though I've always been a little saver and saved lots of money by sharing living and food. But I finally just wanted to get a job and live well. A lot of them had grown up in rich families; everyone was content with antimaterialism except me."

Back in Boston, she found a job by going through the phone book. "I got to the letter *M*. Marvin and Leonard needed a typist. I spent four years learning to write retail furniture ads, which is about four years more than you need. Then Marvin and Leonard laid me off. I went downstairs to Hill Holiday, who gave me a raise to $5,000 a year. I was still the archetypal sixties girl. I had hair to my ass and tie-dyed this and macraméd that. But then I started to dress differently, putting on suits and heels like the character in *Working Girl.*"

Chris is now a chic platinum blonde, much younger looking and more fashionable than most of her classmates. And her twentieth reunion prediction—"It's definitely beginning to look like I'll get a neck lift before I have children"—has come true. "Advertising is full of twenty- and thirty-year-olds and I didn't want to be obviously older than my peers. The neck lift was great. I got the whole lower face thrown in as a bonus. I don't even have those little lines between my nose and upper lip. They pull up everything behind the ears." She celebrated her new face, and a home renovation completed at the same time, at a "neck and deck" party for all her friends.

Playing earth mother or parochial school girl is one thing. Playing vixen is potentially a more treacherous game. A woman leaning on her sexuality risks not being taken seriously, becoming a target for parody: When Hillary Clinton attended the Miss America Pageant, *The New York Times* mocked Miss Delaware's talking about changing American demographics "from atop spike heels." And if to get what she wants a woman must be able to stir male desire, her power is highly perishable and, in fact, not her own. "Left-handed, sidelong in the right-handed upright world of men," wrote poet Randall Jarrell, "they try to get around by hook or by crook, by a last weak winning sexual smile, the laws men have made for them."

Though some young "postfeminists" claim to be breaking new ground by enjoying and exploiting their sexuality in their public dealings with men, in fact numerous women—from Lola Montez to Clare Booth Luce to Pamela Harriman—have used sexual allure to rise above their origins; those who lived before this century have even been made heroines by recent feminist biographers. A *Fortune* magazine article in 1996 profiled seven successful businesswomen, noting that they all knew how to "skillfully exploit" their sexuality; among them was Ogilvy and Mather executive Charlotte Beers, Wellesley, '57. Madeleine Albright, Wellesley '59, is also a recognized master at flattering powerful men.

Michelle Lamson, '69, has always used her exceptional beauty without qualms. A cheerleader and runner-up for homecoming queen as a girl in Des Moines, she was "spoiled silly by my daddy," who sold road-building equipment and ran a giant mobile-home park and made lots of money and bought her show horses and ballet classes and Afghan hounds. Modeling couture in Paris after graduation, appearing on the cover of *Women's Wear Daily* and in French *Vogue* while also attending the Institut des Sciences Politiques, Michelle knew that some thought her a bimbo. "I just made use of that perception. I think it's fun if I'm having trouble changing a tire to play the weak silly woman to get some man to do it for me. I was never one to grow the hair under my arms because I was becoming an object. Should I quit wearing perfume? Perfume is one of life's wonders. Should I make myself ugly to prove that I'm smart? The fact is, I dominate men all the time. Women are harder to seduce. But with men you can be so obvious and they never see through it."

Married, but then left by her husband for another woman soon after her modeling career came to an end, Michelle worked as a freelance translator but grew lonely and became manager of a hunt shop in Paris, selling jodhpurs, bridles, and guns. "When some guy storms into the shop demanding to see the manager and is met by a tall, green-eyed blonde looking down on him, he'll generally drool and stammer and forget his complaint. I don't flirt. Never in my professional life have I felt they misinterpreted my actions. I simply use whatever weapons I have at my disposal to carve out a life for myself and my son."

As yet, the prospect of losing her power to mesmerize men as she ages has not worried Michelle too much. "I don't have the skin anymore. I don't have quite the body I had. I'm not going to put a glass bell over myself to protect myself from getting older, or worry if I have a chipped nail. But I still get attention on the street, and like it. I always return it with a smile. Though now when the boys whistle, I say, 'Thanks, I could be your mom,' and they say, 'I wish you were.' "

That the competition for men's approval has historically divided women also does not concern Michelle. "It's not my problem that I'm prettier than Mrs. A but that Mrs. B is prettier than me. There's always somebody uglier and prettier. And I'm not using my beauty to be an object for men's consumption—I'm using it to get my own way. I was the opposite of what we were all supposed to be at that time. I guess I still am."

CHAPTER SIX

Balancing Work and Family

W hen it was first published in 1899, Kate Chopin's novel *The Awakening* was branded a threat to woman's virtue and the nation's good. "Too strong drink for moral babes," one critic wrote, "should be labeled poison." Now revered as an early classic of feminist literature, the novel tells the story of a married woman with two young sons who finds her creativity awakened outside of her marriage and struggles between her responsibility to others and her imperative to be true to herself. "Think of the children," the heroine is told by the "good mother" of the novel. And Edna Pontellier does think of the children, understanding that "wanting my own way is wanting a great deal when you have to trample upon the lives, the hearts, the prejudices of others." In the end, she decides that her "husband and children could not possess her body and soul," and steps out of the shelter of her husband's home and into the wider world, a rebellion against convention clearly admired by the author. Finally, being a creature of a less-tolerant century, Edna walks into the sea.

Whether a woman can fulfill herself within the family; whether she ought even to seek her own fulfillment; what it might mean to "think of the children"—a century after *The Awakening*, these questions remain unresolved. They are not, strictly speaking, only women's questions: The tension between freedom and responsibility is the central American story. But for a woman, that tension has been felt most often at home, because it is within the family that she has been expected to work out her destiny.

The analysis of the family has therefore been from the beginning a core preoccupation of feminism. Even while drafting the Declaration on the Rights of Woman demanding suffrage, Elizabeth Cady Stanton avowed that "the whole question of women's rights turns on the marriage relation." The remaking of family life was necessary not only to secure women equality at home, but also as an essential precedent and template for the remaking of power relations between men and women in the world. "The public and the private worlds are inseparably connected," wrote Virginia Woolf. "The tyrannies and servilities of the one are the tyrannies and servilities of the other."

While feminists undertook to reinvent the family, their alarmed detractors saw them out to destroy it. Their warnings grew particularly vehement when Hillary Clinton first stepped onto the national stage. Christian leader Pat Robertson preached that "feminism encourages women to leave their husbands and kill their children" (and also to "practice witchcraft, destroy capitalism and become lesbians"). Others of slightly more temperate mind cast Hillary and the women she stood for as man-haters who "throw away marriages like paper towels," sanction illegitimacy, devalue the role of fathers, and disparage cookie-baking moms. Critics found in the recent abundance of memoirs and novels and self-help treatises propaganda against the family as a site of violence and incest and little more. They saw these women suckering their young, impressionable sisters into turning their backs on the joys of hearth and home in favor of the ultimately barren satisfactions of career. In her 1994 memoir of infertility, *Motherhood Deferred*, Anne Taylor Fleming cursed "the old haranguing chorus . . . aping the cultural dismissal of women, femaleness, motherhood, our mothers . . . Hey Hey. Gloria! Germaine! Kate! Tell us, how does it feel to have ended up without babies? . . . I want to crawl back into my female sex . . . where oh where do I go to trade a byline for a baby?"

In fact, far from scorning maternity, first- and second-wave feminists more often rhapsodized what Marguerite Duras called "the colossal swallowing up . . . the only opportunity offered a human being to experience a bursting of the ego." By virtue of her capacity to bear children, many claimed, a woman had a depth of heart and moral authority superior to man's, better equipping her to manage economic and political power. Because she knows "the months of weariness and pain while bones were shaped within, [the] hours of anguish and struggle that breath might be," as Olive Schreiner wrote, a woman could not look upon slain soldiers except as "so many mothers' sons." Were she to govern alongside man, she would bring an end to war: "she knows the history of human flesh; she knows its cost; he does not." Marxist feminists argued that the "unpaid labors of reproduction" should be rewarded; antiwar marchers in the sixties flew banners announcing "ANOTHER MOTHER FOR PEACE." Feminists led the fight for prenatal care, nutrition, and health-care programs for mothers and children, protection against discrimination against pregnant women and mothers, child care in the workplace, and parental leave.

Some feminists did renounce family outright, pessimistic that it could be transformed enough to permit women the same autonomy and creativity granted within it to men. Susan B. Anthony, who never married, believed that "a woman who will not be ruled must live without marriage." Long before the class of '69 arrived at Wellesley, the college's more radical faculty had been advancing the view that like a nun taking vows, a woman bent on an intellectual career must remain unwed. "How many women of rare capacity have blotted themselves out," asked Professor Vida Scudder, who had trained at Oxford with John Ruskin, "from a mistaken sense of duty?"

While some turned against marriage and motherhood because they promised to swallow a woman whole, others focused their critique on the ideology: They fought against the narrowing of women's dreams, the confining idea that maternity was the only way for them to be happy and real. For some women, it surely was. For others, the "recipe for happiness" contained some other mixture. The women of '69 knew well that not all women love motherhood: Raised by women with no other acceptable destiny, many had seen firsthand how chilly and miserable an unmotherly mother could be.

Yet even in its most antimaternal moments ("stop rocking the cradle and start rocking the boat"), the whole feminist chorus was still only the faintest chime against the massed voices of parents and experts and fairy tales and Wellesley College exhorting girls to seek safety and satisfaction with a successful husband and babies. Certainly, for all that the feminist harangue caught them full in their young faces, the class of '69 still pursued marital bliss in the same proportions that women had for a century. Eighty-eight percent have married (a proportion typical for college-educated women in their age group, though lower then the 93 percent of Americans in their overall age group). One in three who married also divorced, but most of those have remarried. Three quarters of the graduates have children. Half of the ones who don't, wish they did. The vast majority of those who have children have also tried to combine motherhood with paid work, in all manner of arrangements.

Jan Dustman Mercer's dream of a literary life lasted as long as it took to get her first job offer as an "editorial assistant," which she soon discovered meant she would do secretarial work for almost no pay. She quickly changed course and entered management training in marketing at a large Boston bank. It was the only division where women could rise beyond clerical positions. "It didn't occur to me to be angry about that. It was just a fact that we all accepted."

For thirteen years, Jan was "gung ho" in her career. "I felt like a pioneer, forging new territory. It was great, but also uncomfortable at times." She endured the usual hazings: the appalled stares when she first set foot in the officers' dining room—a grand, formal club until that moment open only to men—the constant and explicit sex talk by a senior officer. "He would get himself titillated. He was clearly repressed; pathetic, really. And he wasn't the only one. I was once at a dinner with my husband, Tom [who also worked at the bank], and another guy, also very senior, was fondling my legs under the table. I didn't know what to do short of leaving. If I offended him, he was in a position to hurt both my and Tom's career. Nobody really knew what the ground rules were; we were all floundering. It was the first time that men and women were doing things like traveling together for business. Was it acceptable to have a drink with the married men you were traveling with? There were a lot of illicit relationships going on: Women may have realized what power they had and that it could be used to their advantage, or feared the consequences if they didn't. Anyway, at that dinner I finally just left the table. He visited me in my department after that, and invited me for drinks. I rebuffed his advances, which I don't think had negative consequences. But I did not tell Tom until many years later, because he respected this guy and I knew he would get angry. I carried it around by myself."

The insurmountable obstacle for Jan turned out to be pregnancy, an event she had postponed for several years. "All through my twenties I'd thought I'd have my first child at twenty-eight. Then I got to be twenty-eight and thought, Nah. In the early seventies it was very unusual for a woman to have a baby and continue working, and I didn't want to quit working. But when I was thirty-one, Tom and I were struck with this powerful yearning." They stopped using birth control, and Jan got pregnant right away. She also was promoted to vice-president. "It was a wonderful year. Here I was the youngest female VP in the bank's history and I had this baby growing inside of me. But I thought, Oh my word, I wonder if they know I'm pregnant. I was certain that if they had known, I would never have been promoted. But I knew I was in uncharted territory anyway, and I figured that this extra little glitch—it wasn't exactly a glitch—this glitch was going to have some unknown effect on me and my career. Little did I know how much of an effect."

Having never before had a pregnant vice-president, the bank had no policy for officers taking maternity leave; when Jan finally broke the news, her supervisors proved totally inflexible. The senior officers agreed that Jan could take unpaid leave for six months. When, after two months, she wanted to come back two days a week and ease up from there, they said no. At the same time, one officer who was running the United Way campaign asked her to help from home. She felt obligated to say yes because he had influence over her career. "But I resented the immense amount of time I had to spend calling on people when they wouldn't let me come back to work part-time."

When Jan did return to work, the couple hired a full-time nanny, a woman from Trinidad. Tom's job at the bank was also flexible enough that he could go home when he needed to. Still, going to work was for Jan "the hardest thing I'd ever done in my life. I had such guilt about leaving Tommy; he had never even taken a bottle. And I had no flexibility. I wasn't in an income-producing position, where I could be judged on the bottom line. In staff jobs like marketing and personnel, where women typically worked, performance is more difficult to quantify. How many hours you sit at your desk is the way they judge you. I didn't want to stay really late. I wanted to get home and see my baby, and I felt tremendous conflict. But I also knew that there were people watching my every move to see if I was really committed, if I was at my desk as many hours as before." It wasn't only from above that Jan felt pressure. She recognized that what she did would have consequences beyond her own life. "I had one young woman come up to me and say, 'I hope you understand how important it is that you do this well, because it will determine whether any of the rest of us can do it.' And I was flattered on the one hand, but my overwhelming feeling was, Oh my gosh, this is not just me. I'm carrying this huge weight around with me, the burden of being a symbol. I was not just trying to forge my own compromise for motherhood and career. I felt I was doing it for all the women at the bank. If I failed, I failed for everyone."

Caught in a classic bind—between wanting to demonstrate her dedication and toughness and wanting to transform the workplace by pressing for more flexibility—Jan ended up feeling she had to prove that work came first. She stayed two more years at the bank, working fifty hours a week. "I was on a merry-go-round, and like lots of people who step on them, it never hit me how stressed I was until it stopped. Finally, in 1981, I told the bank I was leaving. No one asked me to stay, which was painful. No one even asked why I was leaving. The ranks closed quickly behind me.

"In the end, I went to the head of personnel and gave my unsolicited critique of their mistreatment of women with families. I finally shook off the passive stance of the patient good girl. I think a lot of women in our generation waited for outside forces to make decisions for us. We weren't brought up to believe that women could control their own destiny. We grew up in the days when boys called you, and you sat and waited expectantly by the phone. We were taught to be passive, and that carried over to our early careers. We thought that if you were a loyal, good employee, the powers that be would take care of you. What we needed to do was take charge of life for ourselves."

Jan worked in real estate for a year, and then Tom was transferred to Dallas. She hated the idea of moving, and briefly contemplated a commuter marriage. Instead, she quit her job, moved to Dallas, and became a full-time mom, giving birth to a second son six years after the first. "The move turned out to be a godsend. In Boston, it would have been difficult for me to drop out. We needed my income. And it would have been almost impossible for me to go against everyone's expectations. In Dallas, no one knew me or had expectations. Most of our neighbors had no idea that I'd been a high-powered banker for thirteen years. They never thought to ask. It just wasn't the norm. At parties I would sometimes say, 'I used to be a banker,' as if it were my real identity that I'd just temporarily given up. At times I longed for the sense of being somebody. But the compensation for this enormously long sabbatical is that I got to know my kids, their day-to-day stuff. And I've had time for friends, who are in ways even more central than your kids, who, after all, go away.

"When I got to enjoy Tommy with no pressure and deadlines, I realized how much I'd missed. I'm glad that I shaped my sons' values, that they won't feel they had absentee parents. And after a while, I got okay with being just another mom. We lived in a neighborhood with lots of mothers of young kids. There was a real support system for the mother side of me; if I was lonely, I could just walk out on the street. At first I felt kind of cut off intellectually, but fortunately I had Wellesley friends." For her twenty-fifth reunion, Jan wrote to her classmates of her "decade of eating crow. . . . Who would have believed that I would abandon my hard-won banking career to raise two boys full time, live in the Dallas 'burbs, wash out the gray, appease my children with junk food and TV? . . . Making each day meaningful takes more self-discipline. . . . I've come to think maybe you can't have it all at the same time, but you can have it serially. I proved I could do it all, but chose to do part of it even better."

Jan's decision to drop out in 1982 was a textbook case of the phenomenon that Felice Schwartz would famously name the "mommy track" in a 1989 *Harvard Business Review* article, "Management Women and the New Facts of Life." The article contended that women are more prone to "career interruptions, plateauing and turnover" than men, and that it cost companies money in lost training dollars and expertise when middle- and upper-level women retired, like Jan, to the nursery. Though Schwartz's thesis would be misused as an argument against squandering corporate resources by admitting women to management ranks, Schwartz was actually arguing that corporations had to make it possible for women to pursue both serious careers and motherhood. It was not enough for the bank to treat Jan's departure as her "personal choice": If her only two choices were to work as if she had no family or not to work at all, the line between choice and coercion blurred.

The mommy track has been traversed by many in the Wellesley class of '69. Half the graduates stopped work when they became parents, (compared to just 3 percent of the men of Harvard '69). Some stopped more than once: Pathologist Linda Davis had to quit and find a new job after every one of her four babies, because none of her employers would grant her extended leave. A quarter started or resumed work only after age thirty-five. A majority believe they have "not fully fulfilled their potential" because of sacrifices made for child rearing. And nearly all who interrupted their careers to be with their kids paid a price: On average, they earn 20 percent less than their classmates who've worked nonstop since graduation. Those lower earnings, in turn, have often trapped them in a familiar cycle. As the gap between their wages and their husbands' grew, it made more sense for the men's work to take precedence and for the women to assume more responsibility for the kids. The problem was particularly acute for those like Jan, whose professions made the greatest demands on them at the peak of their child-rearing years. Eldie Acheson, who developed the first maternity policy at Ropes and Gray, watched female colleagues going crazy trying to time their babies just so: " 'Well, let's see, I can't do it in the first three years because I'm brand-new; but I can't do it in my fifth, sixth, or seventh years, because that's when I'm being assessed for partnership.' It leaves a ridiculously tiny window. It ought to be safe for a professional to have a baby anytime." (For some it is: Hillary Clinton was thirty-two and pregnant when she became the first woman to make partner in a major Little Rock firm. She was also the First Lady of Arkansas, which no doubt helped her colleagues overcome their doubts.) Thirty years after these women entered the workforce, having children still makes it harder to advance: In 1998, while just 5 percent of executive men had no kids, 37 percent of executive women were childless.

Many in Hillary Clinton's class have enjoyed what Elizabeth Tracy Hayes, '69, described as the "advantages" of flexible or part-time work— "such as a sub-living wage, and no benefits or promotions." At Ropes and Gray, says Eldie Acheson, "women were definitely at risk raising questions on maternity and family-leave policy during their interview." Though there were two women partners at the firm who were married with children, "they were making it happen by virtue of their personalities and their relationship with the boss. But it shouldn't be something each woman has to work out for herself." When drafting the law firm's maternity policy, Eldie recalls, "we had fights over the tone. They wanted something that seemed less encouraging, more dour." And even when the policies are in place, says Eldie, "it's only a tenth of the battle. You're still dealing with evaluations, and the one thing the boss always remembers is when that associate was out. That inevitably hits women hardest. There's still the expectation that it is the wife who will produce the flexibility, especially at the last minute. If the husband has to, there's lots of slamming of stuff into briefcases, an attitude that it's a management failure on her part, and, afterward, a great sense of heroics on his part. There's still the operating assumption that the husband is more important on the work front and less good at home."

Perceiving the double bind—that good mothers are deemed bad bets for employers, and good workers are deemed rotten mothers—Mary Catherine Bateson proposed in *Composing a Life* the possibility that motherhood and work might enhance each other, offering "a different clarity of vision, one sensitive to ecological complexity, the larger whole." Biopsychologist Martha McClintock, who gave birth to Ben in 1986 and adopted Julia in 1993, describes having children "as so profoundly important that it's beyond words. It's the most important thing. Before I had my children, I felt the strangest thing, as if I had no arms. I felt this metaphor viscerally. Now, with the kids, I feel whole. My arms are full. In fact, my life is full to the point of overflowing. It's too much. But choosing between a life that's too empty or too full—that's a no-brainer." Her graduate students describe her as tireless, but also as committed to going home for dinner with the kids and happy if they do the same. "I actually think having children has allowed me to do better work," says Martha, "because they're such a source of joy and fun that you have the energy to be creative and flexible."

Satisfactory accommodations of work and home are not rare in the class of '69, though they have often taken some time to discover or devise. Jan Piercy's first marriage at twenty-four to an older man who was "very steady and certain in his convictions and direction," brought her a measure of security after her mother's stroke. But her husband's encouragement and faith in Jan's abilities coexisted with what she calls subtle acts of sabotage: When Jan was working on the McGovern campaign, her husband planned their vacation in France—before Election Day. "Like a lot of men," says Jan, "he valued equal partnerships in the abstract but had a history which didn't equip him to practice that."

After a divorce and years alone, nearly forty and "in terrible travail over the biological clock," Jan met Glen. They married and she was a mother by age forty-one, thrilled and terrified both. "In your twenties and thirties, people expect that you could become a parent and that will change you. But when you're forty, people's expectations of you are fixed and you're at a point in your career of more responsibility and your life is organized around work. It's the professional spurt years." Though she was thoroughly satisfied at Shorebank—"I'd finally found my life's work"—Jan could not find a way to limit the job's time demands and felt terrible conflict at her long absences from her daughter. She finally left for the MacArthur Foundation and more flexible hours, but gave up that flexibility again when she joined the Clinton transition team and took her position at the World Bank.

Jan's second marriage has supported her in all the ways her first failed her. It was her husband who pressed her to seize the rare opportunity afforded by her friends' ascendance to the White House, though he had to make immense accommodations. Glen stayed in Chicago with their daughter, Lissa, while Jan commuted to the capital, uncertain whether she would stay in the administration; she did not feel well suited to the White House's "ugly undertow."

Finally, after several months of her equivocations, Glen packed a U-Haul and moved the family to D.C. "My husband loved what he was doing in his own law practice and managing properties, and left that behind to support what I was doing. It has not been easy or particularly fulfilling for him, and I've thought more than once, Wow, this is what women have always done. I don't like seeing what it costs Glen, but you do it sometimes for a limited time. And I think Lissa has come out way ahead. She has more than most kids of her father, who loves her and believes in her so totally. She and I get to have complicated conversations about what it means to be a woman; when I travel, I tell her I don't want to be away from her, and she says, 'You have to, Mommy. It's your job.' We both tell her, 'What you will be is inside you. Listen to your own desires, and resist others of us wanting you to be things you may not be.' "

While Jan and I were talking one afternoon in her office, Spain's ambassador to the United States called, hoping to reschedule a meeting to Friday or Saturday morning. Jan told him that Saturday would require juggling on the home front, and "since it's easier to negotiate with almost anyone other than a five-and-a-half-year-old, I'll try to change Friday instead." She hung up the phone, apparently still slightly stunned that such calls were everyday fare. "I am the same person, so I have to laugh at how, overnight, it's become so easy to make things happen. Things I could only think about before I now have the standing to do."

Jan has used her standing to make children a more acceptable intrusion at work. "With colleagues I know it won't annoy—and I think people without children have a right to be annoyed; you have to understand who you can do it with—I will blend the two and work around the edges." When a high-ranking Treasury official dropped by, the women discussed their kids' after-school programs and Halloween. "At seven o'clock this morning I was still in bed with Lissa coloring beside me. I was talking on the phone to my deputy, and at one point I said, 'No, you can't,' and he said, 'Oh, you don't think I should raise this?' and I said, 'Oh no, I was talking to my daughter.' I've brought Lissa to the office with me. You've got to create paths somehow."

Having produced a son that *Sports Illustrated* has called "a cross between Michael Jordan and Mother Teresa," Janet McDonald Hill has become a public paragon of working motherhood. The cover story in *Essence* magazine on Grant, a superstar with the Detroit Pistons, began: "Janet and Calvin Hill did something right."

Janet was a senior at Wellesley when she met Calvin, an honors student in history and star running back at Yale, at a party at Harvard after the Ivy League championship game. Janet was one of the few black girls at the postgame mixer. She was leaning awkwardly against the wall "trying to figure out what to do with my arms" when Cal, who had just been recruited by the Dallas Cowboys, walked into the room. "Every head turned," she remembers, "as if a spotlight had switched on." Janet didn't know that Cal had been injured in the game: In a fall, he'd badly split his tongue. Though nervousness churned her stomach as he crossed the room to ask her to dance, her flutterings ceased the moment he opened his mouth: All he could manage was inarticulate mumbling. To the amazement of everyone looking on, Janet coolly turned him down. He called a month later, mostly to prove, Janet says, that he could in fact speak.

For two years, the couple dated long distance while Janet got a

Lonny and David Higgins set sail aboard the *Deliverance*, which served as both nursery for their two small children and floating medical clinic. (*Courtesy of Ilona Laszlo Higgins*)

Lonny and David celebrated her fortieth birthday at midnight on Arno Atoll in the Marshall Islands when the women attending Lonny's health clinic woke them up bearing gifts of shells and basketry. (*Courtesy of Ilona Laszlo Higgins*)

Lonny's youngest son, Tucker, was born in 1996 when Lonny was almost fifty years old. (*Courtesy of Ilona Laszlo Higgins*)

Hillary Rodham, 1969. Her impassioned calls to political activism were a counterpoint to ads in the *Wellesley News* that urged women to "Protest boxy suits!" and "Protest big ugly shoes!" (*Lee Balterman, courtesy of* Life *Magazine and* Time Warner, Inc.)

RIGHT: Kathleen Smith married Roger Ruckman on August 9, 1969. Her mother had warned her against going to Wellesley, since "a smart girl would scare boys off." (*Courtesy of Kathleen Smith Ruckman*)

BELOW: Rob, Karen, Stephen, and Jonathan Ruckman, Kathy's "string quartet." As a full-time stay-at-home mom, Kathy found herself in a distinct minority among her Wellesley classmates. (*Courtesy of Kathleen Smith Ruckman*)

Roger and Kathy Ruckman in July 1998. Kathy and her husband joked that "I should go to my twenty-fifth [Wellesley] reunion barefoot and pregnant with him following me around with a whip." (*Courtesy of Kathleen Smith Ruckman*)

ABOVE: Thanksgiving with the Young family in Lynnfield, Massachusetts, circa 1957. (*Courtesy of Nancy Young*)

BELOW: Nancy Young's self-portrait in 1970 at age twenty-two. She described Wellesley as "the worst four years of my life." She felt scorned as a "scholarship girl" by upper-class princesses obsessed with maids, bridge, and the perfect Villager blouse. (*Courtesy of Nancy Young*)

In 1998, at age fifty, Nancy graduated from Boston College's School of Social Work. Her battle with cancer has sparked a spiritual search. (*Courtesy of Nancy Young*)

Matilda Williams in 1992, during her years as a Buddhist nun in Thailand. Matilda understood that the nuns regarded having one's picture taken with a fully opened lotus as arrogant, because it implies one has achieved complete enlightenment. (*Courtesy of Matilda Williams*)

RIGHT: Nancy Wanderer (left), all-American girl, playing "Curly" in *Oklahoma!* in 1960. (*Courtesy of Nancy Wanderer*)

BELOW: Nancy as a high school senior in 1964. She beat out Hillary Rodham as representative to the National Student Association when they were juniors, had a storybook wedding by the end of 1968, and shortly thereafter became the class's youngest mother. (*Courtesy of Nancy Wanderer*)

Nancy and her partner, Susan, in 1993, the "love of her life." (*Courtesy of Nancy Wanderer*)

Dorothy Devine at her wedding to Daniel Gilbarg. Dorothy was engaged in the fall of 1968 and was married by January 1969—a "ring by spring." (*Courtesy of Dorothy Devine*)

ABOVE: By the winter of 1969, Dorothy was cutting cane as a political activist in Cuba. (*Courtesy of Dorothy Devine*)

RIGHT: Dorothy being crowned with blessings and laurel at a recent Goddess Group meeting. (*Courtesy of Dorothy Devine*)

Alison's adult life has been consumed with caregiving for her children and in-laws and battling her own ill health. (*Courtesy of Alison Campbell Swain*)

Alison "Snowy" Campbell (left) at her debutante ball; she later turned down *Glamour*'s invitation to be featured as a deb of the year, citing her grandmother's rule that "a lady is in the paper only when she is born, when she marries, and when she dies." She spent her youth among Rockefellers and Bouviers. (*Courtesy of Alison Campbell Swain*)

ABOVE: Kris Olson's wedding shower for her marriage to Jeff Rogers was attended by Mrs. Spiro T. Agnew, Mrs. George Bush, Mrs. John Connolly, Mrs. John Ehrlichman, Mrs. H. R. Haldeman, Mrs. John Mitchell, Mrs. Elliot Richardson, Mrs. George Romney, and Mrs. George Shultz. (*Courtesy of Kris Olson*)

LEFT: Kris with Hillary and Bill Clinton in 1993. Kris was appointed by President Clinton as the first woman U.S. attorney in Oregon. (*Courtesy of Kris Olson*)

master's in math at the University of Chicago and Calvin attended
Perkins Theological Seminary—and also made Rookie of the Year with
the Cowboys and the cover of *Time* magazine. In 1971, they were married
by the black Catholic bishop of New Orleans before four hundred
guests, including Cowboys' quarterback Roger Staubach; Janet wore a
floor-length white gown and was attended by six bridesmaids. Two days
later, she started teaching public school. She quit after a year, twenty-
three and pregnant, and stayed home with Grant for the next four years,
grateful for an option that her own working mother had never had. "I
could only do it because of Cal's income. I didn't love teaching; frankly,
saying I wanted to stay home with my kid was an out." When Calvin was
traded to the Washington Redskins, the family moved to Virginia and
Janet resumed work, doing research for the Pentagon before launching
her consulting firm.

As the young wife of a famous man, Janet learned early and well what
Hillary Clinton learned late and imperfectly: how to polish her surface—
her public persona—to such a high sheen as to be impenetrable. Janet
presents such a practiced package that the glare of publicity merely
glances off, lending her a brilliant glamor but exposing nothing beyond
what she wishes to expose. The famous Janet Hill is therefore, paradoxi-
cally, the most private of all of her classmates. Far from blurting confessions, she reveals only as much as she chooses; her stories and aphorisms
have the ring of tales told many times.

Even as she has secured her privacy, however, Janet has also refused
the segregated existence she lived as a child, although now her family
would be the ones in the "big house" sheltered by the walls of privilege.
Though Calvin was making lots of money, Janet insisted that they raise
Grant in an ordinary suburban tract home. When Cal moved to Cleve-
land to play for the Browns, Janet stayed behind so as not to disrupt her
career ("I was not going to be Mrs. Football Player, polishing the tro-
phies") and to keep Grant in public school. Far from spoiling her precocious son, whose athletic gifts were revealed early, she was as strict as her
own mother had been. "When I was a kid, there were places I couldn't
go. I couldn't talk on the phone till my homework was finished; I always
had a bedtime, and I was punished if I broke the rules. I raised Grant the
same way. He had curfews when he was six feet five and a junior in high
school." John Nelson, a Yale classmate of Calvin's who married Janet's

Wellesley classmate Kim Ballard, lived a block from the Hills when Grant was in high school. Nelson recalls a summer evening, just past sundown, when he heard a knock at the door. When he opened it, he found on his front step an already towering fourteen-year-old Grant. "Hi," Grant said. "Can you give me a ride home? My mother won't let me walk home after dark."

Like Janet's father, it was Calvin who played the more tenderhearted role in his son's life. Separated from Grant for most of his elementary school years, Calvin "missed the mundane things I got to do with Grant," says Janet, "like driving the soccer team to Annapolis or listening to slide-trombone lessons. That made it harder for him later, when Grant left the nest. His apron strings were stronger." Janet, who felt close to her son "no matter where we each were in the world," found it easier to be away. When she had to work twelve-hour days or travel for weeks at a time for the Pentagon or her consulting firm, she would call Grant every day after school and "have the same conversation a mom at home would have." She suffered little guilt over her absences, not only because "Cal made accommodations for my life and work as often as I made them for his," but also because she remembered her mother's work life without resentment and believed her own work just as worthy. "I'm proud of Cal and Grant's careers. I'm also proud of my own."

Neither did Janet, who both owns her own consulting firm and sits on the boards of numerous corporations and Duke's business school, rely for her sense of success on the reflected glory of her husband and son. When sportswriters ignored her, "writing about Grant as if he were his father's immaculate conception, as though he'd sprung full-blown from Calvin's head," she reminded herself of the lesson of her childhood, a lesson many of her classmates would struggle to learn later, as they attempted to wrestle free from confining social expectations: that self-pride does not depend on the world's admiration or fail with its disregard or contempt. "I never much cared if *Sports Illustrated* knew what my contribution was. I knew, and that was enough." It is a lesson she now repeats to her son as his fame grows, warning him not to get hooked on it or succumb to its temptations. "I tell Grant not to believe too much of his press, even when it's good. I also tell him that I don't respect all athletes simply because they're famous; I think talking trash or having sex with seventy-five women does not make a man; it diminishes him. I have advised him to use his father, who's always been respectful to women, as a model."

The idea of role models—so central to Janet's professional concern for the "talented tenth," and yet another variation on the idea that an individual's personal behavior can have public meaning—is equally strong in her prescription for parenting. She admires "the picture my husband and son offer the world, of strong black men and strong black male role models." She believes more strongly still in "cross-gender" and "cross-race" role modeling. "My father, my husband, my son, my business partner—all have encouraged me and shaped me. All successful women, I believe, have been influenced by men. And all successful men have been influenced by women. I like to think I'm a role model not only for my son but for lots of young men—especially white men. When I hear my classmates worry about what kind of models we provide our daughters, I find myself hoping that they worry just as much about the model we offer our sons. I hope our sons see in us women they can look up to, so that when they grow up they will do better than their fathers at creating respectful relationships with women at work and at home. I've encouraged my son to find someone to love who has her own commitments, who does not define herself through him."

Though Grant is as polished as his mom, his assimilation of her moral lessons seems genuine. Shortly after becoming NBA Rookie of the Year, he launched (with Fila, with which he signed an endorsement contract worth $80 million) the Grant Hill Summer Youth Basketball and Literacy Program for boys and girls, prompting *Gentleman's Quarterly* to dub him, on its cover, "the savior" of sports. *Esquire* also put him on the cover, and lauded his elegance: "He calls coaches sir and does no big mouth or dances." *Sports Illustrated* deemed him "wise beyond his years . . . a counterpoint to the spoiled behavior of some of the league's other young players. . . . He has gracefully borne the burden of being perceived as Mr. Virtue."

Grant, a three-time All-Star and 1996 Olympic team player, has often publicly credited his parents for "teaching me right from wrong." At his 1994 farewell banquet at Duke, where he led his team to three national championships, he devoted his brief speech before thousands of fans to righting the misperception that his mother's achievements were all by association. "It's about time, Mom," he began, "you get the credit you deserve. No more wife of, no more mother of, and especially no more classmate of. Tonight I am the son of Janet and Calvin Hill." When his sports career ends, he says, he would like to join Janet's company. "I respect my mom's spirit and activism. She taught me not to limit myself. She taught me about love and loyal friendship. My dad and I compete for the spotlight. She can live without it. She knows she's the real backbone. Really, the thing I admire most in my dad is his choice of my mom. If I could find someone like her, I'd be fortunate." The question of whether he is a feminist evoked a shy grin. "Yeah, I suppose I am. Mom taught me to respect women because she commands so much respect. I believe the people who really change the world are people like Janet Hill, who work at it every day." Again, he flashed his trademark multimillion-dollar smile. "She's got it goin' on. If you're gonna step to her, you better be right; don't be half-stepping. We can call her Janet X."

There is one member of the Wellesley class of '69 who has managed a nearly perfect integration of home and work, of her private and public lives. In an era when the moral life is increasingly defined as a matter of honoring "family values," Dr. Lonny Laszlo Higgins has consistently honored responsibilities of kinship that go far beyond simple blood ties.

During the summer of her junior year at Wellesley, Lonny worked with the Frontier Nursing Service in Appalachia, riding horseback with midwives to help with home births in the coal-mining country around Hazard, Kentucky, and assisting Mary Will, a woman doctor whose work among the poor made a lasting impression on Lonny. While in medical school at Tufts, Lonny married David Higgins, a handsome and wealthy Harvard-educated lawyer who had rowed in the 1968 Olympics and served in the Navy Reserves. She was a fourth-year medical student when she gave birth to their son, David, and a resident when their daughter, Jessica, was born. Whenever she was on call, David would bring the babies to the hospital so Lonny could nurse them, and the whole family would sleep together there.

Offered a job in obstetrics, Lonny set about transforming the hospital's "cold, antiseptic" approach to delivering babies, which she felt robbed a woman of the full experience of birthing and distressed the baby, who was typically whisked abruptly away and not returned to the mother for many hours. Lonny became one of the first obstetricians in America to use the Leboyer birthing technique—underwater delivery, in dimmed light, with the baby left at its mother's breast. The method received a great burst of publicity when Lonny was made the subject of a documentary on PBS.

The women's health movement was then just beginning to emerge, helped along by a groundbreaking book developed in a 1969 workshop in Boston. *Our Bodies, Ourselves* advocated self-care and natural remedies, taught women how to look at their own cervix and masturbate, inspired thousands of women's health groups, and—millions of copies and several editions later—is still in print. More change followed, for both women practitioners and patients. In 1971, pressure by women led to congressional hearings on the high-dosage birth control pills then routinely prescribed and the passage of legislation requiring that patients be advised of such side effects as thrombosis and embolism; the same year the Women's Equity Action League successfully sued the nation's medical schools for sex discrimination, forcing them to open their doors to many more female students. In 1972, Barbara Seaman's *Free and Female* became a best-seller, challenging the practice of having "women shaved, humiliated, drugged, painted and stuck up in stirrups to deliver their babies." Theologian Mary Daly's 1978 *Gyn/Ecology* targeted paternalistic doctors who treated women as children. Drawing on French eco-feminism, she linked men with everything technological and artificial, from anesthetics to polyester; because they were alienated from nature, Daly argued, men could not lead a revolution against its destruction. It was women, with their deep connection to the earth, who would recover natural childbirth and foods and remedies, replace their mother's Valium with calming herbs, and dump their damaging IUDs and hormones in favor of barrier techniques, like the diaphragm brandished by the heroine of *Fear of Flying*, Isadora Wing.

Lonny did not remain in conventional medicine very long. When her son was two, she was working a hundred-hour week. "I didn't want a whole period of time to go by without my knowing him; I needed to feel my influence exerted on him. And David and I were barely seeing each other." The year after Jessica was born, in 1979, the couple chose a radical solution: Selling their house in Boston for $60,000, they bought a wrecked ninety-six-foot schooner that David fixed up and, with their six-year-old and one-year-old, set out for what they thought would be an eighteen-month journey around the world.

Their shipboard life ended up lasting more than a decade. They spent the first five years sailing through island groups in Central America, French Polynesia, Tonga, Fiji, and Papua New Guinea; with a nurse and donated emergency supplies aboard, Lonny was able to provide medical care along the way. She soon realized, however, that she was potentially doing more harm than good. "We'd come in on this magic ship with medicine and sutures and perform miracles, and then we'd leave, and all we'd done was undermine the local health workers." They shifted their focus to education, training locals in primary maternal and child care.

Educating their children and sleeping aboard ship was, Lonny says, like "camping out with them for years." The family's adventures were occasionally terrifying. Twice their daughter went overboard—at age two and, again, at four in Tonga. In Fiji, David and Lonny had to swim out together into the surf to rescue a drowning mother and son. In Papua, New Guinea, Lonny took it into her head to go after pirates making off with a stolen ship; when her Boston Whaler struck a submerged rock and began sinking, it was only Lonny's brazen bluffings, in David's telling, that saved them from doom.

In 1983, the Higginses' journey came to a seven-year halt in the tiny coral atolls of the Marshall Islands in Micronesia. In this tropical land of abundance, they found four of every one hundred children dying of dehydration and malnutrition, a mortality rate four times that in the U.S., though the islands had been an American protectorate since the end of the Second World War. The U.S. still had responsibility for health, education, and economic development, which it fulfilled in two ways: by providing flights off-island for those suffering from radiation illness in the wake of the sixty-six American nuclear tests conducted on Bikini atoll, and by importing foods. The food imports' main effect on the islands was to undermine local agriculture and fisheries and erode the indigenous diet; high in fat, salt, and refined sugar, the imported food brought an increased incidence of diabetes and high blood pressure. Breast-feeding was abandoned in response to Western advertising; Lonny regularly saw children with malformed teeth, the result of suckling on Coke. Social traditions also broke down. The islands had the world's highest suicide rate among adolescent boys: one in four tried, and one in ten succeeded.

After discussions with the Marshallese health ministry and community leaders on how they might help islanders scattered across a million square miles of ocean, Lonny and David created the Marimed Foundation and raised $4 million to build a tall ship, a three-masted topsail schooner, with a shipboard laboratory and X-ray facilities, that could sail through the Outer Islands full-time to train and support local public health workers. The Marshallese children christened the majestic vessel with her big-bellied sails the *Tole Mour*—"Gift of Health and Life." In the four years it took to build the ship, Lonny and her team flew to many of the islands, most of which were without electricity or clean water.

They sterilized instruments in water heated over a coconut-husk fire, and Lonny did pelvic exams with a flashlight in her mouth—on women who were stretched across school desks with their feet in buckets. When the time came for training, Lonny herself stretched across desks and let island women do pelvics on her, again and again. To treat prostitutes infected with syphilis, who were too ashamed to come for treatment, Lonny would go to the discotheques, take the women into the ladies' room, and give them shots.

Lonny's kids often helped—weighing babies, assisting with immunization—all the time living barefoot and learning the language and ways of the Marshallese. Lonny also learned, developing great respect for traditional healers. "If someone was sick, they would ask, 'Did he steal his neighbor's fish? Was there a curse put on him?' I could give the guy ampicillin, but he wouldn't get better until he made amends. I came to understand that you don't come in as the great white fixer but as the guest of the healer, to learn: What are the poultices that draw out infection? What are the uses of taro and breadfruit? I learned that you have to be a listener, notice patients' body language, what's in their eyes. The body tells a story, which I would try to frame for them in a way that matched their reality. I would tell them, 'If the lungs sound like water crashing on a reef, that's the sound of pneumonia.' "

By the time the Higginses launched the *Tole Mour*, dispensaries were in place and locals had been trained on most of the islands. In another few years, the system was so self-sufficient that Lonny and the *Tole Mour* were not needed at all. In anticipation of that time, Lonny and David had begun sailing between the Marshall Islands with troubled adolescents. Though the kids' grandfathers had been masters of the sea, those seafaring skills had been mostly lost to younger generations. "By sailing on the *Tole Mour*, the kids reconnected with those traditions and returned home heroes, with a great sense of honor," Lonny says.

That experiment became the basis of the Marimed Foundation's on-

going program in Hawaii for adjudicated youth. As an alternative to incarceration, teens who have been convicted of crimes, often violent
ones, can spend six months aboard the *Tole Mour*. They sail the Pacific
and sometimes through the Panama Canal, learning the complex skills
needed to take such a ship through fierce storms and endless calms.
They stand night watch, taking full responsibility for the ship's safety,
and sleep entrusting the same to their shipmates. "Structure and duty
are easier to accept when imposed by nature," says David. "The sea becomes a metaphor for the kids' struggle to weave their way through
chaos and powerlessness. The journey is a rite of passage into adult life.
Most of these kids were abandoned or abused. They'd been handcuffed
and chained, but until they met our staff, a lot of them hadn't been held
much in human arms. Half are parents themselves, but for many it
was the first time they felt they belonged to something, that they had
a family." Though a single act of violence lands a kid immediately in jail,
all make dire mistakes, again and again. "You just keep loving them
through it," David says.

Recently, Lonny and David have brought the ship closer to home,
sailing mostly among the Hawaiian islands, sometimes bringing a kid's
family along for a day sail. Again, Lonny's holistic principles are at work:
"You need to work with the family system; you can't just change the
child." To prevent recidivism, Lonny and David also created Kailana, a
residential center on Oahu for the kids returning from their sea journey
and for other kids not able to live at home. At Kailana the teen residents
learn to build their own little wooden nutshell prams and sail them in
the turquoise bay. "They develop manual skills and build a sense of who
they are," says Lonny. "There's a kind of therapy in physical labor." The
boats are launched with native rituals and ukulele songs under palm
trees and cloud-draped mountains; punk boys with tattoos sing songs
they wrote of returning to "my people's past, a time of happiness."
Lonny is Kailana's medical director. In a session for the girls on safe sex,
she acts out the womb—her arms, fallopian tubes holding ovaries; her
language blunt and slangy: "I haven't found a penis yet that's totally
healthy."

In 1991, Lonny founded a women's health center near their home on
Oahu and returned to obstetrics, putting into practice the spiritual understanding of illness she learned from the Marshallese. "The body has

cellular memory; emotional pain is somatized," she says. "If a girl has painful periods, I ask, 'What does it mean in your family to become a woman, to draw the attention of men?' With fibrocystic breast disease, I consider the breast a symbol of nurturance. I still do D and Cs, of course, and Pap smears to rule out cancers. But I've found that hormone imbalances can be redressed by naturopaths, using things like creams made from yams. Sometimes I prescribe ayurvedics, Tai Chi, meditation, or acupuncture. You'd be surprised how much less medication you use."

Much of her practice is with teens: "I see fourteen-year-old pregnant girls with their cell phones and beepers and the hyped look of methamphetamine; I took enough speed to get through exams to recognize it. I tell them that if they'll admit they're using, I'll put them in detox. If not, I'll randomly screen their urine, and if they don't stay off drugs, I won't see them."

Lonny's approach to delivering babies has deep echoes of the eco-feminism to which so many women in her Wellesley class subscribe. "I help my ladies deal with their fear of giving birth by telling them, 'You are three women. You are the ancient woman, the Clan of the Cave Bear Woman, with the power of millions of years of success, a vessel superbly designed to carry on the species, with a purpose for every bone and muscle. You are also the modern woman, with all her intellectual preparation. And you are the infant who remembers your own birth.' You'll see a woman get claustrophobic and panicky during delivery, as if she were the passenger. I tell them you can rock that baby you were, tell it 'you're safe,' and both babies will get the message. The cervix just opens. The Marshallese don't push a baby out, they let it out; only at crowning do they begin to grunt. They're matrilineal, and celebrate giving birth as a rite of womanhood. We've lost that reverence for who we are at each life stage. A woman never gets another chance to feel herself that real. Birthing is a primal rite of passage, to be revered and shared; my son was there for the birth of his sister."

Lonny also shares her classmates' belief in a woman's way of healing. With her patients, she is intimate, warm, and physical. "Men are excellent technicians, but a lot are prima donnas; there's lots of emotional arrest. A woman brings a different kind of compassion. I've given birth; I can relate to the stresses of motherhood and menopause. It's not unfem-

inine to share tears. I have an easier time holding a patient than a male
doctor would. And a woman is more comfortable educating and sharing
responsibility with the patient; she hasn't such a need to exercise control."

Lonny's success at integrating work and family is to a great degree a
consequence of the success of her marriage. David's mother was a professional, which perhaps better prepared him for a professional wife. He
and Lonny also avoided all possibility of competition with one another.
Each had clear, separate domains of authority. David was financier and
ship captain. Lonny did what she calls "the traditional woman's work"
as mother, teacher, and healer, and "yielded to his command in public."
Temperamentally, too, David and Lonny seem ideal complements.
Lonny has a great gift for commotion; when she is inflamed by some
cause or memory, her pale blue eyes deepen with a fierce intensity and
she speaks almost too quickly to keep up with, hyperalert and pacing like
a high-strung thoroughbred with long athletic strides. She is a great jolt-
ing pleasure to be with, and exhausting as fireworks. She is both candid
and inaccessible to the extreme. Her rush seems at moments a rush past
something, some fear or pain that would paralyze her if she slowed for it.
David, by contrast, is endlessly calm, a steadying ballast in her life.
Thirty years after he first began pursuing Lonny, he seems still fascinated
by her; he was happy all those years aboard ship, he says, to have been
the conveyance carrying Lonny to her work.

More than such particularities, the success of Lonny's experiment
seems a consequence of her having broken open the nuclear family. The
Higginses have never been shuttered in safety, seeking in their small clan
all companionship and intimacy and mutual obligation. Rather, they
have always lived with some larger definition of kinship. At sea, there
were the crew and medical team; aboard ship, as in a frontier town, all
depended on one another for their very survival. In their house on Oahu
and, since 1998, on the Big Island, there is Dana, a young woman who
fled a marriage to a violent drug dealer and, with her three boys, found
shelter with the Higginses. Dana earns their keep by managing the
house—overseeing repairs, paying bills, shopping, and cleaning. There
is also a foster son, a kid of desperately troubled parents, who has been
in and out of jail and substance abuse programs since the age of thirteen.
For a time, there was a second foster child: After Lonny delivered the
baby of a homeless schizophrenic woman and Child Protective Services

insisted on removing the child, Lonny herself became the infant's foster parent, so the mother could make daily visits. Lonny's work frequently places her in such exceptionally intimate relations with strangers. Historically, it has always been women who helped other women give birth. In that role, Lonny and her fellow midwives have crossed in and out between the public and the private: learning secrets of the family and carrying knowledge among women—of erotic pleasures, fertility, contraception, abortion.

It's not mysterious what makes it work for these women—for Janet Hill or Lonny Higgins or the numerous other working mothers in the class who are faring just fine. All have in common, first, great flexibility in their work, in terms of both the time and the place in which it gets done, a flexibility often won by educating themselves into a high degree of leverage or by going into business for themselves, as 30 percent of the class has done. All also have husbands with flexible jobs who are themselves deeply engaged in child rearing. All have money. All have relatively few children, and most had those children either early or late (though for those who married young, divorce was also more likely). Most important, all have fairly porous boundaries as to who counts as family and where children belong. Their experience contravenes the much-advertised conclusion by Judith Wallerstein in her 1995 study of "the good marriage" that the dual-earner couple—pulled apart by competitiveness, loneliness, and stress—is "frighteningly fragile."

Working motherhood has been much harder, of course, for those women in the class who have not had flexibility or money or engaged husbands or who have had to contend with divorce or stepchildren or illness.

Ann Landsberg married shortly after graduating from Wellesley, "because I was frantic to get settled and didn't think I'd get another shot, and had found someone who seemed a good match: John had this long Yankee pedigree, everyone from the best colleges." They settled in Somerville, a faded working-class suburb of Boston, and Ann began working with poor children in the community mental health center. When her son, Jamie, was born in 1979, she went to a half-time work schedule in order to be home after day care and school. When Jamie was four, Ann's marriage came to an end.

"My husband had been ambivalent about getting married, and after thirteen years he still was. Then he read a book about people needing their own space, and took it to heart. We had a lot of marriage counseling. But there was no hope of creating either the sort of relationship I wanted from him or the kind of nonrelationship he wanted from me. We did almost nothing together, except for a lot of unilateral fighting. I was forever going after him trying to engage him; when I quit, there was nothing happening at all. After a while, all James was seeing was fighting. All I heard from my parents was, 'Think about the child; think about the child.' I did, and decided he did not need to grow up in a house with a woman who was a shrew and a man who was a patsy. And I could not continue my slow death. John and I were not even like roommates, there was so much tension. It was so awful. I finally decided an intact family of any sort is not better than none."

Remarried in 1984 to a man she had met in church, Ann stumbled on the effort to mix two families. "In the blush of first romance, everything seemed fine. Tim was just a boyfriend, and Jamie's father was four blocks away. For a while, they mostly avoided each other. But the fact was, Tim and Jamie did not like each other for a long time and I was in high denial about that. I kept feeling divided loyalties. When I would get on a tirade at Jamie, Tim would join in: 'You heard what your mother said,' and my fury would turn on him. I did not need a cheering section. Then I got pregnant. I was thirty-eight. I worried what it would do to Jamie to have a sibling with a live-in father. My attachment to Jamie knew no limits, and I felt treasonous. We also had two days a week with no kid, when James was at his dad's house, and I thought, Oh my God, *it* is going to be here every day. Did we really want to start over again, voluntarily throw ourselves into chaos? But an abortion would have devastated me. I would still be trying to get over it. Finally, we just threw ourselves into the joy of it. This is a much better marriage, even though Tim and I have radically different backgrounds; his dad was a traveling salesman, and he was the first in his family to go to college. But our marriage works, because he is quite selfless, and I'm a lot less needy, and we were best friends before we were lovers, and because both of us had trashed a marriage and knew what we didn't want to do again—that we wanted to deal with difficulties and not just try to bury them."

Ann's second marriage has been greatly tested. At age four, their son, Max, was diagnosed with Tourette's syndrome. "I knew something was wrong much earlier, but I was patronized by the medical profession for two years. They wouldn't even say, 'Yes, something's wrong, but we don't know what it is.' When they finally made the diagnosis, I wanted to say, 'You assholes, I told you my kid had a genetic disorder. What, am I only the child's mother with a graduate degree in child development; should I know anything?' We went through a great period of grief and stress. Sometimes still, it hits as if the first time. Then you weep until you're done weeping, pick up the laundry, and move on."

For more than a decade, Ann has worked as a mental health consultant for Head Start. She observes classes, advises teachers, and makes visits to homes and emergency shelters to talk to parents with toddlers, giving them the address of a food pantry or sitting on the floor to play with the babies and help parents understand their kids' development. It is a job faithful to her youthful idealism and to her generation's belief in the need for social involvement in family life. "The first mom I hooked up with had just been released from jail. This was the first time she'd been alone with her nine-month-old; they were in a room with three pieces of furniture, no toys, and a box of doughnuts, and she looked utterly lost."

When these children enter the Boston public schools, often classed as special-needs kids, Ann frequently acts as their advocate. She has been especially distressed, therefore, by another dilemma familiar to her classmates—the difficulty of keeping her own kids in public school. While these women were at Wellesley, many were deeply affected by Jonathan Kozol's *Death at an Early Age*, which exposed the damaging inequalities in public schools. A number volunteered at his storefront learning center, and most embraced the principle that well-educated parents ought to keep their kids in public schools and commit their own energies there. Ann had not been happy when her first husband insisted that Jamie attend private school. "It was all white and precious. I had one of the few non-Jaguars in the lot. It was the last place I wanted my kid." Because she worked for the public schools in the progressive suburb of Brookline, Ann was able to move Jamie there. "I was thrilled he could be part of a whole ragtag mix, with Cambodian and Costa Rican and black kids all bused in."

By the time Max was entering kindergarten, the Brookline schools were overenrolled; the budget had been cut; Ann was laid off, and Max could not get in. Though fearing it would be "a snake pit" for a kid with Tourette's, his parents saw little alternative but to send him into the notoriously troubled Boston public schools. Bright and eager, Max skipped a grade. But he hated school. "He wasn't getting what he needed intellectually. The homework was boring, and the atmosphere was smallminded and managerial: 'If you're noisy in line, you can't go to science class.' I understand it. They had too many kids with problems, and resources were strained way beyond capacity. They did their best, but that was not very good. Max was with kids with legitimate reasons to be off the wall—one kid's mother had been murdered and he was living in a group home. But it was an impossible place for him. He contaminates easily, and doesn't have brakes. He'd get set off and just keep going. I decided it's not fair: He's a sponge; he's fascinated; he's got a zest for life you can't imagine; and he's withering in this environment. None of the good stuff has a chance to blossom. It's so demoralized and hopeless." Ann's sense of defeat came through in a letter she wrote to her classmates. "Yesterday, Max's hard-won collection of trading cards was stolen by a classmate in the second Max was getting his jacket. Max was devastated. He could not comprehend how someone could be so mean, and he hopes the cards will be returned following his teacher's intervention. I am not so sure.

"The kids I work with professionally in Head Start and early intervention are not in public school yet, but they will be. They'll be sacrificed soon. Here I've been fighting for twenty years with Boston schools on behalf of kids that weren't mine; how ironic that my son would end up a special-needs kid in the very schools that never provided for all the others. In the end, I thought, I've got to pull this one out and save him, and I'm sorry we have to leave the others behind. Ideals and vision are a lot easier in the abstract. It's something else to sacrifice your child.

"The private school we picked is racially mixed and has the same social values we have; it's not all blond and blue-eyed Volvos. The kids learn their way around the city and how to use public services. They use the Boston Common as their playground, check out books from the public library, go to the YMCA for gym once a week, which all helps keep the tuition down, but also expresses a certain ethic—that we're like everybody else. They develop street smarts: This is how you cross the street; this is how you step over a drunk. That's important to me."

The school is also three blocks from Tim's office, which meant that for the first time in sixteen years, Ann stepped out of the role of parent on call. If Max gets sick, Tim goes to get him. "That's mind-blowing to me. I've always been the one to cancel a client because my kid fell off the swing and needed stitches. I've made uncountable compromises; nothing has ever looked elegant. Sometimes when I look at people like Eldie Acheson, I think I should have gone all the way one way instead of doing everything half-assed. For a time, it seemed like everywhere I turned a '69 grad was in my face—Hillary, Jan Piercy, Janet Hill. I turned on public TV one day and there's Alvia Wardlaw talking about a show she'd curated of African-American art. Tim came home, and I burst into tears. 'I can't stand it. I'm nothing. Look at all these women.' It was hard for me to say, 'Yes, me and my Maytag and my minivan and the dinner I threw together and my twenty-hour week of frustrating work is really good in the face of all this success and fame.' On the other hand, my heart aches for the children I work with. I see daily evidence of how we have failed them, how careless we've become with our human responsibilities. My work feeds my soul. We need the money, little as it is. And Tim thinks the world of what I do. So some days it doesn't feel like I've failed."

Mothers who work are frequently accused of selfishness, and rarely more harshly than they accuse themselves. "For all the talk about doing things for community and changing the world, we are pretty self-centered people," Betsy Griffith, a mother of two and also headmistress of Madeira School for Girls and author of a biography of Elizabeth Cady Stanton, said of herself and her classmates in Wellesley '69. "Those of us who have thought about and invested in careers, that's taken time away that other generations of women would have given to family."

But the charge of selfishness made against women who work outside the home rests on a narrow notion of moral responsibility. That there are larger duties as authentic as those to one's own family was part of the nation's founding ideology: John Adams argued that a virtuous republic required "a positive passion for the public good . . . superior to all private passions." Only in the late nineteenth century did an overriding commitment to the nuclear family come to be seen as the first of all moral obligations. With the triumph of that ideal came the repudiation of obligations to a larger brotherhood; as historian Stephanie Coontz writes, "family decency, duty and altruism became less a preparation for civic responsibility than a substitute." The reciprocal relation between family and society broke down: A man could now be ruthless and rapacious in his public life, as long as it was on behalf of his family, and society could deny families support and leave them to fend for themselves.

The larger duties can be honored, even by the mothers of children. It is simply a diversion to turn questions about the self, and the stepping beyond the self, into a matter of whether women work or stay at home.

CHAPTER SEVEN

Full-Time Moms

The women in the class whose lives most resemble their mothers'—those whose principal occupation has been child rearing—would seem to have had the most well-worn path to tread. But as the world changed around them, these women, too, have had to reconceive themselves: devising more conscious justifications, asserting the real autonomy of their choice, and struggling to find ways not to drain themselves entirely in caring for others or to burden their children with their own frustrated ambitions.

When Kathy Smith Ruckman's first baby was still nursing, she was urged by friends to give him a bottle and get out in the world. "I finally gave in. When Rob was nine months old, I decided to take a course, because I thought I should.

"I hated doing it. Something inside me just wouldn't let me leave my children. And I think mothers are having to cut that faucet off if they're high-powered career women and allow other people to do for their kids. I hear women say at eight weeks, 'I can't wait to get back to work and out of the house.' If that's how they feel, they should probably get out of the house. If whatever you're doing is making you unhappy, you're not going to be a good parent. I wouldn't condemn anyone for their choices. But I think such a mother misses a lot. When I see nannies pushing babies, I feel sorry for the mothers and for the kid, who needs someone who loves them all day long."

Though her own mother had been desperately bored with maternity, Kathy knew from a young age that she wanted to devote her life to children. "There probably haven't been too many people who wanted a baby more than me." Like her father, she is, seemingly by nature, maternal: warm and patient, gentle and confiding. In high school, she baby-sat at every opportunity. At Wellesley she majored in developmental psychology, and as a newlywed right out of college she taught elementary school until the first of her four children was born. Then, supported by her high-earning husband, Kathy stayed home.

It was an unusual choice for a woman of her generation: Less than 10 percent of her classmates have been full-time moms. But it satisfied Kathy's heart's desire and, she believes, also provided the best life for her children. It also became the platform on which she stands; though of all in her class Kathy would seem to have most turned away from the political and toward the personal, even she warmed to the role of being a public advocate for the choice of full-time devotion to one's children. "I am acutely aware that my lifestyle is a luxury, and becoming increasingly so in our economy," she wrote to me not long after we first met. "But unless I'd been forced by financial circumstances, I could never have left my kids with someone who didn't care that much about them. It may be right for the parents, but I don't believe it's right for the kids. People don't recognize how hard it is to be a parent, how much time it takes— not scheduled time, not just all the driving them around, but being there at the moment when they need you. Kids are not regular; they get sick at odd times, and have crises. It's a mistake to think they just need custodial care. It's all the little things that add up. Doing it all, as so many of my classmates do, means a frenetic life that leaves no room for quiet, for spiritual renewal. I believe that the most stable arrangement for children is a family with two parents, with one of them giving the kids lots of time and attention."

Kathy's work as a tutor at several Washington-area private schools only deepened her conviction that children whose parents both work are deprived. "I can see for the parents that public recognition would make you feel like somebody, feel important. But if you're in a career getting so much attention, you get increasingly absorbed in yourself. And parenting is 99 percent giving. The kids that I tutor are far from poor, but they are needy. I recently did a workshop on learning disabilities; they presented research showing that kids have noticeable deficits compared to a few decades ago. They're not reading or talking; they're in front of TV and computer screens or with nannies who don't speak English, and so even affluent kids are coming into school language-deprived. I've seen it as a tutor. Tutoring is popular because parents need you to do what they don't have time to do; they need you to be a surrogate parent. But people don't respect it. I hate more than anything the question at cocktail parties: 'So what do you do?' I answer: 'I am a mother to my children,' and get blank stares, from women and men. Look what we pay day-care workers and teachers. The whole business of being with children is undervalued; there's a sense that anyone can raise kids, that there are more important things to do."

Kathy's husband, Roger, has had a nearly all-consuming professional life. Absorbed first in training as a pediatric cardiologist and later with the dual demands of academics and medical practice, he has always worked long hours and come home exhausted. Kathy moved her growing family eight times in ten years for his career. Never in one place long enough to make friends, she felt isolated and often alone with all the responsibilities of children and home. She wouldn't hire household help, believing, somewhat ironically, that it would be a degrading job for whomever she hired. "It always felt like paying someone to clean my house would be like saying, 'I'm more valuable than you. You do this dirty work, and I'll go do something more important.' So it all fell to me: I would vacuum, iron Roger's shirts, fix whatever was broken, make the meals, clean up, deal with the babies. When we were first married I came home one day and Roger was vacuuming and I burst into tears. It was as if he was saying I couldn't handle it.

"Then, I realized it wasn't fair. I'd read Betty Friedan and I thought, 'These are his kids, too.' But by then it was too late. It turns out it's impossible to change someone. I went into marriage thinking I could tinker with Roger's personality; instead, I had to keep readjusting my expectations. Like his father, Roger came home from work expecting to relax. He'd been taught by his mother that kids were not his business. She told me, over and over, that the children should be in bed before he got home so he wouldn't be bothered by them. Of course, Roger married someone very different from his mother; I could see what Hillary was in for with Virginia Kelley. My mother-in-law is very old-fashioned and formal. Coming from such different backgrounds, Roger's and my values often clashed. Roger wanted the kids to conform to what his family believed. But because he abdicated, my values got transferred more loudly. We live casually. At her house, every meal is served on good china. At my house, I still use the unbreakable Corelle."

Kathy's life is hardly spartan: Her house in the rich suburb of Chevy Chase, Maryland, is huge; her kids are at private schools; she has the requisite car phone in her four-wheel-drive van. But she is determinedly neither gorgeous nor grand. Her home has a generic quality, pastel and orderly, with a few folksy touches like painted ducks on wooden panels winging across one wall. For dinner she serves frozen breaded chicken and string beans and nonfat, artificially sweetened ice cream. She offers sardonic commentary on some of her classmates' "perfect coiffures" and expensive clothes. "The thing I hate most about being a woman is being judged by your appearance. I am not interested in makeovers or in decorating the perfect home."

She is also adamantly not "the Phyllis Schlafly" of the class. "I'm not so unselfish that I've become nothing but my kids and husband. On Sundays, my sister makes meals for the whole week and freezes them; when she had her babies, each time before she went into the hospital, she spent weeks stocking the freezer. My kids can order pizza. I will not be a slave to them. I guess I'm in the middle on feminism and traditional roles. I feel like I've taken the best from both, rejecting housewifery while hanging on to what I consider important roles for women: time with my kids, involvement with schools and church and community. I think it's a mistake to turn women into men. If anything, I'd like to see women and men both find a balance, so that career success does not equal having others raise your children."

That her husband failed to find that balance has been for Kathy disappointing. "I think Roger's choice to go into academic medicine was a big mistake. It's terribly competitive; that's where the egos go, and it means not only practicing medicine but also doing teaching and research. When our kids were little, he was simply never home."

That absence turned out to have serious consequences. "When our daughter Karen was two, she was missing all her milestones. She was tiny, the size of a one-year-old, and just barely able to walk. And she was not getting any real help. At birth, her doctors had misdiagnosed the problem as a minor heart defect that would correct itself. I knew they had to be wrong; I was seeing this child really struggling. But they didn't look at her as a kid; they looked at her as a bunch of test results. Finally, they did open-heart surgery and discovered the defect was major. Here Roger was training in pediatric cardiology and his own daughter's heart problems were being overlooked. Because he wasn't home, he wasn't seeing what I was seeing, or maybe he didn't have the emotional energy to pay attention. It's not just him, of course—it's all of medicine. When I was delivering my fourth baby, they told me to go home; they said I was not in labor. They wouldn't listen to me even though I had given birth three times; then the baby was born within minutes. The doctors demonstrated that same deafness with Karen; I knew she was sick, but I was made to feel that I was a nervous mother, that I should go away.

"Off and on, I've been angry about my husband's absorption in his career. But he's now seeing what he has lost by not being involved with the kids. I got the better end of the deal. I don't envy him, and I would not wish his life on my children."

Roger is a tall, soft-spoken, somewhat awkward and formal man— formal even with his children. He believes his family arrangement has been close to ideal. "I would have liked to have done more, but there were lots of demands on my time. If you judge it in terms of my work environment, where there's virtually no flexibility, I've done everything I could to be supportive of my family. I also believe it's best that children be with their mother; there's a special attachment there. Men are just not as nurturing by nature. A mother's consistent nurturing gives children self-confidence, stimulation, trust, an ability to share intimate feelings.

"Kathy could have chosen any profession but valued the welfare of our kids, which I greatly admire. Our kids understand the hardships on both sides, the pressures on the sole breadwinner, the courage required of a woman to stay home in terms of her peer relations. Though I think even Kathy's Wellesley classmates may finally be coming to grips with limits, understanding that if you're trying to be at the top of your profession, a strong marriage and kids may not be doable."

"My kids probably haven't seen my work as being as important as Roger's," says Kathy. "Though it frustrates them that he comes home too tired to give, they know a doctor is what people respect. When my oldest son, Rob, changed majors at college, giving up his chance at medical school, his brother Jonathan, said, 'Well, what's he going to do if he's not a doctor, be a garbageman?' Somehow, the message had come through that those were the only choices. I want my kids to know that there are other choices, like being a teacher, which is wonderful if terribly undervalued. I don't think that serving the community even requires a profession or public life. For most of my married life, I have served the community as a volunteer. The more that kind of parental involvement dries up, the more schools are collapsing.

"I have demanded that my kids not put me down as a woman. They respect that I gave much and that it was a sacrifice in some ways, that I could have done other things. Life involves making choices where something goes by the wayside. What I got from them is unbelievable; they're wonderful people. But who knows what I could have done? I never experienced that other world—my few years teaching hadn't brought accolades or even much intellectual stimulation—so I've never really known what I missed."

Denied her own wish to study music as a girl, Kathy has raised, as she likes to say, a string quartet. All four of her children are accomplished musicians; they have played for U.S. presidents and won national awards. When she was not carpooling or tutoring or conducting the handbell choir at her Presbyterian church, Kathy spent her time scheduling violin lessons and arranging for accompanists and preparing recitals, including one in her living room for my benefit. "It's, of course, the obvious thing to see my kids as somehow fulfilling my thwarted desires, to think that I've foisted my life on them. But that would be a terrible burden. When the fourth came along, I thought, What if he has a tin ear? By then it was clearly a family identity. If he had been miserable in music, I would have accepted that. I don't want to be one of those skating parents. I tried not to say, 'Everything you do is a reflection on me.' That was said over and over to me and was really damaging. But our family is not a democracy. Adults too often abdicate their responsibility to set limits and insist on what's best for kids. My kids did not see an R-rated movie till they were seventeen." (She also had a lightning reflex, her kids report: If there was any nudity in a PG movie, her hands went right over their eyes.) "When Jonathan told me he didn't want to stay at music camp, a democratic mom would have taken him home. I insisted he stay.

"My biggest fans have felt that though I wasn't get paid or getting public recognition, as a mother I was doing a full-time job requiring the same kind of dedication and energy and intellect. I always researched the best way to go about this or that. I don't want dabblers. We're committed to excellence. And I have kept my kids so busy they haven't had time for hanging out in malls. Music has brought discipline and a spiritual dimension to their lives."

Articulate and well mannered, all four of Kathy's children speak their minds with confidence and strong echoes of their mother's worldview. The youngest, Jonathan, born in 1981, wants kids, but not four: "My mom seems stressed-out having to deal with all of us. I wouldn't want my wife to work that hard, and I wouldn't want a job like my dad's, where he's barely here. Sometimes my mom's way overprotective; I don't like having friends over, 'cause she'll hang around. But I wouldn't want to have parents like my friends' parents, who are super-rich, with huge jobs, and give their kids everything but are never home." Stephen, born in 1979, doesn't want to get married. "This family has been an enormous help to me in knowing where to stand and what to value. But there are many aspects of family I couldn't commit to. I feel I'd have to be a breadwinner, but I'd want time with my kids. And I don't think I could accept kids, or a wife, warts and all."

Karen, born in 1974, who since her early illness has struggled with learning disabilities and after high school enrolled at Lawrence Conservatory of Music, "almost had a breakdown in high school, wondering, Am I doing music for myself or for my mother? I do think we're living her dream. But I can live with that. At times I feel sorry for my dad; I know he doesn't feel as close to us. There's not much he could have done, but I wish he'd been here more. If I raise a family, I want to be with my kids. I don't think it's right to go off. I don't know what I'd do without my mom. She's been there behind me my whole life." Like each of her three brothers in turn, Karen makes sure I know that, while at Wellesley, her mother was a presidential scholar.

The eldest, Rob, born in 1973, a graduate of Williams College, wants to be a househusband. "It's hard to say if my mom is happy. I guess she's happy with her marriage. They have incredibly happy moments together. If love exists, I do feel they've come close to it. I would like to emulate that, and to believe that love would transcend all differences. But their marriage is not a model of the marriage I want to have. So much of their interaction is so frustrating to watch. They hardly ever seem in sync. There's always underlying tension. I think it's because they're such opposite people. My mother is emotional. My dad hides every emotion; he has, like me, a strong aversion to conflict. He can't stand fights, because they're not rational. He clams up, and then for my mom it snowballs.

"I also push my mom away: I get uncomfortable when she gets too involved in my life. I look down on her for being so irrational, and then I look down on my dad for being so unemotional. I can't really figure out what is an acceptable way for me to be. I see elements of both my parents in me, and I'm trying to figure out which I want to kill and which to grow. My dad feels guilty because he knows so little about music, and she places so much value on it. It's who she is, so she makes it out to be incredibly important. I'm always in conflict: Should I be practicing tennis for my dad's sake, or violin for my mom?

"What my mom really resents is that my dad didn't make time to be with his kids. He threw himself into his work; that's what he's best at. But by the time he comes home, he's given all he has. He has no patience with us. He's not really a kid person, even though he's a pediatrician. My mom felt burdened. She literally does everything here. My dad did nothing. We've started doing dishes, but only recently. I think she resented that we just took her for granted. That's the central problem my mother faces, in all spheres. She was apprehensive going to her twenty-fifth reunion at Wellesley. Even though she's of equal quality as those women, she hasn't done as much according to what society thinks is something.

"The only goal I have in life is to be a father, a househusband. I love kids—that rubbed off from my mom. I'd like to be seriously part of children's lives; that's why I was leaning toward going into pediatrics. At the playground I see all these kids with nannies. The nannies have their own families but have to be parents to kids whose own parents won't make time. I do think I'd have some of the same difficulties as my mom with staying at home, in terms of feeling unappreciated. Though I've already accepted my mediocrity. Not that being a househusband would be a mediocre thing to do. I would love to be a world-famous pediatrician, but if I was a father for a living, that would be equally hard, but not something I could, or would, run away from. My mother hasn't run away from anything. She's made her decisions and stuck with them. Whether they've made her happy is another question.

"There must be a self-defeating gene in our family. I think in fact my mom's not terribly happy that she just stayed home with the kids; so many times she felt she could have done more. She'll go to a party, encounter women who've done all kinds of things, and feel she's not treated as an equal. There's a tendency in this kind of neighborhood to devalue people who take care of kids. And what's unfortunate with me and my mom is that we place a lot of stock in what society thinks; we too often compare ourselves with society's idea of what's best. I have a friend with the perfect *Leave It to Beaver* mom, and my mom doesn't like to be thrown in the same pot with her. My friend's mom spends her time keeping her house totally spotless and hosting parties and keeping up the appearance of a perfect family. My mother sees herself as a Hillary Clinton–type person, who has just chosen the field of raising children.

"When our quartet plays a concert, my mom gets in a complete frenzy, upset and yelling at us till we get there. Then we give the performance and she's the happiest person in the world, overflowing with love for us. At those moments she's genuinely happy with her decision to raise kids. I don't think my mom gave up at all. She made the decision she thought best. Where for me to choose househusbanding, well, there's the baggage that I didn't have what it takes to do something else. At Williams, I had to change my major because I failed a class. That was rough. I wanted to just leave. My parents thought I could do anything, but discovered I wasn't so good at a lot of things. So child rearing is not the only thing I wanted to do but the only thing I can do. In an ideal world, being a father would be just as important. But a pediatrician does seem a higher calling.

"As a kid I hated playing violin; I felt I was just living out my mom's dreams and it felt like a burden. But more often I felt like I was a burden to her. I would see how hectic her life was, how often she would get upset with me if I didn't take out the trash or something. I felt I was screwing up her life. I blamed myself for her unhappiness. I did see a lot of unhappiness, more than happiness. I always felt like she was trying to prove herself. She is what she acts, but she tries real hard to create an impression of satisfaction. She loves kids and definitely wanted to raise them, but I question whether she truly believes it's as valuable as the alternatives. She seems to have to try real hard to prove to herself that it's okay to be who she is."

"We have a better marriage than the kids think we do," says Kathy. "Kids are always an interference in a marriage. They take away opportunities for intimacy; they demand energy. Roger is not demonstrative, so our close time is not visible to them; more often they've seen ships passing in the night. But our cement is the love between us; Roger has provided unceasing love and is unbelievably supportive of me. Which is not to say we couldn't have a better marriage. I would hope for them that their marriages are warmer than ours."

In raising a family, Kathy has also found, like many in her class, a large measure of understanding and forgiveness for her own parents. "It's not very complicated why the life at home with children that made my mother so miserable could make me happy. I loved kids and actively chose what was right for me. My mother had no choice; she didn't love being a mother, but she wasn't ever allowed to express who she truly was. She was much more confident and happy when she went back to work as a secretary, which became possible only because the world had changed around her. By the time she died, I understood that she had done the best she could and she understood that I had been right in my choices. I'd never heard her tell me she loved me until she was sick and dying, but I did get to hear it finally. I felt sad she had suffered so much. But I certainly don't blame her. She was a victim of her times: I would never advocate going back to the demeaning role of women in the fifties."

A week after my first meeting with Kathy, I received a letter from her. "At the risk of seeming defensive," she wrote, "I am sending you this résumé so you can see what I did while I 'wasn't working.' " The résumé detailed her years of volunteer activities in the church and schools. "I would urge you not to make the common mistake of assuming that a woman who chooses to stay home with her children is doing nothing." Soon after the profile in *U.S. News* appeared, we spoke again. "I can't say it's not true, everything you wrote. But it sounds so awful, like I'm a subjugated woman and Roger's an ogre who drags me around by the hair. It made a friend of mine—the woman who had encouraged me to go to Wellesley—extremely angry. She said you were using me. And Roger and I joked that I should go to my twenty-fifth reunion barefoot and pregnant with him following me around with a whip."

Such a performance, she believes, would only have confirmed her

classmates' disdain, though as Kathy speaks of her classmates, she seems
not to hear the echoes of her mother's warnings thirty years earlier
about "those people with their fancy ideas who think they're better"
than everybody else. "It took me fifteen years after Wellesley to recover
my confidence that I was smart," says Kathy. "I felt like a nothing there.
I haven't come through life with my classmates' sense of entitlement—
that I was born to achieve greatness and be better than other people. At
the reunion there was still so much posturing. At the class meeting we
discussed what messages we should give our daughters. They were all
still talking about modeling the fact that women can do anything. I wish
I'd had the nerve to say: 'What we need to do is give them unconditional
love.' They don't see that what matters most is your relationship with
people. They come across as: 'Here I am, world; I'm so wonderful, and
who are you and why should I talk to you?' People looked right through
me, though now I don't care. Now I trust my own opinions. I'm more
willing to do what makes sense for me, regardless of what people at
Wellesley value, and I certainly don't think they value who I am, or ever
will."

Dismissed and Defensive

In 1977, living gloomily in Washington, Nancy Wanderer, '69, wrote to
the Wellesley alumnae magazine: "I feel motherhood in the first years is
an extremely important and time-consuming profession, one that merits a higher status. It also can be extremely rewarding. I just wish more
women of ability and talent would consider it a worthwhile profession."
In 1984, Susan Fowler Bryant, '69, wrote "of the difficult discovery that I
don't need traditional titles to feel a sense of accomplishment. I had felt
self-conscious and dull that I was careerless, and discovered this was a
myth." In 1989, Karen Cheses Sanders, '69, wrote of having her Ph.D.
framed alongside her M.S. and her Wellesley B.A., "all of which makes
me an educated person with a career in family administration." "What's
really important," class secretary Shaunagh Guinness Robbins asked in
1986, "a successful law practice or the local PTA?" Time and again, one
finds the women in the class who have stayed home with their children
defending and burnishing their choice for their peers. Nancy's sister-in-
law, Katherine Harding Wanderer, calls herself a "home executive."

Others object to the phrase *working mother,* insisting the proper distinction is between an *employed mother* and a *career mother,* the latter being a woman "who, having the choice, chooses to commit herself to raising her children."

An occasional note of defensiveness is heard from other women in the class as well: Betty Demy, '69, a divorced, employed, single mom, was not alone in being angry at Kathy Smith Ruckman's fervent advocacy of her brand of motherhood. "I don't like her setting herself up as some kind of paradigm. Those who made a good marriage and could stay in it are lucky. I would have chosen the same. It's best to have two parents. But it's not the only way to raise a healthy kid."

Of all the women in Hillary Clinton's class, however, it is the stay-at-home moms who seem most to feel the need to defend their lives. Two or three decades ago, that made sense. Feminism's furious rejection of the feminine mystique did for a time sabotage the movement's deeper aim of expanding the range of women's choices. As Jan Piercy says, "Its short-run outcome was to substitute one set of options for another, so that we shifted from an environment in which women who worked outside the home were censured to one in which women who didn't work were regarded as not fully using their talents. It was a natural pendulum swing."

Now, however, such defensiveness seems an anachronism. Much is still made of the so-called mommy wars—with full-time moms scorning working mothers for their pallid commitment to their families ("Oh, you *bought* Johnny's Halloween costume?") and working mothers retaliating with condescension. But in none of my conversations with Kathy Ruckman's working classmates did I find the disdain she perceives. Rather, most recognize an immense debt to the women who hold their neighborhoods together and volunteer in the churches and schools. "We are incredibly lucky to have a stay-at-home mom next door," says Nan Decker, '69, a mother of two who works a twenty-eight-hour week. "She is a big boon, a linchpin of the neighborhood. Today I heard all the kids out front singing, 'I see London, I see France,' and it warmed my heart." World Bank executive Jan Piercy echoes Kathy's words. "The pool of talent, largely women, who were able to commit themselves to work that wasn't compensated, has been the backbone of much of the social progress in this country. Women who cared passionately about the quality of education for their children, for instance, got engaged in the schools as volunteers in a very professional way, and it's partly as that pool disappears with more women in the workforce that the problems of urban education are becoming more acute."

Oddly, the greatest symbolic moment in the mommy wars—Hillary Clinton's infamous remark "I suppose I could have stayed at home and baked cookies and had teas," which presumably marked her as contemptuous of non-wage-earning moms—did not alienate many of her "traditional" classmates. Alison Campbell Swain "knew she wasn't saying stay-at-home moms weren't contributing but asking why she should waste her training, especially since she only has one kid." In 1994, Kathy Ruckman wrote a letter to *The Washington Post* defending Hillary as one of the few public figures standing up for children. "I have been amazed by the criticism and vilification of such a good, intelligent woman. I see her as just another in a long line of capable, ambitious and frustrated women who are forced by society's expectations, and their husbands' powerful positions, to operate behind the scenes . . . forced into the background by outdated stereotypes of her 'place in life.' "

The root question, of course, is: What is best for the children? Kathy's answer—the full investment of their mother (even if with a mostly absent father)—is the answer implicit in most discussions of day care or nannies; even by those who use it, nonmaternal child care is generally begrudged as second best.

Yet while the superiority of maternal rearing is treated now as an eternal verity, the conception of what a child needs, and even of what a child is, has varied radically from one historic era and culture to the next. Puritan children needed most their father's stern hand to drive the devil from their corrupted souls. Victorian children were also their fathers' before all: The preservation of their innocence and obedience could not be entrusted to their emotionally inconstant mothers, but required tutors and governesses supervised by the man of the house; in the event of divorce, custody was automatically his. The early-twentieth-century enthusiasm for Taylorist efficiency (Frederick Taylor was the American engineer who invented time-and-motion studies) bolstered the idea that men, especially expert men, ought to supervise child rearing, applying the principles of scientific management. Mothers were instructed to rear their children by the clock, as picking them up when they cried would only create moral laxity and unwholesome dependence. The influence of Freud reversed those verities but preserved the place of the male expert, who now warned mothers that repression, especially in toilet training, would scar children for life. Mary McCarthy mocked the women who bowed to such fickle and bullying experts: *The Group*'s cowed Priss Crockett, "married to a pediatrician of the six, ten, two, six, ten, two school of scheduled feeding, who trained her never to pick up their son between feedings except to change his diaper," meets in Central Park Norinne Schmittlapp, who fancies herself "advanced" because she lets her Ichabod run naked and feed on demand; she "predicts he'll give up his anal pleasures under peer pressure at nursery school."

In just the span of the lives of the class of '69, the experts have swung from a spare-the-rod advocacy of dunce-cap humiliation and corporal punishment to a Spockean condemnation of "toxic parents," who criticize or punish too harshly. The idea of family as a democracy—which has shaped most of the '69ers' approach to child rearing and informed Hillary Clinton's legal advocacy of children's rights in decisions about their own abortions, schooling, and employment—now coexists with a kind of counterreformation, demanding a return to clear lines of authority and harsh discipline. Breast-feeding has been in, then out in favor of "scientific artificial feeding," then in again. The warnings in the fifties about overinvolved "viper" mothers have resurfaced in mockeries of yuppies competing to get their progeny into Ivy League–prep nursery schools, or neo-Taylorist moms creating "child development oversight systems," with week-by-week development flow charts, educational toys, and Gymboree; such complaints coexist with those against careerist and underinvolved moms. Expert studies prove that working mothers are happier mothers, or unhappier; that men and women with multiple roles and complex lives have more stable, or more fragile, marriages; that kids fare better, or worse, with stay-at-home moms; that kids in day care learn to compete aggressively for attention, or are better socialized and have more self-control and independence. From evolutionary psychology comes the argument that the "public nature" of ape and cavewoman child rearing suggests a biological basis for working motherhood: "It is unnatural for a mother to hand her child over to someone she barely knows and head off for ten hours of work, but not as unnatural as her staying home alone with a child," writes Robert Wright. "Women naturally have a vocational as well as maternal calling. . . . The notion that infants are better off at home gives short shrift to the innately social nature of infants and mothers." Feminists have mostly been what might be called old-fashioned in their views of child rearing: Though they are attacked by neoconservatives for deeming men superfluous, they have in fact been the most consistent agitators for paternal care. Feminist psychologists like Nancy Chodorow were arguing for more fathering long before antifeminists like David Blankenhorn (author of *Fatherless America*) began to do so: Only with fathers involved more than the few hours a week most spend with their kids, wrote Chodorow, would children grow up to be more nurturing and less emotionally distanced. More recently, in *Motherguilt*, sociologist Diane Eyer has revisited the influential studies by John Bowlby and such successors as T. Berry Brazelton on infant attachment and bonding, noting that their conclusions that neglect by *mothers* damages children were based on studies of infants deprived of *any* consistent, loving relationships. Eyer challenges the experts' indifference to the value of paternal attachment; she also challenges the damning premises these experts begin with: that a "well-bonded" mother is defined as one who doesn't leave the house or feels guilty if she does. Several members of the class of '69 have been professional advocates of paternal responsibility. Connie Hoenk Shapiro published a book on preventing teen pregnancy that explored the usually ignored role of the adolescent male. Hillary Rodham represented a father in a child-custody fight.

Though nearly all the mothers in the Wellesley class of '69 have struggled to get their husbands more engaged in their children's lives, only a third report having achieved equality in caring for their children and nearly all have failed to persuade their husbands to share housecleaning, grocery shopping, and cooking; the division of household labor in their class is only marginally different from that of classes their mothers' age. "My husband, Jock, loves being at home," says Johanna Branson. "But it never occurs to him to do dishes or laundry unless he's asked." She worries that for her daughters it will be worse still. "My feminist friends haven't raised sons who will be that different to be married to than our husbands," she says, but *have* raised daughters who expect to share domestic responsibilities and pursue aspirations in the wider world. "I worry we've set our daughters up—that there's now a two-generation lag in expectations between women and men. I don't want my daughters to have to be suspicious and angry to achieve some fairness." That the "new man" does far less cleaning and cooking than he does child rearing would seem to contradict the familiar argument that women do more at home because of their biological endowments. Surely breast milk and a nurturing nature are not assets in washing floors.

A Life Well Spent

Alison Campbell had been resident among the Celtic wood sprites and elves of Findhorn for more than a year when she met Bruce Swain, a journalist and teacher who had joined the community after visiting it to write a newspaper story. The two fell quickly in love, and in 1977 returned to America.

Alison's marriage to Bruce, sweet of temper but unremarkable of lineage, saw her banished from the Social Register, though her father still occasionally sends her an application to get back in. She has spent most of her adulthood as a thrifty midwestern wife, tending her garden, vacuuming furiously in anticipation of a visitor, meeting her youngest child as he tumbles off the yellow school bus telling her excitedly of learning how to pump his legs on the swing. In manner and voice, she has remained the debutante, though she is no longer slender and her blond hair has gone brown; she crops it short and prefers snowflake sweaters and blue jeans to her mother's knit suits and pearls. Rather than ripen into her mother's elegance, she has stayed girlish—gushing and slightly awkward, with a breathy, piping voice.

Like Kathy Smith Ruckman, Alison chose on principle to be a full-time mom to her three children, April, Elizabeth, and Steven. "I believe in being there all the time for my kids and not parking them for the sake of my career. To watch a baby come out of you creates a powerful blood love. Nobody can do a better job with your kids than you, who love them." Unlike Kathy, however, Alison assimilated nearly every one of the sixties tenets as to how to birth and rear a child. All three of her babies were delivered by midwives, the first one at home. Doctors, Alison felt, "way overmedicalized" birthing. She didn't like drugs and had read that you should move around to speed up labor "instead of being stuck with your feet up in stirrups." She'd heard about bonding and didn't want to be separated from her baby. She breast-fed "on demand," though her mother had not nursed her at all. ("She thought it was yucky; she was very proper and private about her body. And wealthy women generally bottle-fed so as not to be tied to their baby, to remain free socially.") She always used cloth diapers. "My skin breaks out with synthetics; I realize this is the princess and the pea, but what's the benefit of having Baggies on your bottom?" And she let all of her kids come sleep in her bed. "I based a lot of what I did on feminist research, like Virginia Axline's theories about validating your children by really listening to them. I tried not to treat my son differently from my daughters; I gave them similar toys and required they all clean their room and learn to cook and sew."

Mindful of her own misery under strict surveillance at Miss Porter's, and eager for her daughters to have the freedom to develop their strength and autonomy, Alison sent them to Montessori and Waldorf schools. "I shared the Steiner principle of trusting a child's inner direction rather than viewing them as objects to be molded. The Waldorf school was artsy and hippie and free—the kids had no homework or tests or much science; they raised goats and made pottery and tie-dye." Her mother-in-law was scandalized: She regularly reminded Alison that when Bruce was a boy, she'd made him sleep on the front porch and every morning saw he had a cold shower and two hours of piano before school. But Alison stood by her choice to be "looser" with her kids. "I don't believe in running arbitrary power trips. I talk things through with my kids. I like to give them more choice than I had. I believe that the way you help your kids not become victims is to let them know that you love them but also to trust them and give them room to make their own decisions. April knows that she can come to me and we'll deal with birth control. I've told her that sex is powerful, that making love can be a cosmic experience, but that treating it as a sport or doing it because you've gotten drunk can leave you feeling rotten, or be dangerous. I've encouraged her to learn to protect herself; I have a black belt in Tae Kwan Do."

Alison had just given birth to their third child, Steven, in 1988, when they learned that Bruce's mother had Alzheimer's and was in rapid decline. Bruce's father was much too frail to take care of her, so Bruce and Alison decided to move his parents in. As she had been after every pregnancy, Alison was in extremely poor health, weak and exhausted and unable to sleep. She felt no match for her mother-in-law. A "cranky, dominating" southern matriarch, Mrs. Swain had from the beginning disapproved of her son's choice of a liberal Yankee bride, and had never forgiven Alison for marrying her only child. Even as her illness progressed and she grew more deluded, Mrs. Swain remained ferociously strong. "She was running things, but she was out of her gourd," said Alison. "Her hours were completely kaflooey. And every so often she'd freak out; she'd suddenly become a child needing to get home and would just head out the door and wander into other people's houses. We finally had to move out to the country, where there were no houses in sight."

The family moved to Lawrence, Kansas, settling in a beautiful old schoolhouse in the middle of cornfields, where their closest neighbors were hawks and coyotes and an occasional bald eagle wheeling in the washed-out skies. For the next seven years, Alison spent her days feeding and bathing and chasing not only her three children but now also her frightened, miserable mother-in-law and her increasingly fragile father-in-law. She could have bought herself freedom from the ceaseless toil— she'd recently inherited enough money to hire as many servants as she herself had been surrounded by as a child. Instead, she gave all that money away, sending anonymous checks to people she'd read about in the paper who were wiped out in a fire or hit by devastating illness. The one fragment of her legacy she kept was the family silver, cherishing the link it afforded to her female ancestors; she kept it in a shoe box stuffed in a kitchen drawer.

Alison had looked forward to the freedom she would gain as her kids got older; now, instead, her responsibilities grew heavier by the day. She persevered in her caretaker role, reminding herself of her great love for Bruce, swallowing each day a bit more resentment, scolding herself for her selfishness, sinking ever deeper into depression. If she ever protested, it was in her most childlike voice and hummingbird manner, apologizing and revoking her complaint almost before she'd finished making it: "I felt frustrated and trapped as my caregiving duties went on and on and on, but I felt guilty feeling that way. I have a hard time dumping anyone. Even with boyfriends, I used to get them to break up with me. I never wanted to regret that I hadn't been there for my kids or that I had pressed my husband to put his parents in a nursing home."

Her childhood of privilege had persuaded Alison as thoroughly as any in her class that how one lives one's personal life is a political decision: She had fallen in love with Bruce because he seemed to be a man who lived what he believed, and she wanted to join him in that effort. She spoke proudly of his heroism as a young man, protesting the war in Vietnam by dropping out of mandatory ROTC and facing court-martial: "I knew people who ate balls of aluminum foil to have weird X rays, or who acted crazy or homosexual. I admired Bruce for having the courage to fight it head-on. He would have gone to Leavenworth if he'd lost." She is equally admiring of him as a husband, father, and son. "I've never felt exploited by him. He has done many things I don't think most men would." After Steven's birth, Alison was so weak that her doctors made her quit breast-feeding and take Halcion to sleep, which plunged her into "huge clouds" of depression. Bruce cared for Steven all night while working all day, and continued his habit of doing much of the housecleaning. When he decided, at the same time, to move his parents in, Alison worried but couldn't help but honor his devotion. "You see what kind of a person someone is by the way they treat people when they're most helpless and the power is most unequal. My sweetie stood by us all faithfully, and I wanted to repay him with the same devotion."

Alison's affection for her father-in-law, a doctor, was nearly as great. "He's amazing and deserved every bit of tender care I could give. He was an orphan who ran away to vaudeville and worked his way through medical school during the Depression and became the only doctor in his Georgia town who would treat black people. I was so startled when I saw the separate waiting room he had to keep. He was such a generous man; even in 1981 he charged five dollars for an office visit and seven dollars for a house call." Over time, she even softened toward her mother-in-law. "After all her hostility, in her last years she said over and over how glad she was that I was part of their family. Hearing that, I forgave a lot of the bother. You can do a lot if you think people appreciate it. I also saw how my kids benefited from having them there. Dr. and Mrs. Swain were the devoted grandparents. My parents were always busy and far away."

For years Alison did not paint. Though she set up a worktable in the middle of the living room, she was always far more interruptible than Bruce in his study, which was a separate room with a door he could close. She suffered the paradoxical unhappiness of the housebound woman—loneliness and no solitude, all the while comforting herself with the thought that though she hadn't "done great deeds," she had "raised good people, which is a contribution." She repeated to herself the Buddhist aphorism "Before enlightenment: carry water, chop wood. After enlightenment: carry water, chop wood."

After fifteen years of complete dedication to the care of other people, Alison began to wonder "if I knew who I was anymore," and finally turned on Bruce in anger. "Gosh, I got mad. My own needs and interests had gone completely by the wayside. I felt that I had no life. Sometimes I was unbearably bored. Taking care of people doesn't use your whole brain, but I had no time for anything else. At moments I wondered if I even knew what I wanted anymore, I was so oriented to other people's needs. I would not wish this on my children. I've told them to put me in a home."

It was a "blessing in disguise," she says, when in 1992 Bruce's mother broke her hip; at last Dr. Swain agreed that she could get the care she required only in a nursing home. He remained with the family, but Bruce hired a visiting nurse to help out two hours a day, which gave Alison her long-wished-for chance to go back to school for a master's in social work. "I loved being with adults and talking about social justice, and got all A's." The same year, she wrote to Hillary Clinton asking if she could come to the White House to make a painting of the Rose Garden for her old employer Mrs. Mellon, who had designed the garden for President and Mrs. Kennedy.

Alison's respite from full-time caretaking proved to be short-lived. April had blossomed into a strong, self-possessed teenager: "She doesn't have that problem of 'Oh no, someone needs help so I must rush in,' " says her mother. "April has her goals and is not easily diverted." Elizabeth, however, had not fared so well; for years she had been battling poor health, enduring recurring bouts of mononucleosis and pneumonia and terrible insomnia. While April had absorbed Alison's vision for her daughters—"to have adventures and careers and do something for the world before they marry and become moms, not just blindly follow what I did"—Elizabeth (named for death-and-dying guru Elisabeth Kübler-Ross) seemed to have been shaped less by what her mother said than by what her mother was. Pale, waifish, and tiny-voiced, Elizabeth has, like her mother, suffered chronic debilitating illness and fatigue.

Again and again in elementary school and junior high, doctors prescribed antibiotics; when she repeatedly failed to respond, they suggested Alison take her to a psychologist. By ninth grade Elizabeth was so weak she had to finish the school year at home.

Alison, meanwhile, had contracted Lyme disease and Epstein-Barr virus and also had to quit going to school. "I thought, There goes the social work; there goes anything to do with my own abilities. I felt all doors closing. I was on the brink of lymphoma or leukemia, which we fortunately caught before chemo and radiation were necessary. My immune system was shot. I'd needed to make caring for us a priority; instead, I'd been caring for Bruce's parents and quietly going down the tubes. I finally had to decide, Was I going to flame out taking care of other people?"

Since 1994, Alison has turned all her energies to getting herself and Elizabeth well. She has read widely and decided, despite her doctors' skepticism, that Elizabeth was suffering chronic fatigue syndrome. Perhaps she inherited an immune-system weakness from her maternal grandmother, who died of lymphoma and lupus, or from her mother, who had polio as a child. Alison is now fluent in the language of T cells and lymphocytes and retroviruses and musculoskeletal degeneration. And she has made progress; first with an immunologist in Tucson, who treated Elizabeth with acupuncture and herbs, then with a move to Hawaii, where Elizabeth dramatically improved. Alison and Hillary Clinton have even traded notes on alternative healing. The First Lady did finally arrange for Alison to paint the Rose Garden (a project she later set aside to cope with her daughter's health crisis) and startled her one evening when Alison was in the garden sketching by suddenly appearing, wearing a baseball cap, big sunglasses, leggings, and headphones. The two classmates chatted for an hour in the waning light. Alison told her that Bill's astrological chart had aspects that make him see all sides of things, which is why it's hard for him to make up his mind. Hillary told her about Chelsea's bout with mononucleosis, and suggested homeopathy and acupuncture.

Chronic fatigue syndrome remains a controversial diagnosis. Most common among white women, it is widely dismissed by doctors as a psychosomatic "yuppie flu"; those who take it seriously are mocked for "performing million-dollar workups on neurotic women," according to

Hillary Johnson, author of a history of the medical establishment's response to the illness. Though it is now on the Centers for Disease Control's list of infectious diseases, and the National Institutes of Health funds research on it, and though the work of scientists like Martha McClintock, '69, has increasingly documented the effects of the mind and social relations on the body's health, many doctors still share the view argued by Elaine Showalter in her book *Hystories*: that CFS is a somatization of emotional privation; that for people who otherwise feel they have no right to ask for attention and care, a physical illness becomes "a culturally permissible language of distress," which entitles them to the "privileges of the sick role." (The men most susceptible to such illnesses, Showalter notes, are low-ranking soldiers. The wars that are meant to deliver manly activity instead trap them in feminine passivity, at the mercy of other people's command; "battle fatigue," or "shell shock," is the erosion caused by months or years of stress in a situation they can't escape.) Unlike the inward, self-gnawing symptoms of depression, Showalter argues, such "hysterical" illnesses have historically manifested outward symptoms that demand attention; as they grow "epidemic," they create a community with a shared story.

The community of CFS sufferers and health activists has provided Alison a new vocabulary to describe her life. And though she resented her doctors' dismissal of her chronic fatigue as a matter for psychotherapy, she herself sees her physical malaise as an illness of the spirit, a perception reinforced by her New Age beliefs. She describes her constellation of illnesses as most common in people who "put other people's needs first and run around whipped" all the time. "It would kill me to think I'd looked out for myself and others had suffered. But I wonder whether, if I'd been able to say to my husband, 'No, we can't take care of your parents in our house' or insisted we bring in a visiting nurse sooner, it might have been easier to protect Elizabeth's health, and my own."

Alison's confusion is an honorable one. To love generously, limitlessly, is one of the highest virtues, but so too is the capacity to recognize when the spending of oneself has gone too far. Alison realized that she had begun to collude in her own exploitation, in the snuffing out of her own passions and voice.

"It's funny," says Alison. "All along it was my father and brother, not my mother and sister, who said to me, 'Get out and do things; take control of your life.' It's clear they feel that kind of control over their own lives. They were never burdened with the sense of automatic responsibility for caring for others. My brother is an involved father, but when he comes home from saving lives all day in the emergency room, fussy babies don't seem so worthy a demand on his energies. He'd tell me to 'get free,' but I couldn't. I believed that to be good meant not to change."

Alison has lately resumed painting and recently illustrated a children's book. At the same time, she is seeking new ways to serve. She would like to work in a hospice attending the dying. "My spiritual experiences have made me unafraid of dying. And if a dying person told me they saw angels or loved ones waiting, I would not pooh-pooh those experiences. Long before the angels fad, I felt the presence of invisible good guys, especially at birth and at death." She would also like to paint murals in hospital pediatric wards, of meadows and flowers.

Feminism helped Alison, she believes, in her erratic wrestling with the proper balance between selfless love and self-preservation. She had more freedom than her mother, and her daughters are freer still, because "feminism changed the world." "Most of my classmates at the Inauguration party were in power suits and I suspect most had résumés in their pocketbooks. I've never owned a power suit; my idea was not to be more like men, more ambitious and less cozy. Helping other people was my humble career choice. But the thing is, I *had* choices. All along, I was making the choices, even if they were pretty darn traditional. I find ridiculous the idea that our generation made life harder for our daughters. Oh gee, we have to apologize because they can do more than our mothers did? Thanks to the women who came before us and women like Hillary, my daughters have the freedom to make up their lives as they go along without feeling like odd ducks. How nice to feel you can write your own script."

The women of Hillary's class fought their mothers and became their mothers; their daughters' inheritance is no less complicated. Like Alison, Ann Sherwood Sentilles, '69, poured her energies into raising her children, felt herself disappearing in that effort, and then watched a daughter fade. Ann's daughter, however, chose a more active self-erasure: Sarah learned to starve.

Though Ann would ultimately choose to stay home, her aspirations had not at first centered on maternity. She discovered early a passion for newspaper writing, starting her own paper in sixth grade and then becoming editor of her high school paper and the *Wellesley News*. She earned a master's at Columbia Journalism School and became the first woman on-air reporter in Columbus, Ohio. In a miniskirt, her straight blond hair hanging to her waist, Ann reported on school integration and civil rights. "When they hired my replacement, I heard them reject one woman because her legs weren't as good as mine. I wasn't conscious that it was a bad thing; it seemed kind of flattering at the time."

Ann had returned to Ohio from Wellesley when her boyfriend, Irwin, began Yale Law School and failed to give her a ring. "My dad told me, 'Come home. That boy's not interested in marrying you.' Then I landed my TV job, and Irwin caught the next flight and proposed. He was everything I wanted: smart, responsible, honest, my soulmate. I loved him completely, and I still do.

"I also loved my television work, but I gave it up in a second to marry him the next year, which, I'm glad to say, my daughters struggle to understand. I did feel a vague foreboding. As a kid, I'd sometimes gone to work with my dad and watched him do surgery; I remember being struck by that intensity versus the chaos and laissez-faire of my mother's household and knowing I didn't want to spend my life waiting at home. It just didn't occur to me that stopping temporarily would be that detrimental to my career."

Ann joined Irwin in New Haven and took a "deadly-dull" job in a bank, which she quit when the first of her four children was born. She continued to work part-time at community newspapers in Brooklyn and New Jersey, assuming she would return to television when the time was right. "I naively believed that I would be able go back whenever I chose. Of course I couldn't, especially not as a woman. Women had to work harder than men; in Columbus, I'd worked twelve hours every day. We had to be more available to prove we belonged. There was a mantle you carried being the first woman who did whatever it was you were doing, and many of my classmates were the first woman in their law firm to make partner, the first woman in that business, the highest-ranking woman in the bank. Unfortunately I think we saw it as a burden—we saw it as an opportunity, but also as a burden—instead of being able to delight in 'Hey, we're here and look what we're doing' and enjoying it. Because if you stepped off that path, it was nearly impossible to get back on."

Ann did knock on network doors, and one summer she worked as a writer for CBS. "But they treated me like I wasn't hungry enough. In a way, I wasn't. I was distracted by being in love and married and a young mother. On the days I worked, I was exhausted when I got home. I didn't want to walk in at six with nothing left to give my kids. I had chosen to be their mother and also discovered the great pleasure in that."

In 1980, Irwin, a corporate lawyer, was transferred to Dallas. Moving to a new city with a six-year-old, a three-year-old, and an infant, Ann felt terribly alone. "I had no help, no support, and I had a husband who was in a new job and that was taking all his emotional energy and his physical energy, too," she told *Frontline*. "I didn't do anything right about it. I did a lot of crying and raging and screaming and I'm not proud of that time in my life. It was not good for my marriage. It was not good for my children. I mean, I began to wonder if my children would ever be happy, because they never saw me happy. I realized I'd made a deal that nobody else was party to, that I had given up several things that were important to me—my independence, my career—and in exchange I expected Irwin to be there for me whenever I needed him for whatever I needed. He didn't make that deal."

In Texas, a fourth baby was born. "My sisters both work full time, but one has two late-in-life kids and, I think, gets more satisfaction from her work than from mothering, and the other has one child and a stay-at-home husband. I agonized for years that I couldn't do it all. I did spend good time doing what I could do, but I always thought I should be doing something more. That made it hard to enjoy what I was doing. It wasn't going to be perfect. It could have been okay, but that's a lesson I hadn't yet learned."

Ann now regrets her lack of attention to what was happening. "It was years before I realized how much I'd given up. I would probably give it up again, but I wish I'd been more aware of what I was doing at the time. If I'd felt, 'Okay, you're making these choices and you're going to have to live with the consequences,' there might not have been so much frustration in everything I did. Instead, it came out as anger at my husband: 'You don't take me out; you don't bring me flowers; why didn't you come home from work earlier?' I don't regret my marriage or children; they are more rewarding and fun and stimulating than any job I've had. I'd just like to say I planned it this way. Instead, I sort of fumbled in and thought, Shit. Here I am."

Her Wellesley classmates became for Ann a measure of all she hadn't done. For years, their notes to the alumnae magazine tormented her. "I'd feel, God, I haven't done anything." More than once she defended her own choices to them. In 1977, as class secretary, she wrote: "The Word is that 'we' don't like Births and Engagements and Marriages at the front of the column, that as liberated, educated women we should be able to do better and generate more academic or accomplishment oriented news. I beg your indulgence and intellectual tolerance and suggest that all professions, homemaking and motherhood included, be equally important parts of our notes." In 1985 she wrote that "a job and money only take you so far," describing her "greater satisfaction from worthwhile activities in the community." Her insecurity kept her from every reunion until the twentieth. "I let my classmates be my peers," she told *Frontline*. "If I'm going to feel judged, they're my jury. And I think, Well, they must wonder what I do all day. I read other people's judgments and they're really my own. You spend a day running car pool and say, 'Hillary doesn't do this,' and I think, What's my life? Do I measure against Hillary?" Irwin suffered at Ann's distress. "I think Hillary's been really hard for somebody like Ann, because she points up the big question: Has what she's done in fact been meaningful? I think it's been incredibly meaningful. The problem is that you don't get a lot of people reinforcing your judgment."

Ann's two eldest have now left home. Her second daughter, Emily, a graduate of Brown, "is very much a feminist and doesn't want to get pushed around"; she has worked with the NOW Legal Defense Fund and plans to continue activism on behalf of women's rights. Ann's eldest, Sarah, is a Yale graduate who spent a year teaching in an inner-city school and is now going to Harvard Divinity School, with plans for an urban ministry. She is also a recovered anorexic, whose collapse in high school was revelatory for Ann. "Even now, when I hear people say 'You must be so proud of Sarah. She's such a perfect child,' it gives me the chills. She was perfect. She got fabulous grades, was captain of every team, editor of the newspaper, always had friends and a boyfriend, delighted adults. She did everything to please everybody.

"But somewhere after tenth grade, her perfect image and reality began to separate for her. She didn't feel like she was what she was pretending to be, but she also didn't feel she had any options, because we had so rewarded her for her brilliant performance. She was afraid if she didn't perform, we wouldn't be there. It was a crushing blow to me that I had failed her so badly."

A pediatrician raised the first alarm, after treating Sarah for stomachache and fatigue. Then friends called and said they were worried that Sarah talked about being fat all the time and wasn't eating. After the call, Ann went to talk to Sarah and found her curled up on the floor of her room in the fetal position, crying. "I really hadn't noticed—or maybe I had, but didn't see it till someone wrapped it up for me. She had gotten obsessive about food. She declared herself a vegetarian and wouldn't eat red meat, but I just grilled lots of extra chicken and persuaded myself it was all fine.

"Sarah was scared. She admitted being afraid she was fat, though swears she was not bulimic. I have nightmarish recollections of her getting up from the table after every meal and going to the bathroom. She says I don't believe her, and I say, 'It's not you I don't believe but the disease.' It didn't matter what the diagnosis was; it was the manifestation of her emotional troubles, which she went to work on. There were twelve very ugly months in this household where Sarah learned to be angry. I had to walk around reminding myself, 'It's okay for a girl to be angry.' "

Many of the teenage daughters of the women of '69 fit the classic profile of those with eating disorders: White, well educated, and affluent, with high-achieving parents and high expectations, they have both the perfectionist impulses and the vertiginous sense of possibility that typically underlie anorexia and bulimia. They have never known the ideal of female beauty preferred for most of history—an ideal of fleshiness, with its associations of fecundity and wealth—but have seen fashion consistently favor narrow hips and slender limbs. Inheriting a world both more fluid and seemingly more perilous than their parents', they have tried to substitute self-control for their lack of control over the world. Though her kids are sophisticated and well traveled, says Ann, "they seem to need small secure places, which I didn't, even though as a kid I'd barely gotten off the farm. They're more intimidated, fearful of being far away from home. Sarah is an extremely mature woman intellectually, but immature emotionally. She hated the transition between home and college, then got distressed at what had to change when she graduated."

A girl in a family like Ann's has an additional susceptibility: Seeing her principal model of adult femininity chafing against limits, frustrated and angry, a girl may consciously or unconsciously starve herself to refuse womanhood, to war against the mother she doesn't wish to become. Like Alison Swain in her confrontation with her daughter's chronic fatigue, through her daughter Sarah's anorexia, Ann was presented with a new frame in which to view her own life. "I realized I use food as a form of expression," says Ann. "Dinner was weighted with huge significance, which made it a natural place for Sarah to rebel and exert some control. One of the things I did to justify myself as a mother was to make sure I put a lovely meal on. That was my contribution for the day, so I took it quite personally when she didn't want to eat the meals I'd worked so hard on. I never said to her, 'I gave up everything to be your mother and you're starving yourself,' but I came close enough.

"The whole family had to undergo enormous change. I was very controlling and judgmental of Sarah's friends. I'd done an overzealous job of shutting out drinking, because of alcoholism in both my and my husband's families. I'd been rigid in my discussions with her about sex. We overemphasized achievement as a measure of her worth. 'Look at that, Sarah, a hundred on your test,' we'd say, instead of, 'Sarah, tell me about your new friend; tell me who you are and not just what you can do.' My husband and I had come by our concern with success naturally—we'd performed and gotten everything from parental strokes to big paychecks. It took much counseling before I realized my job wasn't to make Sarah be what I wanted her to be but to make her aware she has choices and support her in becoming who she is. My parents had a crystal-clear idea of who I was supposed to be. My father is still hostile that I don't vote Republican. He says, 'I did everything for you. How can you do that?' I say, 'There really wasn't a quid pro quo.'

"Irwin was supportive, but I don't think he got it with Sarah. He felt that I could handle it if I'd just stop crying and do what the counselor said. He still hasn't disengaged from the dance. He pressed Sarah to apply for a Rhodes. It meant more to him than it should, and in the past Sarah would have felt tremendous pressure to please her daddy. He still wants his perfect daughter. I have to let her be imperfect with me. Sarah has recovered, and I feel safe she won't ever starve herself again. But, like alcoholism, it's something she's going to live with the rest of her life.

"Irwin is very much a product of the sixties, caught on the cusp himself. He might have liked to do public service law, but we could not have put our kids through school on that income. Dallas is ostentatious; you can live and die by what you spend. We try not to be part of that, but you still press your jeans. It's a reality Hillary has had to contend with. Bill wasn't making money, and if you want to be a player, you have to have money. So Irwin supported my career and always said the right things, but he was too busy to act on them. He just handed over his pay and left me to run the household. He didn't take for granted that the domestic chores got done, but he didn't do them. He'd scrape the plate but leave it in the sink instead of the dishwasher. Not anything to draw battle lines over, though his daughters have been less tolerant than I am. They refuse to go to his club, because it discriminates against women and minorities; he says he doesn't participate in discriminatory acts himself and needs a place to play."

Interviewed on *Frontline*, Irwin looks the heavy. "I thought we had talked about what we were doing," he says, "but I probably didn't listen as much as I should have to where Ann was. Raising kids takes a lot of time, and that's always been a priority for us. Ann is the one who has executed that priority." From off camera comes a question: "Do you think that's what she wanted, to stay home with the kids?" Irwin squirms. "That's a hard question."

Ann does not blame her husband for her frustration. "When I was so unhappy after our move to Dallas, I felt that because I'd given up so much, it was Irwin's responsibility to make me happy. I finally realized I wasn't taking responsibility for my own choices. I had avoided that responsibility by subsuming myself to everybody else's needs.

"Sarah's illness was the beginning of the reawakening of myself, my sleeping self that had been shelved when I got married and had children. I realized how invested I was in being a good mother. To have it blow up in my face, to realize that I had failed, which is how it felt then, was excruciating, striking at the core of who I said I was. I would sit at the soccer field, the only representative of a fully intact family, the only one who cooks dinner every night, and feel: This is not fair. I'm finally letting go of the blame and guilt, and feel a certain freedom and excitement, as if I'd lived in a small quadrant of a square and am finding a whole cube out there. It's scary doing that when you're almost fifty. It's hard, having trained a whole family to expect Mom to take care of everything, to pull back and say, 'No, you're going to have to take care of that your-self.' "

In 1994, Ann wrote to her classmates that "between PMS and HRT" she was shedding the "fantasies I grew up believing" and wanting "to earn money and status in a real job." The next year, she became editor of *Dallas Family Magazine.* "My kids liked having their mother home, but they also like seeing me published. And I hope that out of my confusion they learned something. My daughters experienced my ambivalence, and also my ability to remedy mistakes. I hope they know that even though motherhood is demanding, it's a job of finite duration, and there's got to be a person underneath.

"Like my mother, I have three girls and a boy. Like my mother, I gave up my career to be a full-time mom and community volunteer. She was on the school board; I've been active in my kids' schools. There are tremendous parallels. It's amazing how powerful that model is; it's un-spoken, but it's the most powerful model you've got. As much as I ad-mired my mother, she is not who I wanted to be. I wanted and demand much more from my life. My mother spent a lifetime keeping my father happy, taking care of his mother, doing all the parenting. She has always been taking care of someone else. As my parents have grown older, I've thought about moving them here, and then I feel myself suffocating under that feeling of, Oh my God, I'm going to do again what my mother did. I'm not going to do it. My mother is an utterly selfless per-son. It took me a long time to see that the word *selfless* cuts both ways."

CHAPTER EIGHT

On Their Own

Selfless. Self-effacing: gone over with a rubber eraser until just a few traces remain. Long-suffering. Eating what's left when everyone else has had theirs. Eating nothing at all. Doubting herself when the ridicule begins. Searching her own faults when her lover or husband is unhappy or unfaithful or cruel. If only she wouldn't provoke him. Keeping her looks, biting her tongue, smoothing things over. Giving attention, giving him space.

Of all the confusions descended upon these women in their reinvention of a woman's role, none has been so brambled as the question of how to measure the claims of love. Many would find in love the richest of all life's satisfactions. But many would also discover that love could weaken and humiliate them. For love, they squandered hours in such helpless trivialities as waiting for the phone to ring, or sifted obsessively through the faintest ebbs and flows of romance—and its wreckage— with their friends. To keep men from leaving them, they acquiesced in arguments, made no demands; not knowing when to stand up for themselves, they swallowed and swallowed until poisoned with their own bile, or they burst with rage, another kind of helplessness, then slumped into fear and regret. They loathed their own cowardice: Abby van Alstyne, '69, a civil rights lawyer living in Alabama, actually bent her head in shame as she recalled an evening, a decade earlier, when her husband had dropped a whole bowl of spaghetti on the floor just as she and a friend were rushing out to the theater. He stood and watched as she got down on her knees to clean it up. Though she would be late to the theater, she put up no fight. Abby was not, as she told the story, a victim: Though she saw herself acting out her girlhood training to always be good and make things right, she blamed herself, only herself, for remaining so thoroughly tamed. Later divorced, she reflected on how her timidity had eroded herself and her marriage.

As the daughters of martyrs, these women suspected love and its sacrifices for another reason: They knew that a woman's selfless attentions were not always a freely given gift but could be a trap, a demand, a means of surveillance and manipulation. Self-abnegating and deprived, a woman might extort an offering of guilt. Long-suffering, she might claim moral superiority. (Hillary Clinton, many have suggested, long ruled Bill by being the righteous one while he was the fuckup.)

To resist collapsing in the name of love, it wasn't enough for these women to know that they didn't, in fact, need a saving prince as their mothers truly had. The belief that they needed protection had been too ingrained, the fairy tale ran too deep to be so easily exorcised; they would have to learn, through willful effort, to trust their own powers. For that they turned, as they so often had, to other women; together they could dash cold water on one another's faces, talk up their courage, persuade one another that they were not damsels but roaring women. Feminism gave them acid aphorisms like Gloria Steinem's ("A woman without a man is like a fish without a bicycle") and Shulamith Firestone's ("Love is the pivot of women's oppression"). A new genre of self-help books, like Colette Dowling's 1980 best-seller *The Cinderella Complex*, scolded them for their childish dependency and warned them not to love too much. In their consciousness-raising groups, they cultivated their anger as an alternative to self-suppression and self-blame: They would quit pleasing him, give as little as they got, stop being a doormat, throw the bastard out. When Alison Campbell Swain read of rumors that Hillary Clinton had hurled things at Bill, she thought: Good for her. Better that than bottle it up.

Asked for their twentieth-reunion book what they strive to teach their daughters, the Wellesley women of '69 spun variations on these themes: "not to depend financially, psychologically, emotionally—on a man." ". . . that relationships with men are not the most important or reliable thing." ". . . to take risks, question, speak up for herself, be neither perfect nor obedient nor compliant nor concerned with appearances and what others think." ". . . to have the courage to act by herself, without fear of being alone." Barbara Furne Simmons, who remarried in desperation immediately after being left by her first husband, and ten months later divorced, once "desired to surrender, to be swept away by someone. After a while, I began to wonder how much of me there was left to sweep away. Maybe just swept under. Now I know I can handle life, that I don't need to grab for someone to save me."

Catherine Shen has suffered none of her classmates' romantic helplessness or excessive docility. Her voice is startlingly free of sentimentality or apology. Divorced twice, Catherine has concluded that she is too selfish to be married. "I don't like to live with someone and have to share. My most successful relationship was with a man eight years younger than me. I was thirty and he was twenty-two when we met, which was great, because he was totally malleable. I could make all the decisions. I need to get my own way. It's difficult for me when the other person is equal. I find the Clinton marriage interesting because I know from classes I had with Hillary how smart and strong-willed and outspoken she is and I'm curious how two such strong people manage a partnership. The only person in the world I'll sacrifice for is my son, Benjamin."

Catherine never liked or wanted children—"I hadn't ever been in a panic I wouldn't have kids, but a few times I was panicked that I would"—but when she got pregnant at forty-one she decided to have the child. She had met Benjamin's father when she was features editor at the *San Francisco Chronicle;* they romanced long distance when she moved to Washington, D.C., to be an editor at *USA Today* and then to Honolulu to be publisher of that city's daily. "I had the baby because, theoretically, the time was ripe; I was the age my mother was when she had me. We got married and I left the paper and moved back to California. I went back to work when Benjamin was four months. Then I discovered that once you have a child, a marriage is renegotiated from scratch. My husband and I split the four hundred dollars a week for a nanny, but he was not one with the idea of a fifty-fifty split as far as keeping house or caring for the kid. Neither of us would compromise. We stick out in the same places, so instead of meshing, we poked into each other. I wasn't going to give, so two years after we got married, we got a divorce.

"I dote on my son; I can't wait to get home to see him, and would have happily stayed home from work much longer when he was born.

But my career has been drastically slowed. I would have gone to the *Los Angeles Times*, but the job required midnight hours, which as a single mother I couldn't do. That's fine after so many years doing exactly what I wanted to do, but I can't imagine making that choice at twenty-eight. Now, like it or not, the next twelve years are centered on my child. I have fewer choices now, which is rarely a better circumstance to be in, in this world."

Divorce is somewhat less common in the Wellesley class of '69 than it is in the nation as a whole. Still, one in three of those who have married has also divorced, and a majority of those divorces have involved children. The causes have been varied. A very few were, like Catherine, motivated to leave their marriage by an admittedly "selfish" insistence on having things their own way. Many more struck out on their own for more inescapable reasons: Some decided, like Ann Landsberg, that a hellish family was more destructive to themselves and their children than the alternative. Some fled physical danger. Some were left by their husbands, despite all pleadings that they stay.

Betty Demy met her future husband at a Harvard Law School mixer. She was attracted to him because he was fiercely smart, like her father. She was also moved by an unhappiness she thought she might ease. It is, for some women, an irresistible combination: a man of accomplishment who is also wounded and in need.

"My husband had lived an impoverished childhood, financially and emotionally," says Betty. "He'd been very heavy as a boy, an odd duck, without many friends. There was a sad yearning in him that I responded to. I didn't think I'd change him, but I thought that I could give him the things he'd always wanted and then he would be happy and his good qualities would prevail."

Betty had every reason to believe in the happiness promised by married life. Her parents were those "rare, lucky people" with a good marriage, a real partnership sustained by lasting love. "They traveled and had interesting friends and were involved in the community and politics and had wonderfully passionate conversations about ideas. My mother was not frustrated; she didn't wish she were something else. I grew up wanting to have just what she had. And I thought it inevitable that I would grow into her life, that I would have a contented family and become Cub Scout leader and join the PTA." Right on schedule, Betty was married a week after graduation in her parents' New Jersey backyard, then moved with her husband to the Midwest for his service in the JAG Corps. "Like Bill Clinton and every other college boy I knew, my husband made a deal to stay out of Vietnam." They soon had a baby girl, Rebecca, and a boy, Doug.

Betty could not, she discovered, make her husband happy. When her new family returned to New Jersey and bought the house she'd grown up in, her husband quickly came to despise it. "Every day he found something new that was wrong. He was the same with our children, constantly disappointed—harsh and judgmental, as his father had been. At the dinner table it was always, 'Put your napkin in your lap; get your elbows off the table.' I played referee, but it was an unpleasant place to be. He complained that it undermined him. He was right. It did."

An animated woman, plump and pink-cheeked, Betty soon began to feel trapped and isolated. She tried to cheer herself up in a 1979 letter to her classmates—"My life revolves around kindergarten and nursery school, car pools and piano lessons, but I feel less frustrated than I did five years ago. Though some days are filled with trivia, I don't feel sacrificed on the altar of motherhood." Three months later she went to work part-time. "I realized it sounded awful to say you were bored raising your kids, but a lot of it was day-to-day drudgery. I needed an outlet outside the house. Mostly, I needed contact with adults besides my unhappy husband. I got a job at the newspaper, where for the first time in a long time I was not somebody's mother or somebody's wife. I felt part of the town, which I loved."

As for so many of these women, it was Betty's emergence into the world that gave her the perspective and financial means to alter, or survive alterations, in her private life. "Once I started to regain my self-confidence, I began to realize how unhealthy my marriage was. Every day, our house was growing more filled with tension. It didn't matter what my husband got—it didn't assuage his need. He just got more and more angry, which increasingly spilled out on me."

Betty did not consider divorce. "I wasn't going anywhere. I'd made a commitment, and I believe in fulfilling my obligations. I wanted to give my kids the best possible upbringing and thought it best to have two parents and the financial security of a marriage. Oh, in the long run, I knew I couldn't stay with my husband. But if we had to split, I wanted the kids to be older so I could get a full-time job. Then my husband met somebody else, and I didn't have a choice anymore. Truly, it was a relief when he left.

"Divorce is awful, even if you're getting out of a miserable circumstance. To divorce a lawyer is worst of all—he fought every step of the way." So did Betty, who happened at the time to be helping a friend write a book about divorce and was alarmed by what she was learning about the way women get burned. Two years into the battle, her own lawyer erupted in anger: "He snapped at me, 'What you need is a man to put you on your back where you belong.'" (He later denied saying any such thing.) By the time it was all over, Betty had won a judgment against him as well. In the end, she believes, she and her kids came out better than most. She had to leave the newspaper for a full-time job in public relations at a local hospital, which she didn't love. "But it kept me in my community and available to my kids."

Since the divorce, Betty's ex-husband has had almost no relationship with his children. He did not attend his son's high school graduation. Though he met his financial obligations, for long periods of time, he had no direct contact with his kids, though his office is a mile from the family's home. "I was finished enough with him that he could no longer hurt me, but what he's done to my kids has been abominable. It was hardest on Doug, who was eight and idealized his father; he had a tough adolescence. My daughter was eleven, and told me, 'I'm glad he's gone. I never liked him.' The pain hit her later. But I think both, fundamentally, are okay. Doug and I went out to dinner one night before he left for college. He told me that he felt he had to grow up faster than his friends, that he had more responsibility at an earlier age and a more realistic view of life and expectations and that he was glad for that."

Between 1960 and 1980, the divorce rate in America rose 250 percent. For that breakdown of the family, many have blamed feminism: Its rhetoric of fulfillment, they claim, subverted women's natural inclination to place others' needs above their own and substituted self-gratification, no matter the cost to their children. Feminism has actually promoted and celebrated the dissolution of marriage, in the view of some conservatives: Barbara Dafoe Whitehead finds evidence of a pro-divorce feminist culture in such books as Ivana Trump's memoirs, which, she argues, commends divorce as a technique for self-improvement, like a poetry course or a trip to the spa.

The argument is odd, and not only for the obvious reason that Ivana—like many of Hillary Clinton's classmates—did not elect to be dumped by her husband. It is odd also because divorce is almost never the act of casual self-indulgence the defenders of family values pretend, a fact many must surely recognize from their own broken marriages. In the many sorrowful tales of divorce in the class of '69, few resemble the cavalier, untroubled gesture that has become the cliché. Most of these women were lonely and wretched for years before leaving, or being left by, their husbands. They were racked with impossible questions: Could she mend his happiness? What would harm the children least? Was giving herself up to duty a way to avoid responsibility for her own life?

To see the divorce boom as a consequence of feminism betrays as well a shallow sense of history. From the nation's beginnings, as rugged individualists lit out for the territories in search of wealth and freedom, America has been "the place where husband and wife often split," as John Locke wrote at the end of the seventeenth century. The divorce rate has risen for three centuries at a fairly steady pace, doubling at the turn of the twentieth century, as it would again in the sixties.

It is true that first-wave feminists fought against laws that made a woman her husband's property and gave him alone the prerogative to sever the contract and claim custody of the children, and that temperance activists fought for a woman's right to divorce a drunk. It is also true that second-wave feminism helped women secure the financial capacity to leave and raised their consciousness about the limits to forbearance. But the rise in divorce has also been impelled by a commercial culture that continuously stimulates an appetite for the new, and by changes in the economy that have blurred the very purpose of marriage: With ever more domestic services available for purchase, and with most women earning their own wages, men have ceased to need wives to cook their meals or mend their clothes and women have ceased needing husbands to support them. At the same time, as extended families and communities have loosened their ties, marriage has increasingly been expected to fulfill all needs for intimacy and companionship—an impossible, often fatal, burden.

Feminists have in fact often opposed social changes that made divorce easier, like the no-fault laws that many argued would help impoverish women and children. Most such laws eliminated or radically abbreviated alimony, as if women like Betty Demy could quickly match their husbands' earning power—even though they had set aside their own career advancement for years to raise kids and even though they had lost their most valuable common property: the joint investment in their husband's career assets. After divorce, the private inequalities in such marriages become social inequalities, with the husband's household much richer and the wife's much poorer.

Betty's divorce is not atypical: Fathers (and their money) often disappear. A third of the children of divorce see their fathers just once a week and a third not at all. In 1995, half of the 5.3 million fathers who were supposed to did not pay the child support they owe, reneging on $34 billion to 23 million kids. The success of the women's movement was undoubtedly as much a consequence of the collapse of this paternal responsibility as its cause. As women came to see the fragility of the institution that had traditionally sheltered them, they came to see as well the necessity of securing their own independent income.

In the Wellesley class of '69, those who failed to secure such financial independence invariably suffered the toughest divorces, while those who were the principal breadwinners had much greater leverage and latitude in their choices. Susan Alexander and Nancy Young both had violence in their marriages, but because they were also their family's wage earners, they had the wherewithal to leave. Others in the class, also financially self-sufficient in their marriages, have managed what can only be called successful divorces. Newspaper publisher Catherine Shen's divorce cost her a lot: She had far more assets, which in California were treated as community property and equally shared. But, for her son's sake, "I was willing to spend whatever it took to preserve the peace. His father now lives a mile away and we get along better than we ever did before the divorce." Fashion model Michelle Lamson was also the moneymaker in her family at the time of her divorce, which came not long after she adopted a baby boy; on the day she brought him home, her husband disappeared for the night, explaining the next day that "it was all too much for him." A few months later, he left her for another woman. As her ex-husband, he has been a devoted father, seeing Nicholas every weekend, calling him every day, spending Christmas with the family. "I don't think he'd have been such a good father if we'd stayed married," says Michelle. "Nicholas has thrived."

That the children of divorce suffer less if they do not end up poor is obviously true. Beyond that, it is hard to assess how the kids of the broken marriages in the class of '69 have fared; their mothers' optimistic testimony reflects some unmeasurable mixture of truth and wishful thinking. In their usual fashion, these women have foraged among the countless studies for insight, cringing at those that find kids of divorce more prone to substance abuse, depression, and trouble in school, relieved by those that find them faring as well as those in intact families if their family income is adequate and their mothers are well educated and their fathers remain involved. All worry deeply for their children.

Mary Day Kent, '69, was her family's breadwinner. In 1971, she was living in Philadelphia and working for the American Friends Service when her boyfriend moved in. Eight years later, "because I was pregnant and my mother was weeping," they got married. After her son's birth at her midwife's farm, Mary went back part-time to the Friends Peace Committee, working on human rights in Latin America. She earned little, but it had to serve: Mary's husband spent his time putting out a newsletter promoting bicycle riding. Until they had children, Mary did not object to subsidizing her husband's work. "Then money becomes one of those things that is suddenly much more important. When our kids were young and we were broke, it was a source of great stress to be living with someone who could have helped out and just never got around to it. It was always going to happen any moment. He would have had to work just twenty-five hours a week to ease the enormous financial pressure on me."

A number of Mary's classmates have landed in similar circumstances: supporting husbands whose higher consciousness or free spirit required a life outside the system. Johanna Branson never minded that her husband, Jock, didn't get a bachelor's degree, but she was bothered by "his lack of interest in preparing himself to support his family, and that he managed to shed that traditional imperative without shouldering domestic responsibility. I spent a lot of time when my kids were little chafing, wanting to work more. I'd have to get home by midafternoon, then try to work when they were in bed. I was exhausted and sick all the time."

Mary Day Kent was fortunate to have good subsidized day care at her workplace; she could nurse her kids at work and watch them play in the courtyard, and because she set her own schedule, she could take them to the doctor or attend a school play. "My husband wasn't willing to take on those responsibilities any more than he was willing to get a job, and my experience was that when he was taking care of the kids, he would try to combine that with lots of other things. He wasn't giving them full attention. I felt I was carrying 95 percent of the load. I had to make all the decisions about their schools and get them to do their homework. I had to arrange and pay for summer camp. I had to fight to get him to do any household chores."

"Marrying down," in Mary's case, did not turn out to be a liberating choice. "When I was young, I had vowed I would not get into a conventional marriage, feeling that if I married a high-powered man with lots of goals, he'd make all the decisions and I'd never make my own. I way overdid it. We both were terribly unhappy for a very, very long time. I got counseling and suggested marriage counseling, because it seemed the right thing to do. My husband didn't want to do it. Frankly, by that time I didn't either. I couldn't have stayed with him. I would not have been able to stand it. After ten years of marriage, when our kids were ten and five, we got divorced. My mother was heartbroken. But at one point she said to me, 'Maybe it wasn't such a great idea to push you into marriage. It didn't provide you security after all.'

"I have no doubt that we made the right decision, but I don't think it's possible to overstate the devastating impact that divorce has on children, even under good circumstances. My kids did not have to move. They see their father frequently. Their economic circumstances, if anything, improved: My husband does not give me child support, but I don't have to support him anymore. But my ten-year-old son's academic work suffered. He was extremely depressed and had lots of counseling. He's a progressive and sensitive kid, and right now he's doing well in a special arts high school. But I cross my fingers to say that he is through it. I just hope maybe he'll make it to college and get a self-supporting career."

When I first met Kris and Jeff Rogers in the spring of 1994, their family seemed proof that a marriage could be truly equal, granting both part-

On Their Own   225

ners a chance for a deep, sustained relation with their children and for a
dedicated working life. Like Bill and Hillary Clinton's, theirs was a political marriage, though not in the cynical sense that is usually meant; their
alliance was not simply a way to aggrandize their individual power but a
foundation from which to pursue joint aspirations that were public as
well as private. It was, as Jeff said at Kris's swearing in as U.S. attorney, a
genuine "life partnership," a fair sharing of responsibilities and sacrifices
and rewards.

Jeff made the first professional sacrifice: When, on their arrival in
Oregon, Kris landed a clerkship with a federal judge, Jeff gave up a position in the U.S. attorney's office to avoid a conflict of interest, becoming
a state public defender instead. After the birth of their second child in
1980, they became the first couple ever to share a federal Justice Department job—two desks in an office, alternating workdays—so that they
could share fully in their children's care. For years, the couple worked as
a team: managing cases together, co-teaching courses on sex discrimination at Lewis and Clark College, continuing to take turns stepping out of
each other's way. In 1984, after being forced out of her job, Kris took
herself out of the running for Portland city attorney and Jeff got the job,
a favor he returned when Congresswoman Elizabeth Furse came to him
urging he seek nomination as U.S. attorney. Jeff declined and proposed
Kris instead.

When I next talked to Kris, in the summer of 1994, she began our conversation by saying, "There's something you have to know." She then
told the first chapter in what would unfold as a terribly sad story, ending with: "So, if you were planning to continue with this theme of the
perfect marriage, I need to disabuse you of that illusion." The tale would
become more complicated over the years as I spoke with the two of
them, in alternating conversations that made it easy to imagine what
masterful persuaders both must be in the courtroom. While denying
most of the central allegations, Jeff finally did not wish his words to be
on the record, feeling a public battle would only do more harm to his
children.

In the spring of 1994, Kris told me, her mother was diagnosed with
liver cancer and was told she would live only a few more weeks. Kris flew
to New York in May, and for two days sat with her father to watch her
mother die. She remembers those hours with amazement: her mother's

calm; her father's efforts to express what their life together had meant to him. But she also felt afraid. Just two weeks earlier, she had lost one of her closest friends. "I felt the props knocked out from under me. Life seemed terribly fragile."

After spending a month with her father, Kris returned home to Portland in late June. On the Fourth of July, Jeff told her that for more than a year he'd been having an affair with a woman named Kathryn, who worked as his deputy; he was by then city attorney. Kathryn's husband had discovered the affair and was threatening to tell Kris if Jeff did not. "At that moment, I related in a major way to the first Mrs. Newt Gingrich [who was handed divorce papers by her husband the day after her cancer surgery]. It rocked me to the core—such utter deception. I felt like I'd been living with Dr. Jekyll and Mr. Hyde. Twenty-three years. I didn't know what we would do."

Worried for their daughter, Karen, then seventeen, and son, Ty, fourteen, Kris and Jeff went to a therapist. "I was doing my labor breathing to help me through. Not that I was coping. I was in free fall. It was the most difficult period of my life. The sense of betrayal. My total lack of comprehension over how we could have devolved to that point. My fear of what would come." The pain kept being refreshed for Kris: Searching for answers, she found on their home computer a statement Jeff had composed—a statement seemingly meant for his staff, though never delivered—voicing regret at the pain that he may have caused but describing the undeniable intensity of his new love.

By the fall, Kathryn had resigned as Jeff's deputy and left her marriage and Kris had decided to file for a divorce. Jeff was, at the time, in a race for local office and didn't want to move out right away, says Kris: "He wanted to keep up appearances." When Kris filed for divorce anyway, the local paper ran an item: PORTLAND'S TOP LEGAL COUPLE IS CALLING IT QUITS. Jeff moved out, finally, on Labor Day. "I had to threaten to file a motion to get him to go. In the meantime he was . . . well, it was a difficult time. There were days that I could barely get out of bed, when the tiniest thing would put me over the edge. I'd never been that despondent, for months on end. I felt particularly precarious after the Republican triumph in the November elections, knowing my professional position might crumble. I was kicking myself, thinking if I'd only come to terms with this when I was younger, knowing how difficult it is for women my age to find someone new. I felt my life was over."

Kris's friends were "extraordinarily supportive," especially Hillary Clinton, who happened to visit Portland on her health care tour in the midst of the marriage's collapse. Work also provided some respite, giving form to Kris's days. Like many in the Wellesley class of '69, Kris counters the perception that women are incapable of separating enough from their feelings to function well in the impersonal working world; many have in fact found there the same diversion from painful emotions historically used as an escape by men.

Kris thought about leaving town—moving east to be near her father, becoming a tribal lawyer, joining the Peace Corps, taking a trip with women friends. Her beautiful home in the woods, once so serene in its silences, had come to feel secretive and airless. The smallness of Portland also closed in. "I felt like my nose was being rubbed in it all the time." To illustrate the point, she sent me an article from a local weekly paper, *Willamette Week*, published after the divorce, when Jeff rehired Kathryn. Headlined DANGEROUS LIAISONS, the piece asked, "Should the city of Portland allow managers to supervise workers they sleep with?" It described Jeff as "the son of Nixon's secretary of state . . . law school chum of Bill Clinton and former husband of U.S. Attorney Kris Olson." Kris's accompanying letter struck a note of bitter satisfaction: "He always said he wouldn't stand to be known as S.O.B [son of Bill], F.O.B. [friend of Bill] or S.O.K. [spouse of Kris], but there it is."

Drowned for months in waves of rage and self-recrimination, tossed up eventually on an unfamiliar shore, Kris began to reflect on her marriage from her new vantage. As she did, she began to discern a story different from the one she had so long told herself and the world. Again experiencing the ricochet between the personal and the political, Kris was spurred on in her reconception of her marriage by an unlikely catalyst: the passage of the Violence Against Women Act, which made domestic abuse a federal crime for the first time. Charged with new prosecutorial responsibilities, Kris began looking through materials from a local women's shelter, which included two warning lists outlining the signs of an abusive relationship, one detailing "emotional and economic attacks," the other "acts of violence." While Kris had never experienced physical violence in her marriage, many of the signs on the other list, ranging from lying and infidelity to "not giving support, attention, or compliments," she concluded, "described my own marriage."

That private conclusion brought with it, for Kris, a sense of public obligation. "I feel fortunate that I don't need to keep up appearances the way Hillary does. In fact, I feel this absolute compulsion not to cover up anymore, to share the experience so that people can learn from my mistakes." Kris acted on that compulsion quickly, in the fall of 1994, when she gave a talk to women lawyers at the annual Oregon Bar convention. Because she'd been with the Clintons for the signing of the crime bill, the convention organizers asked her to talk about violence against women. "I ended up tossing the talking points from D.C. and speaking totally from my own heart. I told them that I believed the sixties had been a true revolution, with women daring finally to speak out, but that we'd hit glass ceilings and backlash and the religious right going on about women 'forsaking' their families and that we were losing ground. I'd just read Peggy Orenstein on the collapse of self-esteem in girls; I'd seen my women law students unwilling to speak up and the women in my office sniping at each other because they were afraid to confront problems head-on. I'd seen women lawyers who felt stuck—either they swallowed shit and became one of the boys, or they fled. They had no ground on which to fight; there's rarely strength in numbers inside the firm, and it's taboo to go outside for support: If they press, they end up blackballed as troublemakers. I told those women that we need to sustain our support networks, that consciousness-raising is not outdated, that we need to shed our shame and talk to each other in order to break these cycles. Then I told them what I'd learned about myself. I said, 'Look at me, I'm the first woman U.S. attorney of Oregon, and I've let this happen to me, and I'm not sure how and it's a really slippery slope.'"

Kris's public declaration was in fact veiled, but the message got through. "It was the most nerve-racking talk I've ever given. I felt like I'd stood up and said, 'I'm Kris Rogers and I'm an alcoholic.' I just felt it necessary that we face the degree to which women who gain power are subjected in the workplace and in intimate relationships to a backlash, to people's efforts to control them and put them in their place. I asked all the women in the room to do some group comparison of life experiences, 'Right here, right now.' I read them the list of abusive behaviors, and asked how many had experienced any of them in the workplace or with their partner. I guessed that because they are more public and so more threatening, they would have experienced abuse more than women who aren't pushing the edges. Of the two hundred women there, about eighty percent raised their hands. It was a collective coming out that left me drained. When it was over, my Wellesley classmate Susan Graber [then an associate justice of the Oregon Supreme Court, now a judge on the Ninth Circuit U.S. Court of Appeals] had to help me down off the podium and out to my car."

For a woman left by her husband for another woman to diagnose abuse retrospectively sets off every alarm: She has jumped on a bandwagon, cloaked herself in the victim's mantle, is out for revenge. Kris herself acknowledges having "seen countless examples of women who are hurt and lash out and demonize their ex-husband." But the question is more complicated. Women have long been mistreated by their husbands—but secretly, and without language to talk about it. Only with feminism did women begin publicizing those private miseries, developing in the process a new vocabulary. It is possible, as some argue, that this new vocabulary has mostly had the effect of leading people like Kris to see pathology where there was just ordinary human unhappiness, that it has turned the confused misdemeanors inevitable in a relationship into stark crimes. The problem with the word *abuse* is that it conjures an abuser and an abused; it obscures the collaboration not only in destructiveness but also in the aspiration to integrity and love.

But it is also possible that the new language has given women the capacity to recognize mistreatment that they had previously explained away or blamed upon themselves. Having insisted on stepping free of the shields of the old social rules and making their own choices about sex and intimate relationships, women soon discovered that they needed new, publicly agreed-upon rules, rules that they participated in crafting and that made finer distinctions as to what was an intimate injustice or a sexual crime.

There is no question that Kris's reexamination of her solitary experience through this new collectively built—even if perhaps distorting—lens freed her to see the collapse of her marriage as something other than simply her private failure; she achieved internal resolution only through public solidarity. "I had been denying, denying, denying, even though friends told me that my marriage was often painful to watch and my mother had been voicing her worries for years. She told me that I wasn't making compromises but that I was compromised, that I'd given up part of myself, that I often seemed lost and my eyes dulled."

Jeff never physically harmed Kris. Instead, she speaks of infidelities, public and private humiliations, Jeff meanly deriding her for having "her mother's fat body." She describes growing isolation. "He weaned me away from my close friendships, told me I was emotionally promiscuous and that my friends would come between us. Once I was crying on the phone with a friend; he took the phone out of my hand, told her I couldn't talk now, and hung it up. I acceded to it: I was too bewildered and ashamed to embrace the company of women the way I later would." In her journal, she wrote: "I don't feel safe and loved. I feel like a lab rat cowering, fearing random shocks. How do you know when you're selling yourself out?"

Most strange and most sad is an incident Kris describes around the time of her fortieth birthday. "On New Year's Eve, Jeff and I started to reminisce. But over and over, he'd recall an event and I'd say, 'That's not the way I remember it.' I finally got out the journals I'd been keeping for many years and began to read to him. He was upset by what I'd written, said, 'We can't have that be our history. We have to make a fresh start. What if someone should ever stumble upon these?' He persuaded me I should burn them. So we sat down together by the fire and threw them in, one by one." Kris's interior dialogue with herself had been erased. She didn't write in a journal again until 1992.

Though Kris recalls bitterly Jeff's reminder to her at the end that they had written their own wedding vows and that he had nowhere promised to forsake all others—"Oh yes, I'm a lawyer. Of course I should have vetted the language of our vows"—in fact, their marriage *was* built on the contract model. It was a partnership conscientiously negotiated by equals, with the goal of achieving at home the same kind of justice tempered by compassion that Kris aspires to at work. The view that marriage ought to be regulated by principles of justice came out of feminism, which rejected the conventional notion that the family did not need such principles because it was better than just, a place where each was as concerned with the other as with himself. In fact, feminists argued, there were often great inequalities of power and resources at home and there was, therefore, a pressing necessity to address the politics of personal life.

"Jeff and I both truly wanted the perfect marriage. We strove for that constantly and came close to pulling it off; we did great teamwork in teaching and working, and the thing we did best together was raising our kids. I endured so long because I kept clinging to that ideal. I didn't want to admit it couldn't be done, or that I had failed. I'd think, If we can just get over this hump. I also hung in for the sake of the children. Jeff is a wonderful father. The kids inspire us to transcend our differences. But we lacked what Bill and Hillary have—a real partnership. Bill has truly supported and promoted Hillary; he is intensely fond of her and reliant on her in a way Jeff never was with me.

"At bottom, I think that the equal relationship and the job sharing took a much greater psychological toll on Jeff. He had a harder time with his colleagues. He was viewed as wimpy or not properly ambitious or not fully committed to his career, traits which were expected of women, but not men, while I got positive strokes for being pioneering. Jeff worked hard not to become his father. He married a strong woman and always promoted women professionally," and refused the U.S. attorney job in part, Kris believes, because he worried that his pursuit of it would be wrongly motivated, as a way to achieve success in his father's eyes. "But the fact remained that he'd had a very traditional upbringing, and kept one foot in the fifties all along."

Kris believes that Jeff resented, ultimately, his sense of being eclipsed by his wife and her power in the world. "There was this public persona of a liberated man, and then Jeff would need to control me at home. Anything I did that got public recognition would spark a flurry of behavior by him to undermine me." After he recommended her for U.S. attorney, Kris wrote in her journal, "he grew distant, dour, snappish and mean. . . . He says I'm patronizing him when I don't talk about it, but he doesn't see his body language when I do." When Janet Reno called and in passing mentioned being dumped out of her canoe into the Potomac, he seemed unhappy "that I didn't take that opportunity to mention him and his love of canoeing. . . . The thing he said over and over was 'I grew up in the shadow of my father and I'll be goddamned if I'll be in your shadow now.' "

In conversation and in her journals, Kris turns the story over and over, swinging from recrimination to self-recrimination and back again. In her journal, she wrote: "When he's distant, I think I'm turning him off because I'm too fat . . . or wonder if I haven't drawn him out because I'm self-absorbed. . . . Is Jeff right, am I icy? . . . I am about out of empathy. And if I keep trying to understand, do I set myself up as a punching bag?" At times, she realized, she *had* neglected her family for her work. "I was full of guilt about my career taking me away from the kids, away from Jeff. I've examined every way I could have shored him up, given more emotional support." Looking back, she says, "I was so confused, so emotionally at sea.

"Women like us think we're above this drivel. I hate all the self-esteem crap, but that's what it was—I had zero self-esteem. Even though I was a lawyer with two kids, I felt desperate and scared, felt I had to make it work." An admirer of Eleanor Roosevelt, Kris mused in her journal over their common struggle. "Eleanor lost her sense of purpose for a decade, seeking to please her husband and his family." She suffered from "the Griselda complex," which counts forbearance a virtue, which means the more you put up with, the more noble you are. "That can lead you to accept too much. It can also lead you to overweight his injustices to enhance your own martyrdom."

That a woman so fearless and outspoken in public would feel so vulnerable in her intimate relations; that a knight in the world becomes a damsel at home, helpless and panicked and determined to keep her protector whatever the cost: That paradox has plagued many women in Hillary's class.

"The woman at home was the core of what I was taught to be," Kris says. "It's easier in the public realm to resist. Your life there is not tied up with vows and kids and the whole history and weight of the model of your parents, and, in my case, grandparents' relationships. My grandparents lived with us. My grandfather was a philanderer and physically abusive, and my grandmother took it as her lot, hung in to the end. She believed that a woman should simply endure hardships, sacrifice herself, suffer quietly and nobly. I also grew up hearing my mother say that the woman gives seventy percent and that's the way it is. By the time I got around to consciousness-raising, I'd already internalized those earlier messages, which are incredibly hard to shake. It took me a long time to realize that forbearance isn't a virtue at all."

Kris has continued, in public forums, to urge young women to resist their own habits of submission. In 1995, she and Susan Graber conducted a women's forum on their "journey" since graduating from Wellesley. "I chided the young women there to get to know their life's partner. There's so much pressure for men to make supportive noises. A lot will know just how to sound, but dig deeper and it's just not there. As women, programmed to be the nurturers, we understand that we must accept the worst in our partner to achieve intimacy. But we confuse the acceptance of the person with the acceptance of mistreatment. We believe that we're loving unconditionally; we try to accommodate his needs while feeling more and more inadequate. Women have got to stop turning this on themselves and feeling guilty. I told them to throw the bum out if he was demeaning them, making them feel shitty about themselves. They have to name it, do something about it, not model a stiff upper lip to their daughters."

What to tell her own children has been for Kris somewhat more confused. She speaks of her shared effort with Jeff to shelter their kids from the worst, to not drag them through an ugly divorce; to that end, she says, she agreed to share custody. At the same time, she continues to use public forums (including this book) to recount the story, and has talked privately with her children. Her journals, she says, are written for her daughter, Karen. "I am convinced that recounting stories such as mine can make a difference in our children's and their children's lives. Though I loathe talk-show confessionals, somehow this seems more akin to warning others to avoid quicksand. Think how much we could have learned from Eleanor Roosevelt—had she been willing to talk more about her personal experience. I have learned so much from women risking openness, and feel so indebted to them, that it seems the only responsible thing for me to do—even if it means some embarrassment. And frankly, Jeff has waived his right to claim embarrassment, because he didn't feel any compunction about exposing us all to it in the first place when his own pleasure was paramount."

With her son, says Kris, she has spent a lot of time talking about how he treats girls. "Ty is tall and handsome and a basketball star. He has a great sense of entitlement. When he dumped a girlfriend in a way that seemed callous to me, I blew up at him, reminding him that he'd once professed to love her. He blasted back at me: 'I'm not my father.'

"With Karen, I've spent time talking about what you don't have to accept, conversations I never had with my mother. I think that if out of some instinct to protect her I'd closed myself, she would have been more distressed. She shut me down when she needed to, reminding me that she'll always love her father. But she's a sturdy soul; she doesn't need to retreat into a shell and would have called me on it if I had.

"When I was going through my mother's things after her death, I

found a letter she'd carried for fifty years, a letter sent to my grandmother by one of my grandfather's mistresses, whom he'd bilked out of
her life savings and then discarded. The woman had written trying to
track him down. My mother carried that her entire life. I would never
want Karen to carry my story through her whole life, not if my story carried so bitter a lesson. I hope with all my heart that she would make different decisions. I sometimes think I should have left the marriage much
earlier for her sake. But I also worry that she will learn too much mistrust. I don't accept the view of people like Catherine Mackinnon that all
male-female relationships are inevitably about dominance and submission. I didn't want Karen to think that I was unforgiving, that the first
time he strayed, I threw him out. I wanted her to know you keep trying,
and recover your hope."

Women Without Children

At Wellesley, Charlynn Maniatis was afraid to go to mixers. "I was a hermit, like my mother. I was scared and shy. I didn't even get my driver's
license till I was twenty-nine." She hid in work: Her accelerated push
through college and law school and medical school consumed her time
and walled her off from society as successfully as her father's pressure to
achieve and repressive rules had isolated her as a girl. Though work de-
voured her, it failed to make her happy. After a residency in diagnostic
radiology, she discovered that she didn't like medicine. But when she returned to trial law, the "sinking feeling" she had every day finally drove
her back to medicine. She now has her own part-time practice in New
York. "I get the worst headaches. I'm going bankrupt. I beg my creditors
to take me to court and put a bullet through me. In school, you're idealistic. You think when you get out, patients will come to you; you'll be
rich. I made the mistake of taking over the practice of a retiree. All his
patients were dying; reimbursements were being cut. I have a few crazy
old patients, who complain about the music, the furniture, my hair; they
threaten us and steal pictures off my office walls. I guess my hermit ten-
dencies are not well suited to New Yorkers." She counts herself a failure
professionally. "I am so paranoid about losing my job that I prefer to
have several part-time jobs so that I will always have some income. But
the money I make from those jobs is far less than other doctors make,

and I have no benefits and am extremely worried about my financial future." The only place she ever felt safe and fully at home, says Charlynn, was in the Navy Reserves.

Charlynn always imagined she would get married, though for long periods she has had no men in her life. She dated an economics professor for ten years, but that relationship ended in 1993. From the outset he told her that he'd been burned once and would never marry again. He also always dated other people at the same time. "I thought it was better than nothing, and saw him every week. Then he decided I'd gotten too fat and too Navy, and that I had too little time for him. He left me and dated someone else for six months, then begged to come back, but by then I was dating an engineer from the Midwest, who was wholesome and religious but boring. I now have dinner once a week with the economics professor, which is an event that I look forward to every week. I also speak on the telephone almost every night to a man who lives on the other side of the country and whom I see very rarely. Most men I meet, after two nights it's tedious. I've only known one or two interesting people in my life."

Charlynn lives in suburban Cos Cob, Connecticut, and spends her free hours in mostly solitary pursuits—flying planes and doing needlepoint. Little inclined toward groups—"I'm in church only for weddings and funerals; I don't even participate in my condo association"—she meets few people. "I've gone to singles' groups, but the women outnumber the men, and the men talk only to each other. I did dating services, which are pretty good, but the men get so many women they can't keep up with you. I met the engineer through a service, but they kept sending him names." She also blames feminism, and especially harassment suits, for making men afraid of women and therefore still harder to meet.

Until her mid-forties, Charlynn held out hope that she might still marry and have a child. She thought of having her ova harvested and frozen, but was too shy to approach a colleague and ask. "Not having children is an incredible sadness. I mean, I have friends who have kids and they're delightful for a few hours and then I stay for a weekend and I'm glad I don't have the screaming and shouting. But my mother has no grandchildren and now it's the option lost forever. When I was thirty I thought I might be artificially inseminated, but the technology was too new. Then I thought about adoption, but they would only give you a child if you were married and I never really wanted to do it by myself anyway. At forty I was dating the economist. Then we broke up and it hit me: 'Now what are you going to do?' "

Her "dearest friends," nearly all of whom are men, have not been encouraging. They tell her that what men want is a woman "half his age plus seven," which means those who would be interested in her are in their eighties. When a blind date waited in his car outside the restaurant where they were to meet and after checking Charlynn out took off without a word, her male friends told her they would have done the same thing: If they don't like a woman's looks, why waste their money and time? "I listen to what they say about other women and then I don't feel as bad; I don't take it all so personally. I realize the pathology is on their side, that they don't really like women."

Pat Sinclair, '69, is also sorrowful at her childlessness. She didn't mean not to have kids, though as a midwestern minister's daughter, she'd been far less taken with the picture of her own mom—a Mennonite immigrant from Russia in an apron baking cookies—than she was with her friends' moms, who did their nails and smoked and drank. After Wellesley, she launched into a vagabond life: waitressing to support her pottery making, selling paper dresses, doing cocaine and LSD, "smoking a lot of reefer and crashing at whatever freak's" house she landed in for the night. A marriage of five years foundered on what she calls her husband's possessiveness, and she has not lived with anyone since. In recent years, she has worked as a bank clerk and a bookkeeper at Kansas University, earning $13,000 a year. In her late forties, having lost many friends to AIDS, she began studying social work, "feeling my life needed more meaning." She worries how she will take care of herself when she is old and at moments regrets not falling for Peter Parker ("as in pens") or any of "those other rich boys" who roamed around Wellesley. "Sometimes I feel I've lived an aimless life: no life's work; no kid. Maybe having a kid, being surrounded by people looking smaller than you all the time, makes you grow up. In the eyes of the world, I feel a freak."

Twenty-three percent of the women in the class of '69 have no children. That percentage is just slightly higher than among baby-boomer women overall but far higher than among the women who graduated ten years earlier (just 9 percent of the class of '59 is childless) and much lower than among women ten years younger: In 1994, when members of the class of '79 were entering their late thirties, 42 percent had still not had children.

Some in the class have never had children because they never found a partner with whom they could make a family. One in five has struggled with infertility, some of it a consequence of waiting too long. "I think a lot of my classmates felt duped that no one clued us in that it was hard to have children in your late thirties," says Jan Mercer, who lost three pregnancies between the births of her first and second children. A surprising number, however, trace their difficulties getting pregnant not to ill-advised delays at all but to the crude and hazardous methods of birth control common in their youth, a twist typically left out of the barren-career-woman story. Jan finally discovered that she had an infection, likely caused by the Copper 7 IUD she had once used. Federal prosecutor Rhea Kemble used birth control throughout her first marriage, concerned that a child would interfere with her career, and was then unable to get pregnant in her second marriage, despite four years of taking fertility drugs; in her case, too, it turned out that an IUD she'd had when young had caused a pelvic inflammatory disease that left her infertile. Cynthia Gilbert-Marlow, who could never conceive a second child, recalls a frightening midnight visit to a New York doctor followed by a horrible abscess: Her Dalkon Shield scarred her fallopian tubes and left one blocked entirely.

Like the mothers in the class, the single and childless women have been whipped this way and that by the media and experts, measuring their happiness and telling them how they ought to behave. When they were girls, they saw "spinsters" painted as a sorry lot: *Time* magazine wrote of "lives of quiet desperation punctuated by pathetic sorties to dating clubs." To remain childless was the worst fate that could befall a woman: Erik Erikson, whose work on identity helped make it a central preoccupation and pursuit, advised that a woman who did not fulfill her "innate need to fill her uterus with embryonic tissue was likely to be frustrated or neurotic."

By the early seventies, that story had been upended, a reflection in great measure of the gallivantings of their generation. *Newsweek* proclaimed singlehood "glamorous." Hollywood celebrated the slow discovery of unfettered pleasures by *An Unmarried Woman* and opened the dark *Diary of a Mad Housewife*. By the eighties, when Hillary Clinton's classmates were in their thirties and watching their biological clocks wind down, the story reversed once more: Single women were again depicted as lonely, depressed, and desperate, both reflecting and shaping how the women of this generation perceived their lives. Typical of those years was *Newsweek's* famous warning to women over thirty-five that they were more likely to take a terrorist bullet than find a husband. Even *Cosmo*, that longtime friend of the sexy single girl, offered up sketches from an unmarried life: "Her will to date replaced by a will to eat" she is "sitting on her huge butt in front of *Kojak* eating injudicious amounts of ice cream. She will have similarly plump pals with whom she'll discuss only one subject. 'Why are all the attractive men either gay or married?' " In the nineties, that story persists. Arianna Huffington has called Gloria Steinem "a pathetic woman who pretends she didn't want a man or child, because she couldn't get one." Easy to see why Pat Sinclair might feel freakish.

Several women in the class have grappled consciously with how this story of the pitiable barren woman has weighed on their lives. Virginia Blankenhorn has wished at times that she hadn't wanted to get married, "since I would have had more freedom . . . but I did want to—or maybe it was social pressure, the feeling that I was finally doing what I was *supposed* to be doing. The nine months of my pregnancy represented the longest period of my life where I could unequivocally approve of myself, because I knew that everybody else (i.e., my mother) could find no fault with me at last."

Louise Carter entered Wellesley believing she would have a romantic life, get married, and let a man take care of her, "maybe even be rich." Then she dated moneyed Harvard men and found them dull and realized that "life in the suburbs, sitting by the pool and just having kids to raise, would be a nightmare." As with so many of these women, her own mother's frustration lingered too freshly in her mind. Having once aspired to work in medicine, Louise's mother had dropped out of college when she fell ill during her first pregnancy. She had "no patience for children. She was constantly losing it with us and telling us how much she hated being a mother."

Instead of marrying rich, Louise moved in with a student she met in Cambridge and followed him into graduate school in psychology. They married and she finished her doctorate and began teaching, but soon became unhappy with her work and family life. In an article in the 1990 alumnae magazine, she wrote: "I had a decent husband, an interesting job, a house that rumbled with helpful appliances," but felt "I'd wandered into the wrong lifeplan. . . . Silently, I admonished myself for ungratefulness. I zapped my doubts and slipped back into the updraft of success. I maintained the purposeful flutter for a couple of years, but my dissatisfaction grew." In conversation, Louise elaborated: "My career had taken off, but it wasn't what I wanted to do. I was on a zooming locomotive and had to leap off. My path was a different path and maybe a dirt path." In the alumnae magazine, she quoted Kurt Vonnegut: " 'You are who you pretend to be, so you better watch out who you pretend to be.' I hadn't noticed when the roles I'd played had begun to define me, distancing me from my True Self."

Louise began to write fiction again in 1978. In 1979, her husband went away to a conference, and Louise found herself writing with a new kind of freedom. When he came back, she told him that she wanted to live by herself for a while. After a year apart, she didn't feel like moving back in. "He wanted me to come back and have kids. I felt like if we had kids, it would all be on me, like everything else had been. Ending that relationship was the hardest thing I ever had to do. I would visit him and drive away and think, I could turn back right now and he would be so happy. And I could never do it. I wanted to get to my own home. I haven't seen him since 1981. He got involved with a student of mine, a woman I introduced him to. They got pregnant that summer, so in September, I said, 'I guess it's time for us to get a divorce.' "

From the alumnae magazine: "At thirty-two, I left my husband, moved to an apartment without a dishwasher, started writing again, quit my job. I'd given up a secure job, marriage, plans for children. I wasn't sure I wanted those things, but I wondered if someday I'd regret not having them. Magazine covers screamed warnings about the man shortage, a contemporary horror story about educated, independent women forever deprived of their chance to live the American dream. I bundled all my fears into a Thanksgiving fantasy, and played it over and over in my imagination . . . a New England saltbox, chubby-fingered cherubs clutching at daddy, mommy smiling in the kitchen, while her childless sister sits in a darkened city apartment."

Home alone on her fortieth birthday, Louise got a phone call from a cemetery, wondering if they might interest her in purchasing a burial plot. Unnerved, she put on her shoes and went out for a run. "I realized with pleasure that age . . . is the antidote to pretending. I could relax." Since 1980, she has lived with a man who has made it plain that he is not interested in having kids. "I know lots of women who have just conveniently forgotten to use birth control. I couldn't do that. And I've been ambivalent; I blamed him, but I also wasn't bringing it up. I've always loved the unpredictability in my life, and I don't think children deal with that well. At the grocery store, I see these women with their well-put-together kids and their full grocery carts and I don't envy them. I do have a close relationship with a number of children of family and friends. I also have a cat, and I'm an incredibly overprotective doting mother and I sometimes think, Oh no, I'm turning into one of those cat ladies. I'm sometimes sad, but feel mostly at peace with it."

It was, for Louise, the story she had to get over more than the fact of not having children. It makes one wonder whether in a place that afforded them a more honorable role, women without children might not feel so miserable. In fact, there are childless women in the class for whom that seems to be the case.

In the twentieth-reunion book, Chris Osborne wrote to her classmates of "an experiment with engagement" that had recently "blown up in my face." It was 1986 and she was living in Chicago. He was a lawyer, about to make partner, when he got the call from God to be a minister and quit the firm. "He was the finest person I'd ever met, and I can make myself very in love with a person based on their values. I find it inspiring when someone appreciates right and wrong on even the smallest things. He was brilliant and holy and sweet and I loved him very much.

"The problem was, well, he wouldn't fuck me. I thought, We'll just get counseling, but he wouldn't. I think he had some weird problem that went deeper than anything he was willing to talk about. I went myself and after two sessions thought, I don't need this. That was it. Twice before that I had lived with men, but I never wanted to marry them, either. I think marriage happens when you're convinced you want a family, and I've never been someone who had to have a baby. I would never get married just for that reason, and that took some of the energy in that direction away.

"For a while the biological clock bothered me; then I read about it and thought, Oh, that's what I had. It's nothing I'm going to regret. I would have had children if circumstances had been right and I could have given them a good life. Maybe that's a legacy of my mother's work at Planned Parenthood: I believe you create a loving home first and then have a child. I would never have done it alone. When I was growing up, my dad may have been in the basement working on his model trains and avoiding my mother, but he was always there. I would have wanted to be home when my kids were little, and since I've always had to support myself, that wouldn't have been possible.

"I am really happy to be single and free and independent. I love exploring new cities, building new nests, making new friends. I also adore being alone. I've always been self-sufficient. I love to read and write and garden, all kinds of solitary activities. Even when I'm unhappy, I'm better alone. The last thing I want is to talk to someone else. I've created a beautiful home for myself, where I find all the solace I need."

Like her classmates who chose to stay at home with their children, Chris at times seems to need to persuade her fellows that she is happy in her chosen life. "I hate to go out," she wrote to them fifteen years out of school. "I come home to my cat Gary, build a fire and pull out the current journal. The collected works now number some sixty volumes, a compendium of thoughts, gripes, dialogues, spleen, prayers, lists, oracles and nasty stuff about other people, all of which must be destroyed upon my death." In the twentieth-reunion book, she was intentionally confusing: "I don't get lonely. Clean air, homegrown catnip and neighboring fish have turned Harry and Ernie into big, strapping boys. We're all digging our first yard, featuring real trees, live flowers and actual birds, rabbits, toads and squirrels."

Chris's comic account of her life at times seems almost a parody of her classmates' candor; she is armored by wit even at her most startlingly uninhibited. At the White House reunion, she paused after saying goodbye to me, then suddenly blurted: "There's something I want to tell you, which I'm hesitant to say for fear in some weird way it might hurt Hillary. I've smoked dope every day since 1965. I'm a responsible taxpayer and a responsible doper, and think it should be legalized. If I'm going to be true to the cause, I need to come clean."

She is still less the "good girl" on the subject of sex. "I don't mind not having someone living with me. Guys around the house are great for changing lightbulbs and fixing things; it's amazing how they can do that stuff. I had one like that once, but he was such a shit head, I'm happy to go without. I'd rather pay Tim the handyman, even though he goes at the pace of a retarded snail and is usually cranky. I do mind not having sex once in a while. It's tough, because sex is so problematic these days. I don't even date anymore, because I don't want to get into that. That's why my idea for a vibrator store is so good. I ordered mine by mail from Eve's Garden. It's a Hitachi, about the size of a washing machine, very useful. But there could be something like 'The Sharper Image,' something that sexless, except they would sell nothing but vibrators. Not a sleazy place. Everyone should be comfortable going there. I'm just waiting for financing. I've made millions of dollars for my clients, but I've not made my own million yet. This could be it: There's so many people who feel like they can't have sex with other people anymore."

Certainly, in the class of '69 the level of sexual dissatisfaction is high. A third of the women, both married and unmarried, report a disappointing or inactive sex life. One in three married women in the class has been unfaithful. Others have every reason to be: An anonymous correspondent to the twentieth-reunion book wrote, "I have been faithful all my marriage, but my husband and I always had too little sex for me, 2x a month and now there has been none for nine months or so."

Like the others in the class without children, Chris Osborne knows she will have to fend for herself in old age. She also knows that "just because you have children doesn't mean you'll be taken care of. I don't see me taking care of my mother. And she seems kind of a lost soul, a bright woman who after years of raising kids and not being out in the world is unhappy most of the time." Chris feels neither such isolation nor such sorrow. "There's plenty of us spinsters and also generous women comfortable enough in their marriages that they don't mind setting a place for a single woman. I think in our sixties and seventies we spinsters, widows, and divorcees will link up more and more. In the meantime, I mother my friends and they mother me; one friend celebrates Mother's Day just with friends."

Maternal Instincts

Finding ways to mother—to care deeply for children not their own or for people just as dependent as children—has been for some of these women a way out of the sense of freakishness suffered by Pat Sinclair or the loneliness endured by Charlynn Maniatis, a loneliness which seems less a consequence of childlessness than of a more universal isolation. Before she had a child of her own, Jan Piercy became guardian to classmate (and single parent) Jinnet Fowles's two children, which through Jan's thirties was the "closest I thought I would come to having children." Lindsay Miller has been a Lamaze coach for a single mom. Dorothy Devine assisted her first woman lover through labor and delivery, and remained close to that child, who is now grown and married. After she broke up with her second serious lover, a wealthy woman who squired her to debutante balls, Dorothy discovered that she missed "suppertime, people coming home, kids, and family life." Since 1983, she has helped raise her lover's two sons while their mother has gone to night school and traveled on business.

For her tenth reunion, Nonna Noto wrote to her classmates: "No family yet; still looking!" On her fifteenth, in the line asking her present name, she wrote, "Still single." At her twentieth, she wrote again that she was still single, adding, "I hold great respect for those of you who have managed to combine a successful marriage, motherhood, and working."

By her twenty-fifth reunion, Nonna, an economist who has worked at the Federal Reserve and the Congressional Research Service on public finance and health care, found herself wanting to get together the fifty women in the class who had never married, "to see if we just never met the right guy or if maybe we were somehow predisposed to stay single. I used to think that I was just one of the unlucky ones who never met the right guy, but then you get old and weird and think, well maybe. . . . Everybody has their regrets. But you have to take the package net, and I think I probably chose the package I most wanted.

"My mother persuaded me not to marry young; then I got to be thirty, and she worried she'd done too good a job. Most guys I met when I was young weren't really ready to cope with a wife who wanted a Ph.D. and serious work. I myself don't think it's ideal for kids to have two working parents. But for a woman to have to give up contact with the adult world for twenty years, and then get left by her husband. . . . In truth, I didn't try very hard to make the necessary compromises. I've had lots of nice boyfriends who wanted to get married, but it wouldn't have worked. I don't spend any time now looking. As an economist, I don't like to put energy into something where the odds of success are so low. The odds of finding a great match—well, I'm not in an optimistic mood.

"Sometimes it would be nice to have help, but I look around and think: There's a commandment not to covet other people's spouses, but I wish I saw spouses I did covet. It might give me some sense of possibility. I just spent the weekend with friends, a couple who bickered all the time. I couldn't put up with that crap. I was an only child. Most people are so terrified of being alone that they will put up with a lot just not to be alone. I'm probably at the other end of that spectrum. And since I turned forty-five, somehow the pressure is off.

"Old age does worry me. I'll have financial security; I haven't had to put kids through college. But I'm responsible for three octogenarians— my two parents and my eighty-seven-year-old aunt. When I'm visiting them, I'm thinking, Who's going to visit me? I should probably start making friends now with someone about forty years younger than me, but they're just starting elementary school. On the other hand, I know people who raised kids and still no one comes to visit. They just fight over their money. There are no sure bets."

For the past several years, Nonna has, like Alison Swain, been overwhelmed by elder-care responsibilities. Her father has Alzheimer's. Until 1993, her mother cared for him. Then one weekend, they came to visit Nonna and never went home. Her mother had a septic shock attack in the car, and Nonna had to suddenly take them in. For fifteen months they lived with her in her apartment. She tried sending them to day care, but to get them ready for a 9 A.M. bus required battling with her mother for two hours. "I'm not a morning person. That was really tough." Every so often, her father would bolt from the house and Nonna would get calls saying, "We found this man with your name and phone number in his pocket." Her mother then broke her hip, and went into a quick downhill slide, losing her ability to walk or talk. Nonna took three months off and nearly lost her job. She had to empty her parents' house to sell it, which proved painful: "I'm not good at getting rid of things." Then her aunt, who'd never married or had children, broke her hip, and Nonna took on her care as well. The aunt's apartment also had to be emptied and sold, and in the space of three months, she had to be moved six times to different care facilities, with Nonna overseeing each transition.

Eventually, Nonna moved all three into nursing homes. When her father realized that his independent life had come to an end, he looked at her and said, "I guess the ball game's over, huh?," which left Nonna unspeakably sad. She still faces mountains of mail each day: their medical bills and financial affairs. She shops for their clothes and diapers. She hasn't had a vacation in five years; to go away for two weeks isn't possible. On weekends she cooks "vegetables and stuff" to take to them and spends a day visiting them. Sometimes, she takes her father out with her to the store or the park and listens to his ceaseless, senseless talk.

Nonna has been for the most part alone with her responsibilities. When her mother collapsed, the man she was involved with helped her through the worst; his mother had a stroke at the same time, so they helped each other. Her closest friends have been gay men who know what it's like to watch people they love waste away. As her other friends had children, those friendships faded away: "They're so wrapped up; they don't have time to hang around." When her parents both fell ill, she found her support network still more broken down. "People who haven't been through it don't understand. They'd ask, 'Does your father drive?' Does he drive? He doesn't know where he is or how to get from here to the bathroom. And people get squeamish, or spooked. They'll entertain you, and a few real gems will help with responsibilities. But not many people will visit an old folks' home. My greatest source of renewal has been church, but I'm a liberal Catholic and most churches leave me muttering angrily in the back row. I like to go to the black Catholic church and hear the gospel choir, but it takes three hours to go to mass, which now I don't very often have."

If there is any bitterness in Nonna, it is well concealed. "This is what I do every weekend. I feel like I have my caseload. These things drain you. But I had a charmed life for twenty-five years. I was carefree. I traveled the world. My parents were good to me when I was a child. So I don't resent it. It's shocking to watch sometimes, unbelievable really, and I often wonder which is harder—to lose somebody suddenly or to watch them slip away and lose their personality. It's probably easier when it happens fast, but I'm glad to have them around, grateful for this chance to nurture them a bit. This is the closest experience to parenting I'll ever have. They are my children." Here is another of these women who, though they have never had a child, have experienced loyalties and loves as consuming and irrevocable as maternity. They have made homes worthy of Robert Frost's description—that place that when you have to go there, they have to let you in.

CHAPTER NINE

Spiritual Journeys

In discussions of ethics and faith, a common metaphor is concentric circles. Each larger circle represents a higher level of moral development. The smallest circle is the self; those caught within that circle, concerned only with the self, are the most stunted of spirit. The next-larger circle is the family, then community, and finally—the highest good, embodied in such beings as the Bodhisattva and Christ—a universal love and concern. The metaphor is complicated. One can advance toward the largest circle by gradually enlarging one's commitments: moving from the personal to the political. But one can also reach the largest circle by traveling inward, finding through meditative and spiritual practices an essential unity of the self with all things, a sense that any need or suffering or joy in the world is one's own. Both paths have been traversed by the women of Wellesley '69.

For many in the class, the spiritual search began in childhood: Nancy Young yearned to be a Catholic nun; Chris Osborne secretly rendezvoused with Alan Watts and Zen. Many more began their quest for the transcendental in the sixties: Matilda Williams's ordination as a Thai Buddhist nun and Alison Campbell Swain's sojourn among the sprites at Findhorn were only slightly more dramatic than the Himalayan treks and sustained meditations in Zen monasteries undertaken by numerous of their classmates. Some sought their spiritual home in the established church, though almost never without difficulty; others have preferred the "New Age." For an increasing proportion of the class, the search is at the center of their lives.

In the Church

After graduating from Wellesley, Susan Alexander, '69, did brilliantly at Princeton Theological Seminary and swept easily through her ordination exams. But then Susan couldn't get a job. To become a minister, she had to get "a call" from a congregation, which in the Presbyterian church demonstrates God's approval of a new shepherd for His flock. No matter how many doors she knocked on, her call to service failed to come. "Most congregations were not into the idea of a woman minister. I got more than one letter from a church telling me that it was clear to them that it was not God's will that a woman should serve in that role. After a while, I began to think they were on to something. I certainly found it difficult to convince God to change His mind."

Instead, in the midst of the 1973 recession, Susan found herself dismally unemployed. Her lowest moment came when she was turned down for a part-time Christmas sales position at Saks Fifth Avenue, New York. She ended up a temp at an engineering firm sending out Christmas cards. "An appropriate job, I thought, for a graduate of divinity school."

Despairing of her prospects in the ministry, Susan began working on a doctorate in psychotherapy and training as a pastoral counselor. Through her work with alcoholics and the recently deinstitutionalized mentally ill at a Bowery mission in New York City, she managed finally to be ordained. At thirty-one, it appeared her life was at last secure. She married a "handsome, charming, romantic" man, a chef ten years her senior, from a big Boston Irish Catholic family, who had been a minor league baseball player and a sailor and a cowboy. They settled on Long Island. In their suburban congregation, she even got a call.

Eighteen months later, Susan was pregnant, which turned out to be more than her new congregation could bear. "The women, who were largely homemakers, had problems with the idea that their minister would be a mother who worked." They asked Susan to resign. Though the Presbyterians had been one of the more progressive denominations—ordaining women earlier than most and championing the exercise of individual conscience in interpreting scripture—"no church always lives up to its own ideals," says Susan. "The institution gets involved in keeping itself going, and sabotages its own higher purposes.

And people in churches are like people everywhere. You can't blame it on God."

Though only a handful of women in the class of '69 have become clergy, the church is the institution class members most often name as the most important in their lives; they are as a group both religious and churchgoing. Fifteen percent describe themselves as "strictly" observant; another 30 percent describe religion as "very important." So though few would have to contend, like Susan, directly with the "stained-glass ceiling," many would endure discordances between the demands of their faith and their politics and professional lives.

With the possible exception of science, the church has been for much of its history the most rigid of all authorities on the question of woman's nature and role. Though Jesus and his earliest followers seem to have espoused a radical egalitarianism, from the time the church became aligned with the politically powerful, that early equality was set aside. Augustine described woman as sinful and "naturally subject" to man's higher reason. Aquinas anticipated Freud in naming her a "misbegotten male," who benefits when she performs the role to which her lower capacities are suited. Nineteenth-century clergymen met feminism's first wave with exhortations to pious men to contain their unruly wives and daughters, quoting a passage of the Gospels lately resurrected by the evangelical men's group the Promise Keepers: "Even as Christ is head of the church, the husband is the head of the wife." Elizabeth Cady Stanton responded with a denunciation of the church's patriarchal structure and of its teachings that women brought sin and death into the world. She created her own "woman's Bible," for which she was excoriated even by her feminist sisters. As Susan Alexander would discover a century later, the patrolling of woman's place in the religious community has often been led not by the male clergy but by the female congregation.

Indeed, little had changed by the time Susan and her classmates were finding their way into the church. While Susan was in college, the Vatican pronounced Simone de Beauvoir's *The Second Sex* a forbidden text; after the publication of *The Church and the Second Sex* (1968), feminist theologian Mary Daly was fired (briefly) from the faculty of Boston College: She had questioned the notion of God the Father and challenged the usurpation of the sacred feminine power embodied in "the hag, the crone, the amazon and goddess." Radical politics were infiltrating the church from the left, with clergy leading civil rights marches and third world liberation movements and burning draft board files, but also from the right, with evangelical ministers preaching against the Equal Rights Amendment as a "satanic attack" upon the home and warning that wife beating would continue as long as women refused to submit to men. (In 1998, the denomination to which Hillary Rodham Clinton's husband belongs—the Southern Baptist Convention—would officially declare that a woman should "graciously submit" to her husband.)

The day after Susan gave birth to her son, her family was evicted. Her husband was, as usual, out of work. And the family was broke: What little money Susan was able to bring in, he spent on drink, which made him turn miserable and mean. Four months from completing a doctorate on which she had already spent four years, Susan had to quit her graduate program. "I was an emotional basket case and in terrible financial trouble. And then it got worse. I'd get up at five in the morning on weekends to go to New Jersey to preach, and my mom would take care of my son. One Sunday, my husband beat her up. Another time he came in with a gun at 4 A.M. and was going to shoot us all. For a while I tried going to AA meetings for help, but I couldn't afford a baby-sitter. And the situation was clearly dangerous. I may make bad choices for relationships, but my child didn't make this choice. I finally had to tell my husband he couldn't be in the house any longer. It was a horrible thing to have to do. I loved him, but I had to fight this terrible battle to get him to go, and still he hung around the neighborhood. He died within a year after leaving, before our son was two years old."

Susan's story contains age-old themes: a wife impoverished and shamed by her husband's drunkenness; a woman chastised by the church for failing to conform to its conception of the good mother; a mother whose choices are narrowly circumscribed by the urgent need to secure the physical and financial safety of her child. Variations on it have played out in the lives of many in the class: 10 percent report having been abused or battered; one in three has been involuntarily unemployed.

But Susan's story is also a new one. Alone and out of work, with a nine-month-old baby, she went back again to a temp agency. Able to type eighty-five words a minute, she qualified as a "superior" secretary and on her first day was sent to Wall Street, to Kidder Peabody's new interest-rate-futures division. In short order, her supervisors had spotted her talents for mathematical analysis and writing and promoted her into a position that she quickly came to love. That a secretary could break so quickly into a high-powered, high-stakes job was evidence of a rapid transformation of the financial markets, and also of how feminism had altered the world. Four years later, having hit a glass ceiling at Kidder, Susan went to Oppenheimer as vice-president in charge of commodities research; she found it a company free of sexism that "judged you entirely on what you did."

The largely female world of social service had been demoralizing for Susan: "Everything was all dingy and broken-down, and nothing worked; it was not an environment particularly reinforcing to my self-esteem." But she loved the ways of Wall Street, strange as it was to be so content in a world she had once despised. "You dress powerfully, you take private cars, your whole environment bespeaks power." Overcome by a sense of powerlessness at home, Susan was rejuvenated at work by the same trappings of power that have sustained many a man. And while in one sense, she seemed to have abandoned her social commitment, for a battered, impoverished woman to move from terrified helplessness to a conviction of her own competency and self-sufficiency could itself be seen as an act of social progress.

Susan did continue to conduct Sunday services at churches too poor to support a full-time minister. "I would go to places that scared me to death, where the church was the only building that hadn't been burned down. It was a fantastic experience. The church mattered so much to people as shelter from their harsh environment.

"I suffered at leaving a life in the church, and never imagined I would end up where I did. But I came to believe that not serving the church in an official way didn't mean that I was failing to live up to my ideals. There's nothing that's really pure. And I had a child to raise, and knew I could do a lot of damage. I had grown up thinking you worked to improve the world. By this time, I understood that work was what you had to do to earn a living; it was how I would support my son.

"When you're young, you have great contempt for the lives people end up living. You think people have more choices than they have. Now I admire people who've paid the mortgage, sent kids to college, maintained a relationship, no matter how pedestrian that all is."

For many years, Katherine Shepeluk Loutrel '69 found refuge in Pentecostal Christianity from monstrous family miseries. Her father was a steelworker, frequently out of work and dependent on his wife's income as a nurse. Katherine, one of ten children, grew up caring for her siblings and shielding them from her father's drunken rages. She found some protection for herself in her accomplishments at school and her dutifulness at home: "They were the only things that pleased my dad, and exempted me from some of the punishments my siblings were subjected to. He wouldn't hurt me if I kept the house clean." Still, the pain in her family reached gothic proportions. One sister was manic-depressive. Another killed herself at twenty-one, leaving behind a young child. Three siblings became alcoholics. The oldest sibling suffered his dad's worst beatings yet remained living with him until his death, unable to drive, unemployed, and "not knowing how to live a life except one of being abused." Another brother died of unknown causes; both dead children were discovered by their mother in her home. Katherine herself has been diagnosed in the last decade with multiple sclerosis and depression, and has continued to deal with alcoholism and attempted suicide in her family.

Katherine survived, she believes, only because of her strong faith. "My mother and I both had a life-changing experience when I was fourteen. After hearing a preacher preach that Jesus died in my place because I was a sinner and that I needed to acknowledge that and repent and then I would have a new life, I would be born again, my mother and I made that commitment." Katherine loved the "noisy ecstasy" of services, where worshipers danced and sang in the spirit and spoke in tongues. While her classmates testified to one another in consciousness-raising meetings, she testified before her congregation and God. "I told God that my life belonged to Him. Then at the end of my freshman year at Wellesley, I was at a church in Boston and felt God challenge me to go into medicine; I said, 'I'll try the doors and if they open, I'll know that's what you want me to be.' I didn't feel or anticipate any great conflict between my science and my faith, though I did feel that Creation should have been taught as well as evolution, which I consider merely a theory that I don't personally hold."

Katherine was accepted to medical school on a full scholarship. Her father was "so proud that I was doing what he might have done if he'd gone to high school." At the same time, after many dry years, he began drinking again. "My mother began having to hide from him in the closet and finally had to leave. I was twenty-eight years old, but it was still painful. I believe divorce is not what God wants, but we have to deal with sinful people and can't always do what God wants. My mother had been a marvelous wife: self-effacing, quiet, caring, and giving. She worked hard and suffered long."

Just before starting medical school, Katherine met her future husband, Lou, at a summer camp where Pentecostal Christians led street meetings to share their faith. They were married, and on the eve of her genetics final, Katherine gave birth to their first child. During her internship, Lou worked to support the family, but as soon as Katherine started her residency and was earning money, Lou decided "someone needed to care for the kids" and became a househusband, which he has been ever since. He didn't mind giving up work, though his dad, a vice-president of Sherwin Williams, thought it a waste of his education, Katherine says, "which I realized was just what had always been said about the foolishness of educating women just to stay home."

The Pentecostal church, clear in its policy that men were not to permit their wives to work, could not accept the arrangement at all. "When I was doing my rounds one evening, I visited a deacon who was a patient in the hospital, and he told me I was violating God's will by being in medicine. I knew I was fulfilling God's call. But soon after that, I was told to leave the church because the powers that be thought women should be at home."

Katherine has remained, nonetheless, a believer in the church's higher authority. After her expulsion from the Pentecostals, her family joined a Baptist church. In 1993, her daughter Becky made front-page news in Champaign-Urbana as salutatorian in her public high school graduating class. She thanked God at the end of her speech, acknowledging His sovereignty in her life and asking that He care for the students who were graduating. "Needless to say, this mother was very proud."

Their collisions with the church have led some members of the Wellesley class of '69 into active efforts to create a larger space there for women. Pam McLucas Beyers became an elder of her Presbyterian church and helped "call" a woman as their new pastor. She also chaired a task force on homosexuality and the Christian faith, believing that "the ordination of gays is an issue of justice and inclusiveness—surely central themes in Jesus's message." Rachel Gorn Tedesco served on the board of the Massachusetts Religious Coalition for Reproductive Choice. Elizabeth Nordbeck, the first woman in 154 years to join the faculty of the Lancaster Theological Seminary in Pennsylvania, taught the history of women in the church and was later named dean; in 1990 she became the first female dean in 183 years at Andover Newton Theological School. Still, she finds "sexism alive and well even in 'enlightened' places," as she wrote to her classmates. "I've considered alternatives ranging from becoming an herbalist to shooting myself."

A few in the class have made equally deep commitments to other established faiths. Phyllis Magnus Sperber married an Orthodox Jewish rabbi and is raising ten children in Jerusalem. Sarah Larabee spent years in Hindu ashrams. Priscilla Raymond Gates Heilveil and her husband are raising ten children, many of them adopted from Asia. "Our family includes Buddhist, Unitarian, and Jewish speakers of Cantonese, Mandarin, Korean, and pidgin English—you cannot imagine the holidays we celebrate."

Outside the Church

A growing number, however, have turned away from established religions, finding greater spiritual satisfaction in the mix of Native American, mystical, and Eastern traditions that has come to be called the New Age. The goddess movement in particular boasts a surprisingly high number of acolytes in Hillary Clinton's class: Finding the two great female characters of the Bible—the fallen and corrupting Eve; the chaste and martyred Mary—uneasy role models for their paragons of female strength and justice, many have turned instead to "woman-centered" traditions and mythologies. On their bookshelves one finds such New Age best-sellers as Jean Auel's *Clan of the Cave Bear* novels, set in an Ice Age matriarchy, as well as the works of Starhawk, "teacher of witchcraft and licensed minister of the Covenant of the Goddess," and Clarissa Pinkola Estes's *Women Who Run with the Wolves*. Estes, a Latina Jungian analyst and storyteller, aims to awaken her disciples' "Wild Woman" with recountings of myths and folktales about bold and cunning females drawn from multicultural sources: pre-Christian European, Egyptian, Tibetan Buddhist, African. Starhawk seeks to "heal the estrangement from the earth that began with the Bronze Age shift from matrifocal to patriarchal cultures." These female spirit guides describe ancient matriarchal cultures as models of a more peaceable and ecological alternative to the destructive technologies of men. They urge a return to the worship of female fertility as a source of power and of greater sensitivity to the life-bearing earth. They offer tales of female heroines and divinities, concerned less with recounting woman's history as a victim of oppression than in offering a proud heritage of woman's wisdom and courage and power.

A number of Hillary's classmates actively participate in rituals meant to evoke such matriarchal traditions. A decade after leaving her husband and their radical collective, Dorothy Devine joined a circle of women who each year gather at solstices and equinoxes and other "pagan holidays" to "celebrate the goddess" in each of them. "Some people also have a patriarchal religion; they might go to the Episcopal church. But as women we come together at somebody's house or in a meadow. In the fall, as the days dwindle, we celebrate Demeter and Persephone. At the winter solstice, we light a hundred candles. If someone is suffering we chant or sing and hug her and tell her positive things and wash her feet. We raise energy for a troubled part of the world or a cure for AIDS, then we feast. Some people wear robes in symbolic colors. At Hallowmass everyone comes as an animal. We've done menstruation rites for daughters, involving a ritual bath and gifts of grown-up jewelry, and also commitment ceremonies between women and rites of menopause. When we part, we say to each other, 'Go with the goddess.' "

Kris Olson has fulfilled her "powerful spiritual longing" by studying for years with the elders of the Warm Springs tribe, learning their language to better understand their cosmology. She has also, in her professional capacity, fought numerous battles on behalf of Northwest Indians seeking to shield their sacred life from predation, most recently arguing against scientists seeking to overturn the Native American Repatriation Act so that they can study the remains of the nine-thousand-year-old Kennewick Man. Though Kris is "wary of wannabes, of the Anglo appropriation of native religions," her Episcopalian upbringing disappointed her: "For my church camp play I was cast once as Joan of Arc.

Getting burned at the stake did not seduce me into the faith." Scattered about her home are various objects of "spirit art" from South Asia and Africa; her office is ornamented with an array of wooden and ceramic turtles given to her by the Zuni as her totem. In the nineteenth century, she explains, the turtle symbolized female endurance: Its heart, legend says, beats even when its brain is bashed. In the twentieth century, the turtle stands for risk taking: She makes progress only when she sticks her neck out and makes herself vulnerable. In the twenty-first century, the creature who carries her own house about and manages life on both water and land will be for Kris "an emblem of versatility and self-sufficiency."

Though in the last difficult years of her life in the White House Hillary Clinton has relied ever more fiercely on her Methodist faith, the First Lady has also dipped into the New Age. In Arkansas, she and her female aides called themselves "the Valkyries" in reference to the wise maidens of Norse mythology who selected warriors fit to die. With "sacred psychologist" Jean Houston, Hillary has explored the ancient Greeks and mythology; she and the President both read Houston's *Manual for the Peacemaker: An Iroquois Legend to Heal Self and Society*. Houston was even an overnight visitor at the White House several times: It no doubt cheered Hillary to hear from Houston that she was single-handedly "reversing thousands of years of expectation, and was there up front, more than virtually any woman in human history apart from Joan of Arc."

In the American past, spiritualism outside the mainstream church has frequently sustained outspoken or rebellious women. The suffragist Grimke sisters attended Quaker meetings, one of the few public places a woman was permitted to speak freely. Other first-wave feminists found in the more radical sects of the nineteenth century whole bundles of liberties, including free love, as well as a faith in private illumination and spiritual healing that allowed them to circumvent the patriarchal church and paternalistic physicians. For women otherwise excluded from sacral authority, the role of prophet or trance speaker or séance medium was a rare opportunity to have a public voice, a voice powerfully authorized from the other side. Even today, most "channelers" are female, though most of the spirits they transmit are male.

It is baffling nonetheless that Hillary and her classmates can find some of these New Age testaments compelling. Much of this literature seems a kind of spiritual cotton candy, weightless and overly sweet, with no sense of the terrifying grandeur of the sublime or the wrenching rigors demanded of the pilgrim, and with none of the subtle, paradoxical poetry of the original cosmologies on which it draws. Most troubling is its exaltation of women, a reverence that is, as always, double-edged. The rise of women's power, says Houston, "is the most important event of the last five thousand years." The "male principle is one of order and mastery; the female is not systematic but systemic." Cultures in which the feminine archetype prevails, Houston claims, are nonheroic; they "emphasize being rather than . . . achieving." Unsystematic in their thinking, indifferent to achievement: Houston's language resurrects some of the most regressive certainties about women.

And yet it is clear that Dorothy Devine and Alison Swain and numerous others in the class have found in their spiritual wanderings a kind of peace they had found nowhere else. These newly told stories of female transformation and heroism perhaps can, as Marina Warner has written, "sew and weave and knit different patterns into the social fabric." Even if they are merely fairy tales (and the archaeological evidence for many of the claims is scant), they still perhaps offer a kind of "useful wishful thinking," stirring the imagination to new possibilities. If the language used by some of the Wellesley graduates to describe their spiritual journey is thin, the experience, it seems, is not.

CHAPTER TEN

In Search of Self

Twenty years later, when people were saying that she shouldn't be a mother to her sons any longer, Nancy Wanderer would remember what it was like to be denied the chance to ever hold her second child.

Thomas had been in Vietnam seven months when Nancy gave birth to their first child, a son she named Andrew. From the day Thomas shipped out, Nancy had been home with her parents waiting, passing the hours with *That Girl* and *Mary Tyler Moore*. Just twenty-two years old, she looks like a child herself in a picture taken late in her pregnancy, her small, sweet face framed by pixie hair and a princess collar. "I was so innocent. The first night I was home from the hospital with the baby, my mother said, 'You should go and check him,' and I said, 'Check him for what?' I was afraid to tell my parents I was going to breast-feed. My mother had not, though I learned later she would have liked to but was strongly discouraged from it. With Thomas away and in danger, I felt this incredible responsibility to keep this child safe for the father who had never seen him. When he was still just tiny, Andrew had to have surgery for a hernia, and I dreamt of being in our VW bus circled by wild animals."

Thomas came home from Vietnam in April 1971 and began graduate school at Harvard that fall; Nancy spent her days at home caring for Andrew. In just over a year she was pregnant again, and on the Saturday after Thanksgiving 1973 their second son, David, was born. Thomas had missed Andrew's birth, hadn't even seen him until the boy was already a year old, so Nancy was thrilled that her husband would be there when this baby arrived. She wanted Thomas to be the first to hold their son. When the nurses brought David on a brief visit from the nursery (these were the days before babies were left on their mother's breast), Nancy asked them to place him in Thomas's arms instead of her own.

There was no second visit. That night at midnight, the lights in Nancy's room suddenly went on and she woke to find her doctor standing just outside the room. "He was throwing words at me about David having trouble breathing and a heart defect and moving him to Boston. I said, 'Will you bring him in before he goes?' By that time he was in an incubator, so all I could do was look at him. I still had never touched him. They moved him to a hospital a half hour away. I was twenty-six and not sophisticated enough to demand to be moved also. The doctor who delivered him never even came past the doorframe. He didn't examine me. He couldn't deal with what had happened. He just ordered a sedative and dumped me. They left me in the maternity ward with a roommate and her newborn. I lay there listening to that baby nurse and coo and cry.

"The next day I was putting on my cheerful self, entertaining visitors, trying to put everyone else at ease, telling myself that things in my life had always turned out right. But by that night I knew somehow he was not going to make it. He died the next night. I had never held him. I had barely laid eyes on him. Thomas and I didn't talk about it. He wanted him cremated and the ashes spread. I knew I had to know where David was; I'd been so out of touch with him in his brief life." They agreed to have the baby's organs donated and to bury him in Thomas's family plot. Nancy asked her mother to take Andrew to the Museum of Science. She went to the funeral home and picked up the small brown wrapped package, which she carried in her lap to the grave.

There was no ceremony. "We didn't know what to do. I put the urn in the hole, saw some acorns on the ground, and put those in as well. We drove back to town in silence. Thomas wrote a letter to Andrew, put it in a safe deposit box, and never spoke of it again. I went home and put the crib and the clothes away. I was so numb, one of Thomas's relatives thought I was heavily sedated. I couldn't talk to my mother about it; she was in so much pain. It brought up her own brother's death when he was sixteen. I was sparing everybody, not wanting to look too miserable. But for a year I couldn't clear my throat. It was the only thing important about me: I was a woman whose baby had died. That was my identity. For months after he died I would get calls from diaper services or photography services wanting to take my new baby's picture. The only time I fell apart was when I had to go for my checkup six weeks after delivering and sit among the newborns and the nurse asked me, "How's the baby?" I kept feeling pregnant, kicking feelings. Thomas is an atheist, and I'm not. I would go to a Unitarian church, sit in the front row, and cry whenever the music was loud enough that no one could hear me. I used to go to the grave by myself, take a pumpkin at Halloween or Christmas holly. I kept telling the story to a friend, over and over, telling her what I thought he looked like. Every time she listened as if she'd never heard the story before."

Only many years later did Nancy get some measure of respite from her grief, through the performance of a public rite. While taking a psychology course toward a master's in counseling, she was asked to reenact a painful episode in her life. She stalled until everyone else had taken their turn. "Then I re-created the whole thing—the hospital room, the doctor. The teacher said, 'Would you like to hold your baby now?' and I said yes, and she handed me a bundled-up sweater and I cradled it in my arms. I'd never held him. I hadn't been there when he was hurting, when he was sick and dying. I needed to tell him that I did care, that he had a mother, that I really was his mother. It hurts now to feel like David will be with Thomas's family. I'm not going to be buried there. I won't be able to check on him in that way."

At her fifth reunion at Wellesley, in the spring of 1974, Nancy discovered she was pregnant again. Like Andrew, Peter required surgery for a hernia soon after he was born; before the operation the doctor insisted that Nancy wean him. "They simply didn't want to deal with me in the hospital. I don't know why I was so deferential, but again I was compliant in things that were wrong. Here my baby was in the same hospital where David died, my breasts were full of milk, and I couldn't feed him. My breasts got so large and hard I could put a cocktail glass on them and it would stay. When he finally came home, I couldn't figure out how to be a mother. The only way I knew to quiet a baby was breast-feeding." Two years later, when a missed period fooled her into thinking she was pregnant again, Thomas suggested she think about an abortion. She couldn't. "I am so pro-choice, but after a baby dying, I couldn't have faced it."

Thomas had spent those years completing his doctorate. He wasn't home much, and Nancy bristled at being treated by his Radcliffe students as "the little woman" with nothing to say. It didn't much matter; she was busy with her babies and content in her marriage. There followed three unhappy years in Washington, D.C., where Thomas got his first teaching job and also worked on Capitol Hill and was away from home day and night. Nancy was lonely and bored; to ease her unhappiness, Thomas finally accepted a job at a small college in Maine. "I thought we'd get back to that woodsy, natural way of his I'd been drawn to originally. And we did find a whole new world in Maine. I had a garden; the kids were flourishing. Peter was a sunny little boy, so happy with everything. We felt settled at last. I felt, this is the right thing. Here are my house and my sons and my smart, strong, important husband."

Nancy's optimism sang through her letter to her classmates for their tenth reunion. "The first five years out of college I concerned myself almost exclusively with my sons and with Thomas, his survival in Vietnam, his success in grad school, his satisfaction in his job. I barely had time to think about where my life was heading. These past five years I have earned a master's in education and started my first honest-to-goodness job. I feel we're finally where we wanted to be, physically and psychologically. Thomas and I share all child care and household responsibilities equally thanks to flexible work arrangements and we truly love our new fully liberated lifestyle." In her classmates' eyes, she was the model mother; when Hillary Rodham went to Maine with her husband for a governors' conference soon after Chelsea was born, she called Nancy for motherly advice on such matters as how to find the best teachers in her daughter's school.

After a few years teaching at a "scruffy little" college and earning a second master's, in 1982 Nancy joined Thomas at his college as associate director of career counseling. Over the course of the next several years, she became increasingly active in campus feminism, becoming co-chair of the women's studies program and chair of the affirmative action committee; she wrote the college's sexual harassment policy and acted as advocate for the first woman to bring a case. Accustomed to persuading herself of her own contentment, she did not at first reflect on what in her own life might be impelling her to take a young woman's side against a faculty member. "Because I was married to the star professor, I had respectability and could push against the edges without as much trouble as other women. It was one of those times it helped to look so wholesome and all-American. I had a nice cover behind which to be radical."

In 1984, Thomas took a sabbatical at the Brookings Institution and began spending every other week in D.C. It was, for Nancy, a transformative year. "I'd never in my whole life been on my own. I discovered I loved it. I was master of my time, which had always belonged to him. For the first time ever, I had complete freedom. I found out I wasn't content with my allotted domain, the homemaking and gardening and work that always came second to Thomas's. I wasn't content with being cast as the less intelligent and important one—a role I'd cast myself in; I can't blame Thomas for that.

"Thomas had always been home a lot doing child care and cooking, and saw himself as an enlightened feminist husband. But as I became more involved in feminism, he treated that as a hobby, as if I'd been playing bridge, as if it didn't affect him. It did affect him, because I was changing, but he caught on too late. The kids were keeping pace; they came along to meetings and films and understood that this was central to me. But Thomas didn't take my feminism seriously, which means he didn't take me seriously."

While Thomas was away, Nancy developed a close relationship with an "out" lesbian on the faculty. They organized a film festival and ran together every day. "What I had with her went deep. I had no desire for anything physical, but our friendship nurtured me in a way I'd never been nurtured in my marriage. Thomas started to have a problem with it. When he came home from Washington, he wanted the relationship curtailed and insisted I run with him instead. For a while I ran with both of them, about six miles a day. I learned later he went to a lawyer at that point to talk about divorce. I think it felt adulterous to him that I preferred to spend time with her; I did find myself not telling him when I was seeing her. In fact, it was like adultery—though it wasn't sex but time and emotion, which may be worth more for some people. He could feel my enthusiasm being channeled elsewhere. He could see I might have passions that had nothing to do with him. I had always had them—for my kids, my mother, other friends—but he hadn't noticed. I'd always had intense emotional relationships with women, but this was the first time I was having one in front of him."

Though Nancy had fulfilled her mother's dream by marrying up in the world, she had come to feel alienated by Thomas's ambition. "Success in the world got very important to him. He had a high position in the administration and wanted a college presidency and started hobnobbing with dignitaries and trustees. I'd never wanted to be part of 'the establishment,' and hadn't thought that when I married Thomas that's what I was getting into. I wanted to be natural, not putting on airs. I always wanted to be my own person in these scenarios, and it never seemed like that's what anyone wanted me to be. I was supposed to behave myself. Thomas didn't tell me this, but I felt there was an expectation of me to be polite, to not be argumentative. For instance, when the trustees would say, 'I never hire women salespersons because my customers would never find them credible,' I was supposed to be gracious and say, 'Oh yeah, I can really understand that.' Instead, I was getting in fights with these people, and doing small subversive things like coming to these dinners after I'd run with my friend and showered and my hair was still wet. I never felt like a wife. I tried to be a faculty wife, to be a graduate student wife, and I just never felt comfortable with it."

A year after Thomas's sabbatical, at a conference on women's wellness, Nancy met Susan, a recently divorced high school guidance counselor from a nearby blue-collar town. "We were immediately drawn to each other, and stayed in touch, and after eight or nine months began to realize what it was meaning; I felt something breaking open in my life. I brought those feelings to Thomas. That's what I'd always done. It was part of my impulse to honesty. I thought it was something I'd just work through. Then by chance Susan and I had three days when everyone in both our lives was elsewhere and we could spend all of our time together. We didn't become lovers physically, but we realized what it felt like to be together, a peace and contentment and energy and excitement I'd never felt before. It touched a deep place, more spiritual than sexual. Those three days shoved us a million miles toward knowing we didn't want to lose this. I knew I couldn't go back to my life as it had been. You know something you didn't know before; you have to do something different. Still, I couldn't imagine not being married to Thomas, not after all we'd come through—Vietnam, our baby dying. We had so much history. I felt loyal and grateful. Everything about being with him made sense. And I loved him. It wasn't the kind of passion I feel now, but I had become passionate about wanting it and about our life with the kids. I was married for life.

"I remember one stormy night, about a month after I met Susan, I went running and Thomas caught up with me and we were out in this wild storm with wind and rain and everything and he just looked at me and said, 'What is wrong with you?' At that moment I realized there *was* something wrong.

"Over the course of the next year, Susan and I grew increasingly close. I decided we could be small-*l* lovers, which meant no sex. It was like my decision in junior high about intercourse: It was too dangerous, so I was going to make a deliberate choice to refuse it completely. I never questioned that I could be happy being sexual with a woman. I never thought there was something bad about it. Susan was divorced, and I had been trying to persuade her that being a lesbian was the best thing in the world. I pictured Lakey in *The Group*: Candice Bergen was my idea of what a lesbian looked like. I thought it would be great, and I thought that Susan would get to be one because she was free.

"In August of '87 we decided to have a letting-go ceremony, to let go of the hope and fear we'd become lovers. We had candles and flowers and music. We drank passion-fruit juice before the ceremony and sparkling apple juice after, to symbolize the transition. Thomas wasn't there, but he was involved in the planning. I asked if he would allow one kiss. He said okay. That kiss lasted twenty minutes. Then we went home and had a gourmet dinner Thomas had fixed for us. During this spell I was more attracted to Thomas than I'd been in years. He was being vulnerable in a way he'd never been. He cried for the first time in our first ever real conversation about our baby dying. In a way, it seemed the best thing that could have happened to our marriage. He was writing letters to Susan, saying he had never been happier, felt himself opening up and growing."

In the midst of all this, Nancy decided, eighteen years after putting her ambitions aside to get married, to apply to law school. Her kids, she felt, were now self-reliant enough to manage without her during the week. Accepted to the University of Maine Law School, she took an apartment in Portland and at age thirty-eight began her first year.

Nancy loved being back in school and finished fourth in her class that year, despite the mounting tumult at home. She went home to her family on weekends, and Susan made frequent visits to Portland. On one such occasion, a month after the letting-go ceremony, the two women "sort of accidentally" came frighteningly close to having sex. "I of course had to tell Thomas, who at the time was flat out with a back problem. He told us to go ahead and be lovers. He spent two days persuading us it was okay. He thought himself a big enough person to deal with it and that the suspense was building an energy and life of its own. We knew it wasn't going to be reversible, but we all had a strong feeling that we could transcend petty jealousies and possessiveness. Thomas and I were closer than we'd ever been, because we were sharing all these feelings. He convinced us both that we were going to do something nobody had ever done before. We'd all read *The Harrad Experiment*. He was going to be a new kind of man. He was going to have a loving relationship with Susan and her kids. It might be the experience of his life. He gave Susan a beautiful gift for her birthday. And we bought a huge new house, with thirteen rooms, because Thomas thought we should all live together. He insisted on showing it to Susan before he would buy it."

Susan was uneasy. "I wasn't jealous of Thomas. I knew Nancy's passion was for me. But I'd just exited a thirteen-year marriage and was in no hurry to give up my new freedom, and here Thomas was coming to my house to lay out the whole plan for my life. When Nancy and I did become lovers, I was mortified. I'd never had a sexual relationship with a woman. I'd had sexual feelings for Nancy, but she was unavailable, so it had been safe. Until 1983, I had been in the Fundamental Church of Christ: Homosexuality was Sodom and Gomorrah; women had to be silent in church. Just once, before I met Nancy, a woman in my church had kissed me on the mouth. I had my two babies with me. It was an earthquake in my life."

Nancy was giddy. "I saw it as a way to have everything. Even after I knew I loved Susan, I worked on the principle that Thomas wasn't going to lose by this. If anyone had to go, it would be her. I still couldn't imagine myself without my husband. The struggling we'd had at the outset felt like it had forged a relationship with steel-like strength—though of course, steel is also a trap, strong but not terribly flexible. By September of '87 I was sleeping with Thomas but also with Susan whenever I could. I was ecstatically happy. For a week it seemed I'd have everything; my family and a full life with Thomas and with Susan. But by that weekend, Thomas was a mess. Until Christmas we went back and forth. I was having a lot of sex with everybody, to convince Thomas it wouldn't take anything away from him, to prove to him I was more attracted than ever. I was terrified it would all fall apart and I'd end up back with him pretending it had never happened. Someone had said to Susan: 'These women, I've seen it a million times. They get involved with a lesbian relationship but can't give up their privilege.' I was terrified that might be true. But it's like trying to put gas back into a bottle. Still, I had no idea what we were heading toward. I'd call Susan and say the marriage was over, then he'd call her and say, 'Let's all do something together.'

"Buying the house was the last unified moment. By the spring of '88 it was all downs. Thomas wanted Susan and me to quit being lovers. I kept buying time. He made me come out to the kids about my relationship, say, 'I'm in love with Susan, and it's a sexual relationship.' Andrew said, 'Oh, you can't be a lesbian; you've been with Dad all these years.' I couldn't go back, but I threw myself into working on that house, even though the relationship with Thomas had completely broken down. There was no pleasure between us. He was like my keeper, permitting me two mornings with Susan, monitoring how many minutes I spent on the phone with her. I had no positive feelings for him, but he kept wanting to make love right up to the last day, which was torture for me. By the fall of '88 I was close to a breakdown, but I still didn't know if I could do what I needed to do. Part of it was wondering if I deserved to have what I wanted. That was the worst three months of my life. I lost all sense of possibility, began to fantasize about moving to another town, where no one would know me, about changing my name and disappearing, which I realized were suicidal fantasies."

At Susan's insistence, the two women quit being lovers. At the same moment, Thomas told Nancy that he had called her mother and told her everything and that Marge Wanderer was coming to Maine. Then, two days before Marge arrived, Thomas told Nancy it was over. "I'd talked him out of ending it before. I could just never bring myself to face really leaving. Finally he said, 'You've got to go.' I'm actually very grateful to him that he was wise enough to know when the end had come.

"I was shocked and scared; I was terribly worried for Peter and knew it would kill my mother. Thomas's mother wrote me and said, 'How can you leave your kids?' But I began to feel better instantly, ashamed I hadn't been able to make a decision but relieved that someone had. When my mother arrived, I told her what Susan meant to me, that the marriage had broken down aside from Susan, that Thomas was not communicating or emotionally available. She helped me, though I learned later that I had completely misunderstood her, but she said this thing that was key. She said, 'Look deep inside and I know you'll do the right thing.' I did do the right thing, which was to go; later she said, 'What I meant was you would do the right thing and stay.' But it was the permission I needed. I also had lunch with my classmate Christine Howe Badgley, who said how excited she was for me, that she could see a woman giving birth to herself. That made me feel like I would still be part of the Wellesley family, which mattered to me enormously."

By November, Nancy had moved into a run-down little apartment in a shabby part of town. "I had no money and felt incredibly vulnerable, but it was the only place I ever had that was my own, and I loved it. I didn't go back to the house; we'd planned for me to have dinner there once a week, but as soon as I left, the door slammed. Then my parents came to Thomas's for Christmas and I had to go act like I lived there. I couldn't bring myself to sleep there. My mother got upset each night when I left. She wouldn't even come into my apartment. She said it was a slum."

At the beginning of that year, Nancy's father had been diagnosed with cancer and had undergone a major operation; that calamity and the breakdown of her daughter's marriage were almost more than Marge Wanderer could bear. "For a time my mom and I talked angrily, with her trying to persuade me to go back. She said she would rather have had me murder someone in an alley than do what I did. For her, my coming out was all mixed up with throwing out my luxury life. She wanted me to be what I'd been—the storybook bride with a successful, nice-looking husband, two great kids, a big house, the picture of a happy family. My mother was ready to sacrifice me to that storybook picture. Her identity was entirely caught up in how her children turned out. I feel my sons' destinies are their own; she saw my divorce as her failure. But I never really thought she'd write me off. I was sure she'd get with this too. It felt so right." To *Frontline*, Nancy said: "As painful as it was, I knew that even if she never came around, I had to do it. Losing my mother is an almost unthinkable thing to me. She is the person I've modeled my life on in all the important ways. I couldn't imagine not having her, but I also couldn't imagine not being who I was. It was an impossible choice, and ultimately I had to choose life for myself.

"For two years I kept calling and trying to talk to her. She, meanwhile, was writing letters to Andrew about not letting me spend the money she'd sent him on my 'friend' and saying how sorry she was that 'you've lost your mother.' Finally in the spring of 1990, my father said, 'Let's just not be in contact for a while.' I ran into them when I went back to my hometown for my twenty-fifth high school reunion. My mother couldn't look at me or say a single word. I told them not to come to my law school graduation if they were going to snub Susan. I won an achievement award; it would have been a great day for them."

At the time of the divorce, Andrew was nineteen and a freshman at Columbia; Peter was fourteen and in the eighth grade. "It would have been much easier if both kids were grown. I kept returning in my mind to the summer when Peter was three, when we were at my folks' place at Deep Creek Lake in western Maryland and I got stung by a bee and nearly died. I had what I can only describe as an out-of-body experience. I was sort of floating above the earth feeling incredibly calm, watching them carry my lifeless body away. Then I saw Peter, and I thought, But he's so young, and it was as if I was suddenly sucked back into my body and resumed fighting for my life. Peter was the one who came after baby David, and I didn't want to lose him, too. And I didn't know if, like my mother, my sons would say, 'To heck with you.' Thomas made it clear that I shouldn't even consider they'd be anywhere but with him. It was a way of punishing me; he did it with the kids and with money. I acquiesced. I felt as if he had the right, and that in some ways it was best: Thomas was home more than me, though he was in his study and had to be formally visited. I also believed my bond with my kids was strong enough that the amount of time we spent together wouldn't affect it. It was strong enough, but it was still painful not to have them in my life all the time. It was heartbreaking to lose that time with Peter. Even now, he probably has no idea how I feel.

"Peter turned out in those early months to be my greatest ally. Andrew went through a time of confusion. At one point he asked me, 'What am I supposed to think?' I said, 'We're trying to work something out you wouldn't understand, but Susan is here to stay and you had better get used to it.' The first year of his life, he had bonded tremendously with my mother. Now she tried to win him away, to lever me back into the family, or maybe just to legitimize her anger by getting him to join her in it. He was in misery about that much more than the divorce. Both kids understood the divorce, because they knew me so well. They think a lot of their father, but saw he was going one way and I another. Both wrote their college entrance essays about lesbians; Peter's was about having a lesbian mom.

"I regret they were hurt by the transition, but it's not always possible to prevent that. Once I knew the truth, I couldn't turn away from it. That would have been a bad example for my children. My most important value to transmit was honesty. All their lives, I could hear almost anything about what they did. Sometimes I didn't like it, but I don't think they ever told me a lie. I wasn't rebelling against anything, but trying to chart a course according to my own inner compass. I've been the same throughout my life, following my conscience. The kids suffered, but it has ultimately been for them a much richer experience to have a mother who acted on her deepest desires rather than denying herself.

"Thomas decided he would work out the financial split, without lawyers. Because I was feeling so vulnerable, cut off from my parents, I just signed off on it. He assured me it was fair, and I still believed he had my best interests at heart. I lost my share of his retirement: For eight years I was raising our kids and earning no income; we were working as a team and were both entitled to the fruits of that. As it is, I'm in terrible shape for retirement; I have to work twenty years before I get anything. He didn't account at all for my inheritance from my grandparents, which should have been mine right off the top. To give you an idea of our relative financial positions immediately after the divorce: I was on full financial aid at law school, while Thomas was able to pay Andrew's tuition, room, and board at Columbia out of pocket. He now of course wants me to pay half that back. I developed great sympathy for women who feel powerless in divorce. I had two graduate degrees, was in law school and a feminist, and still I didn't assert myself. I really didn't want to hurt anyone—not my mother, not Thomas. I didn't expect him to want to hurt me."

The sequel to "marrying up," Nancy discovered, is "divorcing down." She now lives frugally: Out to dinner one night in Portland, she hesitated before ordering eighty cents' worth of coleslaw. After a year clerking for a Maine Supreme Court justice, she worked briefly for the state's highest-paying law firm, but didn't stay. "It was just too much against my grain, very establishment, patriarchal and formal. It was like my marriage—secure, but not a good fit. I had to wear a suit, even though I never saw clients. And there was little recognition of the reality of women's lives. They assumed all lawyers were young and single or had full-time wives and could be there six days a week and wouldn't want to be home with their partner or kids. I made it a point not to work Saturdays, which was not viewed favorably. I was advised to come in just to schmooze with the other attorneys. One partner said to me, 'The day will come when you have no work, it's a beautiful afternoon, and you want to see your son play soccer. But you're going to remember that would not be professional.' The same attorney wanted to have a conference call with me in Andrew's dorm room over Thanksgiving. When you're twenty-five, maybe you put up with that stuff as the ropes. I don't have that many years. Part of me felt I should stay and try to make partner and change the rules, but it was so dispiriting; the only women who seemed to be thriving were more like men than the men. And what mattered most to me, as always, was the freedom to be exactly who I am."

Taking a pay cut from $55,000 to $34,000 a year, Nancy went to work for the Maine Health Care Finance Commission, an office of mostly women lawyers. "It was worth every penny. The work wasn't fascinating, but because of all the women it was a collaborative environment. I could use all my counseling skills and often get to a compromise before litigation; in a big firm they'd just want you to roll out the heavy guns." Nancy has been co-chair of the Maine Bar Committee on the Status of Women Attorneys, helped create the Commission on Gender Justice in the Courts, addressing such matters as the legal system's treatment of battered women, child support, and conditions of incarceration for women, and served as president of the Maine Women's Fund, raising money for projects on women's health, aging, and economic independence.

Wanting to avoid "forcing our relationship or their new siblings down our kids' throats," Nancy and Susan lived apart for two years. When they did move in together, they had a commitment ceremony attended by twelve women, including a Wellesley classmate and her companion, who "kind of rolled their eyes at the whole thing." The gathered women read from Anne Morrow Lindbergh's *A Gift from the Sea* and collectively wound together a rainbow of embroidery threads; then Nancy and Susan exchanged rings.

They have made a cozy and peaceful home together, filled with country antiques and quilts and cut flowers and many books. A Wellesley sampler hangs on the wall and a Wellesley chair has pride of place in the living room. Pink curtains hang in the kitchen, and in the bathroom are matching HERS and HERS pink towels. The backyard is planted with a bountiful vegetable garden and abundant flowers. An array of pinks—hollyhocks, phlox, impatiens, peonies, coralbells, and begonias—grow in the shape of a Gay Liberation triangle; whites grow in a half-moon and bright yellow and orange blossoms burst the edges of a round sun. Both women wear L. L. Bean T-shirts, khakis, and Birkenstocks; Nancy's hair is now very short and gray at the temples, and her blue eyes are framed by wire-rimmed glasses. They joke that they blend in well in Maine, where all the women look like lesbians. Nancy sings in a group called Women in Harmony. She and Susan both love the outdoors; they regularly go camping with their kids and tour with the Amelia Wheelheart Feminist Biking Club (which at one point explored patenting Susan's invention, "the Bobbitt," a toilet seat with a spring that requires a man to hold it up while he pees, then snaps back into place when he's done).

In one sense, Nancy's story is a classic romance: Through passionate love she found the self she had failed to realize in her marriage. But in another sense Nancy's is a political story. Nancy released her true being not simply by yielding to her passions but by finding a new (shared) story that seemed to describe her better than did the old story that she and her mom and Thomas had once agreed upon. She achieved personal fulfillment by drawing strength and self-understanding from a collective movement: lesbian feminism.

Nancy and Susan's kids have settled slowly into the new arrangement. Andrew would not see Susan for some months and refused to come to an early family gathering. Peter once asked them to turn off a song about a daughter and her mother who come out to each other. Susan's thirteen-year-old son, Seth, "acted out" with Nancy, stealing her wallet. Only Susan's daughter, Saren, thought from the outset that it was cool to have a lesbian mom. Now the kids, all heterosexual, are outspoken allies of their mothers. While in college, Peter performed as a gay man in *Torch Song Trilogy* and wore a pink triangle and went on an AIDS walk with Nancy. "I think everyone thought, What a nice mom, out there with her son." Seth defended a gay rights ordinance before his hostile classmates in high school.

One morning while I was visiting, Peter arrived for a breakfast of fresh blueberry pancakes with warm hugs and kisses for both women. "When I was a kid, my friends were jealous of what seemed my perfect family. I thought it was perfect, too. I believed a relationship like that could never fail. I can't remember a single fight. Now I realize how much unhealthier that is; all the stuff was kept under the surface.

"The year my mom went to law school was hard. I wanted her to be happy, but it's not easy when you just have your dad. That year ruined things. Or, I suppose, it exposed what was always there. Then Susan was there all the time. At first it seemed like she was bringing them closer together, because they all did things together. Then my father saw it escalate between them. He gave his permission, but reluctantly.

"My parents tried to make it work, and to hide the worst from us; I remember they once locked themselves in the bathroom to fight. Andrew and I both tried to persuade them to stay together, and they did delay splitting up for us, I think. But over time I became confused. I didn't know if I wanted them to stay together, but I knew I wanted them to stop fighting. The lesbianism didn't bother me; I've always been taught to respect all relationships, though that doesn't extend to extramarital ones. But when I was seven, I'd asked my mom to promise she'd never get divorced, and then she did. I felt betrayed by that. I also found myself having to defend my mom to my grandparents. I would say how much she loved Susan, that she'd always been the way they could now see. Grandma thought the marriage had been a perfect relationship and then Susan came in and *wham*. But I could grasp how my parents had become different. My father assumed Mom wanted just to be sure of everything. He wants contentment and security. But my mother wants fulfillment, to go forward and discover new things. She was changing. The whole thing with including Susan was my dad's effort to be there with her during the changes. He wouldn't tell her not to think what she was thinking. My father is not that direct, anyway—he implies things. That was hard on my mom, too, my father's refusal to confront problems. Even now when he's angry he doesn't express it; he just becomes very rational.

"My parents' divorce was the defining emotional moment in my life. It affected the next five years of my life. I'd come home and shout at the walls. I felt they were fighting for my loyalty, trying to one-up each other. I had trouble making friends or relationships; I was afraid of being hurt. But it wouldn't have been better for us if they'd stayed together. The damage was done. And they would be teaching us the wrong thing. If I ever had a romantic view of relationships, I don't anymore, but that's good. When something's wrong, I don't sit back and hope it will pass. I talk about it right away and don't stop till it's resolved. I learned to try to rectify things but to realize that when things are irreparably broken, it's time to move on, to make decisions for myself and to not stay in relationships for anyone's sake but my own.

"The relationship between my mother and Susan is the strongest I've ever seen. They are truly linked, like one person. I think my father has found happiness as well; he has left that part of his life behind. He's stopped bad-mouthing my mother. My stepmother [whom Thomas married in 1992] has the same outlook on life as he. She wants stability, while my mom has found someone willing to go on adventures with her. I call myself a boy with three mommies." I ask if he's a feminist. "I don't know how to use that word anymore. I believe that there is sexism in much of society, that boys are still taught to be aggressive and girls submissive. I'd like a job that allows me to be home a lot raising kids. Yeah, I guess that makes me a feminist."

Peter is sweet and a bit guarded; Andrew, who followed close on his mother's heels at the University of Maine Law School, is more blunt and less qualified in his feminism. "If [NOW president] Patricia Ireland and Bill Clinton agree on something, I'll be there." Like his brother, he is less distressed by the fact of the divorce than by the way it was carried out. "When my parents got married, I don't think either realized who they were—not for another fifteen years down the road, when my dad went away for that year and my mom was forced to get more self-reliant. By the time the divorce happened, they were so different I don't think it would have been possible for them to stay together. Anyway, I'm way past the point where I think putting things back together is always better than letting it go. What bothered me was that everybody wanted me on their side. For a while I was angry at Susan—not because of the nature of their relationship, but because I saw her as a divisive element; I thought she played a critical role. My senior year in high school, the three of them were spending a lot of time together. It didn't seem natural. When I asked them about it, they told me it was their business. I think there was a lot of confusion; neither of my parents really had control. Bad decisions were made all around. After the divorce, my grandmother, whose basic view was 'He's a good catch; why is she letting him go?' invited my dad down to visit her in Pittsburgh. My grandma is great; I could see why my dad would want to keep a relationship with her for selfish reasons, but visiting your ex-in-laws is kind of odd, and it was really hard on my mom. I ended up being a go-between for Grandma and Mom. For a long time I don't think either made a reasonable effort. My mom wasn't trying hard enough and my grandma had to be more open-minded, accept the way it is. I don't blame her for being jarred. In her day, people didn't do that. And my grandfather clearly had a moral problem with the whole thing.

"Is life after the divorce better than it was during the collapse? Definitely. But is it better than twenty years ago, when I was a kid and my parents seemed okay? I don't know. It's different. But I certainly don't see that anything my mother did was an abdication of her responsibility to us. It's judgmental and old-fashioned to see it that way. Some relationships might be fixed. For my parents, it was being kept together as a front and nothing else. I'm just glad it's over. Though it has made me a lot more cynical. I'm in no hurry to get married. You tie yourself into a family; if it doesn't work out, you have to get out, without losing half your stuff. I hope my mom and dad each stay in their present relationships, but I'll never be able to say anything definite again."

After three years of estrangement, Nancy also reconciled with her mother. When Peter won the lead in his high school production of *Bye Bye Birdie*, his grandmother very much wanted to come. "The women in her book group said, 'You go home and call Nancy and tell her you're coming to this play or you're not welcome in this group anymore.' They knew that the connection between a mother and daughter was more important than anything. She did it, and agreed to have lunch with me and Susan. I didn't push her to stay at our house. But that was the beginning of the change."

Nancy's father died soon thereafter and Nancy went to stay with her mother for the first time since her marriage's end. "We did everything that needed to be done. And we went together to see his body, which she wouldn't have done alone. She told me a few months later that she felt like a dog who had spent its whole life in a fenced yard; she said, 'Now the gate is open and I'm scared to walk through.' My father was a disappointment to her in many ways, but her mother had told her that she should not expect to come home if her marriage didn't work out. My dad died with my mom still frustrated in her effort to get him to say 'I love you.' He was always paternalistic: 'We don't need any more dessert, Marge; we don't need more talking.' She's enthusiastic, large-spirited; his job was to squelch those enthusiasms. When I told her I was going to law school, she asked, 'Did you get your husband's permission?' I was enraged that she thought I needed to, but the fact is I did get his permission. I wasn't so very different. I never would have thought I needed assertiveness training, but when I reflect on it, I wasn't assertive at any critical juncture. We did *Father Knows Best*. But ultimately I made the decision not to be defined by my husband."

Marge Wanderer explained the break with her daughter to *Frontline*: "We couldn't understand it, we didn't want to understand it, because it was just something that we just didn't want. And so we didn't go into it. It wasn't so much what I thought, it's what I thought that other people would think. But I don't think I realized, I know I never realized, what it is to walk away from a child that you've had, and it took me a while, but I couldn't walk away, and I think when I came back, I came back as a better mother. Her father never came back."

Nancy: "She knows she has some finite number of years left, and wants to get the most out of them and doesn't want to do that without me, and of course that means me and Susan also. I think we've got it now. I don't think anything like this will ever happen again."

Still, Marge keeps parts of the story at bay. "My mother likes Susan," says Nancy, "because she fixes everything in her house, and she can certainly see how much happier I am. We visit her together. It's absolutely clear what our relationship is. But people can take in just as much as they can take in. Right after my twenty-fifth Wellesley reunion, she said, 'You're a feminist, aren't you?' I said, 'Yeah.' Then she said, 'But you're not a lesbian, are you?' and I said, 'Mom we've been through this. What do you think those three years were about?' "

Nancy's brother, a retired career navy officer as conservative as her father, was initially unhappy about the radical change in his sister's life. His wife, Nancy's Wellesley classmate Kate Harding, had to serve as a bridge between the siblings. So did Andrew, who has been well looked after by his uncle since moving to D.C. Relations with Thomas are also now "cordial," Nancy says, "thanks to my mother paying half the kids' college costs. Once money was not an issue, I was able to let go of my anger. I think he's furious at me, and I don't think he's begun to touch it because he's so controlled, but he did tell my mother he believed Susan was the love of my life. And after the *Frontline* thing, his mom wrote me to say that she was beginning to understand that the marriage wasn't the right life for me." When Thomas and his new wife had a yard sale in 1995, Susan and Nancy went. His wife gave them a tour of the redone kitchen, and Nancy bought a few of Peter's old shirts and pants for herself.

Nancy's classmates at Wellesley have had mixed responses. After her coming out on national television, Nancy became for a time a kind of public spokesperson on behalf of lesbians, speaking with her old Girl Scout's enthusiasm to groups of young women—at tea talks at a bed and breakfast in Bluehill, Maine, and fund-raisers for the YWCA. Her sense of mission has irritated some of her classmates; they complain that she seems to expect their admiration. At her twentieth reunion, one of Nancy's close college friends reacted coldly to news of Nancy's divorce: "She said to me, 'Well, you liked it all well enough then.' And that's right. I shared the mythology. I wanted a husband I could look up to; it's not surprising he would expect his work and his judgment to take precedence. She and I had made similar choices, and now I was disavowing them. I think it left some people feeling that if it wasn't enough for me, why should it be enough for them?

"I wouldn't wish to change anything—not the twenty years of marriage or the years since. It wasn't a sham that we were a close, connected family. Thomas was a rock. But in the end, security wasn't enough. I couldn't get him angry, sad, joyous, no matter how I tried. I couldn't get him to fight, and I needed him to fight with me. I felt myself dying daily. It was placid; when you're dead, what could be more peaceful? I don't mean that to slam Thomas, but he didn't love anything I did. He was so solitary in his study. I'd be casting about, but accountable to him for my time. With Susan, we're either ecstatic or wrestling something to the ground. I've cried more since I met her than I did in the previous twenty years, so I must be happy. I feel like since I've been on my own and sharing a home with Susan that I'm an adult for the first time. I look forward to growing old with her, which I couldn't imagine with Thomas. How could any of it have been otherwise? If you're already married, the only way of coming out is falling in love with someone. You don't come out in the abstract, you only know you're a lesbian when you discover that love.

"I know other friends who live with women who are their life partners but find a way not to say that. They say they're single mothers; they say they're divorced. None of that felt right to me. I've never been very good at not telling the truth. Lesbianism is not, for me, a sexual orientation, but something broader. Though I think sexuality is a life spring, a great source of power, the sexual part was not leading—that could have gone either way. The main thing was wanting to have unity between my sexual life and my emotional life. I always wanted to be in communities of women. As I look back over my whole life, it has been women who have sustained me and energized me and appreciated me and collaborated with me. Except for my kids, who are in a class by themselves, men have been a disappointment, including my father. I didn't need men except to get married and have children, so at first sex went with that, but ultimately I wanted a relationship where could I put everything together. It was a question of where could I have a more fully integrated life, where could I feel whole? I kept hoping Thomas would be that person. But I discovered that the kind of connection I was seeking wasn't possible with him, which is not to say it isn't possible between women and men. My whole life I was looking for a partner with whom I could re-create the intimacy I had with my mother. She gave me a tremendous gift in that way."

The summer before she met Susan, while vacationing at a country motel with her children, Nancy had read Kate Chopin's *The Awakening*. Thomas wasn't with them; he'd had too much work to come along. Nancy read the book in a single night, sitting alone on the porch amid Maine's pointed firs, listening to the sighs of the sea and her sons asleep in the room. She was moved by the heroine's decision to leave her wealthy husband's mansion and move alone into a small "pigeon house," animated by her recognition that "she must free herself of that fictitious self which we assume like a garment to appear before the world" and claim "that which her newly awakened being demanded . . . all life's delirium."

Simone de Beauvoir deplored the fact that women were relieved of the existential struggle; a woman did not find herself or forge herself but gave over that responsibility to a man, who defined her by making her his wife. "Man . . . will undertake the moral justification of her existence; thus she can evade . . . the metaphysical risk of a liberty in which aims must be contrived without assistance. . . . It is an easy road; on it one avoids the strain involved in undertaking an authentic existence." Though nearly all the women in the class of '69 would balk at that surrender, for a few, the quest to discover or build an authentic identity and life would entail truly radical risks and change.

As a girl, Nancy Young dreamed of joining a convent. She took her Catholicism deeply to heart and suffered that no one else in her family seemed to. "My parents went through the motions. They went to church every Sunday and didn't eat meat on Friday, but it was just a way of keeping on the right side of the debit-and-credit ledger. The church they raised me in was a collection of laws you had to obey; I didn't learn for a very long time that I could turn to God for help." At Wellesley's church, she found the same rigid stance. "Sometime in my first year, I was struggling and went to confession at St. Theresa's in town. I told the priest I could not find meaning in the mass. He reprimanded me and told me that attending mass was a law of the Church. Being strong-minded, I stopped going to mass and no longer considered myself a Catholic."

Nancy found a new spiritual path in the commune in Cambridge where she lived while working on a master's in drama at Tufts. "We were all in a women's group and belonged to a food co-op. This seemed like real life. We had our own drug dealer right in the house, and we all smoked up a storm. People were dropping Owsley acid [LSD made by the man who supplied psychedelics to the Grateful Dead], though I backed off: I was a little scared of acid after one of my close friends had a breakdown and was hospitalized. But we'd drop Quaaludes and run around naked and have sex with everyone in sight. I was completely into sexual freedom. I did everything my father never wanted me to do."

Though she continued acting in repertory companies, Nancy finally had to quit when she fell seriously ill. She had long struggled with her body. While at Wellesley, she never had periods; she was always too thin and stressed to have normal cycles. Senior year, doctors had put her on

massive doses of hormones, birth control pills ten times the potency
they are now. They left her sick every morning, and scared, in retrospect,
that she had soaked her body in such hormone baths. Now, in graduate
school, she began developing ovarian cysts, which twice burst and sent
her rushing to the emergency room with life-threatening peritonitis. "I
was so frightened. My body seemed out of control. And my whole thing
with acting got derailed."

Nancy's spiritual teacher arrived a month later, in an unlikely guise.
"I was in a fragile, confused place. And none of the fellows I was meeting
really captivated me. They were all too privileged—Harvard and Yale
types. Then one day, when I was working on a hot line for street people,
this wasted-looking guy showed up, with long hair and a beard and almost no teeth: He'd lost them because of all the speed he'd done. He was
divorced and had never graduated from high school, a tough kind of
guy. He'd been going to Canada, armed and transporting drugs, until he
got deported as an undesirable after selling to the Canadian police.
When I brought him home to meet my parents, my father hated him on
sight. I'd known him for six weeks, decided he was perfect, and married
him. Really, it was Barry's idea; he didn't want a flaky relationship. He
was a Jewish guy from the Brooklyn projects. These people weren't hippies. They didn't march for peace; they were into the hard-core drug
thing.

"We got married in a church in Harvard Square, with witnesses we
pulled off the street. I was wearing a ridiculously short Mexican Indian
dress with a red woven belt. The minister was dour and told us the marriage wouldn't last, but he did go with us to a deli afterward for beers
and sandwiches—that was our reception. We'd packed up my Volkswa-
gen and after the wedding we headed for Colorado, doing our Kerouac
thing. I called my dad from a Howard Johnson's along the way to say
we'd gotten married. It was the perfect revenge.

"At the time, I didn't see it that way. I was drawn to Barry because he
was working-class and I identified with him and, even more, because he
seemed to have figured out how to leave an unhappy past behind him
and find his way into a spiritual life. He'd given up drugs after years and
years because he'd gotten into Meher Baba, who was a Sufi teacher from
Puna, India, and called himself the avatar. Meher Baba's followers believed he was a realized soul; they would pass out cards to strangers that

said, 'Don't worry, be happy.' He had taken a vow of silence; for most of his life he would spell out what he wanted to say on an alphabet board, and a close disciple would speak for him. He had washed lepers and was beloved in India. I still consider him the real thing, a genuine teacher, a genuinely advanced soul. And I admired that Barry so much loved this person that he had gone to India and changed his whole life. Meher Baba was completely opposed to drugs. People were taking psychedelics and having mystical experiences; we all got way deluded that because we could have these experiences, we had arrived on some different plane. Meher Baba was one of the few saying drugs are not the way to satisfy this craving; the soul does not evolve that way; you're doing damage because you're going someplace you haven't earned. Drugs had been alluring to me, and I was drawn to Barry because he'd worked through it, investigated, and came out the other side. After we got married, he took the Owsley acid I'd tucked away for later and put it down the toilet. He also dumped all my medicine. He said, 'Your problems are because of your head.' Remarkably, my health got much better, in spite of our rugged lifestyle. I was initiated into transcendental meditation, read about Hindu masters, did yoga. In Colorado we were planning to live at the Naropa Institute in Boulder and become Buddhists."

The couple stayed just one afternoon in Boulder. Barry decided it was too fancy, and turned the car toward New Mexico. A month later they were back in Brooklyn, as resident staff at a home for delinquent boys. That ended a week later, when Barry got in a fight with the director. "By that time I was beginning to realize that he fought with anyone for any reason." After a couple of weeks in a commune in New Haven, the couple finally returned to New York so Barry could finish his education (he had dropped out after eighth grade). Their VW had given out by then, so a friend drove them to the city, dropping them off in Hell's Kitchen outside their new apartment, a fifth-floor walk-up with a shared shower in the basement and gaps in the wall so wide the snow came in.

"In New York, I was supporting us, and there was no way I could do that with an acting career. Barry's only income was federal money, a grant from the Higher Education Opportunity Program that he got by persuading them that he was underprivileged. He never paid back those loans; he declared bankruptcy instead."

Nancy became a waitress, a children's librarian, a counselor in a Jewish group home for kids, an assistant editor on an encyclopedia for Columbia University Press. Though she was accepted into a master's program in counseling, Barry pressed her to go to business school so that she could earn more money. She finally gave in, quit the counseling program, and got an MBA at New York University at night. "It was a time when women were going to business school in droves. It was a way of mounting the barricades: 'We're going to be decision makers, become empowered. You're not going to hold us back from those incomes.' " Nancy also became a CPA, again at Barry's urging, "though a less CPA-like person than me would be hard to imagine. That was the stupidest choice. Accounting really does attract microminds—not stupid, but just not interested in most of life."

While Nancy was still at work on her degrees, Barry decided he wanted children. "I thought it'd be neat even though we were totally unprepared; I didn't yet know that the cysts had scarred my fallopian tubes and left me infertile. It's just as well, since the marriage was falling apart by that time and I didn't want to be a single mom. He was at Columbia working on a master's in social work and struggling; he thought the stuff was horseshit and was terribly frustrated; really, really angry. I suspected he was having affairs. And he was controlling and had a terrible temper. He threw things, usually at me. I'd be screaming. He'd be throwing. We had no glassware; the TV and every plate and lamp in our house were smashed to smithereens. I had to move out.

"I stayed with him for seven years. I stayed for the classic reasons women stay: I felt maybe I could help the guy. I loved him. I thought in some ways he was a good person, a bold, daring person, a real risk-taker. When my father left my mother, Barry was incredibly helpful to her. He loved crises. I thought that if he could finish school and get a job, he'd get better and settle down and be a mensch. I was naive. And I bought into the idea that I was doing something to provoke him. My father had told me I was provocative. I'd made my father angry, so why not this guy? Even if I did what he wanted, I was doing something wrong. I didn't have a strong enough sense of myself. Since I didn't believe I had much legitimacy, I was easily undermined. Two conversations were going on in my head at the same time—one said I had a right to be treated better, and two said, 'Oh, you're really fucked up.' I was relieved when he left, though I still talk to him. With the O. J. Simpson thing, I said, 'Barry, that brought back to me what our marriage was like,' and he said, 'What are you talking about? It wasn't that bad. We just weren't compatible. We didn't have good chemistry.' He's been married more than once, sold insurance, and now does corporate training.

"I do regret the decision to marry Barry. It's too bad I spent seven years in such a prison. Because of financial pressure, I made decisions I wouldn't have made, that he foisted on me. If I hadn't been supporting him, I would have done the NYU counseling program, just been a poor grad student doing what I loved."

By the time the marriage ended, Nancy was an accountant with Peat Marwick Mitchell, and unhappy. She went to Chase Manhattan, and hated that; went to another job and was fired in a week; became comptroller at a consulting firm, then to a bank in mutual funds. "I kept getting bored and never felt a confluence of my values with my colleagues'. Everywhere I went, they all thought I was the weirdest person. I had aced business school, but I hated the environments it landed me in, which were steady but utterly colorless. The corporate world seemed stuck in the fifties. You had to look like everyone else, and if it took snorting coke to achieve that, then that's what you had to do. A headhunter once told me that high-powered types want someone 'in their likeness.' But I could never be like the people I've met in business who spend sixteen hours a day thinking about the bottom line, and then consider themselves dedicated family men. More than intelligence, corporations want your endurance, a willingness to shut everything else out. Nothing in me could allow such single-mindedness about success. That always showed, that I did not consider these jobs the most important thing."

In 1980, having just lost her fifth job that year and been dumped by her boyfriend, Nancy began reading the works of Baghwan Shree Rajneesh. "They seemed to cut through the bullshit of organized religion and get to the core of what the spiritual life was about. They stirred my spiritual hunger, and also appealed to the social critic in me, to my alienation from the business world. Baghwan is an anarchist. He doesn't believe in organized religions or long-term relations. He did believe in getting high on meditation and sex, especially sex. I started hanging around the ashram in SoHo, where there were intense meditations every night and everybody was sleeping with everybody. At that point I had this ridiculous job at Citibank. I was wearing my dress-for-success suit and also the "mala," the beaded necklace bearing the Bhagwan's picture. My co-workers were always madly squinting trying to see what it was; with his long white hair and beard, some thought it was a picture of my Afghan hound."

After a few months, Nancy was hired to be chief financial officer at the Baghwan's ashram in Vermont. "I went in with both feet and became a disciple and changed my name to Nagara, which means 'beautiful love,' and wore nothing but red. In those first few months, I felt the most balanced, centered, chilled-out feeling I'd had in a long time. It was working. The dancing and music were really powerful; you'd come out of them high. Baghwan's message was freedom. Instead of, 'Here is the trinity and you have to align yourself with it,' we were supposed to discover for ourselves what to feel and believe. We had some stupid arguments, like about why we all had to wear red—if we discover for ourselves what is right and wrong, why is there this heavy rule? But it wasn't just lost souls; there were many well-educated people, professionals, passionate students of human nature, seekers who couldn't see themselves in a traditional religion. Sexually, we were just insane; this was where God really took care of me. We were trying to reach enlightenment through sex, with tantric weekends, where we were all nude for days with something like thirty partners. Never again will anyone be able to do that. Just as I was leaving Vermont in 1981, someone started telling me about this gay virus.

"I left after ten months because after the initial rap wore off, I realized a lot of these people were opportunists and Baghwan was a crook. The guy he had running it was a real operator. We had seventeen dollars in the bank and they'd brought up dozens of people, mostly women, and had no money to pay them or even feed them, and Baghwan was in Oregon buying up land and a Rolls-Royce fleet and I was chief financial officer, so the bankers were screaming at me. The people who went to Oregon had to sign over all their money and were defending the compound with AK-47's." (In an unwitting crossing of paths by class members, in 1995 Kris Olson would win a guilty verdict against Bhagwan followers, for conspiring to kill U.S. attorney Charles Turner, the man who had forced Kris out of her job.) "Our relationship with the outside world was increasingly tense. This was just a few years after Jim Jones and the mass suicide in Guyana, and the revelations that Rinpoche was an alcoholic and sleeping with his students; people were increasingly scared of cults. I finally got burned. They didn't pay me, and stole my belongings, and a bunch of Senyassens [disciples] turned my apartment in New York into their crash pad, then told me I was negative. It took me a while to figure out what to do."

While still at the ashram, Nancy had met a man named Steve, who'd reluctantly come to Vermont with his Boston-based management consulting firm. The firm's senior vice-president, George Littwin, was also Swami Prem Dharmo; it was his idea that the firm get away to the ashram for a brainstorming session. Snowbound, the group had to remain for several days. Reclusive and shy by nature, Steve was embarrassed by the Rajneeshies' antics; he told Nancy that he thought it was all bullshit, but he was also attracted to her wildness and joined her in the dancing every night. When Nancy abandoned the ashram, it was to Steve's little Cambridge attic that she fled. She spent a month there, "a sweet, happy time," while seeking a job and an apartment, then spent the next two years persuading him that they should live together. He would realize he wanted to spend his life with her only when crisis struck.

CHAPTER ELEVEN

Life's Afternoon

The year that Hillary Clinton moved into the White House, Nancy Young was passing the hours watching chemicals drip into her veins, poison for the cancer that had overtaken her ovaries. It was another extreme turn in a life that had always seemed wilder and harder than her classmates': from her blue-collar childhood to her volatile husband, her night school MBA to tantric sex at the Rajneesh ashram to the illness that had suddenly accelerated her life, leaping her twenty years ahead of her generation.

Nancy's life may have been an exaggerated version of her classmates'—more damned with men, more misfitted at work, more ceaseless in her search for meaning, more fragile in her health. But it has confronted her with the same essential and complicated negotiation between the personal and the public that has shaped all their lives. Like all of them, Nancy would struggle to reconcile her own values—etched into heightened clarity by her cancer—with the values of the wage-paying world. She would grapple with the official stories—medical, theological, psychological—that describe her place and her prospects. She would seek communities of support. She would insist on being loved, and also try to transcend her small, needful self.

When she found the lump in her breast, the size of a coffee bean and rock hard against her rib cage, she was living with Steve but deeply unhappy and close to leaving. "I was tired of having always to be the emotional leader—this will be the universal story. I kept saying we should commit ourselves. He would be, like, 'What's the hurry?' Even when I got him to agree to buy a condo together, we had to draft an agreement so he could get out of it the minute he wanted to. He kept saying he wanted time alone, and to see old friends by himself, many of whom were women. It was a game, a head trip to say, 'You're not going to run my life.' But I also think that commitment is genuinely harder for men. Women are better at knowing what we feel, so we can say, 'This relationship has enough that is good.' Men don't pay the same attention to their feelings; their inner dialogue does not include the constant examination of where they are emotionally. I see so many relationships where the women do all the emoting while the men watch TV and go to work. I'm not talking about dumb guys. I'm talking about my own relationship. I'll think, 'Today I have this little edge of feeling.' Steve thinks you deal with emotions when there's a crisis but it's not something you work on all day long."

Over time, Nancy's dissatisfaction grew. "Steve continued to insist on his independence and remained fairly closed off from me. I felt I still didn't really know who he was." Frustrated, she turned her attentions to her old, crippled dog, a German shepherd she had carried with her from her first troubled marriage. "Over time I became more and more the dog's nurse—I couldn't bear to put her down or leave her—and Steve spoke to me less and less. By the summer of 1986, when I finally put her to sleep, Steve and I had become strangers. Our relationship lacked life; it still had little intensity or commitment. And it had not healed by the following March, when I found the lump."

The doctor ordered a biopsy, which brought good news: The tumor was benign. A week later, Nancy went to have her stitches removed. The doctor met her with an apology. He'd been wrong. The growth was malignant. "I started pounding the table and screaming. 'It can't be; it can't be.' I was totally unprepared and furious. This had totally derailed my plans. I was only thirty-nine; I was just starting a new job; I thought Steve and I were going to split and I was going to have to build a new life." The doctor listened, then told Nancy that while she was in the recovery room, drugged and gape-mouthed and drooling, Steve had turned to him and said, "You know, I really love her." This is not the time, the doctor told Nancy, for you to leave this man.

"I went crazy, and turned on Steve. He wanted to be in there with it. I told him to go away, that this was a poisonous relationship, that I'd put enough into it and didn't get anything back and wasn't impressed with his eleventh-hour protestations of how he really cared about me."

The doctor sent her to a breast surgeon, who advised a mastectomy. Though the tumor was small, he believed that it wouldn't respond to radiation. Nancy refused and went to a doctor at another hospital, who told her that the idea of a mastectomy was "off the wall" and ordered a lumpectomy. Nancy had a stage-one cancer with no lymph node involvement, the doctor said, and would probably not need radiation. Days later, she called to say she'd made a mistake; there were cancer cells on the margin and they might need another lumpectomy. They finally decided on radiation—every day, all summer long. It exhausted Nancy and burned her skin, but she never missed work. "Right away you're looking for lifeboats. I was utterly uninterested in my job but grateful for someplace to go.

"Then it was pretty much over and done. I had an 80 percent chance of surviving, which I thought nice odds. And I knew at last that Steve really did care about me; I finally had what I wanted from him. When I finished treatment we went to California, to a beautiful inn by the Pacific, and decided to get married." A justice of the peace performed the ceremony in their apartment, witnessed by Nancy's brother and his boyfriend and a few friends.

For the first time in her life, Nancy felt that she wanted children. She went to a fertility doctor and learned that her tubes were scarred and could probably not be unblocked. In vitro fertilization seemed to her too much like the hospital again; she was not prepared to "pay any price" to have kids. "I wasn't terribly disappointed, because I'd never really expected it to happen. My life had never had the stability children need, and my own miserable upbringing had convinced me that you should only have kids when you can make the right environment for them. I wasn't heartbroken. But as time goes on, I grow more sad about it; having children is such a big part of being a human being."

The day Bill Clinton was elected in 1992, Nancy got much worse news. For fifteen months she'd been having a heavy vaginal discharge, enough to soak her underwear, and long painful periods. They'd done Pap smears, but found nothing until an ultrasound located a mass the size of a grapefruit on one of her ovaries. Told she would need immediate surgery, she left the doctor's office and ran as fast as she could all the way home, desperately trying to outrun her terror.

Her doctor sent her to a gynecological oncologist. "He had a horrible personality and was not the least bit reassuring. I wanted him to leave an ovary, because I knew I couldn't take estrogen, which tends to grow tumors in the breast. I tried writing an agreement: 'If you find this, then you can do that.' He was bullshit about it. Going into surgery, he was furious at me and I was terrified. I had to give this guy I didn't like, who seemed to have no feeling whatsoever, a blank check. When I woke up from surgery, he said: 'This was quite an afternoon you gave me. The tumor was cancerous. The lymph nodes were full of it. There was a second tumor. It took me four hours to clean it out.' He really was a dodo. I had stage-three ovarian cancer." For a tumor so advanced, the doctors told her, the survival rate was 10 percent.

For the next six months Nancy had chemotherapy, an "unbelievably horrible" experience. Each time, it took an entire day to get the full dose. The drip burned out all the veins in her hand, and several times she had to be hospitalized and given intravenous fluids, because she couldn't keep anything down. Her hair thinned and the weight on her five-foot-seven frame dropped to 105 pounds. Every tremor in her body became a cause for alarm that the cancer might be coming back, in her bladder or her colon.

Through it all, Nancy felt an unexpected, wonderful peace. "It was a kind of religious conversion for me, which transformed something that most people would find unbearable into a profound experience. People don't know how you can bear it. They don't think they could ever muster the grace of acceptance. I couldn't, the first time. All I could think was, Why are you doing this to me? But this time I felt chosen, given a deliberate message. I believe in reincarnation, and that you choose the life you need for your consciousness to evolve. In this lifetime, illness is my teacher. Most of what I will learn I'll learn because of my illnesses. The moment I got the diagnosis, I knew I was looking at my life from its end. From that vantage, for the very first time, I had clear knowledge of what mattered to me.

"I finally understood that what's important to me is the spiritual life, finding a path that keeps me aligned with God. Not that God is ever out of sync with us, but your actions can bring you closer or pull you away. If you expose yourself to all the junk that tells you over and over again all day long that what's important is being young and beautiful and having lots of money, if you're bathed in that, with nothing that guides you to

compassion, to being sensitive to other people's sufferings and not turning away from them, then your ability to feel close to God is going to be
compromised. It takes work and a supportive community to be a tran-
quil and kind person. So while I could never say this illness was good, it
has been an illumination, a great spiritual challenge."

Nancy has a deep, sonorous voice, which, as she tells her story, is dry
and matter-of-fact; it neither breaks with tears nor works too hard to
prove her uplifted state. "I'm not like an enlightened being, where all the
terror and anger goes away. I'm afraid of dying—the actual physical
process. It's hard to imagine there won't be panic at the moment of giving up, losing absolutely everything. I don't think there's a beautiful
light you follow and feel no pain. But I do believe that you can die well.
Thich Nhat Hahn [in *The Tibetan Book of Living and Dying*] says that the
monastic path is preparation for death. When I was in the hospital, I realized I was not prepared, that I must become prepared. I started reading
about death and went to a workshop with hospice workers and people
who'd lost friends to AIDS. I saw that some people die in an inspiring
way. To die that way myself, and maybe help other people do so, seems
important. And to savor the life I have, the prospect of good work.
Thich Nhat Hahn says that every time he wakes, he celebrates that he
can breathe."

Though she had been absorbed in her adult life mostly with Hin-
duism and Buddhism, in crisis Nancy found herself turning back toward
Christianity, "the religion most deeply imbedded in me." Buddhism's
universe of emptiness offered too little comfort. "It doesn't have the
same heart quality as Christianity. There have been great, good Christians, even if it has become a withered affair in most churches, obsessed
with people's sex lives, a haven for bigots. It moves me with its dramatic
stories and tenderness." After her experience with the Rajneesh cult, she
had no desire to join another religious community; "the conformism
would drive me up the wall and a lot of those people are crazy." But she
found an Episcopal church with an interfaith spirituality institute,
"where they were not fazed by a Sunyassen who had hooked up with
Rajneesh. One priest said, 'Oh, he had wonderful meditations.' I felt my
sins forgiven for having dipped into this and traipsed into that. They saw
it as a natural seeking."

Nancy wished her husband, Steve, would join her in her spiritual search, but in vain. "My husband has been very loyal and very stoic. He has kept most of his fear to himself. He believes life is as it is, that you can't measure it by what's fair, that you have to make the best of what you're given. But he's not interested in my meditation groups or retreats. He's skeptical and doesn't like groupy feelings and is not a person of great spiritual yearnings. I sometimes wish he were. I know people who pray with their families every day, and would like it to be part of my home life."

The integration of her spirituality into her work life has seemed to Nancy more urgent. "Certain things that were never good for me, like corporate work, are now out of the question. Most of those jobs were an immense waste of my time. They gave me nothing but money, and time is too precious now. I probably couldn't get hired anyway. Not many employers value the wisdom of a cancer survivor, someone who has faced death. You have to do your best to conceal it; they worry you'll rack up their insurance bills or take off too much time. But I've had to face the question: How do you make a living in this world knowing more than it wants you to know?"

Her solution was to apply for a joint degree in social work and pastoral ministry at Boston College, with the intention of working with the dying. The college turned her down, explaining, with no apparent irony, that "she didn't have recent experience working with the target population." They advised her to spend a year doing volunteer work and reapply, so she began visiting the chemotherapy ward at Brigham and Women's Hospital. She was well suited for the work: Where others might have shrunk in horror from tipping juice into the mouth of a man who'd lost an entire shoulder to lymphoma and spoke through a voice box, or tucking in the sheets around another, who was having bone marrow transplants and had to be completely covered except for his eyes, for Nancy it was a familiar environment. She spent her days greeting patients, helping them find a place to sit, and bringing them food, all of which gave her "a tremendous high." "It did not feel like work, but an opportunity to have a powerful experience. Illness called me out of my small self."

Harder for her was listening to cancer patients tell their stories. "My own story is in there, which leaves me tongue-tied. I have an overwhelming reaction to people who are in late stages of treatment, having bone marrow transplants. I see my worst fantasies played out. It stirs my dread: the paralyzing fear of the unknown. I do keep trying. Thich Nhat Hahn says you should seek out suffering to grow. I guess I feel there's no way out but through."

When Nancy finally began Boston College, she again felt as she had at Wellesley: deeply alienated. She was briefly thrown out of the school after dropping a mandatory course in racism, which she saw as "an opportunity for black faculty to get up and revile white people." She was also put off by what she thought to be an excessively politicized perspective in the pastoral program. "They were busy with feminist and Marxist liberation theology; their concern was justice, not spirituality. Their Old Testament was not about a personal relationship with God but about a people working out their political problems, with God just a player in those politics. They would get angry if I asked about the soul. But I kept wondering: If the Bible is just about some third world country two thousand years ago, why would it be of any use to us?"

The feminist analysis was somewhat less alien to Nancy. "We were taught by ex–Catholic nuns who had left the order because they couldn't find a way to be a woman in a church that excludes them from the priesthood and magisterium and consigns them to a life much poorer and more obscure than men's. They were trying to redeem the Bible and Christian tradition from its patriarchal orientation. I could relate to that. The woman thing is why I'm not a Catholic; what do a lot of dried-up old men have to say about my life?" Nancy read Sandra Schneiders's *Beyond Patching* on the exodus of women from the church for the goddess movement, and Elizabeth Schussler-Fiorenzo's argument for a woman's church and Bible. "I do question Christianity's androcentrism, with God the Father and His only Son. The Virgin kind of fades out of the story. Mary Magdalene is central, present at the Crucifixion and the tomb, but she has been terribly slandered by being called a prostitute. I realize the power of symbolism, and that the basic stories in my religion give women second status. So I tried to read people who would help me re-image this stuff, like Elizabeth Johnson, who argues that Jesus is the incarnation of Sophia, the goddess of wisdom, or John McDarr, who shows how we project our own family dynamics onto God. Until I got sick, my God was authoritarian and remote with bursts of love just like my father. Now, like my father, he has come closer. But again, it was more about politics than transcendence, which brought a lot of confusion in my mind."

Nancy was still less at home with the medical model employed in the social work school, where she spent half her time. "They taught us to listen to a patient just to pull out their symptoms and then look at the diagnostic manual, which is like a big reverse cookbook: You have all the ingredients and try to find the recipe, then do the prescribed drug and behavior therapy. They viewed as suspect any behavior that was too religious; psychotic people are always having religious experiences. I discovered I'm not comfortable approaching people as insects, pulling off that leg and an antenna to figure out what kind of bug it is and then make a better bug."

The New Age alternatives repelled Nancy just as thoroughly. She despised the idea implicit in the New Agers' self-healing practices that illness is a kind of failure, proof that one has lived with too much bitterness or anger; she would not accept that cancer, as Camille Paglia once wrote, was "nature's revenge on the ambitious, childless woman." She also found visualization, which she had tried at a mind-body clinic after her lumpectomy, "really kind of stupid. Golden beams of sunlight come into your body and seek out the cancer cells and beat them up and now you're healed. It was so obvious and without imagination and grating. They would critique your visualizations. 'Oh no, you've got the color yellow in there. That's the color for disease. That's a bad visualization.' "

At the interfaith institute, leading a group called Cancer and the Spiritual Life, she was stunned to find so many educated women "into" what seemed to her simplistic and narcissistic nonsense. "They think that if we can think good thoughts, we won't have cancer. What, you think we're that powerful? There are Zen monks who have died of cancer. It's not a disease of neurosis. One guy, a psychiatrist, had a wife with breast cancer. She was doing visualizations, refusing conventional treatment, casting herself as the guru, and is now dead. We had an Irish Catholic nun in the group talking about bioenergetics. I left. All the crystals and massages don't have a lot to do with the spiritual life, as I understand it, which is not about aggrandizement of the self but about a relationship with the Other."

Her classmates' sojourns into the New Age also perplex her. "Angels?

Well, what's the theology here? Are they just benign spirits? From where? These people seem to have no questions. On other subjects they'll be scientific and rigorous; on this they lose their critical faculties. From what I've seen, the goddess movement does no grappling with tough issues. You still have the issue of evil and suffering no matter who you put up there. Make it a goddess. If she's a real goddess, she's been there all along, so why hasn't there been all this peace and ecological harmony? And why were all those pagan goddess worshipers, like the Canaanites and Egyptians, not terribly nice? If you start making up your religion, it's shallow. I'm always looking at the dark side. How does this work on the dark side? I take it deadly seriously."

Nancy's story is more harrowing than the stories of most in her class, but in midlife she feels their same mixture of sorrow and acceptance. "Sometimes I think, Shit, why haven't the things that have come to others also come to me? Why don't I have children? Such a natural thing. I'd love to have some kids around, to have a sense of life on the upswing and not just in decline. Why doesn't my life make sense, have some coherent direction? Why have I had this incredible amount of illness? It never stops, you know. I've had carpal tunnel surgery. Now a doctor wants to operate on my sinuses, and I think, Leave me alone. But I don't cry much, not too much. Oh, I cry over day-to-day disappointments. But I don't wake up in panic; I don't often feel overwhelmed. I've accepted that I live in a new place, that I can't go back to where I was. My life has been shipwrecked. Illness has thrown me out of the ship onto some other shore. All I can say is, 'Well, who am I now, and what do I have?' and go forward from there.

"The cancer diagnosis forced me to come to grips with deep wounds. Knowing I might die very soon, I wanted to make peace with all that I'd hardened my heart to. I tore the cover off a lot of things where the story had been written, realized I couldn't hold on to the set stories that protected me from having to reevaluate my life."

"I wanted to understand my parents and not hate them anymore. I found I could love them even with all their limitations. I try to help my mother, who nearly died from a thoracic aneurysm and is by herself. I've quit being angry at her for not developing her mind more. I see now that her father was so intimidating—he would not have permitted her to do other than what she did. When my father left her, she was fifty-eight and had never worked, but she got a job at Filene's and became a terrific saleswoman, working till she was seventy-three. She made the steps she could, and was forced to, make.

"She was ghastly when I was in the hospital. She talked about what a hassle it was to get into town to visit me. I finally said, 'Look, my life is in jeopardy here.' And she said, with this look of utter terror on her face: 'I just ask God, Why didn't this happen to me? You're a young person, and I've lived my life.' I was touched by her wish to sacrifice herself for me, the ultimate motherly impulse. I saw that she really does have feelings she can't ordinarily articulate. It would have given me a lot of consolation along the years to know that she was behind me in that way.

"My father, I also realized, has had a fairly miserable life. He was acutely unhappy with my mother. He'd loved being an auto mechanic and would have loved to go to college, but he felt forced to do things he didn't love to make more money, to satisfy my mother's desire to be more securely middle-class. He considers himself a failure; to me, he no longer seems a villain, but a victim of the times and men's assigned roles. That he had to be the sole breadwinner limited his life terribly.

"He waited a long time to leave my mother, feeling it a bad thing to do, a great taboo. He's a pretty tightly bound person. He wouldn't be in the vanguard, but then the changes initiated by our generation rippled upward. He finally left, and moved into a one-room apartment, and has been married three times since, not so happily. His second wife died. His third was a disaster: He was with her when I had cancer, which seemed to make no impression on them at all. His fourth, well, with her he seems pretty happy. He's certainly ended up in a far better place than he ever would have with my mother, which I guess is an argument for people to make the changes necessary to try to keep some happiness for themselves. He calls a lot now, and I go to see him.

"My parents are in their eighties, but there's this funny bond, like we're all old people wondering how much longer we have. I drew up my will and then made sure my mother's was in order. I jumped into their generation. Everyone will enter this place in time. But somehow a young person faced with her mortality, well, I speak from a place most people my age don't know.

"I never thought I'd go back to a Wellesley reunion, but for the twenty-fifth I sought them out. I was apprehensive, but wanted to understand why I'd hated it so badly, why it had been so traumatic. I ended up loving it, and came to think less about how fucked-up the college had been and more about who I was when I arrived there. I saw myself as a victim: that they were privileged and I was not, which I now think was mostly my inherited paranoia. And as much as I wish it had been happier, given who I was and my family, it was the only experience I could have had.

"In many ways, the sad tone of my life was set there. I hoped I'd find a place, and didn't. To me it felt like a cul-de-sac, that things were closing down instead of opening up. Other people whose families thought they were great had a stronger sense of themselves, and just flowered. Martha Teichner knew she was a good storyteller and found her place in TV and . . . zoom. I wish I'd had that sense of myself early on, but I couldn't have: My father was too critical of who I was, and what he told me about life was too poisonous and frightened. I thought you had to sell your soul to have a secure life. I felt alienated and lost, and that feeling stayed with me.

"At reunion, I stood up and said, 'Here's the most important thing that's happened to me,' and told them about my cancer. People were really moved, which moved me to tears. I thought, How kind to give me that recognition, to offer courage. And what a shame I had felt so isolated as a student, when I feel so close to these women now. What a terrific community I might have found. All the time I thought we had nothing in common, that they all had it made. Now I see they've struggled, too, that their lives played surprises on them, that everyone has endured grief. No one has gone unscathed. We had more choices than we knew how to deal with, and most of us still are confused. Should I be doing this, or that?"

New Thresholds

The story ends where it begins, with most questions unanswered and with these women crossing thresholds once again: into empty nests, menopause, late pregnancies, altered ambitions, new reflections on their past, gentled relations with their parents, and deepened friendships with each other.

At Wellesley, they had crossed the threshold between the personal and the political. One by one, they had left the domestic shelter of their childhood families for a larger world. Together, they had enacted the same leave-taking on a historic scale: ending a long epoch of women's confinement to the private sphere and marking out the forward edges of a new era, when women would take their full place in public life. They began, at Wellesley and in the years after, mixing the language of the two realms, bringing the vocabulary of maternity and nurture to the workplace, the language of power and justice home. They began publicizing their private confusions and struggles, and also requiring of themselves that their political values be enacted in their personal lives.

In midlife, the thresholds they are crossing again bridge the boundary between private and public life. Some are, at age fifty, only now completing that earlier crossing: coming out of their homes into school and work, or deepening their public commitments; more than half say they are more ambitious now than at graduation. Some are working for the first time, or again, or more than before out of a legitimate fear of poverty in old age: Their part-time and short-lived jobs and lower wages have left many ill prepared for retirement. Others are being pushed outward by menopause and empty nests, which foreclose for good their reproductive and maternal roles. A few are reversing the motion: Having rushed into the world after graduation, they are turning back to home and their inner life. Nearly all feel as Lonny Laszlo Higgins described feeling each time her family set sail, leaving a familiar island for some unknown part of the archipelago: filled with terrible nostalgia and exhilarating freedom.

For the moms in the class who spent their years mostly at home, the new beginnings at midlife have usually meant a return to school or to work. Fifteen years after leaving her vice-presidency at the bank, Jan Mercer has started a landscape-design business, just as her husband decided "by merger" to start a new career. She is torn about whether to expand the enterprise. "The overachiever says crank up to something that will impress everyone. But I don't feel the drive like I used to. I used to love the adrenaline rush. Now yoga deep breathing feels much better." Kathy Ruckman, with just one of four children still at home, has entered George Washington University's night law school. She was not, after all, immune to the frustrations that had plagued her mother. "I realized that I was bored and going nowhere with my tutoring job, that I wanted something exciting instead of make-do work. I gave up the bell choir and my other volunteer work, quite happily. Then I tried writing a résumé, which was tricky. If you've run a household you have managerial skills, but that's hard to put in. I tried to make my volunteer things look like executive work. I finally faced that I needed some real skills to do a real job. I don't think teaching ever really did captivate me. What I'd love to do is work for the Children's Defense Fund, making a difference and using my brain. Roger's glad. He's seen my frustration, which would sort of boil over periodically. He knows he's had all these wonderful opportunities to develop a career and that I've not had intellectual excitement or any of the outside encouragement that comes with a career."

Lorna Rinear has been a single mom since 1976; she sought a divorce after moving seven times to new horse farms with her volatile husband, who verbally warred with his bosses and his eldest son. Her mother, still living in Manhattan opulence, told Lorna after the divorce, "You've made your bed and you should lie in it," and suggested she apply for welfare. Lorna did, unsuccessfully, then spent the next fifteen years supporting her sons by working in electronics factories, sometimes holding down two or three jobs. At forty-seven, she returned to Wellesley to finish her degree, with her son footing the bill. She is now pursuing a Ph.D. in nineteenth-century women's history. For her fiftieth birthday, she bought herself a retired racehorse to ride. "This is a wonderful time. I had the life of being the perfect child, the wife, the mom; now I'm not responsible for anyone but myself. Of course I have regrets. When my son would ask me to play badminton, I wished I'd done more of that, because now there's no one to play badminton with. But people think I put myself places inadvertently, and I say no, I chose this."

When Betty Demy's children left home for school, the prospect of living alone for the first time frightened her: "It's much easier for me to take care of others than to take care of myself." She was in a job she didn't like, trapped there by her need to keep her health insurance. She was dreading menopause, "which for married women may be liberating, but for women who aren't is just another reminder that you feel less desirable." Though she always had a "strong and rich group of women friends," she was unsuccessful at meeting men. For years, she had traipsed to singles' events, but found the men there to be "professionally single." After a while, she gave up. "I hadn't had positive experiences, and kept being drawn to smart, screwed-up men. Why be masochistic and keep seeking experiences that don't feel good? The prospect of being alone for the rest of my life isn't very happy, but I've pushed it aside. I have to build a life for myself without depending on someone else to make it good for me."

Betty has succeeded in beginning anew. After "talking to Prozac" for a while, as she put it in a letter to her classmates, she dusted off an old fascination, returning to school for a master's in museum professions. She is now director of external affairs at a girls' school, which her son calls her "mini-Wellesley," and has been traveling extensively, to Moscow, Paris, and Prague. "I come and go as I please, and do what I want to do, which is incredibly liberating. I'd always regretted that I hadn't made a giant professional splash, and now I'm thinking it's not over."

A number of women in the class are scaling new professional heights in their fifties. In 1998, Susan Graber was confirmed for the U.S. Ninth Circuit Court of Appeals, one step below the Supreme Court. The same year, Crandall Close Bowles, '69, was made chairman, CEO, and president of Springs Industries, a $2.5 billion textile company, leading *Business Week* to name her "one of the top two or three women executives in the country." (Her husband, Erskine, was until 1998 Bill Clinton's chief of staff, and has had to testify before the grand jury as to why he tried to line up work for Hillary's old law partner, Webster Hubbell.) Pam Colony, after more than twenty years, won tenure at last. She now directs the histotechnology and Women in Science programs at the State University of New York. She also, after her second marriage came to a horrible end, moved with her two sons to a farm and spent her fiftieth year building a barn, lifting and nailing the six-foot boards herself. Nancy Gist manages the largest grant-making organization in the U.S. Justice Department, dispensing nearly $2 billion a year to state, local, and tribal criminal justice systems. Because she is doing "the people's business," she travels widely to learn from communities how they are solving their problems. When she traveled to Oregon, her classmate Kris Olson picked her up at the airport. "Here comes the U.S. attorney with the Grateful Dead blasting on the car radio. We were hooting with laughter. Everywhere we went, people were so solicitous, as they tend to be with people who have power or money. We never imagined that either of us would have any power or money, much less official photos in front of the American flag."

Returning Home

While those who remained mostly home have come out into the world in midlife, some of those who have lived more publicly have turned increasingly inward. After her divorce from Jeff, Kris Olson began spending more time on the Warm Springs reservation, talking with the elders, fishing, walking the land. She also remarried, to another lawyer, whom she first described to me in terms of the political work he's done: representing young black criminal defendants in Mississippi in the sixties, suing the makers of breast implants and the Dalkon Shield. She then added that in her new marriage, "I am experiencing for the first time in my life what it is to be really loved." And though she has expanded her professional responsibilities, joining Janet Reno's national advisory committee and working on matters like campaign finance reform, she looks forward to working on a smaller scale after 2001. She may teach at an Indian high school, surveying the history of federal Indian policy so that "these kids know why their parents and communities have been through such wrenching changes."

Lonny Higgins renewed her private life in a more dramatic fashion. In 1995 she discovered that she was pregnant. She and David were both ecstatic. "We felt rejuvenated and rewarded." Then six weeks later she realized that the embryo had stopped growing. She lost the fetus but never bled. "I said to the baby, 'You don't need to go away, you can just come back into me,' " and then watched on the ultrasound over the course of several days as the fetus was resorbed. "Strangely, contemplating new life made me face my own mortality. It's like Timothy Leary said, 'When you take off your watch, that's when time stops.' "

With her two kids in college, Lonny felt urgently that she wanted to be pregnant again. She had just been through a grueling, if vindicating, professional ordeal: successfully defending herself against two malpractice suits for deliveries she'd performed fifteen years earlier, then countersuing the plaintiff's attorney for defamation and malicious prosecution, winning a public apology and a half-million-dollar award. Demoralized by the effects such suits have on obstetrics (causing, for example, doctors to resort more often to cesarean delivery), Lonny quit delivering babies. Her motives were also personal: "My life has been defined by what other people needed, which in some ways is a very easy position, a 'call.' I wanted to learn to take care of myself."

Having tried in vitro fertilization with her own eggs without success, Lonny went in search of an egg donor. She didn't care if it was her genes in the baby; what she wanted was to give birth, which, "beginning with the intrauterine environment," she counts "the ultimate form of creativity." David resisted: "It's you I love, and I only want to fertilize one of your eggs," but after meeting the young woman Lonny had chosen, he agreed. Their grown kids were involved from the beginning, watching the embryos grow outside their mother's body before implantation. At age forty-nine, Lonny gave birth to a baby boy, with whom she now happily spends all her days.

As with the women who stayed home, many of the working women's mid-track switches have been involuntary. Linda Gibson Preston was living in Houston with her husband and four kids, getting rich in real estate and banking, driving lavish cars and working out in her mirrored home gym when oil prices crashed and wiped the family out. "You couldn't sell, rent, lease, or develop real estate. The banks were underwater. We lost everything, including our confidence, and there was no way out." They moved to New Jersey and, fifteen years later, are still "edging back." More than her husband, Linda was able to find useful lessons in the disaster, believing it a good thing for her children (one of whom has Down's syndrome) to have endured. "I think women may be better at changes that come because we've always had to anticipate abrupt disruptions in our lives."

The belief that they have reaped good things from all the sidetrackings and collapses and rebuildings runs deep among these women. Johanna Branson told *Frontline*: "It really hit me at our tenth reunion. We were in our early thirties, so we still were optimistic about getting married, about having children, and everything still seemed to be going our way, and I remember looking around in this room full of women, all dressed in bright, solid-color jackets just ready for network news interviews that might drop on them and clutching these thick leather appointment books and running around networking, and I was thinking, This is getting borderline insufferably smug. The optimism was turning a little bit to something that seemed to me to be unfounded. And it was a different world five years later, for the fifteenth, because women were in their late thirties. Carter wasn't in the White House. People had lost their snazzy jobs; maybe they were having to reinvent new jobs for themselves. There wasn't a track they could follow. Maybe people's marriages weren't existing anymore or they still hadn't found somebody, and a lot of people were facing real fertility problems. So as a whole, I remember looking around that room and thinking, This is a much humbler but a much more interesting group of women, much more complex."

Their new beginnings have also, like Nancy Young's, frequently "rippled upward." Many have been divorced and, later, watched their parents split; many have also seen their mothers bloom late in life. Louise Carter's frustrated mom got a job at the law firm where Louise was working the summer after her sophomore year. She loved it, went back to school, and worked until retirement for Bell Laboratories; "for a while she was the breadwinner, and her whole self-concept really changed." Charlynn Maniatis's mom had never learned to drive and had never shopped for groceries without her husband's supervision when he abruptly left her, taking nearly everything they owned. "The first six months were incredible. She didn't know how to balance a checkbook, but she started to take trips. She would visit me in New York. You saw this flower blossoming." Nancy Wanderer's mom, Marge, also began traveling after her husband died. "She has taken great interest in managing her money and has become a regular visitor to Merrill Lynch and the bank." Dorothy Devine's mom published her first book at age seventy-four, a collection of short stories dedicated to Dorothy's grandmother, who "hid her typewriter in the laundry basket." She is now at work on a novel about a mother and daughter whose family was destroyed by the Vietnam War. Though she cried when she figured out that Dorothy was gay, after her husband died she announced that she would never marry again and take care of a sick old man. She told Dorothy's partner, "Women are the only ones who talk about anything real."

Their mothers' renaissance has often helped these women make peace with their parents and their past. After a long estrangement, Dorothy found her chance to reconnect with her family when her father fell ill; as his only daughter, she went home to help her mother take care of him. In twenty-five years, father and daughter had never reconciled; he could never forgive her for her years in Cuba and the SDS. But he developed Alzheimer's "and forgot that he was angry," and by the end the family was integrated again. Like Nancy Young, Dorothy developed empathy in midlife for the struggles her parents had endured. "Looking back, I realize that my father's breadwinning role isolated him, that he was connected to his children in only the most tenuous way, which was why the ideological splits broke the family apart. If he'd been more involved in raising us, we would have been more people to him. He would have understood better the choices we made." Her view of her ex-husband and his radical colleagues also softened. "A lot of what we did, like trashing Cambridge, I look back on as a sad waste. Aggression breeds aggression; by being radical we just made everything polarized. People hated their kids; kids hated their parents. But I don't anymore think that all men are spiritually lacking and dangerous and have ruined the world. My experience since has taught me that there's violence in men, but in women, too."

The once homeless Dorothy now holds a job that could seem the proper punch line for the most radical member of the class: She is a graphic designer, creating images for a management consulting firm. She has not, however, abandoned her political commitments. In fact, in midlife she has resumed her activism, though her concerns are now more local and small-scale. Living on a pond in Peace Dale, Rhode Island, where "it's wonderful to come home from work and launch the canoe at the bottom of the back yard and follow the herons, glossy ibis, kingfishers, ducks, and swans around the pond as the day cools and the sun sets," she has joined a neighborhood group trying to protect that environment. Having once tried to remake the world and bring down the enemy, she now believes that change happens only bit by bit, and by finding common cause. "As kids, we staked out the margins and became marginalized. Now, if my neighbors join me in my concern for the pond, I'm not going to test them on abortion or gay rights. It's not a compromise of principle to try and make things better, a little better, where you are. That's the kind of real work that has been done by women all along, at the church and the PTA. Though to say that it is up to women to clean things up in the world, well, that's like saying it's housework. I believe anyone can learn to be ecologically sensitive and nurturant."

Dorothy's peacemaking extends even to her own mistakes. "I wasted my twenties. I was in pain for a long time. I'm only now coming into my own. But I learned things. Ten years of living on less than ten thousand dollars a year, that makes you understand more kinds of people. My mother is liberal, but when she talks about welfare mothers . . . well, if you spend your whole life protected, you don't understand. Our generation didn't want to be just safe and meet people only like us. Because I walked in more dangerous places, I can understand what it is to feel trapped and out of control."

As in their prior life stages, the way these women see their own midlife has been strongly shaped by—and has also shaped—the many studies and books that invariably follow in their generation's broad wake. Many of these have focused on the body—the fading of beauty, the onset of menopause—and most have been determinedly cheering, painting the end of the reproductive years as another rejuvenating passage, a liberation from the need to attract and please men, a time when women can become demanding, unruly, politically and spiritually bold. Jan Mercer wrote to her classmates that she "welcomed the freedom from the hormonal ebbs and flows." Nancy Wanderer sees her "warm flashes" as a "sign of ripening." Betty Demy thinks it "might be fun to just break out. On my kindergarten report card, my teacher wrote, 'Betty is a happy conformist'; it was true then and ever since. Now is my chance to be eccentric."

Some are enjoying a new sense of matriarchal responsibility to younger women. When Ann Landsberg's stepdaughter had a miscarriage, "I felt catapulted into my new generational slot, became acutely aware that I am the mother of this clan. I had a grown daughter to deal with. I had to draw on my own experience with childbearing to bring her empathy and support and wisdom, even though it was only eight years since my son was born." When, after her mother's death, Ann's father began calling to ask how to cook this dish or get out that stain, she realized that "my mom's history and everything she knew is gone. I am the bearer of whatever she passed on."

Others have set out to reclaim for "the old woman" her premodern stature as venerable, visionary, wise. Dorothy Devine's goddess group marks a woman's entry into menopause by seating her upon a "throne," garlanding her with flowers, and rubbing her with fragrant oils. Then they all "sit humbly at the crone's feet and say, 'Please tell us your wisdom.' It's a counterweight to the Madison Avenue culture that says you're old and ugly and your husband will leave you. It will be a fabulous experience when my sisters do that for me."

Not all are aging so happily. Their twenty-fifth-reunion book is striking in the number of women describing serious illness, such as Epstein-Barr virus or chronic fatigue syndrome. This may reflect the emergence of new viruses and environmental insults to the immune system, or it may provide these women a legitimate reason to finally take care of themselves, or even justify stasis or middling success. A great many women in the class are consumers and practitioners of New Age therapies: Cynthia Gilbert-Marlow still works as a flight attendant but suffered an injury on the right side of her neck and back, "where you store anger." The wife of her acupuncturist, she was glad to discover, does telepathic psychology: "We get in harmony with the universe. Then she senses my body's responses. She'll ask yes or no questions, and her body moves with the answers." Menopause has given some a difficult time. Kathy Ruckman suffered hot flashes and interrupted sleep, and was anxious to get estrogen. Her doctor started hormone therapy but then stopped it when she began bleeding, and "wanted at the drop of a hat to do a D and C." Others are more suspicious of hormone replacement, worrying that it perpetuates the view, well known to their mothers, that menopause is a deficiency disease requiring treatment so that women remain supple and desirable for men.

Though most in the class are aging "naturally" and are, like Louise Carter, "not very depressed by my older face and streaks of gray hair," the altered face in the mirror does dispirit a few. Susan Alexander finds much to celebrate about midlife. She describes an abundant creative life, writing novels and musicals and films, directing theater, performing professionally on violin, piano, and flute, growing herbs on her balcony, loving and valuing her friends. She speaks rapturously of her son, "tall, handsome and athletic like his dad [with] a wonderful capacity for friendship with women." She has reconnected with the Church, helping the Presbytery of New York City create an Internet site, which she hopes will serve as a platform for some of the poorer churches and social service organizations. She appreciates her matured confidence, the sure knowledge that she can survive anything. All of it makes for what she calls an "intense core of joy at the center of my being, [that] runs from finding delight in small things to the borders of spiritual ecstasy." The "lengthy and arduous process" required to uncover it, she says, was "a most wonderful journey."

At the same time, Susan "loathes and struggles against aging." She hates "the gray hair and bags, the sagging, wrinkling hagdom, the feeling that there's so much more I want to do and that time is slipping away and my vitality is waning. It sucks to be fifty. I have ulcers and am overweight. And ageism, let me tell you, is lots worse than sexism. For women it's death. Men may tolerate thirty-year-old competent females, because they like to have them around, but fifty-year-olds—forget it. Aging women are even less valued than mothers and wives." She "burns with resentment" that her justice-minded generation does not resist more fiercely the relegating of women to the category of "old cow." "The men I know who turned fifty threw spectacular bashes and invited everyone they knew to party the night away. The women took trips to Italy, quietly, by themselves."

TV correspondent Martha Teichner has felt as much as anyone in the class the punishments meted out to aging women. "After nearly seventeen years at CBS and almost that many wars, I was reduced to the 'woman's page,' [covering] royals and fashion for the morning news."

Martha wrote that to her classmates twenty years out of school, one of a thousand messages these women have sent to each other over the years. Indeed, of all the public supports they have found for their individual searches and transformations and painful declines, none have mattered for Hillary's classmates more than their friendships with women. Their devotion to one another is utterly unlike the wary distance often maintained by their mothers and earlier generations, who were schooled to see other women principally as rivals, battling to be the fairest of them all. In *A Room of One's Own*, Virginia Woolf writes about coming across the revolutionary sentence "Chloe liked Olivia" in a contemporary novel by a woman. "Chloe liked Olivia perhaps for the first time in literature. Cleopatra did not like Octavia."

Even where friendships among women had existed, they had been at best what Carolyn Heilbrun has called "societies of consolation": Women soothed one another as they waited for their men, who had gone forth to the world. Only recently, Heilbrun writes, have women's friendships become what they were for men, a bond that "comprehended details of a public life and the complexities of the pain found there."

More and more, as the years have passed, Hillary's classmates have become protectors and teachers to other women. Pam Colony, who for so long fought the male scientists barring her way at university, works nights at a community college, teaching "older women who were intimidated early on but have come back bolder." Within the class, they have forged ties stronger than at any time since their years together at Wellesley. Jan Mercer is grateful for her classmates' candor, "a consequence, I think, of our age. Wellesley was where I learned how valuable female friendships were to me, as important as my family. But even ten years ago there would have been prevarication, more effort to put the gloss on things. By now we realize that everyone's been knocked around." Their youthful commitment to consciousness-raising, to speaking publicly of their struggles in order to discover which are shared and might be fixed together, is fulfilled now as it could not be when they were more callow and preening. Ann Sentilles "was haunted for years by the sense that other people were managing it all. Now I'm aware of everybody's compromises, everyone whose marriage has failed, people struggling with their kids and illness and alcoholism. We all realize we made choices at times blithely and that there's a cost at every turn. If there's recrimination, it's more of ourselves than of our parents or the world. We all recognize our extraordinary privilege, most of it unearned. For most of us now the quest is for some secure inner meaning. We're no longer just collecting gold stars."

Hillary Rodham Clinton has been an important center of gravity in this coming together. For many, she represents the larger effort they are part of, that river of history to which each has been tributary. "Thanks for being me—in a higher place," Jayne Baker Abrams wrote to Hillary in a public forum in the alumnae magazine. "Having you there validates me . . . my nonprofit work, my concern for children." Sue Barnard wrote: "Every increment of respect you garner will increase the leverage the rest of American women have in their marriages, families, and the larger world. If Bill Clinton and other important men can be less defensive in their relationships with women, maybe other men will be less likely to resort to violence and intimidation."

Most have taken heart from Hillary and continue to admire her for her grace and unflinching strength and for her complex understanding of human character and life. They dismiss, for the most part, evidence of her ethical lapses and fall silent "so as not to add to her pain," on the matter of her long sufferance of her husband's infidelities and her own public humiliations. A few, however, have openly cringed at her choice to go on protecting her husband even as he engaged in what one called the "most callous, exploitative treatment of women." They have worried about the message sent to girls about what they should put up with and to boys about what powerful men do. Most of all, they mourn the dissipation of so much of the possibility they'd imagined for their gifted classmate. "Hillary has the whole world," says Nancy Young, "but she can't use what she has. She's cornered. What little spontaneity she ever had is gone. She has become just robotic, a cardboard person. And every time I hear her say *my husband*, I shudder. It's degrading for her, and she's not acknowledging the degradation. She's so compromised having to play this role; it makes her harden or empty herself. He, on the other hand, should be more guarded. I was shocked at our reunion dinner; at one point, he and I happened to cross the room at the same time, and walked past each other. When he looked at me, the overwhelming sense I had was of his availability. I thought, 'This is the president; he should not be so available.' "

Nancy Wanderer has, she says, always measured herself against Hillary. "On the whole, I've felt I haven't come through the way she has. I still agonize. What if I hadn't gotten married senior year? What if Hillary and I had run against each other for college government and what if I'd won? What if I had gone to Yale Law School instead of waiting until I was thirty-eight and going to the University of Maine? I would have been in that early group of lawyers who had the chance to be seasoned. It took me twenty years to get back to where I was in 1968."

Nancy's regret at losing the competition gives way quickly, however, to the more self-comforting notion that she merely chose a different balance between her personal and political life. "I think Hillary's idea was to get to the top of the power structure as quickly and securely as she could. She felt she had important work to do. For that, she was able to accept dissonant chords in her life with Bill, to look the other way, put it aside, put up with it. I think passionate relationships are not the center of her life, as they are for me, which is why I didn't end up where Hillary is. She's done a lot; those White House appointments of women wouldn't have happened if she weren't there. Yes, she had the entrée. I turned my back on that with Thomas, and I'm glad that whatever I achieve I'll have done on my own. But I'm not going to make a national difference and I'm not going to criticize Hillary for how she got there."

As a practical matter, Hillary has also been a unifying force in the class. Among the guests in the Lincoln Bedroom have been many from Wellesley '69: Johanna Branson, Jinnet Fowles, Susan Graber, Connie Shapiro. When the First Lady hosted a twenty-fifth reunion for her class at the White House, 305 of the 430 graduates gathered. They were herded through metal detectors, "overseen, startlingly, by a big, brightly smiling photograph of Hillary," in Lindsay Miller's account, and entertained by Kathy Ruckman's kids, performing a string quartet.

For three days during that reunion, Hillary hung out happily with her classmates—listening attentively to their symposia, participating in the Sunday morning service performed by the pastors in the class, bringing her husband along to the Saturday dinner at the Mayflower Hotel. Nancy Wanderer sat next to Hillary at dinner. They talked for an hour about how they were cutting back on meat, coping with menopause, and worrying about osteoporosis. Hillary asked if she could touch Nancy's nearly crew-cut hair and said, "Maybe I'll get a haircut like this and really shock everyone." She seemed fascinated by Nancy's information that the Meyers-Briggs personality chart would categorize Hillary as an introvert but her husband as an extrovert, "talking to clarify his thinking and soak up energy." She wanted to know all about Nancy's partner, Susan—how they met, what she does for a living. "She was curious to know what kind of person I'd wanted to make my life with." Recalling how charmed she'd been by Nancy's mom in the *Frontline* documentary, particularly Marge's recollection of how she'd wished she could have stopped Hillary's disruptive commencement speech, Hillary wrote Marge a message on the back of Nancy's meal ticket, commending her courage in sticking by her daughter. At one point, Nancy snapped a picture of a scene that amused her: Hillary was huddled with a bunch of women, and all were ignoring Bill, who idly looked about the room for diversion. The class took obvious pleasure when their own president, Karen Williamson, kept Bill Clinton waiting for the microphone while she instructed them to put out their little ticket saying if they wanted the chicken, though many also told me later of the heady moment when he'd locked onto their eyes. He was, many said, the sexiest man they'd ever seen.

The transformation of the personal into the political undertaken by these women—moving from wholly domestic to partly public lives; publicizing issues that had once been considered private; scrutinizing the politics within the home—has had complicated and mixed effects. Most are obscured in the usual attacks: that these women, and their entire generation, have settled into one long confessional whine; that they have abdicated personal responsibility by blaming all their problems and failings on social causes; that they have turned the mysterious realm of relations between women and men, a realm where the erotic imagination and inarticulate feeling could live, into a starkly lit, rule-bound world.

If such generalities fail to describe a more complicated reality, the life stories of the women of the Wellesley class of '69 do reveal the high costs exacted by their generation's success at having breached the boundaries. There are moments when these women do perhaps say too much, jeopardizing their own dignity and sometimes their families': As Eudora Welty once warned, "We can and will cheapen all feeling by letting it go savage or parading in it." There are times when they have misused the public light: Like Princess Diana, who won both sweet revenge and the "love" of a million strangers by publicizing her humiliation and betrayal, Hillary's classmates have at times gone public out of motives beyond the honorable forging of solidarities. Those solidarities, in turn, have had their own trapdoors. The affiliations, the new shared stories, have sometimes freed them from one box only to become equally limiting, reductive, closed. Resorting to canned language and analysis—of the recovery movement, or the New Age, or even feminism—these women can sometimes wind up erasing their own singularity, inhabiting their caricature, settling for too simplistic explanations of their own lives. They can get caught in the therapeutic trap, letting talk substitute for action, ritually repeating insights but failing to act, letting past damage absorb the best part of their present energies.

Their kids, too, can suffer. Hillary's protest in her commencement speech against her generation's "inauthentic" lives was a complaint against a world where too much was hidden or lied about. The children of the class of '69 also have a sense of inauthenticity, but one that comes from too much being seen and so being hollowed of meaning. Living amid all the skeletons dragged from all the closets, their children have sometimes become timid, pessimistic, more ironic than idealistic, lost of an innocence they never had. Having witnessed the fracturing of their family life, Nancy Wanderer's sons are both steering clear of relationships: Andrew sees himself as a perennial bachelor; his closest relationships are with his grandmother and his mom. Many in the class have wavered between the wish to let their kids see "reality" and their equally powerful wish to protect them. Jan Mercer has brought her sons "in on life's struggles, so they know they happen in all families and you handle them and move on"; she has also spent $300,000 to put them through private schools.

Feminism as a movement has been equally confused by the toppling of the traditional wall around the private sphere. The demand for more public attention—to discriminatory and harassing behavior in the workplace, to domestic assault and sexual crimes, to the needs of mothers and children—can sometimes collide with the demand for more respect for female privacy, to make their own reproductive decisions, to enact their desires. Hillary Clinton has been one of the most politicizing in the class—arguing, for instance, that prenatal care ought to be required for pregnant women to get public benefits. But she has also tried to claim a "zone of privacy" when the charges of sexual misdeeds piled up against her husband, despite the fact that most of the women involved had worked for him, and so raised all the concerns about how men use their power at work to get sex from women. Some feminists have also worried at the paradox that, having fought against the public shamings of women—for promiscuity or unwed pregnancy—they have now turned that same weapon against men. They see the kind of denunciation made by Kris Olson Rogers of her ex-husband, Jeff, as just another scarlet letter, unfortunate whether pinned on a woman or a man.

If these women's lives have revealed the hazards, however, they have also revealed how much has been gained by breaching the wall. Those gains have been public: invigorating science and medicine and anthropology and law with new perspectives; pressing employers to make room for their workers' family lives. The gains have also been personal. These women have not, like so many of their mothers, silently suffered cruelties behind closed doors. They have not been paralyzed by the shame that once befell a woman who was sexually misused: Telling her classmates that she had been molested and hit as a child helped free Elizabeth Michel to do useful work as a doctor, to raise healthy children. Their earnest candor has been, finally, the source of their great resilience. At the end of *Carnal Knowledge*, the character played by Jack Nicholson tells his buddy (Art Garfunkel) that he is a credulous schmuck, "but maybe schmuckiness is what you need to stay open." The few in the class who have been most brittle and immobile are those, like Charlynn Maniatis, who have lived the most private lives.

The marriage of the personal and the political has had other good consequences. These women have made enduring alliances. They have found new ways to understand their lives and, from those new stories, the capacity for renewal and change. Most have at least partly sustained their vow to live their political convictions in their personal lives. Some have even tried to make their families into an alliance engaged together in civic life rather than a retreat from the world or a substitute for those larger obligations. If their kids have been heavily dosed with reality, they have also been given the capacity to see through the stories that bind them. Mary Day Kent recalls how her ten-year-old daughter analyzed her fourth grade class: She told her mom that the teacher does not call on girls, how her books are full of boys and have no black people in them, things Mary couldn't see till she was thirty. Mary also marvels at seeing her daughter, a talented soccer player, discover what it feels like to be a hero in front of the world. "Sometimes I sit in a gym full of people cheering for my daughter and think: What would I have been like if as a girl I'd had a whole crowd counting on me to make the goal? Not just to be a cheerleader but to be the one to plunge in and kick the ball?"

In discussing her hope to keep other sick people company while they die, Nancy Young quotes Meister Eckehart, a thirteenth-century Dominican mystic. "To the extent that all creatures who are gifted with reason go out from themselves in all that they do, to that same extent they go into themselves." In its largest sense, the dissolution of the boundary between the private and the public is the resolution Nancy describes, the making of binding relations with the widest circle of human beings.

Bibliography

The women of Wellesley's Class of '69 are avid readers whose lives and self-understanding have been deeply shaped by books. In trying to make sense of their world, I was greatly helped by reading a number of the books that have had meaning for them, as well as others that helped me understand the history of feminist thought and women's lives in the last fifty years. Following is a highly selective list of those books I found most helpful or most revealing about these women.

Classics of First- and Second-Wave Feminism

Beauvoir, Simone de. *The Second Sex* (1949). New York: Random House, 1990.

Friedan, Betty. *The Feminine Mystique.* New York: Dell, 1963.

Millett, Kate. *Sexual Politics.* New York: Doubleday, 1970.

Woolf, Virginia. *A Room of One's Own* (1929). San Diego: Harcourt Brace, 1991.

————. *Three Guineas* (1938). San Diego: Harcourt Brace, 1993.

On Writing Women's Lives

Conway, Jill Ker. *Written By Herself: Autobiographies of American Women: An Anthology.* New York: Vintage, 1992.

Heilbrun, Carolyn. *Writing a Woman's Life.* New York: Ballantine, 1988.

Malcolm, Janet. *The Silent Woman: Sylvia Plath and Ted Hughes.* New York: Knopf, 1994.

Moers, Ellen. *Literary Women.* New York: Doubleday Anchor, 1977.

Olsen, Tillie. *Silences.* New York: Dell, 1965.

Wagner-Martin, Linda. *Telling Women's Lives: The New Biography.* New Brunswick, N.J.: Rutgers University Press, 1994.

Welty, Eudora. *One Writer's Beginnings*. New York: Warner Books, 1991.

On Feminist Psychology and Theories of Gender

Bateson, Mary Catherine. *Composing a Life*. New York: Penguin Books, 1990.

Chesler, Phyllis. *Women and Madness*. New York: Doubleday, 1972.

Chodorow, Nancy. *The Reproduction of Mothering: Psychoanalysis and the Sociology of Gender*. Berkeley: University of California Press, 1978.

Dinnerstein, Dorothy. *The Mermaid and the Minotaur*. New York: Harper and Row, 1976.

Garber, Marjorie. *Vice Versa: Bisexuality and the Eroticism of Everyday Life*. New York: Simon and Schuster, 1995.

Gilligan, Carol. *In a Different Voice: Psychological Theory and Women's Development*. Cambridge: Harvard University Press, 1982.

Keller, Catherine. *From a Broken Web: Separation, Sexism, and Self*. Boston: Beacon Press, 1986.

Tannen, Deborah. *Gender and Discourse*. New York: Oxford University Press, 1994.

On Women and Science, the Law, and Medicine

Boston Women's Health Book Collective. *Our Bodies, Ourselves for the New Century: A Book by and for Women*. New York: Touchstone, 1998.

Keller, Evelyn Fox, ed. *Reflections on Gender and Science*. New Haven: Yale University Press, 1985.

Keller, Evelyn Fox, and Helen E. Longino. *Feminism and Science*. New York: Oxford University Press, 1996.

Okin, Susan Moller. *Justice, Gender, and the Family*. New York: Basic Books, 1989.

Showalter, Elaine. *Hystories: Hysterical Epidemics and Modern Culture*. New York: Columbia University Press, 1997.

On Love, the Sexual Revolution, and the Family

Baruch, Elaine Hoffman. *Women, Love, and Power: Literary and Psychoanalytic Perspectives.* New York: New York University Press, 1991.

Breines, Wini. *Young, White, and Miserable: Growing Up Female in the Fifties.* Boston: Beacon Press, 1992.

Coontz, Stephanie. *The Way We Never Were: American Families and the Nostalgia Trip.* New York: Basic Books, 1992.

Grant, Linda. *Sexing the Millennium: Women and the Sexual Revolution.* New York: Grove Press, 1994.

Rose, Gillian. *Love's Work: A Reckoning with Life.* New York: Schocken Books, 1996.

On Theology and Mythology

Daly, Mary. *Gyn/Ecology.* Boston: Beacon Press, 1978.

Dijkstra, Bram. *Evil Sisters: The Threat of Female Sexuality and the Cult of Manhood.* New York: Knopf, 1996.

Lefkowitz, Mary. *Women in Greek Myth.* Baltimore: Johns Hopkins University Press, 1986.

Murphy, Cullen. *The Word According to Eve: Women and the Bible in Ancient Times and Our Own.* Boston: Houghton Mifflin, 1998.

Reeder, Ellen. *Pandora: Women in Classical Greece.* Princeton, N.J.: Princeton University Press, 1996.

Sontag, Susan. *Illness as Metaphor.* New York: Doubleday, 1990.

Warner, Marina. *From the Beast to the Blonde: On Fairy Tales and Their Tellers.* New York: Farrar, Straus & Giroux, 1994.

———. *Six Myths of Our Time.* New York: Vintage, 1994.

On Popular Culture and the "Experts"

Douglas, Susan. *Where the Girls Are: Growing Up Female with the Mass Media.* New York: Times Books, 1994.

Ehrenreich, Barbara, and Dierdre English. *For Her Own Good: 150 Years of the Experts' Advice to Women.* New York: Doubleday Anchor, 1978.

Eyer, Diane. *Motherguilt: How Our Culture Blames Mothers for What's Wrong with Society.* New York: Times Books, 1996.

Faludi, Susan. *Backlash: The Undeclared War Against American Women.* New York: Doubleday, 1996.

Lasch, Christopher. *Culture of Narcissism: American Life in an Age of Diminishing Expectations.* New York: Norton, 1991.

Lord, M. G. *Forever Barbie.* New York: William Morrow, 1994.

On Home, Fashion, and the Female Body

Davison, Jane, and Lesley Davison. *To Make a House a Home.* New York: Random House, 1994.

Hollander, Anne. *Sex and Suits: The Evolution of Modern Dress.* New York: Kodansha Globe, 1994.

Peiss, Kathy. *Hope in a Jar: The Making of America's Beauty Culture.* New York: Metropolitan Books, 1998.

Yalom, Marilyn. *A History of the Breast.* New York: Knopf, 1997.

Exemplary Biographies

Bair, Dierdre. *Anaïs Nin: A Biography.* New York: Viking Penguin, 1996.

Ginzburg, Carlo. *The Cheese and the Worm: The Cosmos of a Sixteenth-Century Miller.* Baltimore: Johns Hopkins University Press, 1980.

Holmes, Richard. *Dr. Johnson and Mr. Savage.* New York: Vintage, 1993.

Lee, Hermione. *Virginia Woolf: A Biography.* New York: Knopf, 1997.

Rose, Phyllis. *Parallel Lives: Five Victorian Marriages.* New York: Random House, 1984.

Historical and Statistical Resources

Anderson, Terry. *The Movement and the Sixties.* New York: Oxford University Press, 1995.

Costello, Cynthia, Shari Miles, and Anne Stone, eds. *The American Woman 1999–2000.* New York: W. W. Norton, 1998.

Maraniss, David. *First in His Class.* New York: Simon and Schuster, 1995.

Palmieri, Patricia Ann. *In Adamless Eden: The Community of Women Faculty at Wellesley.* New Haven: Yale University Press, 1995.

Anthologies

Agonito, Rosemary, ed. *The History of Ideas on Woman.* Berkeley: Perigee Books, 1977.

Davidson, Cathy, and Linda Wagner-Martin, eds. *Oxford Companion to Women's Writing in the United States.* New York: Oxford University Press, 1995.

Pollitt, Katha. *Reasonable Creatures.* New York: Knopf, 1994.

Schneir, Miriam, ed. *Feminism: The Essential Historical Writings.* New York: Vintage, 1994.

———. *Feminism in Our Time: The Essential Writings, World War II to the Present.* New York: Vintage, 1994.

Tierney, Helen, ed. *Women's Studies Encyclopedia.* New York: Peter Bedrick Books, 1991.

Fiction and Plays

Craig, Patricia, ed. *Oxford Book of Modern Women's Stories.* Oxford: Oxford University Press, 1994.

Chopin, Kate. *The Awakening.* New York: Riverhead Books, 1995.

Jewett, Sarah Orne. *The Country of the Pointed Firs.* New York: Modern Library, 1995.

McCarthy, Mary. *The Group.* San Diego: Harcourt Brace, 1991.

O'Connor, Flannery. *Everything That Rises Must Converge.* New York: Farrar, Straus & Giroux, 1965.

Plath, Sylvia. *The Bell Jar.* New York: Bantam, 1983.

Wasserstein, Wendy. *Unconventional Women and Others.* New York: Dramatists Play, 1978.

Index

DIVIDED LIVES
by Elsa Walsh

Despite the large number of books devoted to women's issues in the last twenty years, *Washington Post* reporter Elsa Walsh felt that the literature was missing a crucial element—the voices of women themselves. Setting out to probe the myriad layers of women's lives and to illuminate the interior struggles women face at work and at home, Walsh spent over two years interviewing three highly successful women—*60 Minutes* correspondent Meredith Vieira, conductor and first lady of West Virginia Rachel Worby, and Dr. Alison Estabrook, chief of breast surgery at the country's second largest hospital—about their lives.

Women's Studies/0-385-48447-X

THE HIDDEN WRITER
by Alexandra Johnson

No other document quite compares with the intimacies and yearnings, the confessions and desires, revealed in the pages of a diary. Presenting seven portraits of literary and creative lives, Alexandra Johnson illuminates the secret world of writers and their diaries, and shows how over generations these writers have used the diary to solve a common set of creative and life questions.

Women's Studies/Literary Criticism/0-385-47830-5

MINDING THE BODY
by Patricia Foster

A multicultural anthology of fiction and nonfiction literary narratives which addresses the psychological and political aspects of a woman's body in today's culture. An important and much-needed book for women who seek to understand their bodies and find independent, imaginative ways to cope with aging, beauty expectations, and ethnic comparisons.

Women's Studies/0-385-47167-X

WILD WOMEN DON'T WEAR NO BLUES
by Marita Golden

Bringing together fourteen African American women, Marita Golden has compiled saucy and spicy essays that serve as an exploration into the contemporary black female psyche. Ranging in style from Audre Lorde's classic polemic on eroticism to Miriam DeCosta Willis's deeply moving essay on her husband's last years, "every single one of these essays is terrific." *(The Washington Post)*

Women's Studies/African American Studies/0-385-42401-9

WHOREDOM IN KIMMAGE
The Private Lives of Irish Women
by Rosemary Mahoney

Before the phenomena of Frank McCourt's *Angela's Ashes* and Thomas Cahill's *How the Irish Saved Civilization*, Rosemary Mahoney traveled to Ireland in response to the growing feeling that changes were taking place, and that those changes directly involved women. Written with the art of a skilled fiction writer whose ear for Irish bluster is pitch-perfect, *Whoredom in Kimmage* tells the tale of contemporary Irish women through a series of brilliantly animated scenes.

Women's Studies/0-385-47450-4

ANCHOR BOOKS
Available at your local bookstore, or call toll-free to order:
1-800-793-2665 (credit cards only).